NORTH CAROLINA

An Economic and Social Profile

NORTH CAROLINA

An Economic and Social Profile

by

S. Huntington Hobbs, Jr.

Chapel Hill

THE UNIVERSITY OF NORTH CAROLINA PRESS

PREFACE

In 1930 the University of North Carolina Press published *North Carolina: Economic and Social* by the author of this book on North Carolina. The 1930 volume was the first book of its kind to be published in the United States—a social and economic presentation and interpretation of the home state. At that time it was promised that a somewhat similar volume would come out in the future. This book keeps that promise.

The chief purpose of this book is to present North Carolina as accurately and as faithfully as possible. There is no intention unjustly to criticize nor is there any attempt to glamorize the state. Throughout the book the author has attempted to offer constructive suggestions.

In the preparation of this book the author has received much assistance in many ways. Many of his students have helped in various ways. Among them are Reverend Robert Insco, Mrs. Ivan B. Stafford, Thad Eure, Jr., George S. Willard, Jr., William Geer, Walter Tice, Jr., A. Craig Phillips, W. J. Scott, Wilmer Jenkins, W. E. Rice, and A. H. Young. Special credit is due Dr. W. P. Richardson for help on public health, to Dr. Ellen B. Winston and Miss Elizabeth Fink for help on public welfare, and to Dr. Paul W. Wager on county government. Other credits are listed in their proper places.

The manuscript was read first by Mrs. Harvey Smith who checked the bibliography and did valuable editorial work. It was then read, edited, and checked most thoroughly and competently by Mrs. George V. Taylor. The author is deeply indebted to Mrs. Taylor and to the Institute for Research in Social Science for supplying her invaluable services.

The author is further indebted to the Institute for financial assistance, for typing the manuscript, for editorial help, and for help in many other ways. Special acknowledgment goes to Dr. Gordon W. Blackwell, until recently Director of the Institute, and to Dr. Katharine Jocher, associate director.

S. H. Hobbs, Jr.
Chapel Hill, N. C.

9511

Contents

CONTENTS

FIGURES

TABLES

NORTH CAROLINA

An Economic and Social Profile

Chapter 1

GEOLOGY AND MINERALS[1]

The surface of the state of North Carolina is characterized by a thin layer of rugged soil of loose, earthy materials. Under this thin layer are two major geological divisions—the eastern coastal plain and the western mountains, of which the upper piedmont is considered a part. The eastern coastal plain is underlain with sands, gravels, clays, marls, and shell limestone. The western mountains are underlain with gneisses, schists, slates, metamorphosed volcanics, igneous masses of peridotite and dunite, igneous granite, syenite, and diorite. Areas of metamorphosed but recognizable sedimentary rocks are found in the piedmont.

A brief examination of the geological history of the state helps explain the existence of these formations and gives some indication for the future of the mining industry for North Carolina.

Geological History of North Carolina

Rocks were laid down in North Carolina as early as the Archeozoic era (the age of the Great Granitoid Series). However, the rocks of this age have been so changed that hardly any exist in their original form, and as a result geologists have classified them merely as Pre-Cambrian in age, which places them merely in the era sometime before the Paleozoic.

These Pre-Cambrian formations were made by the deposition of sediments and by the accumulation of volcanic fragmental flows. The earlier igneous rocks then introduced and by folding, faulting, and metamorphizing changed the later formations. Also, a trough was developed where the Appalachian mountains now stand. The slightly metamorphosed sediments resulted in the schists, phyllites, slates, quartzites, and marbles of Cherokee and Graham counties and parts of Clay, Macon, Jackson, Haywood, Swain, Cleveland, Gaston, Lincoln, and Catawba counties in a narrow belt from the center of McDowell county to the South Carolina line, and from the northwest corner of Yadkin county across the center of Stokes county. Dikes in these formations gave rise to the feldspar, kaolin, mica, corundum, spinel, garnet, and manganese of these areas.

---

[1]This section on geology and minerals, with permission, draws heavily from J. L. Stuckey and W. G. Steel, *Geology and Mineral Resources of North Carolina*, North Carolina Department of Conservation and Development (Raleigh, 1953).

The highly metamorphosed Pre-Cambrian gneisses and schists are light to dark and gray through black in color due to biotite mica and hornblende deposits. These areas are in the upper piedmont plateau, in much of the Blue Ridge, and in the area between the Blue Ridge and the Great Smoky mountain chains. The peridotites occur in a fifteen-mile-wide belt from Clay and Macon counties to Ashe and Alleghany counties. In Wake County the peridotites were metamorphosed into soapstone, olivine, serpentine, asbestos, and vermiculite.

The Proterozoic, or Lower Paleozoic, era was an era of weathering, erosion, and deposition of sediment in the western trough and of accumulation of volcanic fragmental flow in the piedmont plateau and western edge of the coastal plain. The era ended in the formation of the Appalachian mountains in the western trough and in the intrusion of granite, diorite, and other igneous rocks in the piedmont and the Appalachians. A period of weathering then set in that resulted in the Huronian, or Volcanic Slate, age of the Proterozoic era, which gave North Carolina her slate belt. Dikes and faults in this slate belt have contained gold, copper, silver, and iron pyrophylite.

The Cambrian age formations of the Paleozoic era were sedimentary in origin. As they gently metamorphosed, they resulted in sandstone conglomerate, shale, and limestone, in association with quartzite, marble, slate, and schist.

Carboniferous age deposits made in the Paleozoic era are widespread in the state. The deposits of this age are granite and diorite mixed, syenite, and pure granite. These deposits are called the Carolina igneous belt, from which comes nationally known Mount Airy granite.

Triassic age deposits of the Mesozoic era appear in the Dan River coal field in a strip five to seven miles wide and in the Deep River coal field. Deposits in this age also were made as beds and lenses of conglomerate, sandstone, and shale. They vary in color from yellow to red to brown to chocolate. These were deposited in an arid climate which had alternating periods of rainfall and drought. As a result the iron deposits oxidized and gave a wide range of color to the formations. They are commonly known as the red beds of North Carolina. The Cretaceous age deposits made in the Mesozoic era are found in the western two-thirds of the coastal plain. These deposits resulted from the lowering of the state along the present fall line (the dividing line between the sedimentary formations in the eastern part of the state and the igneous formations in the west), and establishing the coast line along the western edge of the present coastal plain. The Tuscaloosa formation contains sands and clays. The Black Creek formation contains black sands and clays because of the presence of carbonaceous materials, and also marl and shell limestone. The Pee Dee formation is made up of sand, clay marl, and shell limestone.

Tertiary age formations occurred in the Early Cenozoic era as the ocean receded again. There are four of these. The Castle Hayne formation includes Pender, Onslow, Duplin, Jones, and Lenoir counties. It contains sands, clays, limestone, and phosphate. The Trent formation is in a belt through Craven, Jones, Onslow, and Pender counties and has deposits of clay, sands, marl, and shell limestone. The Yorktown formation lies in the northern half of the coastal plain west from Edenton and New Bern. It contains fine sands varying in color from bluish gray to bluish green which turn light gray or yellow when dry. Clays and marl also are found in this area. The Waccamaw formation is located mostly in Brunswick County; it contains shell marl and coarse sand varying from gray to buff in color.

The Quarternary age formations of the Late Cenozoic era cover the Tertiary and Cretaceous age formations in the eastern coastal plain. This accounts for the fine sands and light colored clays found in the Tidewater counties.

Figure 1 outlines the location of the geological formations of the state and gives information about their age classification and type.

Mineral Resources of North Carolina

In 1954 the total mineral production in North Carolina was valued at $41,700,000, an all-time high and an increase of $3,200,000, or 8 per cent over the 1953 figure, the previous high. Those minerals that showed gains

Fig. 1   Generalized Geologic Map of North Carolina

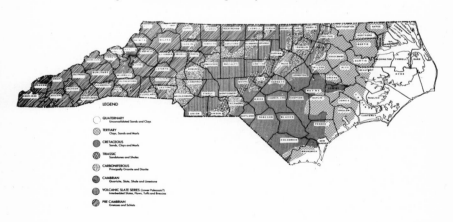

J. L. Stuckey and W. G. Steel, *Geology and Mineral Resources of North Carolina*, p. 5.

during this period were abrasive stones, commercial sand and gravel these categories account for over half the total value), beryllium and tungsten concentrates, miscellaneous clays (mined for heavy clay products), commercial crushed granite, dimension marble, scrap and sheet mica, and noncommercial gravel. These minerals went down in 1954: asbestos, kaolin, vermiculite, feldspar, dimension granite, noncommercial crushed granite, crushed limestone (both commercial and noncommercial), crushed marble, miscellaneous stone (including quartz), olivine, talc and pyrophyllite, and noncommercial sand. Also, for the first time since 1949 some gold production was reported—from a small tonnage of concentrate recovered from mining a gold-silver-copper lead ore; all four metals were reported in 1954. However, no mineral fuels were produced in this period.

Under the Defense Minerals Exploration Administration (DMEA) program, which renders government assistance in the exploration and development of critical and strategic minerals, sixty-one projects were active or completed in 1954, compared with sixty-six in 1953. The total dollar value of expenditures was $193,380, of which the government's share was $163,739 (83 per cent), as compared with $237,736 and $213,960 respectively in 1953, a decrease of 17 per cent in total and 23 per cent in the government portion.

As in 1952 and 1953, the greatest activity under DMEA was in exploration for strategic mica. During 1954, sixty projects in nine counties were for mica and one in one county for beryl-tantalite-tin. Of the sixty-one projects in 1954, twenty-seven were continuations from 1953 and thirty-four were new in 1954.

Metals.

The geological evolution of the state has left many deposits of metals throughout the piedmont and mountain areas. They are as varied and interesting as the geological ages that deposited them.

Chromite deposits in the form of oxide of chromium with peridotite are located at Mine Hill, north of Burnsville in Yancey County; near Democrat in Buncombe County; in Balsam Gap at Dark Ridge Creek in Haywood County; and near Webster in Jackson County.

Although *copper* is not mined in North Carolina at present, approximately 60,000,000 pounds have been produced since 1900.[2] However, this is a very small fraction of the amount produced in the United States as a whole.

Gold in North Carolina often is of more excitement value than monetary. The deposits are native or free gold and usually occur in veins or

---

[2] *Ibid.*, p. 10.

in beds of sand or gravel. This fact accounts for some of the large nuggets found in the past, such as the seventeen-pound discovery on the Reed plantation in 1799.

Silver is usually found with the gold-bearing ores. Small amounts of both have been found from the East Carolina belt of Franklin, Nash, Warren, and Halifax counties all the way to the western part of the state. Although North Carolina was a leader in gold mining before 1849, production value in the past one hundred years has probably not equaled the costs of prospecting.

Iron deposits were discovered as early as 1729 and were mined for a great many years. However, no iron has been mined since the closing of the Cranberry Mine in Avery county in the early 1920's. Pyrite, a mixture of iron and sulphur, is found in Gaston and Macon counties.

Lead and *zinc* deposits are believed to exist in fourteen counties, but few of these have been tapped.

Manganese in very limited amounts has been produced in the state. Deposits are fairly widespread over the mountain and piedmont sections.

Nickel deposits, resulting from the decomposition of peridotites, are found in Buncombe, Jackson, and Clay counties. Production was attempted near Webster in Jackson County but without success.

One of the few known *tin* deposits in the United States is located in Gaston, Cleveland, and Lincoln counties in the form of cassiterite.

Titanium in North Carolina is a source of titanium oxides. These are valuable in the production of white pigment for paint, dye, ink, and linoleum. North Carolina titanium comes chiefly from ilmenite. Ilmenite deposits are located in the Albemarle area as far north as Beaufort County and near Richlands in Onslow County.

North Carolina ranks high in the production of *tungsten*. The value of tungsten lies in the great hardness and toughness that it gives to steel for industrial machines and machine tools. It is also valuable in the manufacture of electrical and radio equipment. Production at present comes from one operation in Vance County. Other deposits exist in Cabarrus County, and more interest has been shown in these as a result of the operation in Vance.

NONMETALLIC MINERALS.

The nonmetallic minerals of North Carolina (roughly 335) have been more valuable to the state than have the metallic. Income derived from them is only a relatively small part of the total state income, yet their value has increased nearly two and a half times since 1927. Still, North Carolina ranks usually thirty-eighth among the states as a mineral producer. Tables 1 and 2 show (1) the increased importance of minerals in North Carolina's economy, and (2) the amount and value of minerals mined in the state in 1953 and 1954.

Abrasive-type stones are found throughout the mountain and piedmont sections. Among these are *emery*, *garnets*, *millstones*, and *grinding pebbles*.

Asbestos deposits are found in Ashe, Avery, Caldwell, Wilkes, Mitchell, Yancey, Jackson, Macon, and Clay counties.

Barite, or heavy spar, has been mined in Gaston and Madison counties.

Clays, which constitute one of the state's most valuable minerals, have been deposited in North Carolina in many types as a result of the weathering of the various kinds of rocks. Some of these types are red-burning clays, pottery clays, buff-burning clays, shales, kaolin, and halloysite. North Carolina is a leading state in the production of brick and tile (fourth in 1954). Red-burning clay, which is found in nearly every county in the state, is used in the production of common bricks; and buff-burning clays, which are manufactured by similar methods, produce face brick, flue lining, and tile. These are buff to pink in color after firing. Pottery clays are found along the flood plains and low places on the uplands. Shale ceramics are manufactured from the deposits in the Carolina slate belt at Monroe, Norwood, New London, Denton, Mount Gilead, and Salisbury. Triassic shale products are produced at Durham, Sanford, Colon, Gulf, Pomono, and Pine Hall. Kaolin deposited after the weathering of feldspar results in true residual clay that is suitable for pottery, china, whiteware, porcelain enamels, tile, and spark-plug insulators. Kaolin has been mined in Haywood, Jackson, Macon, Swain, and other counties. Most of the present mining is done in Mitchell, Avery, and Yancey counties. Halloysite, a clay very much like kaolin, is used with kaolin to produce ceramics requiring glossy whiteness.

Coal deposits in North Carolina are located in the Deep River area from southern Chatham County into northern Moore and Lee counties. Operations in this field were recently closed, however, and approximately 70,000,000 tons of coal are believed to remain. The deposits are shallow and difficult to work, making mining unprofitable at the present. The Dan River coal fields, lying across Rockingham and Stokes and into northern Forsyth County, appear to be of less commercial value than the Deep River deposits.

North Carolina has led the nation in the output of *feldspar* since 1917. Deposits are known to occur in twenty mountain counties. Potash feldspar is mined in blocks and ground for use in pottery, electrical porcelain, and enamel. It is used as the flux for clay and flint in the manufacture of these products, and as one ingredient in glass for china and file. Limesoda feldspar is produced from the granite-type rock alaskite by the flotation process. This type is used in making glass and some pottery.

Gems are collected by hobbyists and in connection with different types of mining in nearly every area in the mining districts of the piedmont and mountain sections. Specimens from North Carolina are found in the outstanding collections of the nation. *Rubies* and *sapphires* have been found in several southwestern mountain counties. *Diamonds* have occurred in small quantities in Burke, Rutherford, McDowell, Lincoln, and Mecklenburg counties, and *beryls*, *emeralds*, and many quartz-type gems occur in several mountain and piedmont counties.

Kyanite, a silicate of aluminum, is found in the crystalline rocks in a belt six to eight miles wide from Swannanoa in Buncombe County to Burnsville in Yancey County and in another belt in a line with Kings Mountain across Gaston and Lincoln counties and into Iredell. No process for extracting the aluminum has been discovered.

Mica has been mined all across the western piedmont, and North Carolina is one of the two leading mica-producing states in the Union. The two big mica areas in the state are the Spruce Pine district (made up of Avery, Mitchell, and Yancey counties) and the Franklin-Sylva district (Jackson, Haywood, Macon, Swain, and Transylvania counties). Sheet mica is used as an insulating material, particularly in electrical equipment. Scrap mica is ground for use in wallpaper, roll roofing, shingles, and paint.

The atomic era has brought renewed interest in the *monazite* deposits of North Carolina, for monazite contains a fissionable element—thorium. But even earlier, from 1886 to 1919, thorium was mined for the manufacture of incandescent mantles for blast furnaces.

The largest deposits of *olivine* in the eastern United States, estimated at 230,000,000 tons, occur in North Carolina. The primary use is as a refractory material in chemical and metal processing.

Sand and *gravel* deposits, of which the state has many, furnish materials for building, plastering, paving, railroad ballast, and engine sand. Nearly every section of the state has pits and beds, but larger production usually occurs along or near streams.

Silica, or quartz, appears in many forms in the piedmont and mountain counties. Silica is used in pottery, glass, wood fillers, and refractories. North Carolina has the distinction of having produced the quartz from which the 200-inch Mount Palomar telescope lens was made. The mineral was mined from the Chestnut Flats feldspar and mica mine near Spruce Pine.

Spodumene is mined as a source of lithium mineral for use in photographic chemicals, storage batteries, dyes, and signal flares.

Stone has long been the most valuable mineral in North Carolina. The value per year is usually about three times that of any other mineral produced in the state. The plentiful supply of stone suitable for crushing has been a great factor in the building of the North Carolina highway system.

Dimension *granite* from North Carolina has become famous throughout the country. Mount Airy granite and Balfour pink from Rowan are outstanding names in buildings and monuments. Granite deposits suitable for crushing and dimension use are found from the coastal plain near Wilson through the piedmont as far west as Henderson County. The State Capitol is built of gneiss, a metamorphosed granite. Burke, Mitchell, and Caldwell counties have used gneiss in public building from the deposits found along the eastern plateau and in the western piedmont and mountain areas. Semicrystalline *limestone* is found in several mountain and piedmont counties. Marls occur in many tidewater counties. The Pender County deposits have been studied as a possible source for raw material in manufacturing cement. *Flagstone* and *crushed stone* are produced from the slate belt in Davidson, Cabarrus, and Union counties. Some production also comes from the gneisses and schists in Buncombe, Swain, and Cherokee counties. Duke University buildings are a good example of the use of slate building stone, mined near Hillsboro.

Fig. 2.   Distribution of Principal Minerals and Rocks

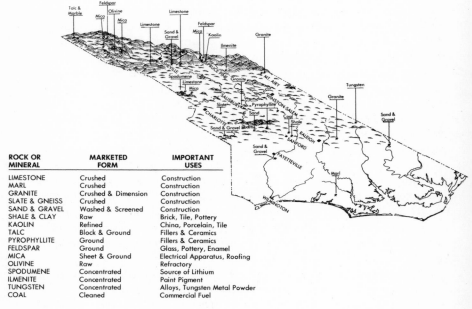

ROCK OR MINERAL	MARKETED FORM	IMPORTANT USES
LIMESTONE	Crushed	Construction
MARL	Crushed	Construction
GRANITE	Crushed & Dimension	Construction
SLATE & GNEISS	Crushed	Construction
SAND & GRAVEL	Washed & Screened	Construction
SHALE & CLAY	Raw	Brick, Tile, Pottery
KAOLIN	Refined	China, Porcelain, Tile
TALC	Block & Ground	Fillers & Ceramics
PYROPHYLLITE	Ground	Fillers & Ceramics
FELDSPAR	Ground	Glass, Pottery, Enamel
MICA	Sheet & Ground	Electrical Apparatus, Roofing
OLIVINE	Raw	Refractory
SPODUMENE	Concentrated	Source of Lithium
ILMENITE	Concentrated	Paint Pigment
TUNGSTEN	Concentrated	Alloys, Tungsten Metal Powder
COAL	Cleaned	Commercial Fuel

Talc, pyrophyllite, and *soapstone* are related to the marble deposits described above and to the altered peridotite and olivine deposits in other mountain counties, and in Wake County.

Zircon is found in Henderson, Madison, Iredell, Burke, McDowell, and Rutherford counties.

Figure 2 shows the distribution of the principal minerals and rocks in the state.

BIBLIOGRAPHY

BROADHURST, S. D. *An Introduction to the Topography, Geology, and Mineral Resources of North Carolina.* North Carolina Department of Conservation and Development. Raleigh: 1952.

BRYSON, H. J. *Gold Deposits in North Carolina.* North Carolina Department of Conservation and Development. Raleigh: 1936.

CROOM, MILTON. *Opportunities for a Portland Cement Plant in North Carolina.* Rural Industries Branch Division of Commerce and Industry, North Carolina Department of Conservation and Development. Raleigh: 1948.

HERMAN, R. E. "Statistical Summary of Mineral Production," *Minerals Yearbook,* U. S. Department of the Interior, Bureau of Mines. Washington: U. S. Government Printing Office, 1954.

HOBBS, S. H., JR. *North Carolina: Economic and Social.* Chapel Hill: University of North Carolina Press, 1930.

Manufacturing China Clay Opportunities in North Carolina. North Carolina Department of Conservation and Development. Raleigh: 1941.

REINEMUND, J. A. "Future Coal Expectancy in North Carolina," in Conservation and Development in North Carolina, comp. C. S. Green. Vol. I. Mimeographed. Conservation Congress Report. Raleigh: 1952.

STUCKEY, J. L. AND W. G. STEEL. *Geology and Mineral Resources of North Carolina.* North Carolina Department of Conservation and Development. Raleigh: 1953.

THOENEN, J. R. AND J. L. STUCKEY. *The Mineral Industry of North Carolina.* U. S. Department of the Interior, Bureau of Mines. Washington: U. S. Government Printing Office, 1954.

WAGER, PAUL AND DONALD HAYMAN. *Resources Management in North Carolina.* Institute for Research in Social Science, University of North Carolina. Chapel Hill, 1947.

Chapter 2

FORESTS

North Carolina's forest resources are among its greatest assets. Many of her leading industries (among them paper manufacture, furniture manufacture, and textiles) are dependent on them, and they help to create superb recreation areas. Of the state's total land area, forests in 1955 constituted 62 per cent, or 19,341,400 acres. Of these, two-thirds are in pine and the remainder in hardwoods. There is a tremendous variety in the timber grown: 24 kinds of oak; eight of nine kinds of American hickories; all six of the eastern maples; all the lindens; all six of the American magnolias; eight of the eleven pines; both varieties of hemlock and balsam fir; three birches; three of the five elms; three apples; six plums; and six cherries. In addition there are the palmetto, American olive, mock orange, and live oak, and in the mountain areas are black spruce, mountain sumac, and aspen. All told, there are 153 trees growing naturally in the state, of which over 70 are of the first size and 57 of great economic value. Fourteen of these trees grow to over 100 feet (three to over 140 feet). Sixteen reach diameters of five feet or over, and five to seven feet or over.[1]

NORTHERN COASTAL PLAIN

This area was first inventoried by the Forest Service of the U. S. Department of Agriculture in 1937. Since then, vast quantities of timber have been cut and new stands have grown up to replace the old. Changes in land use and ownership have been widespread. Improvement in forest protection and management practices has also had an effect on the timber stands which exist today. See Table 3 for figures on use classes in this region.

The twenty-three counties in the northern coastal plain of North Carolina contain a total land area of 6,700,000 acres. In 1955 forests occupied 4,400,000 acres, or about two-thirds of the area. Cropland, pasture, and other agricultural uses occupied 1,900,000 acres, and extensive areas of marsh and sand dunes existed in the coastal region. These proportions of land in forest and agricultural use are almost identical with those found in the southern coastal plain in 1952.[2]

---

[1] *News and Observer* (Raleigh, N. C.), annual farm edition Feb. 21, 1955, p. 34; *North Carolina, Land of Opportunity*, N. C. State Board of Agriculture (Raleigh, 1923), pp. 38–40.

[2] James F. MacCormack, *Forest Statistics for the Northern Coastal Plain, 1955*, U. S. Department of Agriculture, Forest Service, in cooperation with the N. C. Department of Conservation and Development, Forest Survey Release No. 45 (Asheville, 1956); *Forest Statistics for the Southern Coastal Plain, 1952*, Forest Survey Release No. 41 (Asheville, 1953).

The Tidewater, in the eastern portion of the unit, is a low, flat, poorly drained area containing broad expanses of swamp and pocosin. This word is believed to be of Indian origin, meaning "swamp on a hill," and it describes a forest type peculiar to the coastal plain.

The bulk of the commercial forest acreage is in farm woodlands, which contain 2,400,000 acres, or 58 per cent of the total. Industrial and other private owners hold 1,600,000 acres, making the total area in private ownership slightly more than 4,000,000 acres. Public ownership of commercial forest land amounts to 94,000 acres, or only about 2 per cent. Most of it is in the Croatan National Forest and the Cherry Point Marine Air Station in Carteret and Craven counties and along the right of way of the Intracoastal Waterway.

The most important timber tree in the northern plain is loblolly pine. This species alone, with a volume of more than 7,000,000,000 board feet, makes up 75 per cent of the softwood and 45 per cent of the total sawtimber volume. Pond pine and cypress are the only other softwood species of any consequence. In the hardwoods, tupelo, black gum, and sweet gum are the predominating species and together they make up 60 per cent of the volume in hardwood sawtimber trees.

Forests in the northern coastal plain are producing an annual volume of timber equal to 3,300,000 cords of wood, including bark, or 227,000,000 cubic feet of solid wood. This amount includes ingrowth and the growth which takes place on all sound trees 5.0 inches in diameter at breast height (d.b.h.) and larger. Yellow pines are producing at the rate of 1,800,000 cords per year, or about 55 per cent of the total growth of all species. Growth on sawtimber-size trees amounted to 824,000,000 board feet, of which 68 percent was pine. The average production of 423 board feet per acre per year in stands of loblolly pine sawtimber will probably be the highest rate found anywhere in North Carolina.

SOUTHERN COASTAL PLAIN.

The southern coastal plain of North Carolina is a heavily wooded area. Some 5,500,000 acres, or 65 per cent of the total land area, are in forest. Practically all of the forest land is capable of producing crops of commercial timber, but there are 91,000 acres of swampland or pocosin which are so wet or infertile that they will not grow timber of usable size. Agricultural land amounts to 2,500,000 acres, or 30 per cent of the total. The remaining 5 per cent of land area includes cities, towns, rights of way, coastal beaches, and marshland. The actual acreages and percentages are shown in Table 4.

Ninety-two per cent of the commercial forest land is in private ownership. Nearly 3,500,000 acres, or 64 per cent, is in farm woodlands, the remainder being owned by pulp and paper mills, lumber companies, and other private owners. The 455,000 acres of public forest lands are about equally divided between federal and state ownership. The bulk of the federal land is in military establishments, and the state land is mostly in game management areas or in state and school forests.

Softwood species make up 59 per cent of the present sawtimber volume. Loblolly pine, with 4,700,000,000 board feet, or 38 per cent of the total, is the predominating species. Pond pine, occupying the low, wet areas, is next in importance, followed by longleaf pine and cypress. Among the hardwood species, black gum, tupelo, and sweet gum account for 2,800,000,000 feet, 23 per cent of the total volume. Different varieties of oak make up most of the remaining sawtimber.

More than 70 per cent of the commercial forest land is well stocked or overstocked with sound trees of all sizes; yet the trees which provide this rating are mostly seedlings and saplings, all below volume size. Only 13 per cent of the forest land is well stocked with trees 5.0 inches d.b.h. and larger, and the area occupied by well-stocked stands of sawtimber is less than 5 per cent. The comparisons point out the fact that much of the forest area is now actually deficient in growing-stock volume, but at the same time they indicate a better potential stocking in the future as the smaller trees grow into volume size.

In 1952 timber growth exceeded cutting both in sawtimber and total growing stock for all species groups. This favorable trend resulted in an estimated annual increase in board-foot volume of 2.6 per cent and a 2.9 per cent rise in the volume of growing stock.

THE PIEDMONT.

The piedmont of North Carolina is an area of land ranging from rolling to hilly topographically, which lies between the rugged mountains to the west and the flat, level coastal plain to the east. It stretches across the central part of the state in a broad band running northeast and southwest, being a portion of the piedmont plateau region which extends from the Hudson River in New York State to east-central Alabama. Numerous small tracts of forest land intermingled with agricultural land are characteristic throughout the area. Small and highly diverse ownerships are the rule. Table 5 gives the acreages and percentages devoted to specific uses.

The piedmont is the most heavily populated and industrialized section of the state, yet more than half the gross area is still forest land. The 1956 survey revealed that a total of 5,800,000 acres, or 55 per cent was forested. Practically all of this acreage is available for production of commercial timber crops.

Private ownership accounts for 5,700,000 acres, or 98 per cent of all commercial forest land in the area. Less than 100,000 acres are publicly

owned, and most of this acreage is in state parks or in the Uwharrie
National Forest purchase unit. Farmers own or manage nearly 88 per cent
of the forest land, and industrial or other private holdings make up the
remainder. Data taken from the 1950 Census of Agriculture show that the
average farm contains 71 acres, half of which is in woodland.

Shortleaf, loblolly, and other yellow-pine species are under heavy demand for the manufacture of forest products. The shortleaf pine type
occupies 1,400,000,000 acres and is the most important of the softwood
group. Loblolly and Virginia pines together also constitute more than
1,000,000 acres. Loggers operating in mixed stands often cut all the pine
but little of the hardwood timber. Thus the residual stand often becomes
a hardwood type. The most extensive hardwood type is oak-hickory,
which covers nearly 2,000,000 acres.

Sawtimber volume in the piedmont is about equally divided between
softwoods and hardwoods. The leading species is shortleaf pine, which
makes up more than half the softwood volume and over one-fourth the
total volume. Loblolly and Virginia pine are also important. Among the
hardwoods, a large variety of oak species combine to make up a major
share of the board-foot volume. Yellow poplar, most abundant hardwood
other than oak, accounts for 17 per cent of the hardwood volume. The
principal hardwood species include sweet gum, hickory, ash, and maple.

The piedmont contains 83,000,000 cords of wood in trees of various
sizes, species, and quality. Only a third of this volume is in trees which
are large enough and of high enough quality to make saw logs, and much
of the sawtimber volume in the piedmont is in trees capable of producing
only small saw logs. Nearly two-thirds of the softwood sawtimber volume
is in trees which measure ten or twelve inches in diameter at breast height.

THE MOUNTAIN REGION.

The mountain region of North Carolina is located in a relatively
narrow belt running along the western edge of the state. It contains
twenty-one counties (including four counties east of the Blue Ridge:
Wilkes, Caldwell, Burke, and McDowell), and is bounded on the east by
the piedmont and on the other sides by the South Carolina, Georgia,
Tennessee, and Virginia state lines. The steep, rugged terrain, together
with marked differences in the type and composition of the forest cover,
set this region apart from the rest of the state. Table 6 shows how the land
has been put to use in this area.

The mountain region is North Carolina's most heavily forested area.
The 1955 survey showed that nearly 4,000,000 acres were under forest
cover. This is 77 per cent of the total land area in the unit, making the
ratio of forest acres to nonforest acres nearly 4 to 1. The proportion of
forest land by county ranges from a low of 44 per cent in Alleghany County

toa high of 94 per cent in Swain County. It is highest in the western portion
of the unit, where each of seven counties has more than 80 per cent of its
land area in forest. Cropland, pasture, and other agricultural uses occupy
most of the remaining acreage.

The percentage trend in land use is toward more forest and less agricultural land. The trend is unit wide, with each of the twenty-one counties showing a higher proportion of forest land now than it had seventeen
years ago.

Various federal, state, and local government agencies own and administer 1,300,000 acres of forest land in the mountain area. The Pisgah
and Nantahala national forests contain over 900,000 acres of federally-
owned land, with boundaries extending into all but two of the twenty-one
counties. The North Carolina portion of the Great Smoky Mountains
National Park, located in Haywood and Swain counties, contains 270,000
acres of rugged and isolated forest country. The National Park Service
also owns about 28,000 acres of forest along the right-of-way of the Blue
Ridge Parkway, a modern scenic highway built high up along the ridge
of the mountain chain. The Qualla Reservation of the Cherokee Indians
lies mostly in Swain and Jackson counties and contains 53,000 acres of
forest land. Much of the remaining public forest land is found in twenty
municipal watersheds owned by cities and towns, the largest of which is
the twenty-thousand-acre Asheville watershed.

Approximately half of all the forest land in the unit is in private farm
woodlands, where the number of owners is large and the size of the average tract is small. An additional 17 per cent is held by industrial or other
private interests.

Western North Carolina is a region of hardwood forests. Timber
stands composed of hardwood species are found on 3,200,000 acres, or
about 80 per cent of the commercial forest area. The oak-hickory type is
by far the most extensive. In this broad type of classification, the most
prevalent species are white oaks, red oaks, and hickory in association with
yellow poplar, basswood, and soft maple. Limited areas of the northern
hardwood type, including sugar maple, beech, and yellow birch, are
found along the upper elevations. Stands of yellow pine, usually found on
the lower slopes, make up about three-fourths of the softwood type area.
Mixtures of white pine and hemlock are also important, and a small
acreage of spruce and balsam fir is found on the tops of the higher mountains.

The volume of sawtimber material in the unit now stands at
8,700,000,000 board feet. The two national forests in the region contain
an estimated 2,800,000,000 board feet of sawtimber on 891,000 acres of
commercial forest land.

Nearly 3,500,000,000 board feet, or two-fifths of the sawtimber volume in the unit, is made up of various species of oak. The red oaks constitute the largest group, with scarlet, northern red, and black oak as principal species. In the white-oak group, chestnut oak constitutes two-thirds of the volume. Yellow poplar and hickory are also important. The remaining hardwood sawtimber is made up of a large number of minor species including ash, beech, basswood, maple, birch, and locust. Among the softwoods, both shortleaf pine and white pine contain about 750,000,000 board feet. These species are followed in order by hemlock, Virginia pine, spruce, and balsam fir.

See Tables 7 through 11 for more specific figures on ownership and type of commercial forest land, net volume in particular type of timber, and annual volume within tree-size and species groups.

Bibliography

Common Forest Trees of North Carolina. Seventh Edition. North Carolina Department of Conservation and Development. Raleigh: 1954.

Glesinger, Egon. *A Postwar Program for North Carolina Forests*. North Carolina Department of Conservation and Development, Bulletin 45. Raleigh: 1944.

Hobbs, S. H., Jr. *North Carolina: Economic and Social*. Chapel Hill: University of North Carolina Press, 1930.

Larson, Robert W. *North Carolina Timber Supply, 1955*. U. S. Department of Agriculture Forest Service, Forest Survey Release No. 49. Asheville: 1957.

McCormack, James F. *Forest Statistics for the Southern Coastal Plain of North Carolina, 1952*, U.S.D.A. Forest Service in cooperation with the North Carolina Department of Conservation and Development, Forest Survey Release No. 41. Asheville: 1953.

———. *Forest Statistics for the Northern Coastal Plain of North Carolina, 1955*. U.S.D.A. Forest Service in cooperation with the North Carolina Department of Conservation and Development, Forest Survey Release No. 45. Asheville: 1956.

———. *Forest Statistics for the Piedmont of North Carolina, 1956*. U.S.D.A. Forest Service in cooperation with the North Carolina Department of Conservation and Development, Forest Survey Release No. 48. Asheville: 1956.

———. *Forest Statistics for the Mountain Region of North Carolina, 1955*. U.S.D.A. Forest Service in cooperation with the North Carolina Department of Conservation and Development, Forest Survey Release No. 46. Asheville: 1956.

North Carolina, Land of Opportunity. State Board of Agriculture, Raleigh: 1923.

Wood Residue in North Carolina: Raw Material for Industry. North Carolina Department of Conservation and Development. Raleigh: 1955.

Chapter 3

CLIMATE

The state of North Carolina lies roughly between 34 degrees and 36 1/2 degrees north latitude and 75 1/2 and 84 1/2 degrees west longitude. Its extreme length from east to west is 503 miles. Of its 52,712 square miles, 49,097 are land and 3,615 are water (these are estimates, for exact data are unknown). The topography of the state may be described as a vast downward slope, ranging in the west from the summits of the Smoky Mountains at an altitude of almost 7,000 feet to sea level at the Atlantic Coast.

There are considerable differences in the climates of the various parts of North Carolina. In the southeastern corner is approaches the subtropical; in the mountain regions of the west it is of a modified continental type, except that summers are cooler and the rainfall is greater than is usual in the interior states. Some of the mountain districts, notably near Highlands, have more rainfall than is found elsewhere in the eastern half of the United States; again some spots are fairly dry. The climate of the Piedmont is considerably modified by the partial barrier set up by the mountains, and the climate in the more eastern and southeastern sections is modified by the influence of the Atlantic Ocean and to some extent by the sounds and smaller bodies of water found there. The result is that near the coast the temperature changes, both daily and seasonal, are reduced, and there is an increase in the amount of precipitation.

TEMPERATURE.

The temperature of North Carolina is moderate. The state is fortunate in that none of her three regions is subjected to extremes of heat and cold. In only a few localities does the thermometer ever drop below zero and then only for short periods. In fact, it rarely gets colder than 10 or 12 degrees above zero in the eastern and central districts of the state. It is also unusual for the mercury to rise much above 100 degrees and remain there for more than a few hours. The normal annual mean temperature for North Carolina is approximately 59 degrees. In general, January is the coldest month, with its annual mean never having dropped below 31 degrees, while July is the warmest, with an annual mean never having risen higher than 81 degrees. The average is around 38 to 40 degrees for January, and 75 to 77 degrees for July. See Table 12 for average temperatures by regions.

Rainfall.

North Carolina has an even distribution of rainfall. She is fortunate in that the greatest amount of rainfall occurs in the summer period when it is most beneficial to crops, and that the months of October and November, when staple crops are being harvested, are the driest. With an average yearly normal of 49 inches, approximately 17 inches fall in the summer months.

Annual rainfall on a statewide basis varies little from year to year, but this is not to say that various stations will not read wide ranges of differences in any given year. In 1948 Highlands recorded a total of 106.9 inches, while Marshall, some 60 miles to the north in the French Broad basin, had a total of 37.6 inches. The average for Highlands is 79.8 inches.

The coastal plain receives from 55 to 60 inches at Cape Hatteras, about 50 inches at Raleigh, and some 42 inches in parts of the sandhills. Throughout the entire region the maximum rainfall generally occurs in July and August and the minimum in October or November. The piedmont receives between 40 and 50 inches of rainfall annually, usually from 46 to 49. The maximum rainfall occurs in July, almost all of which comes from thunderstorms. The mountain region presents great variations in amounts of rainfall within a relatively small area. Here stations report the highest and lowest annual averages in the state, Jackson, Clay, and Macon counties in the southwestern portion of the state being among the wettest areas of the nation and parts of Buncombe and Madison and other mountain counties receiving only 40 to 42 inches yearly.

Figures 3 and 4 give data on the average winter and summer temperatures and precipitation, and Table 13 shows the average seasonal rainfall by regions.

Hurricanes are not common to North Carolina. By the time they reach this state they have usually spent themselves and are no more effective than moderate windstorms. However, in 1954 and 1955 four rather severe hurricanes did extensive damage to the central and eastern parts of the state.

Growing Seasons.

In order to enjoy an effective growing season, there must be a considerable period between the last killing frost in spring and the first frost in the fall. North Carolina's agriculture depends largely upon the outcome of its warm-weather crops. One, for example, is cotton, which needs a long growing season in order to mature, and another is tobacco, which is admirably suited to North Carolina climate and soil.

As might be expected, the growing seasons and first and last killing frost vary from one section of the state to the other. From Roanoke Island to Southport, the growing season averages approximately 280 days. In

Fig. 3.   Average Annual Precipitation

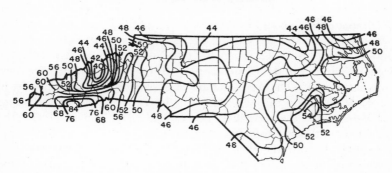

Source: U. S. Department of Agriculture, *Yearbook of Agriculture, 1941* (Washington, U. S. Government Printing Office, 1941), p. 1040.

Fig. 4.   Average January and July Temperatures

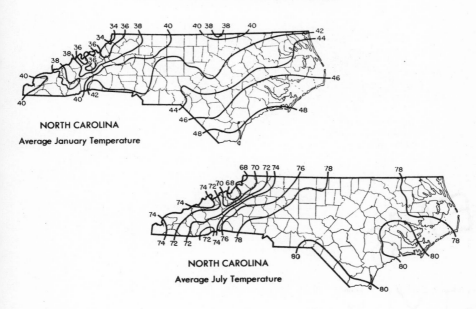

Source: *Ibid.*

Raleigh, the innermost limits of the coastal plain, the last killing frost of spring occurs around March 23 and the first fall frost around November 9, giving a mean average of 231 days of growing season. Charlotte, lying in the piedmont region, has a mean average of 238 days, with its last killing frost on March 18 and the earliest occurring about November 11. The mountain region presents a somewhat different picture. In Asheville, the growing season of 194 days extends from April 11 to October 22. Ashe County in this region has only 150 days of growing season, the shortest in the state. At any point in the state, killing frosts may occur two weeks or more before or after the average date. See Figure 5 for a chart showing the average dates of the first and last killing frosts in a given area. North Carolina's climate features the phenomenon of thermal, or generally frostless, belts which occur in certain mountain localities, especially Burke, Polk, and McDowell counties.

Fig. 5. Average Dates of Last Spring Frost and First Fall Frost

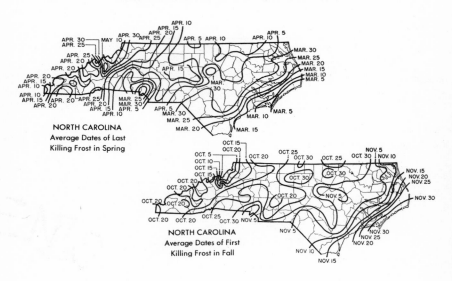

Source: U. S. Department of Agriculture, *Yearbook of Agriculture, 1941*, p. 1041.

BIBLIOGRAPHY

U. S. Department of Agriculture. *Yearbook of Agriculture, 1941*. Washington: U. S. Government Printing Office, 1942.

U. S. Department of Commerce, U. S. Weather Bureau. *Climatological Data, North Carolina Annual Summary*, 1947.

VISHER, S. *Climatic Atlas of the United States*. Cambridge: Harvard University Press, 1954.

Weather and Climate in North Carolina. Agricultural Experiment Station, North Carolina State College, Bulletin 396 (October, 1955). Raleigh.

Chapter 4

WATER AND POWER RESOURCES

North Carolina's water resources are very extensive, and this has had a historic impact upon the development of the state. In colonial times, the sounds and rivers were the arteries of communication and transportation, and nearly all towns and plantations and most farms were located on navigable streams or canals leading thereto. Indeed, the existence of so many navigable waters explains in large measure the wide distribution of North Carolina cities and towns, since there has been no necessity for concentrating settlements at a few sites of water. These water resources are also extremely vital to the agriculture and industry of the state, and in recent years attention has been given to conserving them and to keeping them free of pollution.

Types and Quality of Water Resources

In terms of precipitation, which is the ultimate source of all water, North Carolina is well situated. The amount of precipitation, mostly in the form of rainfall, averages around 49 inches a year, and over a vast part of North Carolina the departure from the average is only very slight. There are small areas of moderately low average rainfall and other small areas with considerably more than the state average. However, approximately 90 per cent of North Carolina has an annual precipitation within four inches of the average for the state.

This precipitation is also very dependable from year to year. There are periods of slight deficits and surpluses but the departure from normal is relatively less in North Carolina than in any other state that has a fair amount of rainfall. This is partially shown by the fact that in the drought years of 1934 and 1936, North Carolina had the best crop indexes of any state. Strangely enough 1936, the nation's dryest year, was North Carolina's second wettest year on record.

There are rivers and streams everywhere in North Carolina. Some of these are small and others carry considerable volumes of water. It is impossible to drive more than a few miles anywhere in the state without crossing bodies of running water. In addition, North Carolina has a unique system of extensive inland coastal seas.

A matter of concern not only to the health of the population but also to industry is the chemical purity of the water, both surface and subsurface. Certain manufacturing processes, notably for textiles and paper, require tremendous amounts of water, which must be of high quality.

Utilization of Water

There are three very important trends which will necessitate care to safeguard the natural water resources of the state: (1) increasing population, (2) expanding use of water, and (3) man's constant interference with nature's water cycle.

The estimated average urban water consumption in North Carolina for domestic and commercial purposes is about 300,000,000 gallons per day, or more than 100,000,000,000 gallons per year. By 1970 the estimated figure will be around 700,000,000 gallons per day, or more than 200,000,000,000 gallons per year. The importance of a dependable supply of water for domestic use has recently been made evident by dry spells which occurred from 1951 through 1954 and the experience of Raleigh and other communities which had taken a chance on a regular supply of water by nature.

In an unpublished report the North Carolina Water Resources Committee presents these figures to indicate the tremendous usage of water:

Some further statements pointing up the demand for water are: (a) a large paper mill may use 50 million gallons a day or more than the total used by the five largest cities in the state. (b) Farm crops are tremendous users of water and the demand is highly seasonal, intensifying the shortage as the peak demand comes during the hot summer months when most other demands are also at their peak. It takes about 100 gallons of water to produce one ear of corn, 21 inches of rainfall to get a yield of 100 bushels of corn to the acre, and more than 7,000 gallons for a bushel of oats. With higher acreage yields in all crops and four summer droughts in succession, irrigation is being considered by thousands of farmers. (c) Farm animals consume vast quantities of water, using increased amounts in the summer months. Cattle consume 15 to 25 gallons per head per day, hogs two gallons per head per day, and 1,000 chickens 50 gallons per day. Both livestock and poultry numbers are increasing rapidly in North Carolina. (d) Municipal use is steadily expanding because of population increases and new uses for water—for example the air-conditioning of public buildings, office buildings, and factories. Fire-fighting and street-flushing services to extended city limits add to the demand. (3) Industrial use constantly expands. Plenty of good water has long been one of the requirements in establishing new industries. (f) Recreational uses of water for swimming, boating, and fishing are more and more popular. Both quantity and quality factors must be taken into account in providing water for recreational purposes.

Average No. of gallons used	Industry or product	Unit
67,000	Wood pulp	Ton
39,000	Paper board	Ton
65,000	Steel	Ton
200,000	Steam generating plant	Per ton of coal used
90-200	Rayon	Pound
8-40	Cotton goods	Pound
240	Meat packing (hogs)	Pound
80	Electric power	Per KWH
2.5	Soft drinks	Case
5	Dairy processing	Per gallon of milk [1]

[1]North Carolina Water Resources Committee, Report to the 1955 Legislature (unpublished; Raleigh, 1955).

Industries which depend upon water will naturally seek out areas that have good-quality waters in dependable quantity. The Davidson River, which flows out of the Pisgah Forest, was chosen for the location of the giant Ecusta Paper Company, the source of the cigarette paper indispensable to the North Carolina tobacco economy, because of the purity of its water.

Too much water has in some respects handicapped certain areas in the state. This is particularly true of the tidewater, with some 5,000,000 acres of wet land. Proper drainage could create 200,000 twenty-five-acre farms on fertile land. Some experts recommend such enterprises as this for the federal government over the more expensive irrigation projects set up in other parts of the country.

The most familiar use of water is the generation of power. For many years the streams of the state were used directly for this purpose—that is, the water was used to turn wheels and the water wheels were hooked up to other wheels which operated machines. About fifty years ago the energy of falling water was first put to use to turn wheels attached to electric generators. Principally because it was almost totally lacking in coal and needed power, North Carolina became a pioneer state in the development of hydroelectric power. For a number of years it ranked third among the states in this respect, and as late as 1950 it ranked sixth in the total output of hydroelectric energy.

Flood control constitutes a major water problem to North Carolina, especially on the Roanoke, the Neuse, and the Cape Fear, but to some extent on all rivers of the state. In planning the use of the state's rivers, it must be considered what the primary problems or potentialities are with a given river. If the chief problem is flood control, then the river will have to be engineered with that in mind. Generally, however, there are few opportunities for drawing hydroelectric power from these rivers. When a river is engineered for flood control and hydroelectric purposes combined, it can never generate as much power as if engineered for power alone. The Roanoke River is now being developed in a combination manner. The other river basins need to be studied carefully and a plan developed for each. Where flood control is a major item, the project will likely be a public one.

Because of its dependable rainfall, North Carolina has never greatly used its water resources for irrigation. However, there are types of agriculture where if maximum production is to be achieved, irrigation may be profitable. At present there are a number of small irrigation projects in the state and indications are that there will be many more in the future.

North Carolina's coastline is often referred to as the graveyard of the Atlantic, and not without justification. In spite of its unhappy record, however, the inland coastal seas and the wide mouth rivers that empty into these are being used more and more for transportation and can be made into greater arteries of commerce. The deep-harbor resources of North Carolina are not the best, but there are assets that can be developed, and with a reasonable expenditure North Carolina could have at least two ocean-front ports and one important and several minor inland river ports. The state is spending modest sums on developing the facilities at Wilmington and Morehead City, and in time the Southport area resources will be developed.

Another use of the state's water resources is in recreation. North Carolina has a frontage on the Atlantic of over 300 miles, with excellent beach facilities. The unique inland coastal seas, with a waterfront of 1,500 miles and an estimated area of more than 3,000 square miles, plus innumerable streams, natural and artificial lakes, and thousands of fish ponds, all constitute tremendous recreation assets, besides the other uses made of these waters. The recreational advantages of North Carolina, particularly those associated with its resources, are increasingly appreciated.

Long-range Planning of Water Use

The need for a comprehensive and effective policy for the use and control of water has been well stated by the National Resources Committee:

> During the last few years, it has become increasingly apparent that such orderless, unintegrated treatment of water problems, however natural or excusable it may have been under pioneer conditions, should no longer be tolerated. Water, though at times a merciless enemy of man, is perhaps the most precious resource of the nation. The supply of water for essential purposes, available and potential, on the surface and underground, is strictly limited, though it varies from time to time at a given place as well as from place to place at a given time.
>
> The further development of large areas in all sections depends even now in considerable part on the extent to which the available supply of water can be increased, by storing surface water, by pumping ground water, or by other means. Sooner or later the wasteful use of water must cease. Sooner or later, the maximum supply of water that can be made regularly available in each drainage area must be put to its best coordinated use.
>
> Under these conditions it would be unwise to depend solely on the long-run tendency of economic conditions to bring about the use of water in the places and ways in which it would have greatest value. Moreover, the sum total of individual and local interests in the water of a drainage area may differ greatly from the best interest of the public at large in their use. Still further, continued uncoordinated development of waters might presently preclude in many basins their later control and utilization in an orderly balanced manner conducive in greatest measure to the general welfare. The inherent conflict of interests in water, between private users, between private and public organizations, and even between public agencies, increases year by year. From every point of view, a practical water development program that can be put into action properly is needed in each river basin. A plan without action is useless; continued unplanned action would be foolhardy.[2]

---

[2] U.S. National Resources Committee, *Drainage Basin Problems and Programs*, rev. (Washington, D.C., February, 1938).

26 NORTH CAROLINA

As a result of this situation the Water Resources and Engineering Division of the North Carolina Department of Conservation and Development has set itself to formulating plans. It has already adopted an eight-point program outlining special activities that cover: (1) surface-water investigations; (2) obtaining authority to approve federal projects within the state relating to water; (3) approval of irrigation and drainage projects; (4) studies of inlets and waterways; (5) studies for stabilization of beaches; (6) encouragement of the development of river-basin associations; (7) initiation and promotion of legislation for control of water uses; and (8) the establishment of the Water Resources and Engineering Division as the state authority in all matters relating to the state's water resources.

The Water Resources Division has agreed that the program should be initiated by: (1) the assembling of data and the preparation of a master map, showing the water resources of the state, and a series of maps showing in detail the various areas affected with their problems and possible development and descriptive material about each; (2) the promotion of river-basin associations on the local level for each of the major river basins; (3) formation of project committees for the various harbor or inlet and beach-erosion areas; and (4) the education of people in general to the importance of the over-all program in order to have their support in the respective projects.

The Water Resources Committee appointed by Governor William B. Umstead has made a report of its study of conditions and needs. It has recommended the establishment of a statewide Water Commission. Such a commission has been created and given broad powers to deal with the vast water resources of the state so that water will be conserved and developed to the greatest benefit now and in the future for all the people of North Carolina. The proposal has been made that the state form a citizens' committee similar to the recent Medical Care Committee and Education Committee to conduct a real education program on this problem.

Power

MAJOR RIVER BASINS.

Figure 6 will be helpful in locating the major river basins of North Carolina, starting in the northeastern part of the state and moving clockwise.

The *Roanoke and Chowan rivers* in a way constitute a single drainage basin. The tributaries of the Roanoke are in both Virginia and North Carolina, and the river meanders across the state line several times and finally enters Albemarle Sound. So does the Chowan. The combined drainage basin of the Roanoke and Chowan is some 10,580 square miles with approximately two-thirds of this total in Virginia. Around one-half of the drainage area in North Carolina is below the fall line.

Fig. 6. Major River Basins

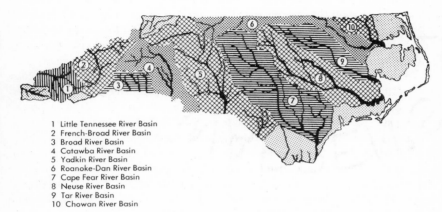

1 Little Tennessee River Basin
2 French-Broad River Basin
3 Broad River Basin
4 Catawba River Basin
5 Yadkin River Basin
6 Roanoke-Dan River Basin
7 Cape Fear River Basin
8 Neuse River Basin
9 Tar River Basin
10 Chowan River Basin

Source: Prepared by North Carolina Advisory Water Resources Committee.

A study by the Army engineers states that there are four hydroelectric sites on the Roanoke River in North Carolina which could be developed to an installed capacity of 76,000 kilowatts, and the engineers specifically recommend the development of the sites of 71,000 of the kilowatts. However, the Federal Power Commission claims that there is a maximum potential of 207,000 kilowatts which could be developed on this river, although it makes no claim that development of all these sites would be economical. Actually, only the proposed project at Roanoke Rapids has been developed.

The *Tar River* rises at Oxford and flows into the Pamlico and thus into Pamlico Sound, entering the Pamlico near the town of Washington. The Tar has a drainage basin of approximately 4,200 square miles, but no important hydroelectric possibilities. It will be developed chiefly for flood control and as a source of water. The Army engineers claim that four projects with a total optimum potential of 13,500 kilowatts could be developed on the Tar River, but no project is actually recommended. The Federal Power Commission reports about the same opinion.

The *Neuse River* rises in Person County near Roxboro and only a few miles from the headwaters of the Tar River. The Neuse enters Pamlico Sound by way of New Bern, where it begins to widen out and becomes almost an arm of the sea before it merges with Pamlico Sound. Again the Neuse cannot be considered as of much importance as a source of power. It is still a small stream as it enters the coastal plain just east of Raleigh, and while it has considerable volume in its lower reaches, the geographic features are such that power development is more or less out of the question. The Neuse will be engineered from the standpoint of flood control and water supply for the cities and towns and potential industries along its course. Stream pollution is already a serious problem on this river.

The Army engineers claim that six projects with a total output of 3,048 kilowatts could be installed on the Neuse River, but does not recommend any of the projects. The Federal Power Commission claims that a potential 41,200 kilowatts are undeveloped, but makes no recommendation. Only 1,845 kilowatts are now derived from the Neuse.

The *Cape Fear River* proper begins above Lillington, where its main tributaries come to a central focal point, and has a drainage basin of some 9,870 square miles. The chief tributaries are the Haw, Rocky, Deep, and New Hope rivers, together with the tributaries of these four rivers. The Haw River, the principal tributary, rises in the northwestern corner of Guilford County and is the chief power river among the tributaries, but there is a modest amount of power on at least two others of these. There is no single important power development comparable with the larger projects in the state. The Cape Fear proper cannot be considered a potential power producer. There is, of course, potential power on any running stream, but potentiality and economic feasibility are entirely different things. It should be mentioned that the South River and its tributaries and the Northeast Cape Fear ultimately flow into the Cape Fear north of Wilmington. The Cape Fear is the only North Carolina river of any importance that empties directly into the ocean. The other rivers either empty into the sounds or pass into South Carolina, where they ultimately reach the coast of that state.

The Army engineers claim that five projects with a total potential of 131,000 kilowatts can be installed on the tributaries to the Cape Fear. The engineers claim that all five projects are feasible. The Federal Power Commission makes a higher estimate but no specific recommendations.

The *Yadkin River* begins with waters that fall from the eastern slope of the Blue Ridge along the western boundary of Wilkes County. This river is made up of innumerable tributaries, among them the South Yadkin, Uwharrie, and Little rivers. The total drainage area of the Yadkin, which becomes the Pee Dee, is roughly 10,650 square miles. The Yadkin is North Carolina's principal power river and has extensive power plants located on it. There are additional power possibilities on the river, but these are approaching the point of diminishing return. One interesting proposal is to build a dam across the South Fork River, which flows into the New River in Ashe County, thus diverting the water of the South Fork through a tunnel through the Blue Ridge and eventually into the Yadkin. It is estimated that a power plant east of the Blue Ridge, which would be several hundred feet below the South River reservoir, would be capable of generating around 60,000 kilowatts. The expectation is that the diversion of water from the present drainage basin will meet with strong opposition.

The Army engineers claim that thirteen additional projects, with a total possible output of 516,400 kilowatts, are possible on the Yadkin-Pee Dee and its tributaries. However, only six of these projects, totaling 296,000 kilowatts, are recommended. The Federal Power Commission is in agreement with the recommended figures. It must be remembered, however, that if some of the proposed installations are made, some of the present hydroelectric developments will have to be scrapped or altered.

The *Catawba River* rises near Ridgecrest and has a number of tributaries entering in a section lying from a point south of Blowing Rock to below Marion. Some of its chief tributaries are its various forks and the Linville River. The Catawba with its tributaries has a drainage area of 3,250 square miles in North Carolina, and then it becomes the Wateree in South Carolina. It ultimately flows into the ocean through the Santee River—or through the Cooper River, since the Santee has been largely diverted into the Cooper River in connection with the Santee-Cooper Power project. The Catawba and its tributaries in North Carolina have been harnessed by the Duke Power Company. There is not much power remaining to be developed on this river in North Carolina.

The Federal Power Commission claims that an additional 115,000 kilowatts could be installed on the Catawba and its tributaries, but this is in excess of any private estimates.

The *Broad River* rises near Chimney Rock. It and its tributaries, chiefly the First Broad and Second Broad rivers, have a drainage area in North Carolina of about 1,450 square miles. The chief power project is at Lake Lure, near the river's head. The Federal Power Commission claims that 91,000 kilowatts can be installed on it, again more than any private estimates.

The *Hiwassee* lies beyond the Blue Ridge in the southwestern corner of the state. This river has a drainage area of 650 square miles. It is the source of power developed by the TVA at the Hiwassee and Appalachia hydroelectric plants. The Hiwassee plant is in North Carolina, but while the Appalachia dam is in North Carolina, its power plant is across the line in Tennessee. The installed capacity of these two plants is approximately 130,000 kilowatts.

Next is the *Little Tennessee River* and its tributaries, chiefly the Nantahala, Tuckasegee, Cullasaja, Oconolufty, and Cheoah. The principal hydroelectric projects are the Fontana, operated by the TVA; the Santeetlah and the Cheoah operated by the Aluminum Company of America; and the Nantahala and some smaller plants of the Nantahala Power Company, a utility subsidiary of Alcoa.

The *Pigeon River*, which has a plant known as the Walters Project operated by the Carolina Power and Light Company has an output of 108,000 kilowatts.

The *French Broad River* has a drainage area of 2,825 square miles. It is made up of tributaries, starting with the Davidson River, and flows northwest, entering Tennessee above Hot Springs. There is a power plant at Marshall and there are plans to develop the power of the French Broad, but altogether the resources are not extensive.

The final rivers of any importance are the *Watauga*, with a drainage basin in North Carolina of 220 square miles, and the *New River*, with a drainage basin of 760 square miles. The South Fork, referred to above, is a tributary of the New River.

In so far as can be determined, there are no separate reports on those rivers in North Carolina which are tributary to the Tennessee. The Federal Power Commission lumps the Hiwassee, the Little Tennessee and its tributaries, the French Broad, and the Pigeon under the head of the Tennessee. The claim is made that these tributaries to the Tennessee could stand additional installations of 242,600 kilowatts. There are power sites remaining on these rivers, a number of which (perhaps half the maximum potential) are economic to develop.

POTENTIAL HYDROELECTRIC RESOURCES.

It is difficult to estimate how much hydroelectric power remains to be developed in North Carolina, even approximately. Some of the rivers have been studied by the Army engineers, some by private utilities, some by the TVA, and some by the Federal Power Commission, and their estimates differ somewhat:

Table 14 shows by river basins the total existing and estimated undeveloped hydroelectric power in North Carolina. It also shows the present power storage at existing hydroelectric plants and the estimated potential power storage associated with the undeveloped power projects, as reported by the Federal Power Commission. This is maximum potential installation without regard to the economic advisability of its development.

It will be noted from Table 14 that the 1951 hydroelectric installations on the rivers of North Carolina total around 961,000 kilowatts. (The 1956 rated capacity is approximately 1,280,000; see Table 15.) The Federal Power Commission claims that the undeveloped hydroelectric potential of North Carolina is 1,225,000 kilowatts. By this it means that there are sufficient places where generating plants could be set up to produce a maximum capacity of this amount. It does not, nor does anyone else, claim that it would be possible to generate this much power all the time or even one-fourth of the time. It does claim that at certain times there would be enough water in the rivers to turn turbines rated at this capacity.

It may reasonably be assumed that the hydroelectric projects which have been developed in North Carolina were the choice sites and that the projects to be developed in the future will steadily run into diminishing returns and thus beyond the realm of economic feasibility. There were in 1955 fifty public-utility projects (excluding TVA plants, which have a production of 404,600 kilowatts) in the state, with a total installed capacity of approximately 581,000 kilowatts. (This also does not include nonutility [mainly Alcoa] plants. There are five major ones rated at a total of 289,500 kilowatts.) If these public-utility plants operated at full capacity, they would generate from four to five times the power that they have generated in recent years. Actually they have in recent years operated at around one-fourth of their rated capacity, and only about one-fourth of all public utility power generated in the state these past few years has come from hydro-electric stations. Calculations from the estimates of undeveloped sites, using Federal Power Commission data, show that the actual output per year is expected to be about one-fourth of the capacity of the generators going at full speed. Unfortunately, this is the fallacy in accepting some statements of kilowatt potential as compared with actual kilowatt-hour output of electric energy. Theoretically steam plants can operate at nearly full capacity, while there is no hydroelectric station now in operation in the state that functions at anything like full capacity.

An analysis of all the available data leads to the conclusion that the hydroelectric installations which are feasible from an economic standpoint will probably total not more than 500,000 kilowatts and that these installations will probably never operate at more than 50 per cent of rated capacity throughout a good year and below that during a dry year. It may be that with public subsidy in connection with flood control, the federal government in the public interest could go beyond this figure of 500,000 kilowatts. So far as is known, no student of the subject believes that it is economically feasible for private capital to go much beyond it.

EXPANSION PROJECTS.

It might be pointed out in this connection that tremendous expansion in steam power is taking place in the state (see Table 16). The Carolina Power and Light Company has recently added large plants at Lumberton, Goldsboro, and Wilmington. The Duke Power Company has more than doubled its steam-plant capacity since 1950. On December 31, 1954,

the rated capacity of Duke Power steam plants in North Carolina was
1,485,400 kilowatts; the eighteen Duke hydroelectric plants in North
Carolina have a rated capacity of 175,843 kilowatts. Incidentally, it is
interesting to note that before 1926 all power generated by the Duke
Power Company was hydroelectric, while all recent additions by Duke
have been steam plants. The *North Carolina Employment Security Quarterly*,
in commenting on plans for expansion of power production, says:

> North Carolina electric-power-producing companies are stretching efforts in
> erection of new plants to keep even or just ahead of the increasing demand for
> electric power for expanding North Carolina industries. Since World War II,
> when most construction was halted, the utilities firms have gone ahead, spending
> many millions of dollars to provide power and lighting current. Estimates are
> that last year (1956) from $80,000,000 to $90,000,000 were spent in building new
> plants, providing high-voltage transmission lines, and developing and expanding
> distribution systems. Indications are that this year that figure will reach
> $100,000,000, since the larger companies have announced greater expansion pro-
> grams, not only for this year but for several years to come.
> Last year the large Virginia Electric & Power Co. hydroelectric plant at Roa-
> noke Rapids on the Roanoke River was completed and placed in operation,
> costing $32,000,000. Carolina Power & Light Co. has spent about $163,000,000
> in the past 10 years, is spending about $8,000,000 this year, and has a $65,000,000
> program for the next three years. Plants at Goldsboro, Lumberton, Wilmington
> and Moncure are involved. The new unit at Moncure, to be completed in 1958,
> will add 150,000 kilowatts.
> Duke Power Co. has invested about $320,000,000 in plants and facilities since
> World War II, and plans call for expenditure of $10,000,000 a year for several
> years to come. Presently Duke is engaged in building two sections of Plant Allen,
> near Belmont, which will cost $41,000,000, and plans three other units which will
> take the entire cost to about $100,000,000. [On May 15, 1957, Duke applied to the
> Federal Power Commission for permission to develop 350,000 additional kilowatts
> in North and South Carolina at a cost of approximately $51,000,000.] Carolina
> Aluminum Co., Badin, has asked permission to build another power dam on the
> Yadkin River to cost around $14,000,000, for use at its Badin smelting plant.
> Nantahala Power & Light Co., in half a dozen far western North Carolina
> counties, continues to add dams on mountain streams, small and close together,
> to turn power generated by the swift downhill streams into electricity for the small
> industries and for lighting purposes in the area.[3]

Hydroelectric vs. Steam Power.

Twenty years ago around 80 per cent of the state's power came from
hydroelectric plants. The percentage is now not quite 25. Many of the
potential hydroelectric installations are relatively small units and are
pretty well scattered over the state. If these units were bunched and could
be developed by one concern with central station control, such as the
Nantahala Power Company now employs, these developmental projects
would be more easily feasible than they would be with a separate maintenance crew at each site. Existing conditions of multiple ownership make

---

[3] *North Carolina Employment Security Quarterly*, XIV (Winter-Spring, 1956), 35.

hydroelectric development less advantageous than construction of steam plants.

The point has been made—based on facts with which power companies and electric-utility engineers are in agreement—that potential power for brief periods of time does not necessarily mean economical power throughout the years or throughout the total life of the project, and further that hydroelectric power is not free power. Setting up a hydroelectric station costs several times as much as setting up a steam station of equal capacity, although after the initial expenditure, hydroelectric stations are cheaper to operate. Improved techniques have greatly increased the efficiency of steam stations, while on the other hand a hydroelectric plant retires thousands of fertile valley-land acres from agricultural use. This is partly offset by the hydroelectric station's recreational potential.

DIVERSION OF POWER BENEFITS.

Not all of the hydroelectric energy generated in North Carolina is used within the state or is used to the best advantage of the state as a whole. For instance, the Aluminum Company of America operated five major hydroelectric plants with an installed capacity of 289,500 kilowatts. All of these plants, except those of the Nantahala Power Company (99,235 kilowatts in 1955), a public-utility subsidiary of Alcoa, were built as aluminum manufacturing plants. This company has no surplus power to let to public utilities. Actually it has a shortage. This means that this vast amount of hydroelectric production (289,500 kilowatts in 1955), far exceeding the output of the Duke Power Company, is of little real benefit to the economy of North Carolina. Also, power generated at Cheoah and Santeetlah is exported to Tennessee, where it is used at the Alcoa plant there. This is no criticism of Alcoa. Rather the intention is to point out that in so far as the economy of North Carolina is concerned, this power could be of immensely greater benefit to the state. The present benefit is rather local.

Again, the Tennessee Valley Authority has an installed capacity at the Fontana, Chatuge, Hiwassee, and Appalachia plants of 404,600 kilowatts—close to 600,000 horsepower, since a horsepower is roughly equivalent to two-thirds kilowatt. Virtually all of the power generated in North Carolina by the TVA at these plants is exported into Tennessee and used in that and other states by the TVA, only a very small amount finding its way back into North Carolina through sale to a rural-electric–membership corporation in the extreme western part of the state. Because of such drainage, less than one-half of the state's hydroelectric power (694,160 kilowatts in 1956) was available for public use, and it was necessary for public-utility companies to expand their steam-power production.

CONSERVATION OF EXISTING FACILITIES.

The need for conserving present sites has become apparent. Every day every hydroelectric project in the state is just a little less efficient than it was the day before—some days much less efficient—for sedimentation is taking place behind every dam in every reservoir in North Carolina.

The chief of the Regional Water Conservation Division, U. S. Soil Conservation Service, H. G. Edwards, writes:

> The greater portion of the sedimentation surveys made in North Carolina by the Soil Conservation Service has been completed on water supply reservoirs rather than on those built primarily for power, but comparisons can be made. Reservoirs, ranging in size from 460 acre-feet to 289,000 acre-feet in capacity and with net sediment contributing areas of five square miles to 3,900 square miles, have been surveyed. Annual storage depletion rates have ranged from 0.20 per cent to 1.85 per cent.
>
> The U. S. Engineers, Department of the Army, have reported an annual loss of storage of 8.7 per cent in a small power reservoir in North Carolina, while the Tennessee Valley Authority reports annual capacity losses of from .023 per cent to .899 per cent in reservoirs they have served in North Carolina.
>
> There are many factors influencing reservoir sedimentation. Among these are the size of the drainage area, the land use pattern of the drainage area, the capacity of the reservoir in relation to the size of drainage area, the rainfall and runoff pattern. It is difficult to give any hard and fast rule concerning reservoir sedimentation and, at present, each site or existing reservoir must be studied individually. [4]

Some hydroelectric plants now in operation will have ceased to operate well within the lifetime of many people now living. It may be that a few will remain efficient for a hundred years or more. One company writes off 2 per cent of its plant investment a year as depreciation. It is impossible to prevent all sedimentation, but it is possible to reduce the rate greatly, and thus extend the life of the project.

Power Rates

There has been a large increase in average residential consumption of electricity, as well as in total consumption by industry and others. That average residential consumption per month has gone up can be seen from these figures covering the 1931–51 rise for both Carolina Power and Light Company and the Duke Power Company: Carolina, from 54 kilowatt hours to 224 kilowatt hours; Duke, from 50 kilowatt hours to 183 kilowatt hours. This rise is typical of other electric-utility companies as well.

The rate per kilowatt hour has gone down for the same years as follows: Carolina, from 6.5 cents per kilowatt hour to 2.3 cents; for Duke, from 6.3 cents per kilowatt hour to 2.2 cents. The Federal Power Commission reports that the average cost per 100 kilowatt hours for the United States in 1952 was $3.76, and for 250 kilowatt hours it was $6.97. In North

---

[4] Letter to the author.

Carolina the averages were $3.60 and $6.99 respectively. Thus North Carolina rates were in line with national rates. Power rates per 250 kilowatt hours range in the southeast from $5.04 in Tennessee to $7.61 in Florida.

Industrial rates for North Carolina plants that use from 375 to 1,500 kilowatt hours per month are about the average for the southeast, perhaps a little below average. For industries using more than 15,000 kilowatt hours per month, North Carolina rates are the lowest in the southeast with the exception of states in the TVA territory. Even the TVA rates for large users are higher in some cities than in Charlotte, Greensboro, or Raleigh, or other places served by the two major North Carolina utility companies.[5]

Rural Electrification

Rural electrification began in North Carolina in 1935.[6] Tables 17 and 18 and Fig. 7 report progress made by 15 public utilities, 32 electric-membership corporations (cooperatives), 58 municipalities, and 3 institutions engaged in rural electrification. The total program represents an investment of more than $250,000,000. Farmer cooperatives have borrowed around $100,000,000.

Fig.7   Generalized Areas Served by Major Electric Utilities

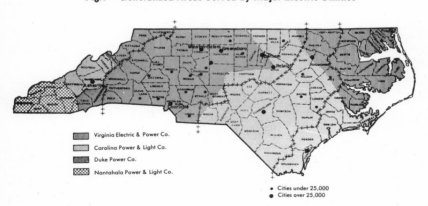

Virginia Electric & Power Co.
Carolina Power & Light Co.
Duke Power Co.
Nantahala Power & Light Co.

● Cities under 25,000
● Cities over 25,000

---

[5] L. M. Keever, Electric Generating and Transmission Systems in North Carolina (unpublished report to Governor W. Kerr Scott; Raleigh, 1952).

[6] *Annual Progress Report*, North Carolina Rural Electrification Authority (Raleigh, 1954).

BIBLIOGRAPHY

Annual Report of the North Carolina Utilities Commission, 1952. Raleigh.

Annual Progress Report, 1954. North Carolina Rural Electrification Authority. Raleigh.

GREEN, C. H. (comp.). Conservation and Development in North Carolina. Vol. I. Mimeographed. Conservation Congress Report. Raleigh: 1952.

KEEVER, L. M. Electric Generating and Transmission Systems in North Carolina. Unpublished report to Governor W. Kerr Scott. Raleigh, 1952.

North Carolina Water Resources Committee Report to the 1955 Legislature. Unpublished. Raleigh, 1955.

Planning Report on Water Resources of North Carolina. State Planning Board. Raleigh, 1937.

U.S. National Resources Committee. *Drainage Basin Problems and Programs.* Rev. Washington: U.S. Government Printing Office, February, 1938.

Chapter 5

COMMERCIAL FISHING RESOURCES[1]

Among the twenty-two states which have a seacoast, North Carolina stands fifth in length of general coast line and fourth in general tidal shore line. Offshore, the state has about 3,800 square miles of salt and brackish-water sounds. It has a total of 6,375 square miles of shallow-water fishing grounds, an area equal to 13 per cent of the entire land area of the state, and 1.6 per cent of the offshore salt-water and fresh-water fishing bottoms of the United States (exclusive of Alaska, or 1.2 per cent if Alaska is included).

North Carolina lies at the divide between the cold northern and the warm Gulf-Caribbean fisheries and has a wide assortment of fish and shellfish, some characteristic of each of these regions. The state is visited by numerous species migrating either northward or southward, and some of these breed in the sounds and in the rivers. The sounds have water of a wide range of saltiness, from pure fresh at the river mouths to nearly pure ocean salt near the inlets, and therefore accommodate a great variety of plant and animal life. These protected sounds afford an exceptionally favorable place for the cultivation of oysters and perhaps other shellfish.

The assortment of fish which naturally occur here includes three of the top-ranking money-value species of the country: shrimp, oysters, and menhaden. Other than menhaden, the fisheries do not include any such cheap and large-volume species as the cod, haddock, and ocean perch; rather, the bulk of them are the choicer delicacies: shrimp, oysters, crabs, scallops, striped bass, shad, white perch, and others.

The state has other natural advantages in location. Experts report that in the warmer water oysters grow much more rapidly, perhaps two or three times faster than they do in the colder northern waters. Certain seasonal species, shad and soft-shell crabs among them, occur earlier in the season, when prices are higher, than they do farther north.

HISTORY.

In the South Atlantic states, including North Carolina, from 1880 to 1950, the federal government has made twenty-four statistical fishery

---

[1]This chapter is deawn largely from Harden F. Taylor, "Marine Resources in North Carolina," in Conservation and Development in North Carolina, comp. C. S. Green, Conservation Congress Report (mimeographed; Raleigh, 1952), II, 212–22.

surveys at irregular intervals, averaging one about every three years, and similar surveys of about the same frequency in other regions of the country. The data from these surveys can be arranged in various ways: if the twenty-nine commercial fishing states (including Alaska as a state) are arranged in rank according to the value of their fishery products, North Carolina has stood in positions from eleventh in the 1880's and 1890's, sixteenth in 1930, to fourteenth in 1940 and 1950, with about two per cent of the total national money values, varying but slightly from one survey to another (see Table 22).

In quantity of fish produced in North Carolina, if we include the menhaden fishery, which began in large volume about the time of World War I, the yield has risen from about 40,000,000 to 50,000,000 pounds in the eighties and nineties to around 200,000,000 pounds since World War I. This seems to be a huge increase, but it has not had a correspondingly great effect on the number of fishermen or their money income. The number of fishermen supported in whole or in part by the fisheries ranged from 6,000 to 7,500 in the 1890's, and reached its all-time high at 11,200 in 1902. The number then declined to a little over 6,000 in 1918 and on through the twenties to 5,200 in the depression years of the early thirties, back to about 7,000 in 1940. In 1950 they numbered 7,580, about the same number as in the 1890's. The money value of the whole fishery, including menhaden, appears to have increased when measured in actual dollars; but when the purchasing value of the dollar is taken into account, the total value of all fisheries, food and nonfood—i.e., the buying-power income of the fishermen—in 1940 was only slightly more than it was in 1902. See Table 23 for a description of the 1954-56 catch and its value.

The production of food fish only, exclusive of menhaden, rose from some 30,000,000 pounds in 1880, to 50,000,000 in 1900, but has changed little since then, averaging around 50,000,000 annually. In 1950 it was 47,500,000 pounds. In 1953 it was 60,543,000 pounds, valued at $6,878,000. Again, in actual dollars received by the fishermen for the total catch, the income was about the same in 1940 as it was at the turn of the century, but in terms of constant purchasing power the total income from the food fishery had declined from about $2,800,000 in 1897 to $1,740,000 in 1940, or the same as it was in 1890. Thus in the fifty years from 1890 to 1940, menhaden was not a net addition to income, but served only to make up for the decline of the value of the food fishery.

Thus whatever the productive capacity of the 6,375 square miles of fishing grounds may be, North Carolina's fisheries as a whole had not made any progress to speak of over the sixty years between 1890 and World War II. Even though the population of the state nearly doubled between 1900 and 1940, the number of fishermen in 1940 was the same as it had been half a century before, and their gross income was sustained only by the addition of the menhaden fishery. The economic gain in the fisheries industry since 1950 has been equal to the total advance of the sixty years before that date, largely as a result of the great increase in demand for and rising price of a few species, mainly shrimp.

POSSIBILITIES FOR EXPANSION.

Experts have pointed out that North Carolina's economy would be greatly strengthened if the state utilized its own seafood products to the utmost and undertook to process them for distribution to other regions. While, considering the immense food-producing potential of the water areas of the nation, the country as a whole takes very little of what it consumes from the sea or fresh-water bodies, North Carolina (which might logically be expected to consume a good deal, being a coastal state) takes even less. If it used its entire production of 12 pounds per capita, or five pounds of edible fish per capita, it would consume only from one-half to three-fourths of the national per capita average. Indeed, a sizable part of the fish products which appear on North Carolina tables comes from New York, New England, Florida, and the Chesapeake Bay area.

The state has faced certain problems in expanding its fisheries industries. The first of these is that the fisheries are not uniformly distributed for efficient operation, either seasonally throughout the year or geographically. The coastal region of the state is subdivided by sounds and rivers, so that no one distributing organization has direct access to the whole supply. This fact, plus the occurrence of the principal fisheries in waves at different times in different parts of the state, make it impracticable, with the present marketing operation, for the state to furnish a continuous and dependable supply of the most desirable assortment of fish, even to its own population. Further, the attempts to legislate in behalf of the fisheries industries have been limited to restrictive legislation, a measure apparently unnecessary. Meanwhile no governmental attention has been given to the basic problems of developing a product which can compete with out-of-state sources of seafood (through greater efficiency and economy in finding and catching, preparing, processing, and manufacturing of the catch; and through more effective and economical methods of sales and distribution.)

The industry has had considerable help of a scientific nature from the research laboratories and institutes, however—some of them of long standing. The Federal government established one at Beaufort fifty years ago, and Duke University founded its marine laboratory about seventeen years ago. There are others operated by the government and other universities, nearby and across the nation. These laboratories have done and are doing indispensable work in discovering the basic facts and laws of nature which give the industry the scientific knowledge on which it bases, or ought to base, its action. However, the point has been made that the failure of the fisheries industries indicates a need for practical efforts in merchandising and advertising in addition to pure zoological research.

The University of North Carolina established the Institute of Fisheries Research at Morehead City. It cooperates harmoniously and directly with the Department of Conservation and Development, from which two members of the Executive Committee of the institute are appointed. The Institute is staffed with scientists and equipped with laboratory, fishing boats, and so on for the conduct of research designed to solve specific scientific problems which the fishery enterprises in their present strength and organization cannot reasonably be expected to solve for themselves.

The Institute, established in 1947, made the shrimp survey authorized by the state legislature for the biennium beginning that year; and also on request of and by agreement with the Department of Conservation and Development, it functioned as the scientific and advisory authority in the Oyster Rehabilitation Act of 1947.

In the shrimp researches, which have been continued by the Institute after the expiration of the survey, a considerable amount of bottom surveying and general oceanographic sounding has been accomplished, designed to assist shrimp fishermen in finding new and productive shrimping grounds. These studies, which contributed new biological knowledge about the brown-spotted shrimps of Pamlico Sound, provide an interesting example of how such research organizations can be of immense practical value to the industry: Some years ago a conservation regulation was made by the Board of Conservation and Development prohibiting night shrimping in Pamlico Sound. In the Institute laboratory, shrimp under observation in aquaria were seen to burrow into the bottom mud or sand when the lights were on. If one entered the darkened room and suddenly turned on the lights, the shrimps were seen to be swimming around, but if the lights remained on they again soon burrowed into the sand. Obviously these shrimps were nocturnal—they were choice prey of many fishes, and in self-protection they kept out of sight in daytime, under cover in the mud; and while a trawl dragged on the bottom in daytime would catch some shrimp, it would be much more efficient if operated at night when the shrimp are actively swimming. Whereupon, on recommendation of the Institute, the Board of Conservation and Development repealed the regulation which prohibited night shrimping.

In the rehabilitation of the oyster, under the act providing a tax-supported revolving fund for shell planting, etc., the Institute has been conducting surveys to find the best spots for planting shells, suitable temperatures, proper saltiness of water, and other conditions that must be taken into account for best results. The Institute has made this information available to the Department of Conservation and Development as a guide to its shell-planting work. It is also conducting other continuous researches on the oyster. In cooperation with the School of Business Administration of the University, it has conducted a study of the economics and marketing of commercial fishing. A report entitled Commercial Fisheries of North Carolina has recently been published. Indications are that a dependable supply of oysters must come in the future from private cultivations on bottoms leased from the state rather than from spontaneous wild growth. North Carolina has both the environment and materials for such an undertaking, and the postulation has been made that this type of controlled cultivation of the sea may be a forerunner of a new facet to North Carolina fisheries.

BIBLIOGRAPHY

COKER, R. E. "Potentialities and Limitations in Fisheries Research," in Conservation and Development in North Carolina, comp. C. S. Green. Vol. II. Mimeographed. Conservation Congress Report. Raleigh: 1952.

FULCHER, CLAYTON, JR. "Conservation Problems in Commercial Fisheries," in Conservation and Development in North Carolina, comp. C. S. Green. Vol. II. Mimeographed. Conservation Congress Report. Raleigh: 1952.

PATTON, C. P. "Inland Fish and Wildlife," in Conservation and Development in North Carolina, comp. C. S. Green. Vol. II. Mimeographed. Conservation Congress Report. Raleigh: 1952.

POTTER, W. H. "Menhaden Industry—Past, Present, Future," in Conservation and Development in North Carolina, comp. C. S. Green. Vol. II. Mimeographed. Conservation Congress Report. Raleigh: 1952.

TAYLOR, H. F. "Marine Resources in North Carolina," in Conservation and Development in North Carolina, comp. C. S. Green. Vol. II. Mimeographed. Conservation Congress Report. Raleigh: 1952.

WOODWARD, GEORGE M. Commercial Fisheries of North Carolina, an Economic Analysis. Bureau of Business Services and Research, School of Business Administration, University of North Carolina. Chapel Hill: 1956.

Chapter 6

Recreational and Wildlife Resources

As a group or taken singly, it would be impossible to give a monetary value to North Carolina's recreational resources, both to the state and to its people, for their moral and aesthetic values outweigh the material values by far. Nevertheless a material value, or economic potentiality, exists and can be utilized; and a systematic, enlightened exploitation of this material value is an excellent way to conserve resources and at the same time further their development, since those measures taken to prepare natural recreational resources for public use also tend to conserve them and promote their well being.

Hunting

Early histories of North Carolina frequently refer to the abundance of game to be found. Time has reduced this abundance in most instances, but a study of North Carolina wildlife will reveal that there is still a large variety of game. The topography, ranging from coastal swamps to mountain peaks, affords habitats for many different types, and the forests and fields furnish the food, shelter, and water necessary to sustain large numbers of animals and fowl.[1] The major factor contributing to the depletion of game is not the problem of food, but rather the ruthless hunter.

Hunting was once necessary for sustenance; it is now largely recreational. Many animal resources have been exhausted and it has become necessary to institute game-protection laws to control hunting and hunters and to conserve wildlife. State and federal regulations now classify practically all hunting as strictly recreational and to be controlled, based on the philosophy that the wealth of a nation cannot be measured according to the size of its bank accounts or the dimensions of its industrial life, but only in terms of its natural resources, and that "renewable resources (i.e., forests, fisheries, animal life, as distinguished from nonrenewable—or mineral—resources) must be carefully managed and protected and planned for so that they are not destroyed.[2]

---

[1] Win Donat, *Our Wildlife and Its Wise Use*, North Carolina Wildlife Resources Commission (Raleigh, 1950), pp. 5 ff.

[2] H. J. Stains and F. S. Barkalow, Jr., *The Value of North Carolina's Game and Fish*, Game Division, North Carolina Wildlife Resources Commission (Raleigh, 1951), p. 4.

This game-and-fish control program in North Carolina is self-sustaining, for it is paid for by the licensing fees from those who actually participate in the sports. Indeed, there is sufficient surplus from this source to contribute a sizable sum to the budgetary General Fund, and over a thousand children are kept in school each year with money derived from fines for fish- and game-law violations.[3]

The game animals include bear, deer, wild boar, squirrel, rabbit, fox, opossum, coon, bobwhite, quail, wild turkey, and ruffed grouse, among others, and hunting draws thousands of enthusiasts from other states as well as from North Carolina because the absence of deep snows and extreme cold weather in the state make it a feasible all-weather sport.

Most sportsmen plan their own hunting parties, but organized and supervised hunts are gaining in popularity. These are sponsored jointly by the United States Forest Service and the North Carolina Wildlife Commission. The hunts are set for specific dates and are held in wildlife-management areas of national and state forests.

Bear, deer, and wild-boar hunts predominate among the supervised hunts. The wild Russian boar is found in America only in areas of the Nantahala National Forest and near the Great Smoky Mountain National-al Park, and hunting it is very strenuous recreation.

Another attraction to hunters lies at the eastern end of North Carolina. Here two migratory wild-fowl-hunting areas attract thousands of hunters annually. Lake Mattamuskeet, in Hyde County, and Currituck Sound are known all over the eastern part of the United States as winter quarters for Canada geese and many species of wild ducks. Lake Mattamuskeet is a federally owned and state-managed waterfowl refuge, open to managed hunting during season. One feature making Lake Mattamuskeet attractive to both the fowl and the hunter is that in spite of its large area (thousands of acres), its average depth is only two or three feet. This makes both feeding easy for the fowl and the erection of blinds and use of boots safe and convenient for the hunter. The Currituck Sound area is not a refuge, and hunting parties are generally serviced by guides who learned wild-fowl hunting from their fathers and grandfathers. The area is so large and uninhabited that a stranger may spend hours, even days, wandering around trying to locate a good hunting spot, whereas the guide can find a choice spot in a matter of minutes. The Currituck area, in general, includes some of the several adjacent counties and that part of the Albemarle Sound out to and including the northern portion of the Outer Banks. While these are best known areas, migratory ducks are found over much of eastern North Carolina and some even in the Piedmont.

---

[3] *Ibid.*, p. 10.

Wildlife in North Carolina[4]

FUR-BEARING ANIMALS.

The cottontail rabbit, now found to some degree in every county of the state, reached its peak of abundance in the central piedmont counties of North Carolina in the early 1900's. During this period market hunting flourished, especially in Chatham County, then known as the "rabbit county." Since that time rabbit populations gradually declined, mostly because of the "clean farming" methods now practiced in the state. However, the cottontail is still one of the most abundant and popular game species found in most sections of the state today.

The only other species of rabbit found in any large number in North Carolina is the marsh rabbit. The marsh rabbit is smaller than the cottontail, and since it prefers swamps, it is found in large numbers only in the Coastal Plains and the Outer Banks.

The gray squirrel, once the most abundant game animal in North Carolina, is still found in relatively large numbers throughout the state in spite of heavy hunting pressure and mass logging operations. Although it is found in every county in the state, the greatest numbers are in the coastal plains, because of the swamps, and the mountain regions, because of the hardwood growths.

The present range of the fox squirrel is the southern part of the coastal plains region and the sandhill region, where longleaf pine and scrub oak are in abundance. The fox squirrel differs from the gray squirrel in that it prefers forest edges and clearings to the deep hardwood forests that the gray loves so well.

The raccoon is a common animal in almost every county in North Carolina; however some game regions possess habitats and conditions that are particularly suitable for this animal, while some sections of several counties in the western part of the state have had a very low raccoon population for the past few years.

The opossum is common in every section of North Carolina. A sharp decline in the value of its pelt has led to a decrease in hunting and trapping of this animal, so that it is rapidly becoming a nuisance in many parts of the state. Although there has been very little interest in the well being of the 'possum, it is certainly near the top of the game list in numbers if not in popularity.

For the past ten or fifteen years the number of gray foxes in North Carolina has been steadily on the increase. The gray fox ranges all over North Carolina in considerable number. Although not so highly regarded

---

[4]This section is based on material from W. L. Hamnett and D. C. Thornton, *Tar Heel Wildlife*, North Carolina Wildlife Resources Commission (Raleigh, 1953).

by fox hunters as its red cousin, the gray fox furnishes most of the sport for North Carolina fox hunters.

The red fox was not originally native to the state but probably came in through the northwestern counties from Virginia, where many were released. In recent years a good many have been released in North Carolina as well, and their range now includes most of the state, excepting the eastern part of the coastal plains region.

Deer, as well as other types of wildlife, must have suitable habitat and management in order to prosper. They have, since 1584, when the first historical reference was made to them, fluctuated in abundance because of different types of management and hunting pressure, and are now making a comeback in North Carolina because of relatively newly enacted game laws and greater emphasis upon habitat improvement. Greatest concentrations of deer in the state are found in the coastal plains region, where there are large areas of swamp and pocosin that furnish food and cover. Many are found in the mountains, especially in and near federal forests and parks. It is estimated that there are between 50,000 and 60,000 deer in North Carolina.

At present the black bear is found in the Coastal Plains and the mountain region. Since the bear is an animal that must have a private habitat not disturbed by men, which it finds most adequately in the swamps and pocosins of the Coastal Plains and the isolated parts of the mountain region, its range is limited to the most remote sections of the state.

The European wild boar probably has the most interesting and unusual history of any of North Carolina's existing types of game animals. This animal is not a native of North Carolina but was introduced about 1912, when a few were released on a private hunting preserve in western North Carolina. For a few years these original animals were kept within the limits of the preserve by means of a heavy wire fence enclosing 600 acres. When an effort was made to hunt these animals within the preserve, some of the boar became excited and broke through the fence, taking up refuge in the laurel and rhododendron thickets nearby. These rugged animals throve in the new country in which they suddenly found themselves and were soon plentiful enough to spread across the state line into nearby Tennessee. At the present time, the wild boar is found in only these two states.

GAME BIRDS.

The eastern bobwhite quail is certainly North Carolina's most popular game bird, and perhaps the most popular of all game species. The Piedmont at one time produced these birds in almost unbelievable abundance. However, with new farming methods and a tremendous increase in hunting, the quantity declined. At the present time, the highest quail populations are found in the Piedmont and Coastal Plains. Elsewhere in the state they are few.

The wild turkey is another one of North Carolina's game birds that have decreased steadily in numbers in the past few years. While it was present at one time all over the state, its range is now extremely limited, principally to the Coastal Plains. Most of them are concentrated on the flood plains of the Roanoke River in Bertie, Martin, Northampton, and Halifax counties. The estimated total of wild turkeys for the state in 1950 was 8,340 birds. North Carolina could have far more than it has by utilizing fully the suitable habitats that do exist.

The ruffed grouse is found only in the mountain region of North Carolina, where it is probably the most abundant game bird present. Once a native of the Piedmont, the grouse was driven further west as the Piedmont was cleared and put under the plow. Mainly a forest bird, it requires less management than any of the other game birds of the state. Grouse hunting is a popular sport in the western part of the state because of the wariness of the bird and the quality of the meat. The grouse also is better able to stand greater hunting pressure in this area than the quail.

Perhaps less is known about the woodcock than any other species of common game birds. The "timber-doodle" remains a mystery, not only in North Carolina but all over the United States. It is known, however, that the woodcock is a migratory bird and that it nests and raises young in North Carolina. In the past few years, it has seemed to be more plentiful in the state but, since very few hunters seek it out, there is very little hunting pressure upon this little game bird at the present time.

The dove, like the woodcock, raises young in North Carolina, and many doves also migrate to the state during the fall and winter. A census taken during the week of February 6, 1950, placed the state dove population at about 257,000. Dove hunting is popular mainly with city hunters and large organized dove hunts are often staged within the state. The dove tends to take some of the pressure off other species of game.

MIGRATORY GAME BIRDS.

Some authorities claim Currituck Sound, Lake Mattamuskeet, and allied spots, to be the best waterfowl wintering grounds in North America. Every year large sums of money are spent within the state by waterfowl hunters from other states who come to hunt ducks and geese in North Carolina. Many species of ducks and geese winter in the state, or at least are present for a few days while they stop over for rest and food during migration flights. Thirty-two different species of waterfowl are known to be present in North Carolina from time to time:

Migratory Water Birds[5]

1. Whistling Swan
2. Geese and Brant

Canada Goose	Blue Goose
Snow Goose	American Brant

3. Ducks and Mergansers

Mallard	Lesser Scaup
Black Duck	Ring-necked Duck
Galdwall	American Golden-eye
Baldpate	Buffle-head
Green-winged Teal	Ruddy Duck
Blue-winged Teal	Old Squaw
Shoveler	White-winged Scoter
Pintail	Surf Scoter
Wood Duck	American Scoter
Canvas-back	Hooded Merganser
Redhead	Red-breasted Merganser
Greater Scaup	American Merganser

4. Others

Rails	Coots

FUR BEARERS OF VALUE.

The annual catch of fur-bearing animals in North Carolina usually amounts to approximately $350,000. This sum, comparatively small as it is, serves to supplement the annual income of many farmers and laborers within the state. Other important fur bearers besides the raccoon and opossum, already mentioned, are the muskrat, mink, otter, skunk, wild-cat, and beaver.

The muskrat usually heads the list of fur bearers taken in North Carolina annually, both in number of furs taken and over-all price received for the pelts. The mink, while very valuable, is not found in the same numbers as muskrat. The quality of its fur, however, is much better. The otter is not very abundant within North Carolina but prices paid for its pelts remain high. For this reason the few animals remaining within the borders of the state are hunted intensively. There are two types of skunks in North Carolina—the striped skunk and the spotted skunk. The present range of the striped skunk includes generally the area east of Stanly County and south of Johnston County and also the mountain region. The mountains are also the only region of the state in which the spotted skunk is found. Wildcats are not common, but a few are still found in the most remote sections of the state, notably in the swamps and pocosins of the coastal plain region and the most isolated parts of the mountains. Beavers became extinct in the early 1900's because of unregulated trapping and

---

[5] *Ibid.*, p. 37.

the great demand for their fur. They have been restocked and are now present in at least seven counties. Because of their limited number, no hunting of them is permitted.

Fishing for Recreation

The Outer Banks, those narrow island strips of sand lying to the east of the mainland coast of North Carolina, serving as a breakwater between the Atlantic Ocean and the sound waters, attract more and more people each year as transportation facilities improve to permit people to get to and fro. This string of islands is primarily noted for the quaintness of its people, the beached shipwrecks, sand dunes, storms, and wild ponies. At present there are not many modern accommodations for the average tourist, but for those who prefer isolation and seashore recreation as nature provides, the Outer Banks can justly qualify, and the completion of the National Seashore Park, now being constructed near Cape Hatteras, is expected to attract additional thousands of visitors to the area each year.

The waters on both sides of the Outer Banks afford some of the best sports fishing anywhere on the eastern seacoast. The 300-odd-mile coastline of North Carolina offers a variety of game fish, some of which can be caught at almost any season of the year. The real saltwater-fishing season does not begin until April, however, when the channel bass school around the coastal inlets, and the bluefish appear around Frying Pan Shoals.

In the western part of the state the mountain-trout season also opens in April. Some twenty-five western North Carolina counties with their streams, rivers, and lakes afford habitat for a dozen or so varieties of game fish. Some of these streams are easily accessible; others require rugged traveling to get to, but they generally have satisfying rewards. In recent years, lake fishing has gained in popularity, particularly in hydroelectric-power impoundments. Smallmouth and largemouth bass, crappie, and bream are plentiful, and in some lakes good trout catches are frequent.

An extensive program of stocking carried on by the state and federal governments assures a steady supply of fish in western waters. State hatcheries are situated at Waynesville, Roaring Gap, Morgantown, Marion, and Pineola.

Parks

During the summer months more and more people are turning to outdoor recreation in the forms of picnicking, hiking, and camping in areas provided by state and federal parks services. Good highways make it possible for individuals and families and even larger groups to travel several hundred miles on weekend excursions to seashore, mountains or some place between. The fact that the North Carolina Highway Department has become aware of the highways' use for recreational purposes is plain from the rather recent appearance of roadside picnic tables strategically located in attractive settings along main highways.

Areas are now being developed by state and federal agencies solely for the purpose of serving the recreational needs of the public. Considerable funds have been spent to make spots of natural beauty accessible by good highways, to restore and maintain places of historic interest, and to arrange for the comfort of visitors. Much progress has been made in developing and maintaining campsites for tents and trailers, and in a few places attractive cabins have been built to rent at nominal costs. In addition, both the State Conservation and Development Department and the National Park Service have developed numerous picnic areas; golf courses and other sports areas; swimming, boating, and fishing facilities.

DIVISION OF STATE PARKS.

The state parks are supervised by the North Carolina Department of Conservation and Development, a board of fifteen members selected so as to represent the various areas and interests of the state, charged with the conservation and constructive utilization of the state's natural resources and the development of its economic potentialities.[6]

Briefly, the job of the state park department is in preserving and protecting the state's major scenic and natural areas; arranging displays and explanations of its natural features—geological, plant, animal, and other; conserving and explaining its principal historical places; and providing for outdoor recreation in natural surroundings.[7] The parks department is charged with the management of all state recreational areas, the first of which came into being in 1915, when the General Assembly provided $20,000 for the purchase of the crest of lands on Mt. Mitchell. Today there are fifteen state parks completed and several more in various stages of development. Those listed as ready for use in 1953 were: Brunswick State Historical Park, Cliffs of the Neuse State Park, William B. Umstead State Park, Ft. Macon State Park, Hanging Rock State Park, James Iredell House State Historical Park, Jones' Lake State Park (Negro), Morrow Mountain State Park, Mt. Mitchell State Park, Pettigrew State Park, Reedy Creek State Park (Negro), Rendezvous Mountain State Park, Singletary Lake Group Camp, Town Creek Indian Mound, and Tryon Palace State Historical Park.[8]

Information about any particular park, as well as on the whole state park system, may be secured from the Division of State Parks, Department

---

[6] P. W. Wager, *North Carolina, The State and Its Government* (New York: Oxford Book Co., 1947).
[7] *Fourteenth Biennial Report of the North Carolina Department of Conservation and Development* (Raleigh, 1952), p. 2.
[8] *State Park Pamphlet Number 1*, North Carolina Department of Conservation and Development (Raleigh, 1953), pp. 3ff.

of Conservation and Development, Raleigh, North Carolina, but salient features are listed herewith:

1. Accessibility: all state parks have paved roads leading to them.
2. Admission and parking fees: none.
3. Operating seasons: all state parks, except Mt. Mitchell, are open the year around.
4. Camping: (a) Cabins, rented; (b) Developed campsites—fee depends on size of group and services required.
5. Boating: where boats are available.
6. Fishing: subject to rules and regulations of Wildlife Commission.
7. Hiking: all parks have foot trails.
8. Nature study: some parks have naturalists on duty during summer.
9. Picnicking: tables, benches, shelters, outdoor fireplaces, and water available.
10. Refreshment stands: open daily from June 1 through Labor Day.
11. Swimming: most parks have pools with scheduled hours with lifeguards on duty.
12. Sanitary facilities: all state parks have water and sanitary facilities.
13. Wildlife: all state parks are wildlife sanctuaries; guns, cats, and dogs not permitted.
14. Rules and regulations: state park rules and regulations are posted in parks, and they are enforced by park superintendents.

North Carolina state parks, in which the natural beauty of the parks themselves are emphasized rather than man-made amusements, attracted more than 1,500,000 visitors in 1955. In addition to the state parks, there are several national parks and national forests under federal supervision which, although separately administered, remain a part of the state's recreational resources.

One of these, the Great Smoky Mountains National Park, drew more visitors than any other park in the nation in 1956—2,886,000, according to official report. The Great Smokies, with their abundant rainfall, produce a tremendous variety of flowering plants, shrubs, and trees—some 1,300 species. This rainfall also forms an integral part of the power resources of the TVA project. The mountains themselves rise to over 6,000 feet, and the park covers approximately 500,000 acres. Besides the magnificent scenery, the park has many other attractions, such as the historical pageants of the Cherokee Indian; the Appalachian Trail, which crosses through the park; fishing in the mountain streams; trailer and tent-camping areas; and opportunities to study wildlife, geology, or mountain flora.

Other national parks, smaller but with attractive features, are scattered along the Blue Ridge Parkway from the Smokies to the Virginia line. Some of these are only parking overlooks, but others have camping facilities, picnic tables, restaurants, hotels, and recreational facilities, all under the federal government. Near the extreme southwestern end of

North Carolina is the Fontana Village resort, with complete recreational and vacation facilities for several hundred people at one time. At the extreme eastern end of the state another new federal park is under construction, the National Seashore Park near Cape Hatteras.

In addition to the parks, there are several national forests located in the state. Although these are not maintained primarily for recreational purposes, hunting and fishing and limited rough camping are permitted during certain seasons. The Pisgah and the Nantahala national forests are the largest of these, and both are located in the mountain section. Others are the Uwharrie National Forest, located in the south-central section of the Piedmont, and the Croatan National Forest in eastern North Carolina.

The North Carolina Recreation Commission works in conjunction with the state park department in promoting and coordinating recreation, town and country, throughout the state.

BIBLIOGRAPHY

DONAT, WIN. *Our Wildlife and Its Wise Use*. North Carolina Wildlife Resources Commission. Raleigh: 1950.

Fishing and Hunting. State Advertising Division, North Carolina Department of Conservation and Development. Raleigh: 1952.

Fourteenth Biennial Report of the North Carolina Department of Conservation and Development. North Carolina Department of Conservation and Development. Raleigh: 1952.

HAMNETT, W. L. AND D. C. THORNTON. *Tar Heel Wildlife*. North Carolina Wildlife Resources Commission. Raleigh: 1953.

STAINS, H. J. AND BARKALOW, F. S., JR. *The Value of North Carolina's Game and Fish*. North Carolina Wildlife Resources Commission, Game Division. Raleigh: 1951.

State Park Pamphlet Number 1. North Carolina Department of Conservation and Development. Raleigh: 1953.

WAGER, P. W. *North Carolina, The State and Its Government*. New York: Oxford Book Company, 1947.

Chapter 7

Physical and Social Economic Areas

The state of North Carolina is located on the Atlantic seaboard of the United States midway between New England and Florida. It has an average width from north to south of approximately 100 miles, and its extreme breadth is 187.5 miles. Its total length from east to west is 503 miles, greater than that of any other state east of the Mississippi River. Its total area is 52,712 square miles, of which 49,097 square miles are land and 3,615 square miles water. As we have seen, North Carolina extends from the crest of the Appalachian mountain system to the Atlantic Ocean and lies across three major topographic divisions of the United States. As a result it is divided into three divisions—its Coastal Plain (including the Outer Banks) on the east (in this book the Coastal Plain is subdivided into Tidewater and Upper Coastal Plain), the Piedmont Plateau in the center, and the Appalachian mountains on the west. Beginning at sea level on the eastern edge of the Coastal Plain, the topography of the state rises in elevation and increases in irregularity through the Piedmont Plateau and reaches its maximum height and ruggedness in the Appalachians.

Running across the state, and somewhat parallel with the shore line, lies the "fall line," cutting the state into two regions of about equal size. East of this line the soils are of sedimentary origin; west of the line they are mainly of igneous origin. In other words, North Carolina is divided into two great soil or physical provinces, the east and the west, an enormous factor throughout the history of the state. It is no less important today than it has been in the past. No other state on the Atlantic seaboard is so clearly marked off in this respect. The east is more or less clearly and equally divided into its two provinces, the Tidewater and the West Coastal Plain; the west is definitely divided into its two provinces, the Piedmont being considerably larger than the mountain region. These divisions must be kept in mind, for they constitute also four clearly distinct socioeconomic areas.

The Rivalry of East and West

Throughout the history of North Carolina the east has been arrayed against the west. At times there have been bitter controversies, but for the most part the two regions have lived together in friendly rivalry.

The War of the Regulators, which culminated in the Battle of Ala-mance in 1771, was a struggle between the small farmers of the upcountry and the great planters of the lowlands for political power. In the Conven-tion of 1788 every county voting for the ratification of the federal Consti-tution but Lincoln was located in the Coastal Plain, while every county in the Piedmont voted against ratification, again excepting Lincoln. The long contest over the calling of a convention to amend the state constitu-tion, which culminated in the Convention of 1833, was likewise an east-west contest for political and economic supremacy; in 1834 every county in the Coastal Plain voted against the calling of a convention and afterwards, in 1835, against the ratification of its work, while every county in the Piedmont Plateau voted in the affirmative on both occasions. The same line of cleavage, though not so marked, is seen in the vote on the proposal to call a convention in February, 1861, to take North Carolina out of the Union, and also on the suffrage amendment of 1900. Professor Collier Cobb used to tell his geology classes at the University of North Carolina that "... the political questions in North Carolina have always been questions of east and west, of the upcountry against the lowlands, of crystalline schists and granites against unconsolidated clays, sands, and gravels."

For a long time the conflict lay between the planters of the east and the small home-owning farmers of the west, with the east generally pre-vailing. As a result of population growth, the stranglehold of the east was finally broken. The chief conflict today lies between the farmers of the east and the factories of the west, with the west holding the whip hand, for today the west has a majority of the population and wealth of the state.

The fact that a governor cannot succeed himself in office is a product of this east versus west phonomenon. Each section alternates, and this agreement has generally been accepted, although Governor Kerr Scott, from Burlington, did break the tradition in 1948 when he succeeded Gregg Cherry from Gastonia. The lieutenant governor is supposed to come from the same section as the governor. The speaker of the House, in order to preserve a balance of power, is supposed to come from the other section, in alternate times. In the same fashion, one United States senator is sup-posed to represent the east and the other the west. Incidentally, history proves that the east, up to now, has shown more political acumen than has the west. The east has dominated in the legislative halls and in im-portant offices held, out of all proportion to population. The west is begin-ning to awaken to its real potential powers. It may be that the dominance of the east will not be so decided in the future.

Other evidences of east–west conflict are seen in the presence of two literary societies at the state university, one drawing boys from the east, the other, boys from the west. This is not so true today as in former years. In high school athletics and other contests, the final battle is generally between representatives of the two sections. In the legislative vote on the secret, or Australian, ballot in 1929, chief opposition came from the east, chief support from the west. Today the stronghold of the Democratic party is eastern North Carolina; of the Republican party, western North Carolina. The cleavage is the result of economic, racial, and historic conditions. As has been noted, the major conflict of interests today is between the agricultural element east of the fall line and the urban-industrial element west of the fall line. The chief point in the conflict at present is over the question of taxation. On this point the east gains much support from the rural counties of the west. Table 24 gives some economic comparisons which shed light on this east-west rivalry.

The Coastal Plain

The Coastal Plain is that region lying between the Piedmont Plateau on the west and the continental shelf on the east. The land lies low (in part submerged) and varies in width, its western boundary passing through Northampton, Warren, Halifax, Franklin, Wake, Johnston, Chatham, Moore, Richmond, and Anson counties. The seashore forms the boundary between its two distinct divisions—the submerged, or submarine, and the emerged, or subaerial. This dividing line is constantly changing imperceptibly, and in past geologic ages has moved several times across the Coastal Plain, at one time located over the Piedmont Plateau and at another time situated well out to sea. The belief is that at present the sea is slowly encroaching once more. [1]

Along its western margin the Coastal Plain is often hilly, the streams frequently cutting through the softer coastal plain deposits to the harder rocks of the Piedmont Plateau below. Several of the more important cities of the South are located on the fall line, which marks the head of navigation of the rivers. In North Carolina the rivers cut deep into the softer sedimentary soils, forming rapids that have been harnessed for the development of electric power. Roanoke Rapids is an illustration.

Along the western border of the Coastal Plain is the famous sandhill country. These often appear as outliers on the Piedmont Plateau, where they attain elevations of from 400 to 500 feet. They were probably formed in somewhat the same manner as the sand dunes along the "banks" today.

East of the fall line, the country declines in altitude, passing from one broad plain or terrace to another until it approaches tidelevel, where it embraces swamps, marshes, bays, and sounds over wide areas, the whole

---

[1] *The Coastal Plain of North Carolina*, North Carolina Geologic and Economic Survey (Raleigh, 1912), III, Chapter 1.

surface for more than 50 miles inland from Hatteras and the Eastern Shore being less than 20 feet above sealevel. The ocean is walled off from this low region by a long, linear chain of sand islands of dunes, ranging from 75 to 100 feet and more in height and separated in a half score places by inlets which connect the sounds with the ocean. The total width of the plain averages about 135 to 150 miles. Its total land area is half that of the state, or some 24,200 square miles, and embraces wholly or largely forty-five counties.

For fifty miles or so the continental shelf slopes out into the Atlantic, the submarine part of North Carolina constituting an area of approximately 16,000 square miles. The submarine division of North Carolina consists of one terrace, the subaerial division of six. These six are the products of the numerous incursions and excursions of the Atlantic, which, as has been noted, appears to be coming in again. Beginning with the highest, they are: (1) the Lafayette, represented in North Carolina by the sandhills of Scotland, Richmond, Cumberland, Moore, Harnett, Wake, Johnston, Nash, and Northampton counties; (2) the Coharie, which is found in the region to the east of the sandhills in Scotland, Robeson, Cumberland, Harnett, Sampson, Johnston, Wilson, and Nash counties (along its inner edges it has an elevation of 235 feet from which it slopes gradually to the eastward, with elevations of from 160 to 180 feet along its outer border); (3) the Sunderland, found principally in Robeson, Columbus, Bladen, Cumberland, Sampson, Duplin, Wayne, Johnston, Greene, Wilson, Edgecombe, Nash, Halifax, and Northampton counties, varying from five miles in width in the northern counties to 40 miles in places near the South Carolina border; (4) the Wicomico, the largest areas being found in Halifax, Edgecombe, Martin, Lenoir, Craven, Jones, Duplin, Onslow, Pender, Bladen, and Columbus counties, characterized by numerous swamps and poor drainage; (5) the Chowan, found chiefly in Brunswick, New Hanover, Pender, Onslow, Jones Pamlico, Carteret, and Craven counties and to a lesser extent in several other eastern counties, varying in elevation from around 60 to 30 feet and containing much undrained land and swamps; (6) the Pamlico, covering the entire area of Hyde, Dare, Tyrrell, Curricuck, Camden, and Pasquotank counties and much of Perquimans, Chowan, Washington, Beaufort, Pamlico, Craven, and Carteret counties. The elevation varies from twenty feet along its western border to tide level. The surface of the Pamlico terrace is covered over wide areas with swamps and marshes and embraces many estuaries, sounds, and bays, including the Great Dismal Swamp and Mattamuskeet Lake.

Thus the whole eastern portion of the state is a vast plain, stretching from the seacoast into the interior of the country, a distance of from 100 to nearly 150 miles in places. From east to west the surface rises at an average rate of about one foot to the mile, the rise scarcely perceptible to the traveler, at the eastern end and much more rapid toward the western edge. Though generally almost level, it is relieved by slight undulations and low, rolling hills along the western border. Over this whole area the rock foundation is covered with a layer, or more accurately many layers, of sedimentary deposits, varying in depth from zero, where it dovetails with the Piedmont along the western border, to around 2,000 feet or more in the southeast along the coast.

The Coastal Plain is further divided into (1) the Tidewater, including the Outer Banks, and (2) the Upper Coastal Plain.

1. THE TIDEWATER

The Tidewater is that vast low-lying, flat, swampy, and generally wet country of extreme eastern North Carolina. There is no clear line of demarcation on the west, since any line drawn is at best only approximate. Ordinary field observation and studies of statistical data clearly show the existence of a region quite distinct from the adjacent area to the west—in soils, drainage, elevation, climate, race ratios, density of population, crops, and numerous other ways.

The Tidewater Region as conceived in this book includes the following twenty-two counties: Beaufort, Bertie, Brunswick, Camden, Carteret, Chowan, Craven, Currituck, Dare, Gates, Hertford, Hyde, Jones, Martin, New Hanover, Onslow, Pamlico, Pasquotank, Pender, Perquimans, Tyrrell, and Washington.

There is no agreement on what constitutes geologically the tidewater region. Some authorities list as Tidewater just the Pamlico surficial formation, which runs straight south along the Chowan river to Newport on the western edge of Carteret county. Others include the Chowan formation, which runs south through Gates and Hertford counties and the center of Jones County and covers most of the coastal tier of counties from Jones through Brunswick. This book considers the Pamlico and Chowan surficial formations as tidewater country.

The following quotation is from a letter to the author by Dr. Jasper L. Stuckey, state geologist:

I have never seen what I consider a perfect definition of the tidewater region. For my own thinking, I place the western limits of the tidewater region at the heads of the various sounds and estuaries. I normally think of the line beginning at about Gatesville and extending to Washington, New Bern, Jacksonville, and Wilmington. Your definition, which includes Gates, Hertford, Bertie, Martin,

Jones, and Pender—to which I would add Brunswick—seems just as good. Like yourself, I have often wondered about the uncertainty of these definitions.[2]

The Tidewater includes the Outer Banks, that series of low-lying sand islands off the coastline from Virginia to South Carolina. Many inlets serve to connect the ocean beyond the islands with the sounds lying between the banks and the mainland. The banks have been formed through successive deposition of sedimentary material brought down by mainland streams on the floor of the submerged portion of the Coastal Plain. Breaker and undertow action caused this deposition to form into reefs lying parallel to the general contour of the shore. They vary in width from a few hundred yards to two miles in some places. Somewhat crescent-shaped in outline, they lie roughly three miles offshore at their northernmost point within the state, but then they swing southeast until at Cape Hatteras they lie twenty miles from the mainland. From this point they once more approach the shore. From Bogue Sound to the South Carolina line, the inlets increase, and often the banks are separated from the mainland only by the channel dredged out for the Intracoastal Waterway. The surface of the banks is uneven, with small hummocks of sand and many very much larger dunes. In general, the banks have a higher elevation than the mainland. The largest sand dunes on the Dare Banks are more than a hundred feet in elevation, and other places they reach sixty or more feet. Beyond the dunes, lying next to the ocean, are many marshes and fresh-water ponds which serve as wintering grounds for marsh ducks.[3]

TOPOGRAPHY.

Perhaps the outstanding characteristic of the tidewater region is physiographic. As we have seen it is a vast low-lying, swampy, and generally wet country. It is sometimes referred to as a peninsula and it is the nearest thing to a peninsula found along the Atlantic Coast. A line drawn from Norfolk to the northeastern corner of South Carolina cuts off a considerable part of North Carolina. Excessive wetness of the land has been the determining factor in the utilization of this area and will continue to be until it is drained.

POPULATION.

The Tidewater is an area of relatively sparse population, having 21.2 per cent of the state's land area and only 11 per cent of the population. Vast areas are uninhabitated and other areas are thinly settled. The population tends to be concentrated in areas that were suitable to settlement without being drained.

---

[2]Letter to the author.

[3]W. L. Hamnett and D. C. Thornton, *Tar Heel Wildlife*, North Carolina Wildlife Resources Commission (Raleigh, 1953), p. 5.

Indeed, the Tidewater is sometimes referred to as an area of static population in that it has grown less rapidly in population than any other region of the state. Only two counties in this region have grown faster on a percentage basis than the state average during the last fifty years. One of these, Onslow, owes its growth to military establishments, and the other, New Hanover, is a city-county, drawing upon surrounding counties for its economic sustenance. Four of these counties—Camden, Currituck, Gates, and Perquimans—have fewer people than they had fifty years ago, and eleven other counties have increased only from 1 per cent to 50 per cent in population during this period. The fifty-year increase in population for the twenty-two counties has been 60.2 per cent, which is considerably below the rate of growth of any other region of the state.

The Tidewater is excessively rural in that a large percentage of the total population lies in places with less than 2,500 inhabitants or in the open country. The main urban places are Wilmington in the southeastern section, New Bern and Morehead City—Beaufort in the central section, and Edenton and Elizabeth City in the Albemarle country. Other mod-est-sized towns are Williamston and Washington.

PRESENT ECONOMIC SITUATION.

The Tidewater is an area of relatively few farms. Only 37.2 per cent of the total area is classed as farm land, and only about 7 or 8 per cent of the total area is actually under cultivation. Again the excessive water ac-counts for this situation. Of these farms, 31.9 per cent are operated by tenants, according to the 1950 census. The bulk of the people live by ex-tractive enterprise—farming, lumbering, and related activities, and fishing, hunting, and other recreational activities.

The Tidewater contributed 9.6 per cent of tax retail sales in 1955–56, a figure approximately comparable with its population ratio. However, it reported only 6.7 per cent of the state's individual net taxable income in 1952, and 7.6 per cent of real and personal property listed for taxation in 1953–54.

In the past the tidewater people have been characterized as individual-istic, and they remain so to a considerable degree, but better transporta-tion and communication facilities have brought them into contact with the rest of the state and introduced a greater cosmopolitanism.

POSSIBILITIES.

The Tidewater has bast possibilities for development far beyond its present status. The major handicap is the wetness, and many experts be-lieve that drainage of such areas as this would be much more feasible and profitable than attempts to irrigate the arid lands of other parts of the country. The United States Department of Agriculture has declared the Tidewater a prospective source of winter truck-garden produce for all of America.

Another possibility is in the development of a food-processing (of canned goods, quick-frozen foods, butter, oleo, preserves, dehydrated food, etc.) industry. The Tidewater has the capacity to grow raw materials in abundance. Hardy vegetables can be produced in the winter time, and during seasons when crops and animals are in short supply, the inland coastal seas and the frontage on the Atlantic Ocean offer great opportunities for canning and freezing of seafood. The area also has both a domestic market in North Carolina and access to other markets.

Development of such an industry, besides fostering the prosperity of the Tidewater, would also improve the economy of North Carolina as a whole in that the state would be able to keep a large amount of her food dollars at home, rather than importing processed food from other states.

Industires related to the forest resources present another opportunity for this region. It already has a sizable lumber industry. There are at present two large pulp and paper mills, and it could support several more. North Carolina is already exporting large quantities of pulp to other southern states.

The Tidewater area has always been handicapped by poor transportation facilities. This defect has been largely remedied by the network of all-weather roads. Inland waterways have been greatly improved during the past quarter-century or so, and this means of transportation will receive much additional attention. Also, the state has begun the development of public port facilities at Wilmington and Morehead City. These ports are chiefly serviced by motor trucks. Whether they can prosper with truck connections remains to be seen. If the railway connections could be greatly improved, their future would be better assured.

2. UPPER OR WEST COASTAL PLAIN.

The Upper of West Coastal Plain lies between the tidewater region and the so-called fall line.[4] The fall line does not follow county lines, and while the Upper Coastal Plain in this book includes twenty-three counties (Anson, Bladen, Columbus, Comberland, Duplin, Edgecombe, Greene, Halifax, Harnett, Hoke, Johnston, Lee, Lenoir, Moore, Nash, Northampton, Pitt, Richmond, Robeson, Sampson, Scotland, Wayne and Wilson), some of the counties listed are partly in the Piedmont and partly in the

---

[4] In a letter to the author, State Geologist J. L. Stuckey says:

The fall line is commonly referred to as the point, or line, at which streams pass from the crystalline rocks of the Piedmont on to the unconsolidated sediments of the Coastal Plain. Theoretically, this should be a line, but practically it is a zone. I was taught at Cornell University, where . . . R. S. Terr made physical geography outstanding, that the fall line is a zone fifteen or twenty miles wide rather than a definite line. In my publication, "Geology and Mineral Resources of North Carolina," I place the western limit of the Coastal Plain along the outcrop of Cretaceous and Tertiary sediments. The western limits of Pleistocene terrace formation crosses Northampton, Halifax, Warren, Franklin, Wake, Chatham, Lee, Moore, Montgomery, Richmond, and Anson counties.

Upper Coastal Plain. Where most of the county lies in the Piedmont, as in the case of Wake and Franklin, the county is classed with the piedmont region, and vice versa.

The Sandhills is a subregion of the Upper Coastal Plain occupying most of Richmond, Moore, and Hoke counties and portions of Montgomery, Lee, Harnett, Cumberland, and Scotland counties which requires separate consideration. Located in the southwestern corner of the Coastal Plain the sandhills appear to be extensions of the Piedmont Plateau, since they attain elevations of from 400 to 500 feet. North of this region, the western border of the Coastal Plain seldom rises above 400 feet. The Sandhills proper comprise nearly one million acres, while patches of its characteristic soils occur in other surrounding counties.

In general the terrain consists of a series of ridges, the surface varying from gentle undulation in the interstream areas to decidedly rolling and broken along the stream courses. The Sandhills are thoroughly dissected by drainageways; and there are no large, poorly-drained areas. Soils consist of sandy loams, and drainage is generally excessive. Until recently much of this area was considered worthless, but today the region is an important recreational center, has considerable agriculture, and is the peach-growing center of the state.

The Upper Coastal Plain occupies approximately 28 per cent of the land area of the state. It is a vast region of level and gently rolling land of excellent quality on which will grow in abundance every crop suited to the mild climate of eastern North Carolina, and there are certain outstanding characteristics that distinguish this area from the other regions of the state.

POPULATION.

It is an area of dense agricultural population, having from two to three times as much land under cultivation as the tidewater region. In 1950, 72.4 per cent of the total area was classed as farm land, and nearly one-third of the area was classed as improved land; the soils of this area are the easiest in the state to manage and respond well to conservation practices. The region contains more than one-fourth of the population of the state, or 26.4 per cent in 1950. It ranks second in density of population with 79.1 persons per square mile in 1950. This is approximately the average for the state.

It is an area with large Negro population ratios. Several counties have Negro majorities and in other counties the Negro ratio runs from 40 to 50 per cent. In no other agricultural region in the United States have the Negro farmer and the Negro population held their own numerically so well as in this region. Negroes and Negro farmers have declined throughout the Negro belts of the South, except in eastern North Carolina. This is due to the increased value of tobacco, which has more than offset the decline in cotton values.

PRESENT ECONOMIC SITUATION.

The Upper Coastal Plain is North Carolina's leading agricultural region, and it is outstanding in farm-wealth production. There is probably only one other area of equal size in the United States, around Los Angeles, that produces more cash farm income than this section. Around half of the cash-crop wealth of the state is produced in these twenty-three counties, for it is the tobacco capital of the world. These counties also produce a considerable amount of cotton and a sizable part of the peanut crop of the state, and also a fair quantity of corn and a number of minor crops. The population of this region is highly agricultural, for townfolk as well live largely from the wealth produced by the farms.

The Upper Coastal Plain is an area of excessive farm tenancy, both white and Negro. Approximately 55 per cent of all farms are operated by tenants, tenants being farmers who own no land and no homes. While tenancy has declined rapidly throughout the United States and in practically all counties in the western half of North Carolina, there has been little change in tenancy ratios in this region during recent years—some counties have lost tenants while others have shown increases. Perhaps the continuation of this system is a result of the fact that tobacco and cotton are crops remarkably well suited to a tenant arrangement. However because tenants move in large numbers each year, this region ranks low in social items associated with stability of population, such as church membership, school attendance, and general interest in community affairs.

The trade towns of this region are among the most attractive and prosperous to be found in purely agricultural regions, for around half the cash-crop wealth of the state is produced in these counties, and the trade towns handle farm wealth both going and coming: the towns supply the farmer with that which he purchases, and practivally all of the crops produced in this area pass through the towns on their way to final markets. There is probably no other farm region of equal size in the United States where towns handle so much farm wealth. In many areas, farm wealth goes to market without passing through its local towns and cities. This is true of the major crops of California, for example.

Livestock raising is the major deficiency in this area. In no other important agricultural region in America does livestock play so small a part in the farm economy, and usually North Carolina ranks last of all states in percentage of farm income derived from the sale of livestock and livestock products. The effect of the tenant system can be seen here, for the Upper Coastal Plain, which dominates the agricultural economy of the state, is a land of tenants, and tenants have little or no livestock. This is particularly true of tobacco tenants, for there is no relationship between tobacco and livestock.

According to state tax records, the Upper Coastal Plain accounted for 20.8 per cent of taxed retail sales in 1955–56 and 16.7 per cent of individual net taxable income for that year. It reported 18.6 per cent of the state's real and personal property listed for taxation in 1953–54. These figures are below the population ratio of 26.5 per cent. Two chief reasons are the dominance of agriculture and the large Negro proportion.

POSSIBILITIES AND NEEDS.

It is probable that the Upper Coastal Plain will always be the chief agricultural region of the state, since it has natural farming assets. There are, however, excellent industrial opportunities, and industry is growing. Industries seeking locations in North Carolina are beginning to look more into the advantages offered by the Upper Coastal Plain, which is somewhat virgin territory compared with the piedmont region. The chief industry thus far has been the overflow of the textile mills along and east of the fall line. A good supply of underemployed labor is perhaps the major industrial resource offered by the region.

A fundamental weakness of this area is the high ratio of tenancy to farm ownership. A higher proportion of farm ownership would result in better-balanced agriculture, better living on the farm, and more wholesome community life. Nor is it likely that there will be much increase in livestock farming until more farmers own their farms.

Somehow there must be a better relationship between the production of farm wealth on the one hand and the retention of wealth on the other. This area ranks nationally far better in production than it does in retention of wealth. Perhaps two-thirds of the cash farm income is produced by tenants, and it is obvious that tenants in general have not accumulated much wealth. More than half the tenants of this area are croppers, which means that not only do they not own their own homes and farms, but they do not own the animals they work with or other forms of farm power, such as tractors.

More farm ownership, more diversified agriculture, and more industry seem to be the chief needs of this region. It has the resources for a truly prosperous economy.

The Piedmont

The Piedmont Plateau lies between the fall line and the Blue Ridge. Geographically it terminates at the foot of the Blue Ridge, but this book considers it to extend to the top of the mountain range. Economically and socially the eastern side of the Blue Ridge belongs to the Piedmont. The term Piedmont as herein used includes the following thirty-eight counties: Alamance, Alexander, Burke, Cabarras, Caldwell, Caswell,

Catawba, Chatham, Cleveland, Davidson, Davie, Durham, Forsyth, Franklin, Gaston, Granville, Guilford, Iredell, Lincoln, McDowell, Mecklenburg, Montgomery, Orange, Person, Polk, Randolph, Rockingham, Rowan, Rutherford, Stanly, Stokes, Surry, Union, Vance, Wake, Warren, Wilkes, and Yadkin. This total comprises approximately 37.1 per cent of the land area of the state or 18,265 square miles, which makes the Piedmont the largest of the four divisions of the state.

The most important drainage basins of the piedmont region are those of the Roanoke, Tar, Neuse, Cape Fear, Yadkin, Catawba, and Broad rivers. These streams reach the Atlantic through a complex system of valleys, 300 to 500 feet below the intervening divides. Most of these streams have their origin in the Piedmont or foothills of the Blue Ridge Mountains.

DESCRIPTION.

The Piedmont is an intermediary region lying between the more rugged mountains and the flatness of the plains. It is gently rolling, a succession of hills with occasional stretches of forestland and here and there an artificial lake. The variations in its topography become more pronounced traveling from east to west, where its ruggedness merges with that of the mountains themselves. The elevation of the Piedmont Plateau along its western margin at the foot of the Blue Ridge is generally from 1,200 to 1,500 feet above sea level, and there are numerous high and precipitous spurs that project eastward from the Blue Ridge. However it has ascended gradually, the eastern edge ranging from around 200 to 500 feet above sea level.

The soil of the Piedmont presents a blending of the soils of the eastern and western regions. It is often deep, with clay and sandy loam predominant. The soil is stiffer and tougher and therefore much more difficult to cultivate than the sandy loams of eastern North Carolina. The climate does not differ a great deal from that of the Upper Coastal Plain. The growing season is somewhat shorter, and the mean average temperature ranges from 56 to 59 degrees Fahrenheit (see page 17).

This region originally contained excellent forest resources, with hardwoods predominating, but the present annual cut is small compared with that of a few decades ago. In general the hardwoods need to be replaced with the better grades of pine, such as loblolly.

One of the great natural resources of this region is the vast amount of water power, much of which has been developed and has played a major part in the great industrial development found here. Water was almost the total source of power until some thirty years ago, and it is still very important in the economy of the state.

PRESENT ECONOMIC SITUATION.

The significant fact about the Piedmont is its strong position industrially. It ranks first in the South in every phase of industrial development,

such as number of establishments, value of output, value added by manufacture, number of wage earners, amount of wages and salaries paid, and
capital investment in industry.

Chief among its industries are its textile mills, and indeed, it stands
as the nation's largest producer of fabrics. There are approximately 1,100
mills in the state, and the total output of these is in the neighborhood of
$2,200,000,000. Perhaps 85 per cent of the total textile industry is found
in these thirty-eight piedmont counties. (The piedmont section of South
Carolina ranks second only to North Carolina's as a textile center.)

Tobacco products, however, are the Piedmont's best-known commodity, for about half the total value of tobacco-industry production in the
United States comes from this section. The entire industry in the state
is located in the Piedmont, and the four major manufacturing communities are Durham, Winston-Salem, Greensboro, and Reidsville.
Factory value of tobacco production, including federal taxes, is roughly
$1,500,000,000, or $750,000,000 without taxes.

The Piedmont also leads the nation in the manufacture of furniture,
especially wooden furniture. There are some three hundred and fifty
factories in the state, and approximately 95 per cent of the industry is
located in this section.

The developing electrical industry is largely located here, and perhaps
three-fourths or more of the so-called miscellaneous industries of the state
also. These are more fully described elsewhere.

POPULATION.

The population density is the heaviest in the state, with 112 people
per square mile. This area in 1950 accounted for 52.7 per cent of the
state's total population, and the population is increasing at a faster rate
than in any other region. North Carolina has no large cities, but it did
have a sizable total urban population of nearly a million and a half in
1955, and two-thirds or more of the total urban population is concentrated
in the piedmont section, where towns and cities are growing faster, on the
average, than those of other regions of the state.

While this area has 52.65 per cent of the total population, it accounted
for 61.8 per cent of the taxed retail sales in 1955–56, for 70.7 per cent of
the state's individual net taxable income in 1952, and for 67.2 per cent of
all real and personal property listed for taxation in 1953–54.

The percentage of the total area classed as farm land, 72.3, is almost
exactly that of the Upper Coastal Plain, 72.4. The bulk of the farms of
this region was operated by white farmers, and only 29.2 per cent were
tenant farmers in 1950.

Notwithstanding the rapid growth of towns and cities, the agricultural
population has held up well. The farm-population density is approximately

that of the Upper Coastal Plain, and both of these regions rank at or near the top of the United States in number of farm people per square mile.

There has been considerable agricultural progress in the piedmont region as the small farmers (who constitute the majority) have come to appreciate the value of nearby markets, and more and more are taking advantage of these by increasing their production of such goods as dairy products, poultry, and beef, which can be consumed locally.

The small farms of this area supply out of their homes a large part of the labor force which operates the industries and other nonfarm activities of the Piedmont, and there is considerable farm-family income derived from nonfarm employment. In a number of counties the family income from off-the-farm jobs exceeds that from the sale of farm products. Almost every farm home is within commuting distance of some kind of nonfarm job, and there has been a great increase in part-time farming and part-time nonfarm employment.

Yet this area still has a great underemployment of rural population, farm and nonfarm, and its vast potential labor force is its greatest asset in future industrial development. This is a condition not peculiar to the piedmont area; it is found all over the state.

The transportation resources of this area are perhaps the best in the state, but like every region in the state, there are deficiencies, primarily the lack of east–west trunk-line railway facilities.

The percentage of the state's bank resources found in this region is about the same as for real and personal property and taxable income, and there has been a tendency for bank resources more and more to be concentrated in the piedmont section, perhaps natural, since the Piedmont is the urban, industrial region of the state.

The Carolina Highlands

The mountain region as delineated in this book lies west of the Blue Ridge. It extends from the Virginia line to South Carolina and Georgia and embraces seventeen counties—Alleghany, Ashe, Avery, Buncombe, Cherokee, Clay, Graham, Haywood, Henderson, Jackson, Macon, Madison, Mitchell, Swain, Transylvania, Watauga, and Yancey—with a broad area of 6,633 square miles, or 13.5 per cent of the land area of the state. Some students include the tier of counties just east of the Blue Ridge. Actually these counties are a part of the Piedmont geographically and economically. Their contacts are almost together with the Piedmont.

DESCRIPTION.

The entire mountain system of North Carolina is regarded as a division of the southern Appalachians. Physiographically the region is a broad, high plateau, bordered on the east by the Blue Ridge mountains and on the west by the Iron, Great Smoky, and Unaka mountains, which form the boundary between North Carolina and Tennessee. Numerous cross ranges—such as the Black, Balsam, Pisgah, New Found, Cowee, Nantahala, and Valley River mountains—divide the main plateau into a series of smaller plateaus, each having its own drainage system. Between the mountain ranges and along the drainageways are fertile valleys of varying width.

The eastern slopes of the Blue Ridge mountains are drained by the Broad, Catawba, and Yadkin rivers, while the main portion of the mountain region is drained westward through such streams as the Little Tennessee and tributaries, and the Hiwassee, French Broad, Nolichucky, New, and Watauga rivers.

The Appalachian mountains reach their climax in western North Carolina. Mount Mitchell, with an elevation of 6,684 feet, is the highest peak east of the Mississippi, or east of the Rockies with one exception. In addition to Mount Mitchell there are four other peaks above 6,600 feet in elevation; six from 6,500 to 6,600 feet; thirty-eight from 6,000 to 6,500 feet; fifty-four from 5,500 to 6,000 feet; and over a hundred from 5,000 to 5,500 feet. The main floor of the plateau, however, averages from 2,000 to 3,000 feet above sea level.

The outstanding characteristic of the Carolina highlands is its rough topography. This section is walled off from the east by the Blue Ridge, and the economic and social development, or lack of development, is largely a result of the isolation inherent in its rough, mountainous terrain. Improved highway systems have meant an end to the isolation, but there remains a carry-over of past conditions.

POPULATION.

The mountain country is inhabited chiefly by native white stock and Indians. There is probably no other area in America where the population has a higher percentage of native born than in these counties. Outside the chief urban centers of Asheville, Hendersonville, Waynesville, and Canton, the population is predominantly white. The roughly three thousand Indians are concentrated largely in the Indian reservations, notably the Qualla tract.

These seventeen counties account for 13.5 per cent of the land area of the state but only 9.8 per cent of the total population in 1950. The total area is some 6,663 square miles and thus it is much the smallest of the four regions of the state. The average density of population is 60.1 per square mile, slightly lower than the average for the tidewater country; the northern half is much more densely settled than the average of the area, the southern half being much less densely populated. It is in the southern half that we find the Great Smoky Mountain National Park and most of the forest land owned by the federal government. Federal forests total considerably more than one million acres, and North Carolina's part of the Great Smoky Mountains National Park comprises about a quarter of a million acres.

Illiteracy was once prevalent in this region. Today illiterates among native whites are largely adults who had no chance at an education during their youth. Strong family ties were once characteristic and family feuds common. Feuding is a thing of the past, but the family ties remain strong, as they do throughout all of North Carolina, which is characteristic of a rural state.

PRESENT ECONOMIC SITUATION.

This area contains far more farms than would be suspected. There are several counties with more than 3,000 farms each, or more than the average for the state. It also has more land classed as improved land than would seem likely. Especially is this true of the northern counties, where mountains tend to be rounded, and excellent pasture land is found on mountain sides and tops as well as in the valleys. Slightly more than half the land area of the mountain counties is farm land, 52.1 per cent. This is considerably higher than the farm-land ratio in the tidewater country, notwithstanding the large federal holdings in the mountain counties. The farm-tenant ratio, as might be expected, is the lowest in the state, with only 10.7 per cent of all farms operated by tenants.

In the year 1955–56, the mountain counties accounted for 7.8 per cent of the state's taxed retail sales; these counties reported 6.1 per cent of the state's individual net taxable income; and in 1953–54 the mountain counties reported only 6.6 per cent of the state's real and personal property listed for taxation.

The mountain region is the chief mining area of the state, the main products being sheet and scrap mica, natural and ground feldspar, stone and crushed rock, and other minor minerals.

There is probably no other sizable region in the nation where agriculture is more self-sufficient. By this term we mean that the farmers consume at home more than half of what they produce. In some counties home consumption amounts to two-thirds or more of farm production. There is relatively little commercial agriculture, although there are some sizable beef-cattle farms and commercial orchards. The burley tobacco crop amounts to some 30,000,000 pounds a year, and cabbage, beans, and other truck crops are grown, although on a more or less minor scale compared with commercial centers.

This region is lacking in extensive industrial development but has considerable possibilities. The chief industries are the Enka mills near Asheville; the large pulp and paper mill at Canton; the cigarette, Bible-paper, and cellophane plant at Brevard (Olin Industries); a few textile mills scattered over the region; and sawmills and woodworking establishments, including a few furniture factories.

The mountain country is the chief tourist region of the state, and the prospects are bright for expansion of this business. As we have seen, more people visit the Great Smoky Mountains National Park than any other park in the United States—nearly three million in 1956. The Blue Ridge Parkway is unique, and literally millions of people travel on it each year. Many religious groups have their summer encampments here, and there are many private camps. The area is regarded as one of the nation's finest recreational spots.

POSSIBILITIES AND NEEDS.

The economic resources of the mountain country are to a large extent untouched. There is considerable room for improvement and expansion in agriculture, particularly in the sale of surplus crops and the development of livestock products for sale. Furthermore there are natural horticultural possibilities that are yet mostly unexplored. It is a natural apple-growing area, and the annual apple crop runs into millions of bushels. The problem here is to grow uniform types of apples, take proper care of orchards, practice scientific harvesting, and package and market the crop efficiently. There are some excellent orchards but apple growing, like many other things in this area, is highly individualistic and haphazard. The solution of the marketing problem remains to be accomplished. Much of the mountain country is well suited to cabbages. The cabbage crop could be expanded and more of it needs to be processed at home. A sauerkraut industry is a natural. Irish potatoes as good as those that now come from Maine can be grown, and a seed-potato crop could be a source of considerable income.

The northwestern corner of the mountain country has most of the sheep left in North Carolina. It is the considered opinion of many students that this area can grow as fine wool as can be grown anywhere. One proposition is to select the best variety of sheep for wool purposes, enlarge the stock, shear the wool, and convert this wool into homespun and other wool products in the mountain area. There is a fine small-homespun business at Biltmore. The homespuns made from locally grown wool can be unsurpassed; instead of being sold for fifty or sixty cents a pound, wool can be converted into homespun cloth that will sell for better than ten dollars a pound. This would give employment to people who really need employment and additional income to an area now deficient in cash.

The wood resources are adequate for pulp and paper mills and other wood-using industries.

Perhaps the greatest opportunity lies in capitalizing on the unsurpassed beauty and general recreational resources of this vast mountain region. Eighty to a hundred million people in the eastern United States have access to the Carolina highlands, and if this land were properly developed and facilities provided for accommodating the tourist trade, the volume of income from this source would swell tremendously.

BIBLIOGRAPHY

The Coastal Plain of North Carolina. Vol. III. North Carolina Geologic and Economic Survey. Raleigh: 1912.

HAMNETT, W. L., AND D. C. THORNTON. *Tar Heel Wildlife.* North Carolina Wildlife Resources Commission. Raleigh: 1953.

HOBBS, S. H., JR. *North Carolina: Economic and Social.* Chapel Hill: University of North Carolina Press, 1930.

Statistics of Taxation, 1954 and 1956. North Carolina Department of Revenue, North Carolina Department of Tax Research, and the State Board of Assessment. Raleigh: 1954.

Chapter 8

POPULATION

When America was discovered in 1492, the territory which is now the state of North Carolina was peopled by only one race and was influenced by the culture of only one group of people. Since that time, many thousands have moved into North Carolina, chiefly from other parts of America, Europe, and Africa. The various groups which will be considered are: the Indians; the English, who comprised the majority of the early settlers; various Scotch emigrants; Germans, Negroes, French, Swiss, and Welsh.

Ethnic Backgrounds[1]

INDIANS.

Modern scholars have estimated that there were about thirty tribes and from 30,000 to 35,000 Indians in North Carolina at the advent of the whites. These were chiefly (1) the Chowanocs, with whom the settlers had their first war, though a minor one; (2) the Tuscarora, the largest, most important, and most warlike tribe of eastern North Carolina, numbering some 6,000 to 8,000, with whom the whites had the most deadly Indian war in North Carolina history; (3) the Catawba, the most numerous and important of the eastern Siouan family in North Carolina; and (4) the Cherokee, like the Tuscarora, of Iroquoian stock.

From the natives the white settlers learned the techniques of wilderness warfare, as well as methods of fishing, trapping, and cultivation of such crops as corn, tobacco, and other vegetables and fruits. However, the Indians unfortunately took more readily to the vices than to the virtues of the whites. Furthermore, the whites did not recognize Indian title to the soil. It has been aptly said that when the English landed in the country "they fell on their knees and then on the aborigines." The Indian population of North Carolina has decreased considerably, and according to the 1950 census there are fewer than four thousand (3,742) now living within the borders of the state.

ENGLISH.

The first European known to have explored the coast of present North Carolina was Giovanni da Verrazzano, a Florentine navigator in the

---

[1]This section on ethnic backgrounds is largely adapted, by permission, from H. T. Lefler and A. R. Newsome, *North Carolina: The History of a Southern State* (Chapel Hill: University of North Carolina Press, 1954), pp. 1–16, 24–28. For a more detailed study, see R. D. W. Connor, *Race Elements in the White Population of North Carolina* (Raleigh: The College, 1920), pp. 7–112.

service of France. His explorations along the Cape Fear River and his later published account probably influenced Walter Raleigh in formulating his plans for planting an English colony in the New World.

A Spanish colony was attempted in 1520 and again in 1526 by Lucas Vasquez de Ayllon, but fever and starvation made the endeavor short lived, and it remained to Sir Walter Raleigh—soldier, poet, favorite of the Queen—to lay the groundwork for future English colonization on the Virginia-Carolina coast. The efforts which he sponsored were doomed to failure, but the knowledge his men had gathered and the publicity he gained for the project were directly contributory to the first successful enterprise at Jamestown in 1607.

Raleigh dispatched two sea captains, Philip Amadas and Arthur Barlowe, in 1584 to explore the country and to recommend a suitable site for settlement. They returned with a glowing report of the New World, and the first English colony, under the command of Richard Grenville with Ralph Lane as lieutenant governor, set out. The group included many scholars, but not those with the training essential for the conquest of the American wilderness. The colony suffered from friction among leaders, Indian hostility, and scarcity of food, tools, and other articles necessary to establish the settlement on a sound basis. Inevitably it failed.

But Raleigh made yet another attempt at colonization. The second colony was under the leadership of John White and consisted of about 150 settlers, including seventeen women and nine children. Soon after their arrival, Virginia Dare was born, the first child of English parentage born in the New World. This colony had difficulties also, and its strange disappearance gave it its famous name the "Lost Colony."

It was not until 1607 that the first permanent English colony was established at Jamestown, Virginia. As the colony began to prosper, most of the good land next to navigable streams was taken up and the soil exhausted. The desire for better land and fresh hunting grounds drove explorers, hunters, traders, and farmers along the streams of southeastern Virginia into the Chowan River–Albemarle Sound area. This movement was a gradual one. Although the exact date is obscure, some writers believe that the first English settler probably entered what is now North Carolina about 1650.[2]

If an estimate of Virginia's population at 22,000 in 1654 is correct, it is easy to understand why many people were seeking new land in Carolina, Maryland, and elsewhere. By this time there seems to have been a steady flow of population from Virginia to the Albemarle region. It is

[2]John M. Mullen, *Facts to Know about North Carolina* (Charlotte: Mullen Feature Syndicate, 1933), p. 9.

known that some of these early settlers brought slaves with them.[3] Some of the towns established during this period were Bath, New Bern, Burrington, Roanoke (Edenton), Currituck, and Brunswick.

At the close of the proprietary rule in 1729, there were only about 30,000[4] whites and fewer than 6,000 Negroes in the province. At this time, North Carolina was perhaps the most sparsely settled of all the English colonies, and most of its population, chiefly of English stock, lived in the Tidewater. By 1775 the white population was estimated at 265,000 and the Negro at 80,000. North Carolina had become the fourth most populous colony.

There were several reasons for this growth. Although the birth rate was high, as in all the colonies, immigration was the major factor. Inhabitants came daily from Virginia and Pennsylvania and other parts of America, and some came directly from Europe, especially from England, Scotland, and Ireland. From the mountains of Switzerland and the valleys of the Rhine and the Danube, thousands of hardy, enterprising pioneers poured into North Carolina, occupying the vacant places in the older settlements, moving up and down the banks of the Roanoke, the Neuse, and the Cape Fear, and spreading out over the plains and through the valleys of the piedmont section.

Table 25 shows the chronology of the introduction of new ethnic groups and the growth in population.

SCOTCH HIGHLANDERS.

The Highland Scots were the only large group to come to North Carolina directly from their native land. As early as 1729 a few Scots had settled on the Upper Cape Fear, and in 1739 Neil McNeill and three hundred and fifty Highlanders landed at Wilmington. According to tradition, they left that town because the citizenry made fun of their peculiar costumes and unusual language and settled instead in the present Fayetteville region. The Assembly, interested in promoting immigration and also prodded by Governor Johnston, a Highland Scot himself, voted to exempt the new settlers from all taxation for ten years. Even more significant than this gesture in the immigration of the Scots, however, was the political situation at home. Since the Act of Union in 1707, Scotland had been resisting the enforced union with England, and the smouldering unrest sporadically broke into open warfare. The Scots were decisively defeated by the British in 1745, and the aftermath of the battle led thousands to North Carolina.

---

[3] Lefler and Newsome, *op cit.*, p. 16.

[4] R. D. W. Connor, *History of North Carolina, the Colonial and Revolutionary Period, 1584–1783* (Chicago: Lewis Publishing Co., 1919), I, 143.

Within a few years there were Highland settlements throughout the Upper Cape Fear Valley in the region now embracing Anson, Bladen, Cumberland, Harnett, Hoke, Moore, Richmond, Robeson, Sampson, and Scotland counties. At the head of navigation on the Cape Fear River a town was begun which was incorporated in 1762 as Campbelltown, although it was renamed Fayetteville in 1783 in honor of General Lafayette.

The French and Indian War interrupted Scottish immigration, but it continued on a greater scale with the termination of that war. The Highlanders who came to North Carolina were among the most substantial and energetic people of Scotland and were referred to as men of "wealth and merit." The Scots continued to use Gaelic, but it gradually gave way to English, although there were survivals of the ancient tongue for more than a century. Most of the Highlanders were farmers, though quite a number became merchants and mechanics. Some likewise entered the professions and made distinctive contributions in politics, religion, education, and military affairs.

Scotch-Irish.

The term "Scotch-Irish"[5] is a misnomer, and does not, as one would naturally suppose, signify a mixed race of Scotch and Irish ancestry. The so-called Scotch-Irish were in reality Scotch people, or descendants of Scotch people, who once resided in Ireland. They invaded Ireland in the seventeenth century and lived as conquerors. The Irish hated them. Thus the Scotch in Ireland remained Scotch, and "Irish" as applied to them is merely a geographical term. In fact "Scotch-Irish" is purely American in its origin and use and has never been known in Ireland, where the descendants of the Scottish settlers are distinguished from the Irish proper by the far more significant terms "Irish Protestants" and "Irish Presbyterians." Another name often applied to them, "Ulstermen," is derived from the province in which they are chiefly found.

Occasional settlers of Lowland Scotch and Scotch-Irish descent were found in North Carolina at a very early date. The first of these who came to North Carolina as an organized group were brought into the province by large land companies. In 1736 immigration began, accompanying a grant of 60,000 acres of land in what is now Sampson and Duplin counties. (A few Irish and Swiss also settled in the same community.) The great tide of Scotch-Irish rolled in upon that section of North Carolina drained by the headwaters of the Neuse and Cape Fear and of the Yadkin and the Catawba and their tributaries. Scattered families were living along the Hico, the Eno, and the Haw. Six new counties were formed within sixteen years as a result of immigration, and Mecklenburg became the center of

_____
[5] *Ibid.*, p. 162.

the Scotch-Irish settlements. Many of the Scotch-Irish moved down from Pennsylvania through Virginia, although it is questionable whether they ever resided in Pennsylvania for any time at all.

The Scotch-Irish made a great contribution to the growth, expansion, and development of North Carolina. With their strong Calvinist background, they were strong believers in education and religion—wherever they settled, a Presbyterian church and a schoolhouse soon were built, and the state is indebted to them. It is interesting to note that all the Carolina-born presidents of the United States—Andrew Jackson, James K. Polk, and Andrew Johnson—were Scotch-Irish.

GERMANS.

Moving from Pennsylvania (in 1775 Pennsylvania was one-third German) along the same route at the same time as the Scotch-Irish, and settling in the same general area of North Carolina, came many Germans. They had emigrated from their homeland earlier because of economic, social, and religious hardships, and it is estimated that by 1775 about twenty-five thousand had settled in the Piedmont.

The Germans belonged to three different religious groups—the Lutheran, Moravian, and Reformed churches, the Lutherans being the most numerous. The Moravian settlement at Wachovia, perhaps the best known, was established in 1753, but soon after came Bethabara, Bethania, and Salem. Many Germans were scattered over the present Rowan, Anson, Orange, Mecklenburg, and Forsyth counties and as far west as Catawba county, especially along the waters of the Yadkin and Catawba rivers.

By habit and training the Germans were industrious, thrifty, and law abiding. Unaccustomed to slavery and unacquainted with Negroes, they were inclined to rely on their own labor. Like the Scots, the Germans endeavored to preserve their language and customs for some time. They had fine farms and plenty of livestock and in general were more interested in business, religion, and education than in politics.

NEGROES.

One large group of people did not come to America from Europe, but were brought as slaves. The exact date of the entry of Negroes into North Carolina is unknown; the arrival of the first slave ship in Virginia is recorded as 1620, and Virginians moving into North Carolina about 1650 are known to have brought Negroes with them. The slave trade was begun by the Portuguese, enlarged by the Dutch, and carried to its culmination by the English. Because of the dangerous coast, North Carolina did not get many slaves directly from Africa but rather received them from Virginia and other colonies.

THE FRENCH, SWISS, AND WELSH.

The French, Swiss, and Welsh population of North Carolina were negligible. A few French Huguenots had settled in Virginia near Richmond and moved to the cheap land in the Neuse–Pamlico section. A Swiss land company was active in the founding of New Bern along with a few early German settlers. The Welsh never emigrated as a group, though scattered families entered North Carolina along with various groups from the British Isles.

Estimated population figures for various ethnic groups in 1760 were: English, 45,000; Scotch, 40,000; German, 15,000; and Negro, 30,000, making a total of 130,000 (see Table 25).

Demographic Characteristics and Trends

GROWTH OF POPULATION.

In 1790, when the first population census was taken, North Carolina had 393,751 people. Only Pennsylvania and Virginia had more. By 1850 North Carolina ranked tenth among the existing states, and at no time has the state ranked lower than sixteenth. In 1950 it was again tenth. Table 26 presents the findings of the census from 1790 to 1956: the percentage increase refers to the rate of increase during the preceding decade. Table 27 gives a supplementary breakdown of the population structure from 1900 to 1950 by age and color, and Table 28 shows the increase in urbanization from 1790 to 1950.

Except for the two decades 1830 to 1840 and 1860 to 1870, the rate of population growth has been fairly constant. The small increase between 1830 and 1840 was due to emigration largely to Indiana and adjacent middlewestern states and to the new cotton states to the south. The small increase from 1860 to 1870 was attributable to deaths during the Civil War. There has been almost no immigration from abroad into North Carolina for more than 120 years, and no state has a lower proportion of foreign born. On the other hand, North Carolina has sent into almost every state in the Union more people than have come from those states to North Carolina. The only noteworthy exchange gain has been from South Carolina.

Table 29 shows the principal population facts for the state, county by county, as revealed by the 1950 census.

PERCENTAGE OF NATIVE-BORN WHITES.

The 1850 census of population revealed that of North Carolina's population, 95.7 per cent were born in the state, 3.8 per cent were born outside the state but in the United States, and only 0.5 per cent were of foreign birth. At that time, North Carolina had the highest percentage of whites born within its own borders, and the smallest percentage of people of foreign birth, of all the states. The 1920 census showed that North Carolina still had the highest percentage of native-born inhabitants; only three of every thousand whites in 1920 were of foreign birth. In 1950 (when the state was tied with South Carolina in percentage of native-born population) only about five of every thousand whites were not native born.

MIGRATION FROM THE STATE.

Historically North Carolina has been an exporter of population to other states. The 1860 census showed there were 272,606 white (*i.e.*, free) North Carolinians living in other states. These 272,606 constituted a number equal to 43 per cent of the resident white North Carolina-born population. At the same time, while this many North Carolinians were living in other states in 1860, there were only 23,845 natives of other states living in North Carolina, effecting a net loss of 248,761. Only two states—South Carolina and Delaware—had received fewer people from outside their own borders, and only New York, Pennsylvania, and Virginia had larger relative losses.

Again, in 1920 there were 443,844 native North Carolinians living in other states. The residents of North Carolina born in other states numbered 157,996, making a net loss of 285,848. Only five states had emigrations to North Carolina greater than the number of North Carolinians who had emigrated to them. The net migrations to forty-two states and the District of Columbia ranged from 123 to Nevada to 75,918 to Virginia.

The decade 1920 to 1930 was one of outstanding progress for the state of North Carolina, and perhaps the only decade since 1790 during which more people moved to the state than left it. In 1930 there were 315,278 people living in North Carolina who were born elsewhere, an increase of 157,282 over 1920.

The 1950 census figures, which reflect a reshuffling of the population in the postwar decade, show a total migration of 900,435 persons from North Carolina to other states, a number equivalent to 20.3 per cent of the state's population at that time. Concurrently, there was a movement of 475,240 people into the state, a figure equal to 11.9 per cent of the state's population. Thus the net decline in population through emigration was 423,195, the largest such loss in any census period in the state's history. Only eight states, mostly southern, experienced greater net losses in this period. (Table 30 shows the estimates of migration from North Carolina from 1900 to 1950.) This emigration process has been an expensive one, since people who have been raised and trained at the expense of the state have gone elsewhere to live their productive lives, and their earning power has not benefited the welfare of the state.

Dr. C. Horace Hamilton of North Carolina State College lists six chief reasons for emigration: (1) Pressure of population, particularly in rural areas where a surplus of children are produced; (2) population vacuums in out-of-state urban areas because of low birth rates there; (3) expansion of urban industry, sparked by wartime production and postwar prosperity; (4) location of war industries in certain areas (few in North Carolina); (5) mechanization of agriculture and changes in the types and amounts of agricultural production; (6) the continued drift of Negroes from rural areas to urban areas in the North.[6]

Subtracting the differential between births over deaths in the period 1940–50 from the net loss through emigration in that same period, we find that North Carolina had an absolute loss of 261,000 in that decade, and according to census estimates, the rate of loss has continued up to 1957. There were seventy-eight counties that gained in population, but in only fourteen did the birth rate exceed the death rate between 1940 and 1950. The largest gains were in urban counties and counties with military establishments, such as Onslow and Cumberland. The largest losses have been principally in the mountain and tidewater areas and in highly rural counties in other regions.

North Carolina's estimated population in July, 1956, was 4,406,000 and its rank eleventh among the states. The census estimates that in recent years some 28,000 more people have been leaving the state each year than have been entering it.

RACE RATIOS.

Both the white and Negro populations in North Carolina have shown considerable increases in every decade since 1790. The actual rates of growth and the ratio of whites to Negroes have fluctuated in this period but have ultimately almost returned to the original figures. In 1790 the white element was 73.2 per cent. From 1790 to 1880 the Negro proportion increased in every decade except one, 1830–40, and that was negligible. Since 1880 the reverse has been true and the white population percentage has increased in every decade. In 1880 whites constituted 62 per cent of the state's population, and by 1950 the percentage was 73.4, almost exactly the 1790 figure.

Expressed another way, even though the Negro population has increased numerically in every decade since 1880, the *rate* of increase has in general been declining. The Negro population is growing, but much slower than that of the white population. Table 31, based on the 1950 census, gives interesting facts about the race ratio in North Carolina by decades from 1790 to 1950.

TREND TOWARD URBANIZATION.

The 1950 census definition of urban differed from the definition previously used. Under the 1950 definition, the urban population consisted

---

[6] C. Horace Hamilton, Net Migration to and from North Carolina and North Carolina Counties from 1940 to 1950, North Carolina Agricultural Extension Station Progress Report 18 (mimeographed; Raleigh, September, 1953).

of all persons living in (a) places of 2,500 inhabitants or more which were incorporated as boroughs, towns, and villages; (b) the densely settled urban fringe, including both incorporated and unincorporated areas, around cities of 50,000 or more; and (c) unincorporated places of 2,500 inhabitants or more outside any urban fringe. The remaining population was classed as rural. The definition used in previous censuses included as urban all persons living in incorporated places of 2,500 inhabitants or more and areas (usually minor civil divisions) classified as urban under special rules relating to population size and density. Thus, using the 1950 definition, there were over a hundred thousand people (129,908) classified as urban who, under the old definition, would have been classified as rural.

According to the 1950 census, the urban element in North Carolina numbered 1,368,101 persons, or 33.7 per cent of the state's total population. The urban component was living in 107 urban places (above 2,500 inhabitants) and in communities included in the fringes of the six large urbanized areas in the state. But more than 70 per cent of this population lived in 31 towns and cities of 10,000 or more inhabitants. Each of these gained population between 1940 and 1950, the increases ranging from 1.0 per cent in Thomasville to 190.6 per cent in Albemarle.

Table 32 shows how the population is distributed in dwelling places of varying size.

THE URBAN POPULATION.

Remembering the new definition of the term urban and how it automatically reclassified over a hundred thousand people who were formerly regarded as rural, we must understand that since we make comparison, we can compare only on the basis of the old definition. On this basis the urban population rose from 186,790 in 1900 to 1,238,193 in 1950. The highest rate of growth in the fifty-year period occurred in the decade 1900–10, when the increase was at the rate of 70.5 per cent. The largest numerical increase took place between 1920 and 1930. From 1940 to 1950 the increase was 264,018, or 27.1 per cent. In 1900 the population of the state was 9.9 per cent urban, and in 1950 30.5 per cent urban (under the new definition, 33.7 per cent). The number of incorporated places of 25,000 or over rose from none in 1900 to ten in 1950, with a combined population of 633,660.

There were six urbanized areas in the state in 1950 under the new definition. An urbanized area includes a city of 50,000 or more plus the surrounding closely settled incorporated places and unincorporated areas that meet certain criteria for being a part of the urban fringe. These urbanized areas were Asheville, Charlotte, Durham, Greensboro, Raleigh, and Winston-Salem. They ranged in size from the environs of Charlotte area, with 140,930, to the Asheville area, with 59,437.

THE RURAL NONFARM POPULATION

The category designated as rural includes not only those people living on farms but also those in small towns of less than 2,500 inhabitants and people living in rural areas but not on farms. In 1950, the population classed as rural was almost equally divided between people living on farms and people not living on farms. This second element—the rural nonfarm—is becoming increasingly more important in the total population picture in the state. By 1930 the rural nonfarm population constituted 24.1 per cent of the state's population; in 1950 it made up 32.4 per cent. The rate of growth has been roughly equal to that of the urban population.

Just who are these rural nonfarm people? First, they are those who do not live in a town or city, incorporated or unincorporated, with as many as 2,500 people, or who do not live in what the census terms the urban fringe of cities of 50,000 or more people. Second, they do not live on farms. (A farm is defined as being three acres or more in size if agricultural products grown on them amounted to a value of $150 in 1949; or when it is less than three acres, if it grew $150 worth of farm products in 1949.) Thus, though 69.5 per cent of the population of North Carolina is classed as rural, only about half of these are actually farm people.

THE RURAL FARM POPULATION.

The farm population of North Carolina is getting smaller and smaller, just as it is in other states. However, North Carolina is one of three states that gained in number of farms from 1940 to 1950. Its gain of more than 10,000 farms was the largest of these three states, the others being South Carolina and California. North Carolina is the only state that gained farms both from 1940 to 1945 and from 1945 to 1950.

In 1940 there were 1,656,101 North Carolinians classified in the rural farm category. By 1950 this group had declined to 1,578,061. This decrease in size of the rural farm population is tied up with the decrease in tenancy in the past two decades, gradual increasing mechanization of farming, and migration of excess farm population to small towns and larger cities, both in and out of the state. North Carolina is still classed as a rural state, but one of the main reasons for this is the preponderance of small towns and villages with less than 2,500 population, which are not classified as urban by the census. As pointed out previously, North Carolina's rural population is almost equally divided between this rural nonfarm element and the true farm population.

At this point we might note the racial differences in urban, rural nonfarm, and rural farm classifications. Table 35 shows that the Negro population is almost 40 per cent farm, while about 31 per cent of the whites are so classed. Another interesting difference is that shown between the

two races in patterns of rural nonfarm settlement. The Negro urban element is slightly larger proportionately than the white. However, only 25.6
per cent of the Negro population as against 34.9 per cent of the white population is classed as rural nonfarm. Some of the reasons for these differences will be pointed out below.

Occupational Distrubition.

Table 34 deals with occupational distribution of the employed population of North Carolina in 1950, and it shows some of the differences in
occupations of the whites and nonwhites by urban, rural nonfarm, and
rural farm residence.

Of those people living in urban areas, very few nonwhites (which includes Indians and a few others) are found in such occupations as (a) managers, officials, and proprietors except farm; (b) clerical and kindred
workers; (c) sales workers, etc. The urban nonwhite population is heavily
concentrated in such occupations as (a) operatives and kindred workers;
(b) private household workers; (c) service workers; and (d) laborers,
especially in the tobacco industry.

In the usual nonfarm-residence category it will be noticed that a much
larger proportion of the nonwhites are engaged in farm and other types
of labor. Another important difference is in the two categories of industrial laborers—foremen and kindred workers, and operatives and kindred
workers. In these two categories are found about 53 per cent of the employed white rural nonfarm population, as against only 26 per cent of
the employed nonwhite.

Under the rural farm designation, exactly the same proportion of
whites and nonwhites are classed as farmers and farm managers. On the
other hand, much larger proportions of the nonwhites are classified as
farm laborers and other types of laborers. Further, almost 20 per cent
of the employed whites in the rural farm population are classed as craftsmen, foremen and kindred workers, and operatives and kindred workers.
Only 5.2 per cent of the nonwhites are so classified.

One of the main reasons for these differences is that many of the textile
mills and small plants are in locations classed as rural nonfarm. Thus it
would be expected that a large part of the population of those farm areas
round about would be employed in these mills and plants. The same racial
occupation differences hold true in the urban areas, where the majority
of the nonwhite employees are in service occupations and relatively unskilled labor groups.

The analysis of the employment situation by race, occupation, and
place of residence in Table 34 indicates that of all the experienced civilian
labor force residing in rural nonfarm locations, almost half of them are
craftsmen, foremen, operatives, and kindred workers, which is accounted

for by the great number of textile mills and other plants which have settled in small towns.

REGIONS OF THE STATE AND POPULATION.

As we have seen, North Carolina is generally subdivided into four major areas: Tidewater, Upper Coastal Plain, Piedmont, and mountain region. Although all regions of the state have increased in population size, the increase has been greater in some parts of the state than others.

The tidewater region is made up of twenty-two counties (as used in this book) in the extreme eastern part of the state. This region has grown more slowly in population than any other. The population has increased from 278,672 inhabitants in 1900 to 446,403 inhabitants in 1950, an increase of 167,731 or 60.2 per cent.

The Upper Coastal Plain contains twenty-three counties. This region had 500,024 inhabitants in 1900 and 1,078,486 in 1950, an increase of 578,462, or 115.7 per cent. It had the second largest growth of all the four regions.

The Piedmont region is the largest with thirty-eight counties, lying east of the Blue Ridge and west of the fall line. There were 892,701 inhabitants in this region in 1900 and 2,138,651 in 1950. This was a numerical growth of 1,245,950 and a percentage increase of 139.6, the largest of the four regions.

The Mountain region is made up of seventeen counties in the extreme western part of the state. In 1900 there were 222,013 persons living in this region as against 398,389 in 1950. This was an increase of 176,376, or 79.4 per cent.

THE COUNTIES AND POPULATION DENSITY.

Seventy-eight of North Carolina's one hundred counties experienced gains in population during the decade 1940–50. Nearly one-fourth of the state's population growth took place in three counties—Mecklenburg, Guilford, and Cumberland. Fifteen of the counties between 1940 and 1950 had rates of growth of more than 20 per cent.

In 1950 the counties ranged in population from Tyrrell with 5,048 inhabitants to Mecklenburg with 197,052. Six of the counties had smaller populations than they had fifty years before. These were Camden, Currituck, Gates, Perquimans, Madison, and Mitchell, the last having lost some territory and population in the formation of Avery County.

In size the counties range from Sampson with 963 square miles to Chowan with 180 square miles, land area, and in density of population they range from 364 per square mile in Mecklenburg County to 10 in Hyde.

AGING POPULATION.

One of the most significant facts of this century is that we now have an aging population. The 1950 census showed that North Carolina had a quarter-million people who were 65 or over, 5.5 per cent. From 1940 to 1950 the state's population increased 13.7 per cent while the population 65 and over increased 43.9 per cent. Better medical care is largely responsible. But derivative of this phenomenon is a social problem. The proportion of old people will rise steadily, and providing for them will be an ever growing necessity.

OTHER POPULATION DATA.

The 1950 census revealed some additional facts about the state of North Carolina: In 1790 North Carolina had 10 per cent of the nation's population. This percentage dropped steadily to 2.4 per cent in 1910 and in 1920, but rose to 2.7 per cent in 1950. Population per square mile has risen from 38.9 in 1900 to 82.7 in 1950. North Carolina ranks twelfth among the states in population density. The state's delegation to the federal House of Representatives was five in 1789; thirteen from 1810 to 1830; seven in 1860; and eventually twelve in 1950. North Carolina ranked fourteenth in the *amount* of population increase from 1940 to 1950, the total being 490,306, and ranked twenty-first in per cent of increase, with a 13.7 per cent gain.

Until 1820, the state's urban population was nonexistent, but by that date 12,502 people could be classified as living in urban areas. Even in 1880, only 55,116 could be so classified. In reverse percentages, the rural population dropped from 100 per cent in 1790 to 90.1 per cent in 1900 to 69.5 per cent, old definition (66.3 per cent, new definition), in 1950.

The median age in the United States in 1950 was 30.2 years. In North Carolina it was 25 years. Only South Carolina has a lower median. In the United States as a whole, 8.1 per cent are 65 years of age and over. The percentage for North Carolina is 5.5, again second lowest to South Carolina, with 5.4 per cent.

North and South Carolina are tied for the highest per cent of native-born adults in the population with 99.4 per cent each.

The median years of school completed by North Carolina's adult population in 1950 was 7.9. Four states ranked below it.

The percentage of the population fourteen years old or older who were widowed of divorced in 1950 was 3.9 for males, the second lowest among the states, and 12.1 for females, the seventh lowest.

The median income of North Carolina urban and rural nonfarm families in 1949 was $2,471. Only nine states ranked lower.

The state's per capita income in 1955 was $1,236, fifth lowest.

In 1950 North Carolina had the largest nonwhite population of all the states. North Carolina had 1,047,353 Negroes and 31,455 other non-whites—principally Indians, 3,742, and all others (mainly those of mixed white-Negro-Indian blood known as Croatans or Lumbee Indians), 27,270.

POPULATION 83

This gives a total of 1,078,808 nonwhite population, as compared with Georgia's 1,064,001, the second highest nonwhite population. Within the state the nonwhite percentage ranges from 1.1 in Yancey County to 66.4 in Warren County. There are ten counties in the state with more nonwhite than white population, and there are sixteen additional counties that are from 40 to 50 per cent Negro.

BIBLIOGRAPHY

ARNETT, A. M. *The Story of North Carolina*. Chapel Hill: University of North Carolina Press, 1933.

ASHE, S. A. *History of North Carolina*. Vol. I. Greensboro, North Carolina: C. L. Van Noppen, 1908.

BARKER, HOWARD F. "National Stocks in the Population of the United States, as Indicated by the Surnames in the Census of 1790," American Historical Association, *Annual Report, 1931*, I, 126–359.

BOLTON, C. K. *Scotch-Irish Pioneer in Ulster and America*. Boston: Bacon and Brown, 1910.

CLEWELL, J. H. *History of Wachovia in North Carolina*. New York: Doubleday, Page and Company, 1902.

CONNOR, R. D. W. *Ante-Bellum Builders of North Carolina*. Greensboro, North Carolina: The College, 1914.

———. *History of North Carolina, the Colonial and Revolutionary Period, 1584–1783*. Vol. I. Chicago: Lewis Publishing Co., 1919.

———. *North Carolina: Rebuilding an Ancient Commonwealth, 1584–1925*. Vol. I. Chicago and New York: The American Historical Society, 1929.

———. *Race Elements in the White Population of North Carolina*. Raleigh, North Carolina: The College, 1920.

DUNAWAY, W. F. *The Scotch-Irish of Colonial Pennsylvania*. Chapel Hill: University of North Carolina Press, 1944.

EHRINGHAUS, J. C. B., AND C. GOERCH. *North Carolina Almanac*. Raleigh: Almanac Publishing Company, 1954.

FAUST, A. B. *The German Element in the United States*. New York: The Steuben Society of America, 1927.

FRIES, A. L. (ed.). *Records of the Moravians in North Carolina*. 7 vols. Raleigh: Edwards and Broughton Printing Company, State Printers, 1922–47.

FRIES, A. L. *The Road to Salem*. Chapel Hill: University of North Carolina Press, 1944.

GEHRKE, W. H. "The Transition from the German to the English Language in North Carolina," *North Carolina Historical Review*, XII (January 1935), 1–19.

GREEN, PAUL. *The Highland Call*. Chapel Hill: University of North Carolina Press, 1941.

GREENE, E. B. AND V. D. HARRINGTON. *American Population before the Federal Census of 1790*. New York: Columbia University Press, 1932.

HAMMER, CARL. *Rhinelanders on the Yadkin*. Salisbury, North Carolina: Rowan Printing Company, 1943.

HOBBS, S. H., JR. *North Carolina: Economic and Social*. Chapel Hill: University of North Carolina Press, 1930.

LEFLER, H. T. AND A. R. NEWSOME. *North Carolina: The History of a Southern State*. Chapel Hill: University of North Carolina Press, 1954.

McKELWAY, A. J. "The Scotch-Irish of North Carolina," *North Carolina Booklet*, IV (March, 1905), 3–24.

McLEAN, J. P. *An Historical Account of the Settlements of Scotch Highlanders in America Prior to the Peace of 1783*. Cleveland, Ohio: The Helmen-Taylor Company, 1900.

MULLEN, JOHN M. *Facts to Know about North Carolina*. Charlotte: Mullen Feature Syndicate, 1933.

NEWSOME, A. R. AND H. T. LEFLER. *The Growth of North Carolina*. Yonkers-on-Hudson, New York: World Book Company, 1940.

NIXON, J. R. "The German Settlers in Lincoln County and Western North Carolina," *The James Sprunt Historical Publication*, under the direction of the North Carolina Historical Society, XI (1912), 25–62.

The People of North Carolina. North Carolina State Planning Board (with the cooperation of the National Resources Committee, Works Progress Administration), Raleigh: 1938.

U. S. Dept. of Commerce, Bureau of the Census. *Seventeenth Census of the United States:* 1950. Vol. II. *Characteristics of the Population*. Part 16. North Carolina. Washington: U. S. Government Printing Office, 1953.

University of North Carolina News Letter, VIII (December 7, 1921); XII (November 21, 1923), (December 5, 1923); XI (December 3, 1924), (December 10, 1924), (October 28, 1925); XII (October 20, 1926).

WITTKE, CARL F. *We Who Built America*. New York: Prentice Hall, 1939.

Chapter 9

Agriculture

North Carolina at present ranks second among the states in total number of farms. There were 267,906 reported by the 1954 Census of Agriculture. Texas has more farms, but the number is declining so fast there that North Carolina may soon rank first. Throughout the United States, farms have been on the decrease for some years. North Carolina is the only state that has shown an increase of farms for each of the two census periods before 1954, an era in which the nation lost more than a million and a half farms. During the years 1950–54 North Carolina, along with nearly every other state, lost farms, but the number of farms in North Carolina has been more stable since 1930 than in any other state.

Farm Size and Population Structure

North Carolina ranks first among the states in total farm population—1,376,560 according to the 1950 census. The farm population has dropped during the last fifteen or twenty years, but the reduction (from 1,500,000 to 1,376,560) has probably been relatively less than in any other state. For the nation as a whole the farm population has declined since 1940 from approximately 30,000,000 to 22,000,000.

Size of Farms.

In 1954 the average farm in North Carolina was 68.2 acres, smallest in the United States. For a hundred years this gradual decline has gone on in North Carolina while throughout the nation, at least for the last several decades, farms have been getting larger. (See Table 35 for data on farm acreage and values.)

This figure of 68.2 acres per farm is the arithmetic average—that is, the total farm acreage divided by the total number of farms. The median farm acreage—the middle-sized farm in North Carolina—is less than 68.2 acres, since a few large farms will offset the number of small farms in an arithmetic average. The 1954 census shows that there are 34,479 farms under 10 acres; 76,672 farms from 10 to 29 acres; 49,329 farms from 30 to 49 acres; and 31,778 farms from 50 to 69 acres. Thus, in 1954 there were 192,258 farms ranging from under 10 acres to 69 acres, total area (see Table 36). It is therefore seen that 70 per cent of the farms of North Carolina average below the state average of 68.2 acres. This is probably the most significant fact about North Carolina as an agricultural state.

It is essentially a state of small farms, and it will never rank high on a per-farm income basis so long as this exists.

Contiguous with the small size of Carolina farms is the amount of land actually harvested per farm. Total acreage includes cropland, woodland, and other, while the true size of a farm is more accurately measured by the number of acres on which crops can be grown. The 1954 census showed that there were 77,423 farms where the harvested acreage ranged from one to nine acres, and 67,558 farms with a harvested acreage of from 10 to 19 acres. Thus about 54 per cent of the farms of North Carolina harvested crops from fewer than 19 acres in 1954. In harvested acres per farm, North Carolina ranks close to the bottom among all the states. There is no way to get an accurate comparison among states, since non-crop pasturelands should be considered as contributing to the farm income. There are one or two states with less cropland per farm but these states have more pastureland per farm.

We have seen that the size of North Carolina's farms has been going down for a hundred years. It may be surprising that in 1850 the average North Carolina farm contained 369 acres and the average crop acreage per farm was 96. Nor has there been any increase in the total amount of land in farms in North Carolina during the last century, although the acreage has fluctuated from one census to another by about two million acres—in 1850 the total acreage of farm land was approximately 21,000,000, and in 1954 the total acreage was 18,260,346.

Fig. 8. Farm Land, 1956

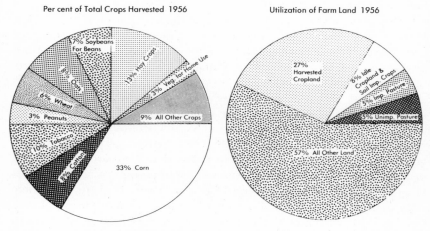

Per cent of Total Crops Harvested 1956

7% Soybeans For Beans
13% Hay Crops
3% Veg. for Home Use
9% All Other Crops
33% Corn
9% Cotton
10% Tobacco
3% Peanuts
6% Wheat
8% Oats

Utilization of Farm Land 1956

27% Harvested Cropland
8% Idle Cropland & Soil Imp. Crops
5% Imp. Pasture
3% Unimp. Pasture
57% All Other Land

Source: North Carolina Farm Census, North Carolina Dept. of Agr. Dec. 23, 1957, Raleigh.

Fig. 9. Crop Reporting Areas

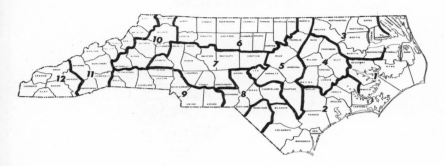

Source: *Agricultural Statistics*, North Carolina Department of Agriculture, 1954.

Fig. 10. Cotton Acreage, 1951

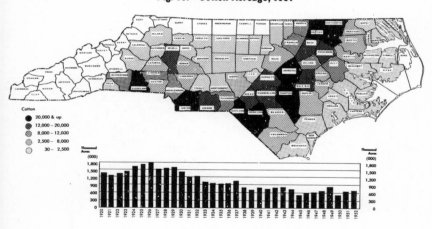

Source: *Agricultural Statistics*, North Carolina Department of Agriculture, 1953.

Fig. 11.   Corn Acreage, 1951

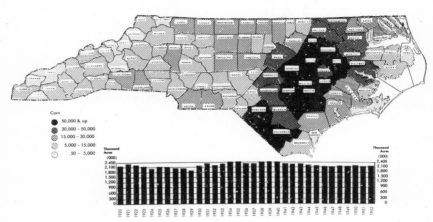

Source: *Agricultural Statistics*, North Carolina Department of Agriculture, 1953.

Fig. 12.   Fiue-Cured Tobacco Acreage, 1951

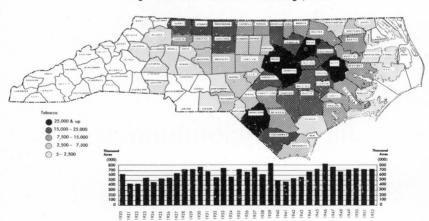

Source: *Agricultural Statistics*, North Carolina Department of Agriculture, 1953.

NEGRO FARMERS.

Another significant factor, leading directly to the problems involved in tenancy, is the Negro as a farmer. Exactly one-fourth of all the farms of North Carolina are operated by Negroes. There has been a slight decrease over the years in the percentage of Negro-operated farms, however the ratio of Negro farmers to all farmers has remained more nearly constant in North Carolina than in any other state where Negroes are important in the farm population. As cotton has faded in importance throughout the Old South, the Negro has declined as a part of the farm population. But in North Carolina the rise of tobacco has far more than offset the decline of cotton, and this fact alone explains why the Negro element in agriculture has not decreased in recent years. The 1954 census shows that nonwhite (almost all Negro) farm operators numbered 66,908. From 1940 to 1950 the Negro farmers increased by roughly 12,000, and North Carolina is the only state that experienced such a gain. Colored farmers are usually tenants and are confined very largely to tobacco and cotton counties.

FARM TENANCY.

The significance of tenancy has to be understood in order to comprehend North Carolina as an agricultural state. As in practically every other state, tenancy in North Carolina is on the decline, but the decline has been slower than in the nation as a whole. Farm tenancy reached a peak in the United States from about 1930 to 1935, when some 43 per cent of all farms were operated by tenants. The tenants in North Carolina for those years number almost 50 per cent of all farmers. From 1935 to 1954, the farm–tenant ratio for the nation dropped from roughly 43 per cent to 24.4 per cent, and the farm–tenant ratio for North Carolina dropped from roughly 50 per cent to 36.9 per cent in 1954 (see Table 37).

The decline in tenancy has not been uniform throughout the state. In a number of counties, particularly in the tobacco belt, there has been little change in this ratio between the total number of farms and the number of tenant-operated farms. In the piedmont and mountain areas, tenancy has declined rapidly, while in Edgecombe, Greene, Wilson, Pitt, Nash, Scotland, Lenoir, Hertford, Robeson, and other eastern counties there has been no net change in farm–tenant ratios. In some counties the percentage of farms operated by tenants has increased slightly since 1940 and in other counties losses have been negligible. On the other hand, in all western North Carolina counties farm tenant ratios have declined. For instance, in Cabarrus County, the ratio declined from 38.4 per cent in 1940 to 21.7 per cent in 1950; in Iredell, from 38.9 per cent to 21.1 per cent; in Graham, from 29.3 to 7 per cent. These are picked at random and are illustrative of the decline of tenancy in the noncash-crop counties of North Carolina.

FARM POPULATION EMPLOYED OFF THE FARM.

An exhaustive study of the nonfarm income derived by farm families has recently been made.[1] Briefly, in 1949 there were some 77,000 farm families in North Carolina with family income from nonfarm sources which exceeded the farm income. There were nearly twice as many farm families in 1949 in which some members worked off the farm as in 1945— 99,109 as compared with 55,212—and it has been estimated that the nonfarm family income for farm families in 1949 was around $166,000,000. The farmers who have nonfarm jobs to boost their farm incomes are principally in the piedmont section where jobs are rather plentiful. Nonfarm income is relatively low in the eastern part of the state, where nonfarm jobs are relatively few. These thousands of North Carolina small farmers situated in industrial areas have extensive opportunities nearby for nonfarm income, and each year the number of farm families working off the farm increases materially. Further development of industries, particularly those in the small towns, villages, and open country, will give the small farmer, in great need of more income, additional opportunities to pad the family finances. (See Table 38).

Agricultural Wealth

FARM INCOME.

All these facts are interrelated, and all must be borne in mind when one looks at the production of agricultural wealth in North Carolina. Further, it must be realized that while on a total basis, North Carolina shows up fairly well in farm-wealth production (and the total figures are the ones generally presented), the important point is not farm income on a total basis but farm income per farm. It is the per-farm and per-family and, even more accurately, the per-farm-inhabitant income that counts. The standard of living of the farmer is determined very largely by the per-farm-dweller income. Since 1950, the cash farm income of North Carolina has been around $900,000,000 per annum (see Table 39 for figures on the history of farm-crop income and the value of the crops that produced it), and in this connection it might be stated that North Carolina's total farm income has held up better than has the nation's since the decline which set in about 1950. While the nation's farm income has declined by some $2,600,000,000 from 1951 through 1956, North Carolina's cash farm income has remained rather static. On a per-farm basis, North Carolina's cash farm income has ranged from about $3,000 to $3,250. Its rank in per-farm income is almost invariably from thirty-eighth to

---

[1] G. W. Blackwell, S. H. Hobbs, Jr., Harriet Herring, G. L. Simpson, and others, Part-Time Farming in North Carolina (unpublished; Chapel Hill: Institute for Research in Social Science, University of North Carolina, 1954).

to forty-second among the states. For instance, in 1954 Arizona averaged better than $35,000 cash income per farm, and West Virginia, at the bottom, averaged $1,512. North Carolina, with $3,211, ranked thirty-eighth. This is its best recent rating. Bear in mind, however, that this income which ranks thirty-eighth is from the forty-eighth-largest farm. It is the high value of tobacco per acre that keeps North Carolina from ranking lower than it does.

The problem of the small farm is shown in the 1954 Census of Agriculture report that there were 58,650 farms in North Carolina with cash income from farm-production sales of less than $250 each. From these come the farmers who augment their families' incomes by working off the farm. See Tables 40 through 43 for data on farm income.

FARM WEALTH.

North Carolina ranks in farm wealth about as it does in farm income. The average value of land per farm in 1954 was $8,105, and North Carolina ranked forty-second among the states. The pressure of population and the high yield in value of cash crops, notably tobacco, give North Carolina farm land slightly higher value per acre.

Principally because the farms are small, the value of farm machinery is relatively low, forty-fifth in value of farm machinery per farm in 1950. The two major crops, tobacco and cotton, are grown with a minimum of machinery in North Carolina.

We have noted that the state places either forty-seventh or forth-eighth in ratio of income from livestock sales. In value of meat and milk animals per farm, North Carolina generally ranks about forty-sixth. In the strictest sense, mules and horses are work stock and thus comparable with tractors, not with meat and milk animals. The small size of North Carolina farms makes the use of mules rather than tractors economically sound, and because of the great number of farms, and the small average size of those farms, the state ranks first in the total number of mules. Without changes in cultivation practices, it would be practically impossible to harvest tobacco, or spray the grown crop, without mule power.

CASH-CROP–LIVESTOCK RELATIONSHIP.

North Carolina's agriculture can be characterized chiefly as cash-crop farming. During the last few years, close to 80 per cent of the cash farm income of North Carolina has been derived from the sale of crops and 20 per cent from the sale of livestock and livestock products. In some years the percentage from livestock has been slightly higher, ranging up to 24 per cent, and in some years it has been less than 20 per cent. Ordinarily, North and South Carolina alternate for bottom position in the percentage of income derived from the sale of livestock and livestock products (although Florida occasionally descends to last position). Although the total income from livestock in North Carolina has increased, there has been a parallel gain in crop income, due chiefly to the gradual rise in importance of tobacco. In recent years tobacco sales alone have provided more than half the total cash farm income of North Carolina. The range varies from around 50 to 58 per cent, depending mainly on how well tobacco does, or how poorly cotton does.

Aside from cash farm income derived from the sale of livestock and livestock products, on the basis of both the actual value of livestock per farm and the percentage of farms having purebred livestock, North Carolina ranks near the bottom, as would be expected from a state whose agriculture is based on a cash-crop economy. At the same time, many farms in North Carolina have high-quality livestock, and their numbers have been increasing. North Carolina's principal gains as a livestock state have been in the number and quality of dairy cattle, the number of beef cattle, and production of poultry and eggs. The expansion in dairy cattle has occurred chiefly in the piedmont and mountain areas, and in beef cattle generally throughout the state; the poultry production increase has been mostly in a dozen or so piedmont and mountain counties.

It is interesting to compare North Carolina as a livestock state today and a hundred years ago (see Table 44). According to the 1850 census, there were 869,039 people in North Carolina and 56,963 farms. In 1950 there were 4,061,000 people and 288,508 farms. In 1850 there were 694,000 cattle reported by the census, and in 1859 there were 698,000 beef and dairy cattle. However, from 1950 to 1954 cattle increased by 251,000. In 1850 there were 595,000 head of sheep and in 1860 considerably more than this number. In 1954 the census reports approximately 46,000 head of sheep in North Carolina. Further, in 1850 the census report 1,813,000 head of swine and in 1954, 1,419,000.

But the growth of the dairy industry has been steady during the last fifty years or so. A recent issue of *Agricultural Statistics* from the North Carolina Department of Agriculture reports that dairy cattle, including calves, have increased from 534,000 to 606,000 from January 1, 1934 to January 1, 1954, and the quality of the cattle (as with all livestock) has risen concurrently with their quantity.[2]

The number of beef cattle dropped, in general, on a per-farm basis after 1860, but it has grown considerably in the last 10 or 15 years, and especially since 1950. Again citing *Agricultural Statistics*, beef cattle figures rose from 145,000 to 355,000 from January, 1934, to January, 1954, and the percentage of beef cattle among all cattle has risen from 21 to 37.

---

[2]*North Carolina Agricultural Statistics, 1953–1954*, North Carolina Department of Agriculture (Raleigh).

The number of hogs fluctuates greatly from one census to another, or even from one year to another. In some recent years the total number of hogs on farms has dropped to below 600,000, while in others the total number has ranged up to 1,250,000 or more.

See Table 45 for figures on cash-marketing receipts on both livestock and cash-crop items and Figs. 13 and 14 for percentages of cash receipts from specific items within both the crop and livestock categories.

Fig. 13. Source of Cash Receipts

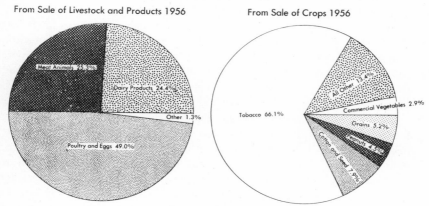

From Sale of Livestock and Products 1956

From Sale of Crops 1956

Source: The Farm Income Situation. U. S. Dept. of Agr. Sept., 1957.

Fig. 14. All Cattle on Farms, 1934–1954

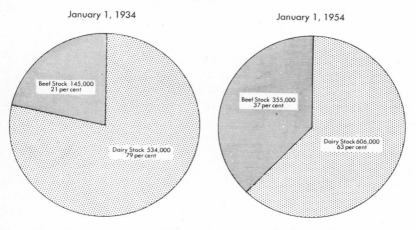

January 1, 1934

January 1, 1954

Source: *Agricultural Statistics*, North Carolina Department of Agriculture, 1954.

Food and Feed Deficits

One of the chief features of the state's agriculture, and lamentable for the total North Carolina economy, is its inability to feed the people and livestock of the state. It is a peculiar situation that a state which ranks second in number of farms and first in farm population, with a ratio of farm to urban population two and a half times that of the national figure, should rely so heavily on other states for food and feed for livestock.

The feed deficiency is the less important (although the state imports large quantities of feed despite its low rank as a livestock state), but in feeding the population of North Carolina, the deficits are astronomical. In so far as the farm population is concerned, the state ranks fairly well in that the average Carolina farmer raises more food for home consumption than does the average farmer in the nation as a whole. As a general rule, small farmers tend more to live off the farm than do large commercial farmers, who generally specialize in one or two commodities. The average consumption from a farm by the family living on that farm, in North Carolina, is valued at $500 a year, according to official estimates. Obviously, the farmer must purchase much in addition to this quantity, because $500 will not feed a typical farm family. Therefore, there is a deficit involved in the fact that a farmer cannot even feed his own family from his farm but must purchase considerable quantities elsewhere; and the vast majority of food consumed by the urban and nonfarm population, now numbering more than three million, is imported into the state. North Carolina does ship out millions of dollars worth of fruit and vegetables, but even as it does so it imports millions more in other types of food.

There is scarcely a single food of which North Carolina has a surplus. This is probably true even of pickles, which are produced in such quantity at Faison and Mount Olive. The state imports fresh milk and most of its butter and other dairy products. It imports beef and other meats. It exports raw peanuts but imports the by-products of raw peanuts. It exports cottonseed but imports the food products made from cottonseed. It exports cabbage on a minor scale and imports sauerkraut. It exports fresh peaches and imports greater quantities of canned peaches and other peach products.

It is well known and obvious to anyone who visits a grocery store and observes where the supply comes from that North Carolina grocery stores are retail outlets for food produced in almost every state of the Union except North Carolina. It is probably true that the food processed in North Carolina and sold throughout the United States does not exceed seven per cent of the processed food purchased in the grocery stores of the state of North Carolina alone. The estimated deficit in food and feed far exceeds a billion dollars, and certainly the food and feed purchases exceed the gross farm income of the state. Around 25 to 30 per cent of the family income is spent for food. The percentage is higher among low-income families and low-income states. The lower the family income, the larger the percentage which goes for food. If only 25 per cent of North Carolina's income goes for food, and if the total income of the state is $5,371,000,000 (1955), then the state spent 25 per cent of $5,371,000,000 —or roughly $1,340,000,000. When the value of all food grown by North Carolina farmers is deducted from this sum, there still remains a deficit that far exceeds the net farm income of the state. The surest way to improve the state's position in income and in retained wealth is to increase its ability to supply itself with home-raised and home-processed food and feed. The surest way for North Carolina to continue poor is to send its dollars to other states that now supply its largest single family expenditure, food.

The 1954 Census of Manufacturers' special pamphlet on processed food in the United States reveals these facts about the industry in North Carolina (see Table 46 for the exact figures): the value of shipments of canned seafoods amounted to $972,000 and was the lowest of all states reporting, equaling 0.4 per cent of the nation's total. The value of canned fruits and vegetables shipped amounted to $1,967,000 and was less than .01 of one per cent of the total. Pickles and sauces shipped amounted to $4,758,000, or 1.2 per cent of the total. The value of North Carolina's total processed food production was $7,706,000, or 0.2 per cent of the national total.

The census report on processed food covered canned seafoods, canned fish, canned fruits and vegetables, pickles and sauces, dehydrated fruits and vegetables, manufactured seafood, and frozen fruits and vegetables, all of which North Carolina could produce and process. And experts who urge the development of a processed-food industry in the state point out the fact that, assuming that her 2.7 per cent of the total population consumed its proportionate share, North Carolina consumed $101,000,000 of the total national production; yet since the state produced only $7,705,000 of above-listed processed food, it manufactured only 7.7 per cent of the amount actually consumed within the state.

Agricultural Needs

Some recommendations have already been made in the discussion above. The Extension Service of North Carolina State College of Agriculture and the state Department of Agriculture, both separately and cooperatively, are constantly pointing out the state's agricultural strengths and weaknesses and are spending millions of dollars each year in efforts to improve agriculture and rural life. Tremendous gains have been made in North Carolina's agricultural economy and will continue to be made, but it appears that the chief remedies for the state's agricultural problems lie in these areas:

1. Farm tenancy must be reduced. While some tenancy is desirable and indispensable, in general cropping is not farming in the best sense of the word. Cropper tenants are not farmers; they are croppers. They are not agriculturalists; they are essentially a substitute for hired labor. The areas of greatest tenancy, the tobacco and cotton belts, are also the areas where the great deficiency in livestock, food crops, and gardens is found. In a word, tenancy produces unbalanced agriculture. Better farming, better living, and better citizenship will result when more farmers own their own farms.

The size of farms must be increased. As we have seen, for the last several years, they have been from 65 to 68 acres. It seems the irreducible minimum has been reached. Throughout the United States the size of farms is increasing, and has been for a number of years, while North Carolina farms have steadily grown smaller until the present size was reached fifteen or twenty years ago.

Apparently we have in this an irremediable situation. Suppose the 100,000 smallest farmers of the state moved to town or in some way disappeared. Suppose the land that they now cultivate were taken over by the remaining farmers. The cultivated acreage of the 170,000 remaining farms would increase by only six or seven acres. North Carolina would still rank near the bottom in size of farms, both cultivated or total acres. If the premise that larger farms are necessary for better income and better living is accepted, then the possibility of achieving these larger farms looks rather remote. Some gain might be made from clearing more land and thus adding to the cultivated acreage, yet when it is recalled that there has been no increase in the total cultivated acreage of North Carolina in the last century, it is unlikely that there will be any significant increase in the immediate years ahead.

3. A better balance must be achieved between crops and livestock. Some progress is being made in this area now, but the discrepancies between their relative values in this state are still vast. North Carolina will never become primarily a livestock state—it is likely that crops will continue to dominate in the agricultural economy so long as tobacco remains at its present high value (there are indications that this desirable situation will not last)—but unfortunately there is no relationship between tobacco and livestock as there is between most other crops and livestock. Livestock is totally independent of tobacco, and vice versa, but nonetheless the state does have livestock resources far beyond those being utilized at the present time.

4. More of the food consumed in the state and elsewhere must be produced and processed in the state.

5. Finally, business interests and other groups with capital to invest, and the populace as a whole, must be aware of the farmers' problems in marketing and willing to the point of investment to help solve them.

BIBLIOGRAPHY

BLACKWELL, G. W., S. H. HOBBS, JR., HARRIET HERRING, G. L. SIMPSON, and others. Part-Time Farming in North Carolina. Unpublished. Chapel Hill: Institute for Research in Social Science, University of North Carolina, 1954.

CATHEY, C. O. Agricultural Developments in North Carolina, 1783–1860. Chapel Hill: University of North Carolina Press, 1956.

North Carolina Agricultural Statistics, 1953–1954. North Carolina Department of Agriculture. Raleigh.

North Carolina Accepts the Challenge. North Carolina Board of Farm Organizations and Agencies. Raleigh, 1952.

SMEDES, H. R. Agricultural Graphics: North Carolina and the United States, 1866–1922. Chapel Hill: University of North Carolina, 1923.

U. S. Department of Agriculture. Crop Statistics, 1866–1906. Bureau of Statistics Bulletins 56–64. Washington: U. S. Government Printing Office, 1907.

———. The Farm Income Situation. Agricultural Marketing Service. Washington: U. S. Government Printing Office (March 6, 1955).

University of North Carolina Newsletter, XLI (March 16, 1955).

Chapter 10

INDUSTRY

North Carolina is not only the leading industrial state of the South, but it is also one of the dozen foremost industrial states of the Union. In all such indices as number of industrial plants, persons gainfully employed in industry, total salaries and wages paid, value of raw materials used, total value of factory output, and total value added by manufacture, North Carolina ranks from tenth to fourteenth. (See Table 47 for data on the state's industrial progress since 1899.) Further, while textile mills, tobacco, furniture, and sawmills and related activities are North Carolina's primary industries, there are a good many others. Altogether there were some 7,500 industrial establishments in North Carolina in 1955; the Big Four mentioned above have approximately 3,250 separate factories, which means that there are some 4,300 miscellaneous industrial establishments in the state. See Table 48 for trends and growth in the major North Carolina industries from 1939 to 1955 and Tables 49 and 50 for comprehensive data on industry in 1954.

At the same time, during the calendar year 1954, the average weekly earnings for all production workers in all manufacturing industries of North Carolina was the lowest of any state. In 1953 the state ranked forty-seventh. In 1954, the average weekly wage was $47.88, compared with the national average of $71.86. This means that North Carolina's average was only two-thirds as high as the national average.

Also, the official records show that the rate of increase in average weekly earnings during the last five or six years has been lower in North Carolina than in any other state. The average North Carolina earnings increased from $39.90 in 1949 to $47.88 in 1954, a 20 per cent increment, while the national average increase rose from $54.92 to $71.86, or 30.48 per cent. The hourly earnings in North Carolina in 1954 averaged $1.25, as compared with the national average of $1.81, and the state ranked forty-sixth in this respect. When we recall that North Carolina ranked last in average weekly income, we see that production workers in North Carolina averaged slightly less time per week than the national average—38.3 hours compared with 39.7 for the country at large.

The discrepancies between (1) the number of industrial plants, total value of output, total salaries and wages paid, etc., in North Carolina and (2) the low income of North Carolina workers make it obvious that

North Carolina industries are low-wage industries. The only remedy is to attract to and develop within the state better-diversified industries that require more skill and pay better wages. (See Table 56 for figures on employment, earnings, and hours worked for all nonagricultural employment in North Carolina in July, 1956.)

Labor unions are weak in North Carolina. The state ranked twelfth in 1953 in number of industrial employees, but thirtieth in total membership in labor unions, with 83,000. In 1939 North Carolina ranked forty-seventh in percentage of nonagricultural workers unionized, with 4.2, with only South Carolina lower. In 1953, North Carolina was last, with 8.3 per cent of workers unionized. The percentage for the nation is four times that of North Carolina, and the percentages for both Carolinas were considerably below the next lowest states.[1]

One of the features which make North Carolina attractive to industries looking for a place in which to locate is an abundant labor supply (see Fig. 15). This body of recruitable labor can be broken into two categories: first, those who are actively looking for jobs; and second, those who might accept jobs under certain circumstances. The first segment includes (1) the unemployed, (2) those working on a seasonal or intermittent basis who want full-time employment, and (3) those looking for a job which gives them greater opportunity or income than their present occupations. The second group includes (1) housewives, who often have to be paid at a high enough scale to cover the cost of domestic help; (2) handicapped persons or older people whose skills might be utilized if the industry were geared to take advantage of them; (3) young people leaving school or military service who might be persuaded to join the local labor force if there were enough economic and opportunity inducement; (4) minority groups who would accept regular work if a climate favorable to their employment existed; (5) workers now commuting to other areas but who would prefer to work in their own communities in order to eliminate the expenditure of time and money in commuting; and (6) agricultural workers who would like to enter industrial employment but must wait on the farm until such a move would materially increase their incomes.[2]

North Carolina is producing the largest total surplus of farm males (and females, for that matter) from 25 to 69 of any state in the Union and has the second highest farm-male replacement percentage of any state.[3] The replacement figure for the years 1950–60 is placed at 20.7 per cent.

---

[1]National Bureau of Economic Research, *Thirty-Sixth Annual Report* (New York, 1956).

[2]*North Carolina Employment Security Commission Quarterly*, XIV (Summer-Fall, 1956), 83–124.

[3]U. S. Department of Agriculture, *Farm Population*, Agricultural Marketing Service, Series Census AM (P–27), No. 22 (August, 1956), p. 9, Table 1.

This means that North Carolina farms, without losing a single person engaged in agriculture, can contribute to nonagricultural employment in ten years a total of workers equivalent to 20.7 per cent of its present agricultural population from 25 to 69. This amounts to 200,000 individuals, plus a considerable element from the rural nonfarm population.

Fig. 15.   Recruitable Labor for Industrial Development by County

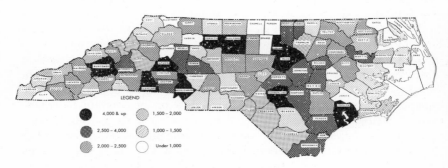

Source: Employment Security Commission of North Carolina.

Chapter 11

THE TEXTILE INDUSTRY[1]

History

The textile industry had its beginning in North Carolina in 1813, when Michael Schenck and Absolom Warlick (his brother-in-law) built a mill on Mill Branch, one and one-half miles east of Lincolnton, North Carolina. Much of the machinery was built by Michael Bean on the premises. The original contract for the machinery is still in existence. For $1,300 Bean built and installed two spinning frames with seventy flyers each and two cards and one picker. John Hoke and Dr. James Bivens bought an interest in the mill in 1819.

In 1817 Joel Battle and Henry A. Donaldson built a mill at the falls of the Tar River (now Rocky Mount), working slave labor. The mill was burned by members of the Union army in 1863.

In 1830 Henry Humphries built the Mount Hecla Mills at Greensboro. It was three stories high, the first steam cotton mill in North Carolina. The machinery was shipped from Philadelphia to Wilmington, thence up the river to Fayetteville and across the country in wagons to Greensboro. Thomas R. Tate was clerk for Humphries and later bought him out. When wood for fuel grew scarce around Greensboro, Tate moved the mill by wagon to Mountain Island, where it was operated by water power.

E. M. Holt built a mill on Alamance Creek, in Orange County, in 1832. W. A. Carrington was associated with him. John W. Leak's mill at Great Falls went up in 1833. (It was chartered as the Richmond Manufacturing Company, later burned by Yankees in 1865 and rebuilt in 1869). Also in 1833 General McDuffe and Mitchell King built a mill at Vaucluse. Francis Fries and Dr. Schumann put one up at Salem in 1836, and in 1838 John M. Morehead built another at Leaksville.

According to statistics, the first five cotton mills built in the South were all on North Carolina soil, and the names Schenk, Warlick, Battle, Tate, and Holt are still prominently connected with the industry in the state.

The industry might have grown more rapidly in North Carolina than it did in Massachusetts, but before the Civil War it was more profitable

---

[1]All data are from the *North Carolina Employment Security Commission Quarterly*, X (Summer-Fall, 1952), 71–139.

to farm with slave labor than to manufacture cotton into cloth, and industrial development was so slow that in 1860 there were only 41,834 spindles and 761 looms in North Carolina. Destruction by federal troops reduced those figures to approximately 30,000 spindles and 600 looms in 1872. The number of spindles in North Carolina had tripled to 92,380 by 1880, but very little progress was made from that date until the early nineties, when the first real movement for expansion of its cotton-manufacturing industry began.

For many years textiles in North Carolina meant yarn mills (the state still shares leadership in spun-yarn production [see Table 57], but the peak for the yarn industry is two decades past), but in 1888 J. W. Cannon, a merchant at Concord, opened up the fabric and finished-article field when he raised $75,000 and built a mill of 4,000 spindles. When he died in 1921, his original mill had grown to 165,000 spindles and he controlled and operated 600,000 spindles and 10,000 looms, with a conservatively estimated value of $30,000,000.

Denim mills by Moses and Caesar Cone and by W. A. Erwin, gingham by C. W. Johnston, damask by S. F. Patterson, hosiery by Julian S. Carr, knit underwear by P. H. Hanes and Sons, and fine yarn by A. C. Lineberger are a few of the pioneer products which established North Carolina's reputation for quantity and excellence in textile products.

In the manufacture of textiles, North Carolina has moved ahead in such an outstanding manner that it has surpassed all other states. From around 1900 to 1925 the emphasis was on increasing the number of spinning and weaving mills and installing more spindles and looms, while in the last quarter-century there has been a marked decrease in the number of spindles and looms. In recent years, the emphasis has swung to finer types of machinery and larger research operations in an effort to develop better yarns and fabrics and better dyeing and finishing techniques.

Although the textile industry has advanced in North Carolina by moderate steps instead of long strides, it has been characterized by a sure, regular progression of determinative consequences. Placing emphasis on progress instead of immediate returns, industrialists have used profits for expansion and for newer and better equipment. As a result, North Carolina's textile industry today possesses some of the most modern plants and latest machinery not only in the United States, but in the world. The textile industry in no other state employs more people or pays out more in gross wages (see Table 58). And more North Carolinians are employed in textile mills than in all the other industries of the state combined.

In contrast with the long working hours and poor pay of the early days of industrial operations, North Carolina's textile employers today provide pleasant working conditions and require only moderate working hours.

The pay scale is well below the national average for the industry—$650 gross wages per quarter as compared with the national figure of $742 (see Table 58)—yet it runs ahead of most other southern states. Realizing that the well being of their employees is significantly related to the success of their enterprises, employers also give much attention to employees' benefits. These include hospitalization and retirement plans, paid vacations, cafeteria service, transportation facilities, and recreation facilities for workers and their families.

In discussing the textile industry, let us first determine what constitutes the industry. Essentially, it can be broken down into four operations which may or may not be interdependent: (1) manufacture of yarn, thread, cordage, and twine; (2) manufacture of woven fabric, carpet and rugs, laces, knit fabrics, and other products from yarn; (3) dyeing and finishing fibers, yarns, and fabrics; and (4) coating, waterproofing and otherwise treating fabrics. All activities in connection with any of these four subdivisions fall into the inclusive term "textile industry." Table 59 shows the wages and number of employees involved in each of the aspects of the textile industry in 1951.

In 1951 there was some textile employment in 72 of the state's 100 counties, although in nine of these the textile industry employed less than 100 workers such as are covered by the Social Security Law. Wages and employment data for 1951 for the twenty-two counties having 2,500 or more workers are shown in Table 60. All the twenty-eight counties reporting no employment in textiles (i.e., employing no workers covered by Social Security) in 1951 are found in either the coastal or the mountain areas. All piedmont counties have some textile production.

Table 61 gives a comprehensive picture of the North Carolina textile industry in 1954, the most recent census data.

Types of Manufacture

HOSIERY.

Fifty years ago North Carolina's hosiery mills were few, and they manufactured just one or two types of cheap cotton hose and socks in limited colors and sizes. Still in the experimental stage, silk stockings were being produced in small quantities, and in only two plants in the entire state.

Statistics from North Carolina hosiery plants today present a striking contrast. Now North Carolina claims 425 hosiery mills which together employ more than 50,000 workers, and they produce much of the nation's supply. According to records from the Employment Security Commission in the second quarter of 1952, the state had 377 hosiery mills operating and covered by the Employment Security Law (that is, with eight or more employees) and those factories employed 49,065 workers. Of these mills, 256 employed 26,048 workers in the production of seamless hosiery, and 212 employed 23,017 workers in the production of full-fashioned hosiery. Many of these mills were producing both kinds. Another 57 mills, with 11,233 employees, were making other knit goods, such as underwear, outer wear, and knit specialties.

Among North Carolina hosiery manufacturers, the trend is toward plowing most of the profits back into the industry. They are continually building new mills and installing the most modern machinery and equipment. The benefit is already seen in full-fashioned hose, with increased production made possible by much larger, more up-to-date machines. And the cheap cotton stockings of fifty years ago, once called seamless hosiery, have almost passed from the scene. Seamless hosiery is made today with improved equipment and includes some of the highest-quality nylon. Also included in the seamless category are fine grades of men's and boys' socks and misses' and children's anklets.

During the past thirty years the importance of North Carolina has risen rapidly in the hosiery industry, and she has outstripped all other states, ranking higher in employment figures, production, and value of production than any other. Some 40 per cent of all American hosiery is made in North Carolina, her closest competitors being Pennsylvania with 20 per cent and Tennessee with 12 per cent. Today North Carolina has about 50,000 engaged in hosiery production and 60,000 in the entire knit-goods industry. These figures are very significant when one sees that the total national employment in hosiery in 1947 was just 126,481. In 1947, out of the 1,355 hosiery firms in the United States, North Carolina had 411.

The state's leading hosiery-producing counties in 1952 (as judged from employment figures) were Guilford (8,250); Alamance (6,150); Catawba (4,250); Randolph (4,250); Burke (3,250); Mecklenburg (2,600); Forsyth (2,875); and Surry (2,400). Fifty-six out of the hundred counties in North Carolina report some employment in hosiery.

From 1899 to 1952 North Carolina's proportion of knit-goods production on a national comparison rose from 1.8 per cent to 40 per cent (in 1899 she had less than 2 per cent of the national employment engaged in the knit-goods industry), and hosiery plants are still springing up throughout the state. In Alamance County alone, almost a dozen hosiery mills have begun operation in the past five years. In the same period of time at least six mills have been set up in Randolph County, ten in Guilford County, at least three in Forsyth, three in Gaston, and nine in Mecklenburg.

During 1951 North Carolina produced 48,000,000 pairs of seamless hosiery out of a total national output of 103,500,000 dozens of this type of hose. It produced 17,600,000 dozens of pairs of full-fashioned hosiery out of a national total of 51,000,000 dozens of pairs. (According to the latest figures compiled by the North Carolina Department of Labor, weekly earnings averaged $59.86 in the full-fashioned mills and $43.84 in the seamless hosiery plants.) During 1951, North Carolina installed 260 multiple-section full-fashioned machines (750 installed during the same period throughout the nation), at between $35,000 and $40,000 each.

KNIT GOODS.

North Carolina is making progress in the development and expansion of the knitting industry exclusive of hosiery. In addition to the more basic production of knit underwear and outer wear, high-quality knit specialties have been developed, and knit-goods operations are being expanded relatively more rapidly than hosiery mills.

As we have seen, seventy-two counties have some textile industry, but most of these are confined to hosiery mills. In those twenty-four counties which have other types of textile plants, there are fifty-seven firms employing eight or more workers, with a total paylist of 11,225 people. Forsyth County has by far the largest employment in knitting, followed by Catawba and Rockingham. Other counties, in order of importance, are Alamance, Surry, Iredell, Gaston, Durham, New Hanover, Randolph, Davidson, Alexander, Cleveland, Robeson, and Guilford.

WOOLENS AND WORSTEDS.

North Carolina's woolen and worsted industry is the largest in the South in terms of number of establishments, employment, or value added by manufacture. Four of the state's thirteen woolen plants are of the regular apparel-producing integrated type; three produce cotton and woolen blankets; one produces only woolen yarn; and five are specialty firms producing home-spuns or similar goods. There has been very little change in the woolen-manufacturing branch of the industry, with only four new plants since 1939. Worsted manufacturing has sprung up more recently, however, all plants having been established since 1939, and most since 1945. The availability of trained textile workers is at least partially responsible for this development.

GARMENT MANUFACTURING.

North Carolina has been engaged in garment manufacturing since early colonial days, and carding, spinning, and weaving of cloth and handmaking of clothes continued in the home for many years. Many of the older generation can still remember the "homemade" clothes generally worn.

Garment making as an industry had its start in the state about seventy-five years ago, but it was close to the end of the last century before it really got under way. The principal product was overalls, but also work shirts and work pants. As overalls and work clothes were improved, workers became more skilled and shirts were added, then underwear and some outer wear, largely of the cheaper grades. Improvement continued and better-quality clothing followed, and overall firms added play clothes. Now North Carolina manufacturers make all qualities of garments, including those in the highest price ranges.

Many of the state's largest garment firms have been long extablished, increasing their quality and output as time passed. Several firms from outside the state came twenty or thirty years ago and have built large industries, and recently their numbers have increased. In 1954 around twenty-five garment firms either began operations in the state or announced definite plans for doing so.

North Carolina garment manufacturing has increased 225 per cent in twelve years over its prewar level. Early in 1954 the 150 firms existent at that time employed around 18,000. There are now about 175 firms and the number of workers unquestionably exceeds 20,000. The new plants, plus enlargements of old ones, constructed in this forthcoming year should run the number of firms to 200 and employment to 25,000. Garment-plant salaries and wages in 1953 amounted to $35,460,000, and present conservative estimates place this figure at around $42,000,000.

BIBLIOGRAPHY

BARNWELL, M. W. *Faces We See*. Gastonia, North Carolina: The Southern Combed Yarn Spinners Association, 1939.

BENDURE, ZELMA AND GLADYS PFEIFFER. *America's Fabrics*. New York: Macmillan, 1946.

North Carolina Employment Security Quarterly, X (Summer-Fall 1952); XI (Winter-Spring 1953).

MORRIS, J. A. *Woolen and Worsted Manufacturing in the Southern Piedmont*. Columbia, South Carolina: University of South Carolina Press, 1952.

Chapter 12

The Tobacco Industry[1]

North Carolina is the foremost tobacco-producing region in the world. In 1954, 913,874,000 pounds of tobacco were harvested from 698,700 acres, for a production value of $495,683,000.[2] This means that North Carolina's tobacco acreage is 42 per cent of the total acreage given to the production of tobacco in the United States, and these acres yield 41 per cent of the total produced. The production of flue-cured tobacco, used principally in the manufacture of cigarettes, has expanded in North Carolina until the state raises about 67 per cent of the total annual harvest in the United States.

The history, development, production, and manufacture of tobacco in North Carolina is closely related to the state's farming and industrial progress: the farmer and his family receive cash income from the culture of tobacco—about $500,000,000 shared annually by half a million North Carolinians living in ninety-four counties; and workers (about 35,000, including those outside the factories) in the manufacturing and processing plants in 1954 received more than $77,000,000 in gross wages.

History

Although authentic information on the early history of tobacco is limited, it is known that Columbus took tobacco leaves back to the Spanish court with him, and by "about the middle of the sixteenth century, tobacco received sensational attention as a divinely-sent remedy for virtually all ailments of the human body."[3] Many recommendations for the use of tobacco came from Portugal, and about 1560 Jean Nicot, French ambassador at the Portuguese court, sent to the Queen Mother of France seeds of the fabulous plant. The leaves of the plants produced in France reportedly cured many ailing Frenchmen, and the remedy was labeled Nicotiene.

The first importation of tobacco to England has been attributed to both Sir Walter Raleigh and Sir John Hawkins. However, it is well

---

[1] The author is indebted to student George W. Willard, Jr., for assistance on tobacco production and to student William M. Geer for assistance on the manufacture of tobacco.

[2] Statistics furnished the author by the North Carolina Department of Agriculture, Raleigh, N. C.

[3] Joseph C. Robert, *The Story of Tobacco in America* (New York: Knopf, 1949), p. 4.

established that Sir Francis Drake substantially encouraged the use of tobacco in 1586 when he returned to England with quantities of tobacco captured in the West Indies. The fashion caught on, and the dandies of London began "an exaggerated and affected display" of smoking.[4] In 1604 King James I felt called upon to write his *Counterblaste to Tobacco*, the most famous of all antitobacco tracts (see page 116).

The story of tobacco in the English colonies began in 1612 at Jamestown, Virginia, when John Rolfe planted West Indian seed, *Nicotiana tobacco*. It is recorded that he had in mind furnishing the requirements of his own pipe as well as the possibility of developing an export commodity. By 1616 the culture of tobacco had become common in the colonies, and in 1619, 20,000 pounds were shipped to England. The 1622 crop amounted to 60,000 pounds.[5] These statistics indicate the trend in the production of tobacco in the United States during the seventeenth and eighteenth centuries: 1639, 1,500,000; 1664, 23,750,000; 1684, 25,000,000; 1698, 30,675,903; 1730, 36,000,000; 1744, 40,357,000; 1763, 80,743,537; 1771, 95,241,937; 1790, 130,000,000.[6]

North Carolina's prominence in the culture of tobacco was achieved gradually. During the first half of the nineteenth century, the dark and coarse North Carolina tobacco was considered inferior to Virginia tobacco—particularly in Virginia. It is recorded that a Virginia minister as late as 1865 described some of his parishes as "sweet-scented" in recognition of the value and fragrance of the tobacco produced in them. In contrast, he referred to North Carolina as an unfavored region where the men of God were paid in tar, pitch, and pork.[7]

The minister apparently was unaware that the tobacco plant was then moving toward a position of distinction in the land of "tar, pitch, and pork," for the year 1852 marked a tremendous change in North Carolina tobacco culture. It was during that year that Eli and Elisha Slade of Caswell County, by chance, produced a fine yellow leaf which they believed to be the result of curing with artificial heat. Experience, however, soon demonstrated that the determining factor in producing the new type was the light, sandy, siliceous soil. The new strain spread into neighboring counties, and that area came to be known as the Bright Tobacco Belt, from the fine bright leaf that it grew.[8]

---

[4] *Ibid.*, p. 5.

[5] Wightman W. Garner, *The Production of Tobacco* (New York: Blakiston, 1951), p. 23.

[6] R. C. Rankin, *Bright Leaf Tobacco* (Lumberton, N. C.: Tobacco Board of Trade, 1954), p. 3.

[7] Nannie May Tilley, *The Bright-Tobacco Industry 1860–1929* (Chapel Hill: University of North Carolina Press, 1948), p. 3.

[8] William Kenneth Boyd, *The Story of Durham* (Durham: Duke University Press, 1925), pp. 57, 58.

In about 1860 John Ruffin Green moved from his farm near Durham's Station into the village and began manufacturing smoking tobacco. He planned to sell his product to "the young University sports from Chapel Hill, who, after their teeth-rattling hack ride of twelve miles, had time on their hands as they waited for the train."[9] The business thrived until 1865 when Union soldiers pilfered so many "free samples" that his stock was depleted. Within a few weeks after their departure, many of the men were writing for Durham tobacco. Green made a new start and named his product "Bull Durham Tobacco."

The bright tobacco, lighter in color and milder in taste, avoided the biting qualities of the original dark leaf, and as the manufacture of tobacco rapidly increased with the invention of the cigarette-making machine in 1884, the production of the bright leaf kept pace.

Tobacco Farming
RAISING AND CURING OF TOBACCO.

Although some light, air-cured burley tobacco is produced in North Carolina near Asheville, Boone, and West Jefferson, the total poundage in 1954 was only 24,384,000 compared with 889,490,000 pounds of the flue-cured types. Four kinds of flue-cured tobacco (classified by the U. S. Department of Agriculture as types 11a, 11b, 12, and 13) are grown in the four tobacco belts in the state. The Old Belt and Middle Belt flue-cured tobaccos (types 11a and 11b) are produced in the Piedmont; the Eastern North Carolina flue-cured type 12 in the coastal sections of the state lying north of the South River; and the Border Belt type 13 in the southeastern counties of the state that are south of the South River.

The leading tobacco market in the Old and Middle Belts is at Winston-Salem, where 56,528,424 pounds were sold in 1954. Fairmont led the Border Belt markets, with total sales reaching 43,530,648 pounds. And Wilson headed the list of Eastern Belt markets, as well as all other flue-cured markets in the world, by selling 88,381,985 pounds of tobacco in its twenty-one warehouses. Table 64 summarizes the production of the flue-cured types of tobacco in North Carolina for 1953-54.

The production of a crop of tobacco begins with the preparation of a seed bed during the winter months. These beds are sowed at different times in different sections of North Carolina from December through the early part of March and are covered with mesh cotton canvas early in the spring to protect the seedlings from the cold and frost. Later the cover is removed and the seedlings are allowed to develop to the point that they may be transplanted.

---

[9] Robert, *op cit.*, p. 123.

The transplanting of the tobacco plants from the beds is started early in April in the Border Belt and is continued in the piedmont and mountain sections of the state through the middle of June. The plants are set from 14 to 24 inches apart in rows which are from 3 to 4 feet in width.

Growing good tobacco requires highly specialized farming, and cultivation of the crop is begun soon after the plants are set in the field. The rows are harrowed and plowed several times to keep down the grass and weeds and loosen the soil. The last plowing is done about the time the plants are knee high. Soon after the crop has been "laid by," the tobacco plants begin to bloom, and then the blooms are generally broken off to allow the top leaves to develop properly. The plants are sprayed and dusted several times during the growing and harvesting season to keep the insects under control.

Harvesting flue-cured tobacco is an arduous job, for an acre yields between 100,000 and 150,000 leaves, all of which are handled individually about ten times. Usually it takes close to eight weeks to complete the curing process. First, each leaf has to be primed, or stripped individually, as it matures and ripens, the crop being primed about once a week with two to four leaves being pulled from each plant. The leaves are carried to the curing barn, looped on sticks by the stringers, and placed in the barn on from five to seven tiers. Artificial heat is used to eliminate the excess moisture and give the tobacco a bright, golden color. The original method required the hand stoking of a wood-fired furnace, but in recent years the majority of the growers in this state have turned to manually controlled oil-burning units.

Table 65 gives statistics on the stemming and drying process in North Carolina as compared with other parts of the country.

After curing, tobacco is stored in a packhouse until all of the crop has been harvested and cured. The leaves are then sorted into about three grades, tied into "hands," and marketed.

Present Status of Tobacco Farming.

No discussion of the production of tobacco in North Carolina today would be complete without reference to what many farmers call "crop control" and "price support." If as many as 66⅔ per cent of the growers vote in favor of tobacco-marketing quotas when a referendum is held by the Production and Marketing Administration of the U. S. Department of Agriculture, they are given the benefit of price-support loans. Under the present (1956) price-support program, each federal grade is supported at 90 per cent of parity. If a grower's tobacco does not bring a price at auction equal to the support price, the Stabilization Corporation of the U. S. Department of Agriculture pays him the support price for the particular grade and takes over the tobacco for future sale.

Perhaps many tobacco growers would welcome an increase in their individual tobacco allotments, but they have continued to give overwhelming support to crop quotas in order to have the protection of loans. In the 1952 flue-cured-tobacco referendum, 99 per cent of the votes cast by 188,487 owners, tenants, and sharecroppers favored the continuation of the quotas. There were only 1,836 votes against the system.

The production of tobacco is now in the midst of a critical period. Growers are being exhorted to keep supplies in line with effective demand, while at the same time the per capita consumption of tobacco products is declining somewhat. It has been estimated that the nation's tobacco growers have suffered an income loss of at least $75,000,000 as a result of medical claims linking cigarette smoking and lung cancer.[10] The tobacco industry has recently appropriated one million dollars for research on the subject.

Tobacco Manufacturing

GROWTH OF THE INDUSTRY.

North Carolina processes more than half of the cigarettes made in the United States and one-third of the nation's smoking tobacco, snuff, and chewing tobacco, as well as a small quantity of cigars. In 1950 North Carolina manufactured more tobacco products than all of the other states combined, 52.2 per cent of the total domestic production.[11] The total value of these North Carolina products, exclusive of federal taxes, was $700,721,441.14, as compared with a national total value of $1,328,464,-386.23. North Carolina's total breaks down thus: cigars, $141,869.73; cigarettes, $685,816,639.11; chewing tobacco-snuff, $14,762,680.30.

The growth of North Carolina's tobacco factories has occurred largely in the last four decades. Before 1910 the state produced what might be regarded as a normal proportionate amount of tobacco products, some 8 to 9 per cent. Several now famous brand names of cigarettes made their appearance in the years just before World War I, and the rate of manufacturing concentration in the state rose sharply. In 1915 it was 16.3 per cent of the domestic production, 36.6 per cent by 1920, 42.5 per cent by 1925, and 56.9 per cent by 1930. Since 1930 the state has made approximately half of the tobacco products of the United States, with a constantly increasing concentration of cigarette production. In the fifty years from 1900 to 1950 the increase in cigarette manufacture in North Carolina was one hundred and fifty times.[12]

---

[10]*News and Observer* (Raleigh, N. C.), June 28, 1955, p. 1.
[11]*North Carolina Employment Security Commission Quartely*, IX (Summer-Fall, 1951), 67.
[12]*Ibid.*, p. 68.

As these developments occurred the industry's contribution to the state's wages and taxes grew larger and larger and the values of its raw materials and manufactured output increased. It is now the second largest industry in North Carolina, ranking after textiles. Its annual output (1953) is $1,580,000,000, (including taxes) or 25.8 per cent of the state's industrial production. The total number of employees (counting factory employees only) is 20,956. Table 66 will give some indication of the phenomenal growth of the industry.

TAXATION.

The tobacco consumer pays a high tax premium for the privilege of smoking, chewing, and dipping, and the tobacco companies act as the user's agent in paying the tariff. The estimate is that almost one-half of the purchase price of a package of cigarettes goes for taxes, based on the federal tax-collection reports.

Federal income from tobacco taxes have soared with the increased cigarette consumption and advancing tax rate. In 1900 total federal revenue from tobacco amounted to $59,333,084, of which $5,173,972 was paid in North Carolina, about one-twelfth of the total. By 1930 the federal take was $480,339,060 from the United States, of which $256,729,938 came from North Carolina, or more than half. This meant a concentration of the industry in the state by that date.[13] In 1940 the federal cigarette schedule was changed from $3.00 to $3.25 per thousand; in 1942 to $3.50 per thousand. This last rate meant, of course, seven cents for the usual package of twenty cigarettes.[14] In 1954 the United States tobacco tax was $1,580,229,000, of which $822,618,000, or slightly more than half, was collected in North Carolina. Table 67 (simplified) will show the growth of national and state collections more strikingly.

Since the industry is considerably concentrated in North Carolina and in four cities of the state, the figures on taxes paid can be broken down to localities and given more meaning. A surprising fact is that the factories of Durham, Reidsville, Winston-Salem, and Greensboro spend more than $3,000,000 a working day for cigarette-tax stamps. North Carolina ranks tenth among the states in the payment of federal taxes. For the fiscal year ending June 30, 1954, a grand total of $1,550,839,000 was paid in federal taxes from all sources in North Carolina, and of this sum, as we have seen, $822,618,000 was derived from tobacco.[15]

The tobacco processors of North Carolina must face many local tax levies on their products. North Carolina has placed no commodity taxes

---

[13] Tilley, *op cit.*, p. 620.

[14] Robert, *op cit.*, p. 276.

[15] U. S. Department of the Treasury, *Annual Report of the Commissioner of Internal Revenue, 1954* (Washington: U. S. Government Printing Office, 1954), pp. 52, 68.

on tobacco, but by 1948 thirty-eight other states were collecting an estimated $339,321,000 annually in tobacco taxes. At least forty municipalities levied an extra tax on cigarettes.

In North Carolina the industry pays state franchise and income taxes the same as other corporations. It was estimated that in 1952 the total taxes due the state from franchise levies was $1,334,995.48. Income taxes amounted to an additional sum of $7,297,626.00. The tabulations of income taxes paid by corporations in the state for 1952 disclose that tobacco manufacturers paid 20.6 per cent of the total, or just over one-fifth of all state corporate-income taxes. Only the textile industry, with a much greater gross sales, paid more. Its levy was $7,534,000, or 21.3 per cent of the total.[16] There is no state property tax, but the tobacco businesses pay local property taxes on a total assessed valuation of $901,214,939.00. Since assessed valuation is usually much lower than actual value, it can safely be assumed that the inventories and factories which produce tobacco products are worth far more than a billion dollars. Table 68 shows recent North Carolina income taxes paid by tobacco firms.

WAGES AND WAGE EARNERS.

In terms of the value of its products, the tobacco industries employ less labor than any other major North Carolina industry. Table 66, which shows the growth of the tobacco industry in the state, indicates a rapid expansion of output in the last fifty years, but a slow enlargement of the working force. The factories which employed 6,585 wage earners in 1899 to produce $13,000,000 worth of goods employed only 20,946 people in 1953 to produce $1,580,000,000 worth of products. Thus, while the output increased by 121 times (including taxes), the employee force only tripled. The industry came into its own with the invention of the Bonsack cigarette-making machine and its acquisition by the Duke interests. Subsequently a main trend has been further mechanization.

Tobacco is a low-wage industry, with an average weekly wage (37,900 employees) of $58.45 in August, 1957. Earnings in the stemmeries and redrying plants, where the labor is largely Negro, are even less. Within the state, however, this wage compares favorably with the state's average weekly industrial wage in August, 1957, of $56.20, or slightly lower than the tobacco industry's average. Cigarette employees (16,100) averaged $74.07 weekly in August, 1957. The total tobacco payroll for 1957 was about $110,000,000, using the August data as average for the year.[17]

---

[16]*Statistics of Taxation, 1954*, North Carolina Department of Revenue, North Carolina Department of Tax Research, and State Board of Assessments (Raleigh, 1954), pp. 42, 72, 97, 152-3, 187.

[17]*N. C. E. S. C. Quarterly*, IX (Summer-Fall, 1951), 68; *Annual Report of the Commissioner of Internal Revenue, 1950.*

FACTORIES AND THEIR PRODUCTS.

The great bulk of tobacco products come from the factories in four cities, located within seventy-five miles of each other in the northern piedmont section of the state. Dominating the industry are R. J. Reynolds in Winston-Salem, American Tobacco Company in Durham and Reidsville, Liggett and Myers in Durham, and P. Lorillard in Greensboro. These four firms manufacture more than 55 per cent of the nation's cigarettes, their leading brands respectively being Camels, Lucky Strikes, Chesterfields, and Kent. All have recently introduced filter-tip brands. The first three companies also manufacture a smoking tobacco. In Winston-Salem the Reynolds firm and two other companies—Brown and Williamson and Taylor Brothers—make chewing tobacco, the Taylor plants limiting their output exclusively to chewing tobacco. Brown and Williamson is the state's only manufacturer of snuff. Altogether these five firms produce in North Carolina 34.8 per cent of the nation's smoking and chewing tobacco and snuff. Greensboro has the state's only sizable manufacturer of cigars, El Moro. The new Kent plant at Greensboro makes that city now an important tobacco center.[18]

These plants account for the greater production of tobacco products in North Carolina, and they control the cigarette and smoking-tobacco branches of the industry. Any analysis of the industry, however, must include the number of manufacturing units which contribute to various stages of production. The *Directory of Manufacturing Firms* for 1944 lists fifty-two factories of all types under the heading "tobacco manufactories." Of these, five factories made cigarettes; four were devoted to chewing, smoking, and snuff products; one produced cigars; and forty-two were engaged in stemming and redrying operations. The stemmeries were located in such tobacco-market towns as Durham, Kinston, Oxford, Rocky Mount, and Greenville. The Imperial Tobacco Company and the Export Leaf Tobacco Company both operated several stemmeries in the tobacco area, and the largest stemmery was the Durham plant of Liggett and Myers.

The *Directory* for 1952 lists seventy-eight tobacco-manufacturing firms but does not analyze them according to specialty.[19] It will be noted that in the century in which North Carolina has manufactured a considerable amount of tobacco, the number of factories has decreased as the output has increased. In 1881–82, for example, a listing of 295 tobacco manufacturing firms was made. These were located in 35 North Carolina counties.

---

[18]*News and Observer* (Raleigh, N. C.), June 24, 1954. This plant employs 1,500 people with an estimated yearly payroll of $5,000,000; its cost of construction was $13,000,000.

[19]*North Carolina Directory of Manufacturing Firms, 1952*, Division of Statistics, North Carolina Department of Labor (Raleigh, 1952), p. 200.

Davie County led the list with 29 "factories." Forsyth and Rockingham
had 27 each; Vance and Surry had 25 each; while Granville and Stokes
followed with 22 each. Trailing along came Yadkin with 16 and Durham
with 12. Obviously these businesses hardly deserved the name factory,
if compared with the modern mammoths. They made the simple products, such as plug and smoking tobacco, with crude methods.[20]

RISE OF CIGARETTES.

The most dramatic change in the production and consumption of
tobacco products in the twentieth century has been the increasing popularity of cigarettes. Total production of this commodity rose from
3,200,000,000 cigarettes in 1900 to just under 100,000,000,000 by 1927.
Thereafter the public taste, encouraged by advertising campaigns of increasing magnitude, lifted the totals to an annual average of 164,000,000,000
in the late nineteen thirties, 256,900,000,000 in the early forties,
364,600,000,000 in the late forties, and more than 400,000,000,000 in the
fifties (see Table 69). It was apparent that the "coffin nail" of 1900 had
become a public necessity by mid century.[21]

The early habit of "rolling-your-own" cigarettes gave way in public
favor to "tailor-made" brands—with Camel (introduced in 1913), Chesterfields (1913), and Lucky Strike (1916) leading all in popularity. All
of these brands were manufactured in North Carolina, Camels exclusively
so.[22]

The importance of cigarette production to the North Carolina industry is illustrated by the fact that 90 per cent of the sales of the R. J.
Reynolds organization is realized from the sales of Camels (the recent
introduction of Winston and Salem brands have greatly reduced this percentage). Chesterfields have dominated the production of Liggett and
Myers, as Lucky Strikes have the American Tobacco Company. Even the
depression did not blight the trend to tailor-made cigarettes, since most
of the smokers preferred to economize on something less essential than
cigarettes.[23] There was only a slight decline in the figures for those years.[24]

Table 70 gives us a concise picture of the affairs of the cigarette industry in North Carolina as compared with the industry in other parts of the
country.

---

[20]Tilley, *op. cit.*, pp. 679 ff.

[21]U. S. Department of Agriculture, *The Tobacco Situation*, Agricultural Marketing
Service (June 10, 1955), p. 5.

[22]Tilley, *op. cit.*, p. 610.

[23]Fred Albert Shannon, *America's Economic Growth* (New York: Macmillan, 1941),
p. 652.

[24]Ben F. Lemert, *Tobacco Manufacturing Industry in North Carolina* (Raleigh: National Youth Administration, 1939), p. 65.

Cigars, Chewing Tobacco-snuff.

The aggregate amount of tobacco consumed in the United States in all forms except cigarettes has dropped some 25 per cent below the level of consumption in 1909. Until World War I about 400,000,000 pounds of tobacco were consumed as chewing and smoking tobacco and snuff. Thirty years later, in the period of World War II, this poundage had dropped to some 300,000,000.[25] Cigars have shown the greatest decrease, from a production of 8,600,000,000 in 1913 to 5,800,000,000 in 1935, a drop of 37 per cent.[26]

Nonetheless, the production of these products by North Carolina factories increased while consumption throughout the nation declined. In dollar value, North Carolina produced $41,478.65 worth of cigars in 1910 and $141,869.73 in 1950. In chewing tobacco and snuff the state produced a total value of $5,728,317.66 in 1910 and $14,762,680.00 in 1950. Figures for the intervening years show a peak of $208,754.00 for the state's production of cigars in 1920, a drop of $25,103.88 in 1930 and a rise in the years since then. Chewing tobacco and snuff reached a peak production of $23,100,937.41 in 1930 (see Table 71).

Money gained from tobacco manufacturing not only supports several thousand working people and a large segment of our agriculture, but also plays an important part indirectly in the life of the citizens of the state. Its tax contribution to the federal government is large in proportion to its gross sales and a handsome sum goes into state and local government as well. It enters into the support of the institutional and trade life of North Carolina. The question of the relationship between smoking and lung cancer is a matter of concern to the state not only for reasons of public health, but also because anything which would vitally injure this large industry would strike a serious blow to the economy of the state.

Cheerful observers take heart at the ability of tobacco to withstand major attacks upon its use. Just before the first English settlement was being made in North America, James I of England leveled a heavy blow at this American importation in his *Counterblaste to Tobacco*. He called its use "a custome Lothsome to the eye, hateful to the Nose, Harmefull to the braine, (and) dangerous to the Lungs . . (a) black stinking fume . . . resembling the horrible Stigian smoke of the pit that is bottomeless."[27] So through the years has the fragrant weed been called into question. But those who enjoy its pleasure continue in their habits, for the most part, probably feeling much like the author of these lines:

---

[25]L. T. Weeks and E. Y. Floyd, *Producing and Marketing Flue-cured Tobacco* (Raleigh: Technical Press, 1941), p. 77.

[26]Lemert, *op. cit.*, p. 59.

[27]Robert, *op. cit.*, pp. 5-6.

Tobacco is a dirty weed. I like it.
It satisfies no normal need. I like it.
It makes you thin, it makes you lean,
It takes the hair right off your bean.
It's the worst darned stuff I've ever seen.
                I like it.[28]

BIBLIOGRAPHY

BOYD, WILLIAM KENNETH. *The Story of Durham*. Durham, N. C.: Duke University Press, 1925.

EMORY, SAMUEL THOMAS. *Bright Tobacco in the Agriculture, Industry, and Foreign Trade of North Carolina*. Chicago: Privately printed, 1939.

GARNER, WIGHTMAN W. *The Production of Tobacco*. New York: Blakiston, 1951.

HOBBS, S. H., JR. *North Carolina: Economic and Social*. Chapel Hill: University of North Carolina Press, 1930.

JENKINS, JOHN WILBUR. *James B. Duke*. New York: Doran, 1927.

LEFLER, HUGH TALMAGE AND ALBERT RAY NEWSOME. *North Carolina, the History of a Southern State*. Chapel Hill: University of North Carolina Press, 1954.

LEMERT, BEN F. *Tobacco Manufacturing in North Carolina*. Raleigh: National Youth Administration, 1939.

North Carolina Agricultural Statistics. North Carolina Department of Agriculture, Federal-State Crop Reporting Service. Bulletin No. 98. Raleigh: 1954.

North Carolina Directory of Manufacturing Firms, 1952. Division of Statistics. North Carolina Department of Labor. Raleigh: 1952.

North Carolina Employment Security Commission Quarterly, IX (Summer-Fall, 1951).

RANKIN, R. C. *Bright Leaf Tobacco. A Statistical Report Showing the Production and Sale of Bright Leaf Tobacco by States and Markets for the Years 1933–1953 Inclusive*. Lumberton: Tobacco Board of Trade, 1954.

ROBERT, JOSEPH C. *The Story of Tobacco in America*. New York: Knopf, 1949.

SHANNON, FRED ALBERT. *America's Economic Growth*. New York: Macmillan, 1941.

Statistics of Taxation, 1954. North Carolina Department of Revenue, North Carolina Department of Tax Research, and State Board of Assessments. Raleigh: 1954.

---

[28]First written by G. L. Hemminger for the *Penn State Froth*, November, 1951.

TILLEY, NANNIE MAY. *The Bright-Tobacco Industry 1860–1929*. Chapel Hill: University of North Carolina Press, 1948.

U. S. Department of Agriculture. *Annual Report on Tobacco Statistics*. Statistical Bulletin 157. Washington: U. S. Government Printing Office, 1955.

_____ . *Crops and Markets*, 1954 ed., Vol. XXXI. Agricultural Marketing Service. Washington: U. S. Government Printing Office.

_____ . *The Tobacco Situation*, Agricultural Marketing Service (June 10, 1955.

WEEKS, L. T. AND E. Y. FLOYD. *Producing and Marketing Flue-Cured Tobacco. Raleigh: Technical Press, 1941.*

Chapter 13

The Furniture Industry

From very modest beginnings, North Carolina has attained leadership in the furniture industry and today it ranks first among all the states in the production of wood and upholstered household furniture. During Colonial times most furniture was hand built in carpenter shops. In addition some was brought from Europe by the wealthier people—especially mahogany pieces, all of which were imported. Furniture making began to differentiate itself from the general carpenter trade in 1812, when Congress imposed a tax of 30 per cent upon all imported articles of furniture. During the last part of the nineteenth century, furniture making in North Carolina began its transformation from a handicraft type of enterprise, primarily in the cabinet-shop stage, to a mechanized operation when William E. and David A. White established their first small furniture factory in Mebane in 1881. Its resources consisted of a secondhand planer, a carload of lumber, and $300 in capital; it is still in existence. However, a larger undertaking which gave the furniture industry its real impetus and beginning was the High Point Furniture Company, established in 1888 by local citizens with the assistance of a superintendent from a plant in Charlotte that had failed.

There are two factors which explain why the furniture industry developed particularly in the state of North Carolina. First, between 1870 and 1890 the population of the South increased from twelve million to twenty million people, which growth called for more housing and more furniture. More significant, however, was the increase in the number of wage earners and the low wages they received, which created a demand for large quantities of cheap furniture. North Carolina was admirably equipped to satisfy this demand. The western part of the state was very densely covered with valuable hardwoods—oak, cherry, yellow poplar, and walnut—and lumber was available at low prices. There were vast supplies of unskilled farm labor ready to move into industry, and skilled artisans of the cabinetmakers' trade from Western Europe had come southward and settled in North Carolina.

Few industries have shown such phenomenal growth and development, especially in view of furniture's extreme sensitivity to general business fluctuation, as the North Carolina furniture industry. In the fifty-six-year period from 1899 to 1955, the number of furniture establishments increased from 44 to over 300, in spite of changing markets and rapid changes in style. With an annual production of over $295,000,000, the industry ranks third in the state, exceeded only by textiles and tobacco. Employment in the industry steadily increased from 1,023 workers in 1899 to a monthly average in August 1957 of 38,500, with an average weekly wage of $55.62.

As early as 1899 the furniture industry was well established in North Carolina; in that year it accounted for 15 per cent of the value of the furniture produced in the South, and in 1909, influenced by expanding markets in the North and Midwest, it accounted for 25 per cent of the total value of southern furniture production. But the home-building program after World War I created a tremendous demand for furniture. During the twenties many new plants were built, and while technologically few changes were made in machinery and operating techniques between 1900 and the mid thirties, late in that decade the principles of mass production were introduced. Great improvements were made in furniture factory layout, design of woodworking machinery, and the manufacturing technique itself. Automatic and scientific control of the drying process, greater use of waterproof resin glues, improved finishing processes, and extensive use of conveyors had an important impact on manufacturing.

As early as 1939 North Carolina ranked first in the country in the total production of wood household furniture, bedroom and dining-room furniture, fifth in kitchen furniture, and eighth in library and living-room furniture. North Carolina ranked higher than any other southern state in each type of furniture produced.

Some indication of the growth of the industry since 1939 is shown by the fact that household furniture production in the state has increased 337 per cent as compared with an increase of 272 per cent for the nation as a whole. In this eighteen-year period, North Carolina's production of dining-room furniture increased from 24.6 per cent to 32.4 per cent of the national total, and for bedroom furniture the increase was from 21.4 per cent to 25 per cent of the total.

Today the furniture factories in the state are located as far east as Goldsboro and as far west as Waynesville. The largest number, eighty-three, are centered in Guilford County. Catawba County has 48, Davidson 27, Iredell 19, and Caldwell 18. High Point has more factories than any other city, and the 150-mile radius surrounding it comprises the greatest concentration of furniture manufacturing in the world. Two-thirds of all the furniture made in the South is produced in this area.

Most furniture is fabricated from raw lumber to the finished product. Honduras and Phillipine mahogany, African mahogany veneers, cherry, walnut, oak, poplar, maple, and hackberry are used as base woods in combination with veneers of Celtis, Korina, cherry, walnut, and comb-grain. Manufacturers of some of the finer furniture products, including eighteenth-century, Early American, and French Provincial styles, utilize a wide assortment of such solid hardwoods as Honduras mahogany, cherry, maple, and magnolia. Popular lines have also been developed in western Carolina white knotty pine.

North Carolina's furniture industry, and its successful progress through-out the years, did not evolve spontaneously. Two primary influences gave this industry the caliber and integrity it now possesses. The Southern Furniture Manufacturers' Association, organized in 1911, has proved to be powerful in national furniture markets. It has taught improved furni-ture production, lower costs, and better management. Also, the location of a permanent furniture market in High Point and the erection of the Southern Furniture Exposition Building there in 1921 stimulate design and selling while publicizing the new southern industry to the entire nation. Starting with 200,000 square feet of floor space, this building has increased to 463,890 square feet of display space, one of the largest furni-ture exposition buildings in the nation. Exhibits of furniture and rugs produced by the North Carolina manufacturers are maintained through-out the year and annually attract an estimated 15,000 to 18,000 buyers from all parts of the country.

RELATED INDUSTRY.

The demand for the resources and the raw material requirements of the industry has created a great outlet for native raw materials and has brought to the state many allied industries, among them logging, lumber-ing, box and container making, and the manufacture of cabinet hardware, veneers, plywood, mirrors, and wood-finishing materials (see Table 72). Many yards of material and cotton batting produced by North Carolina textile mills are consumed by upholsterers. Some sandpaper, abrasives, and finishing materials are imported; however, many paint and lacquer plants have located in the state, as well as hardware, machinery, springs, and glue and resin factories. The total amount of activity relating to the furniture industry is almost the size of the industry itself. North Carolina is the largest consumer of wood in the nation. A striking percentage of the hardwood production of the state, and in many instances the entire output of certain types of hardwood, are used by the industry. North Carolina consumes a total of 350,000,000 board feet of lumber a year in the manufacture of wood products—97 per cent of all the yellow poplar produced in the state, almost the entire output of red and sap gum and tupelo, 60 per cent of the oak production, and 70 per cent of the total maple produced—of which the furniture industry takes 333,000,000 board feet, plus 35,000,000 board feet of veneers.

An industry of this dimension (See Table 73), which hires such a large fraction of the labor force and consumes so many products produced within the state, has a tremendous effect upon the economy of the state, and the prosperity of the industry involved in new techniques and new materials will ultimately be reflected in an increased prosperity to the state as a whole.

BIBLIOGRAPHY

DUNNAGAN, M. R. "North Carolina Furniture Manufacturing," *North Carolina Employment Security Quarterly*, X (Winter-Spring, 1952), 1–67.

TATE, FRED N. "Sketch of Furniture Manufacturing in North Carolina since 1888," *The Carolinas*, IV (June, 1932).

North Carolina Commerce and Industry, III (January, 1926).

Blue Book of Southern Progress, 1955. Baltimore: Manufacturer's Record, 1955.

Chapter 14

The Pulp and Paper Industry

From its origin in Chinese antiquity until modern times, all paper has been made by hand, by which method three men working one vat can produce 130 pounds. A typical pulp company today has a rated capacity of 600 tons of paper board each day. One machine, in a week's time, mades more paper than was manufactured in the entire United States in the full twelve months of 1810, before the use of the paper-making machine.

North Carolina has at least 50 plants, employing approximately 10,500 workers, with average weekly earnings of $89.44, which are engaged in manufacturing pulp, paper, and paper products, in addition to many thousands of workers engaged in gathering, selling, and transporting pulpwood, waste paper, and other products from which modern paper is manufactured.

Manufacturing Process.

With but two exceptions (Ecusta Paper Corporation and Sonoco Paper Products; see pages 126–127), all the state's paper companies use the same process in the manufacture of the pulp. This is known as the sulphate process because of the sodium sulphate used in cooking the wood chips. An abundance of pure water is an absolute essential in paper making, for it is used in every operation from the washing of the peeled logs to the forming of the sheets. It has been calculated that 15,000 gallons of water or more are required for every ton of paper made. Briefly the seven stages in paper manufacture are:

1. The Wood Yard. Row on row, and acre after acre, the pulp wood stretches away in the wood yard. In this vast store of raw material for paper, wood is carefully piled, assuring the mill of adequate supplies for continuous operation. Most is already cut to standard five-foot lengths for ease in handling and stacking, but log-length trees are cut to size at the yard. From the wood yard the bolts of pulpwood travel to

2. The Barking Drums. Into one end of the huge drums the lengths of wood are tumbled. As the drums slowly revolve, the jostling of the logs against each other and the metal plates of the drums removes the bark. From the drums the bark is conveyed to the furnaces, where it is burned to help make the steam required for paper making. The logs, now gleaming white, leave the barking drums again on conveyers. As they travel

they are thoroughly washed to remove all loose dirt and bark before reaching

3. The Chip House. Within the circular housings of the chippers are large rotating discs, on each of which are mounted from four to ten knives. As the peeled logs are fed to the face of a disc at an angle, the revolving knives cut the wood to chips one and one-half inches long and three-fourths inch thick. After the chips are sifted through large screens to insure uniformity of size, they are conveyed to the chip bins, there to await

4. The Cooker or Digester. Tons of chips at a time are fed directly into a "kettle" or "digester." The kettle is closed, a cooking liquor of sodium sulphate is added, and the chips are cooked for several hours at 100-pounds pressure. Under heat and pressure the resins and liquids in the wood enter into chemical reaction, leaving the cellulose fibers or pulp and spent liquor known as "black liquor." The kettle's contents are then blown into tanks for temporary storage. This cooking is known as the kraft process. It was invented by C. F. Dahl, a Swede, in 1879. The name "kraft" comes from the Swedish word for "strength," the outstanding characteristic of pulp fibers by this method. The pulp now goes to

5. The Pulp Laundry. Here pulp is placed in a conventional steel blowtank, where it will be washed on vacuum washers and screened on flat screens. This will remove the dirt, wood shives, and the spent cooking, or black, liquor. This liquid is carefully drawn off to be further processed for the recovery of chemicals, resins, and other by-products. To further refine the pulp it is passed through "knotters" and screens where knots are removed and large bundles of fibers are reduced to pulp. Then the pulp passes to the "thickeners," in which the fibers are washed once more and the water content is reduced to a specific amount. The pulp is next pumped to

6. The Bleach Plant. From the pulp laundry the pulp will be pumped to the bleach plant and bleached, using six stages consisting of chlorination, two caustic extractions, two hypochlorite bleachings, and sulphur dioxide acidification. After each stage the pulp will be washed on a vacuum washer. Now the pulp is ready for

7. The Paper Machine. At the "wet end" of the machine a carefully controlled stream of "stuff"—the diluted pulp—flows into a rapidly moving copper belt known as the Fourdrinier wire, named for the Englishmen Henry and Sealing Fourdrinier, who perfected the entire machine. This belt simultaneously moves forward and from side to side, thoroughly interlocking the pulp fibers. The web next passes between endless felts and pressing rollers, followed by eighty-seven steam-heated drying cylinders. Finally, highly polished steel rollers, the "calendar stacke," give

the required surface and final finish to the paper, which is now sliced and wound into rolls. It is interesting to note that when "stuff" enters the Fourdrinier it is approximately 99 per cent water. Of this about 9 per cent is removed by draining, 30 per cent by pressure, and 55 per cent by evaporation. While the moisture content varies in different papers, 6 per cent is normal—about the same as for a well-aired sheet of linen.

HISTORY.

The first paper mill to be established in North Carolina, so far as information is available, was erected in Orange County, near Hillsboro, probably on or near the Eno River, in the latter part of 1777, but how long or how successfully it operated is unknown. We do know that the colonial assembly, late in 1775, offered a bounty of 250 pounds for the first paper mill established in the state. In July, 1789, Gottlieb Schober built the second-oldest mill at Salem,[1] but the third mill had to wait until 1884, when the firm of Griffith and Jouffray constructed another one, also at Salem. The Memorabilia of Salem Congregation of that year says that "the machinery will run by two engines, one of twenty and the other of forty horse-power. The pure water required for the manufacture of the paper is supplied in quantity by an artesian well. The capacity of the mill will be one ton of paper per day, only wrapping and newspaper will be manufactured at present." The mill was not too successful, however, for in 1904 the Memorabilia reported that "the old paper-mill has given place to a row of neat cottages, greatly improving the neighborhood."[2]

MAJOR PAPER-MANUFACTURING COMPANIES.

The Halifax Paper Company, Inc., of Roanoke Rapids, one of the half-dozen large pulp and paper manufacturing firms in North Carolina, has been operated and enlarged during the past decade by its present owner, but it dates back almost to the turn of the century. Originally the Roanoke Rapids Manufacturing Company, it was incorporated in the fall of 1905, the controlling ownership having been in the hands of W. M. Habilston of Richmond, with a pair of brothers named Edwards as managers.

The pulp mill for converting wood into pulp through the use of the sulphate process was built in 1908 and started operation on February 26, 1909, the first in the United States. Initial production ranged from fifteen to eighteen tons a day. In 1913 the management changed, and so did the name—to Halifax Paper Corporation. Then in 1937 the Halifax Paper Corporation was bought by the Albemarle Paper Manufacturing

---

[1]"The Manufacture of Paper and Paper Products, an Expanding North Carolina Industry," *North Carolina Employment Security Commission Quarterly*, VI (Winter, 1948), 30.

[2]*Ibid.*, p. 32.

Company, Inc., of Richmond and re-incorporated under Virginia laws as the Halifax Paper Company, Inc.

The Champion Paper and Fibre Company opened its plant at Canton (close to suitable water, labor, and timber supply) in 1907 and has been a leader ever since in the production of high-grade paper. Every day it produces 650 tons of chemical pulp, 420 tons of paper, and 200 tons of paper board, plus many tons of by-products. Originally the Canton plant produced pulp only, but in 1922 it began the manufacture of paper, and today it operates some of the largest machinery in the industry, including two Fourdriniers 242 inches wide and two others 168 inches wide.

Champion owns large areas of timberlands in North and South Carolina and Georgia. It practices the best conservation methods and also carries on conservation-education programs among farmers and other timber-land owners.[3]

In 1928 the Mead Pulp and Paper Company (an Ohio firm) opened a mill at Sylva to utilize waste products in making paper board. Formerly the waste leached chestnut chips from an existing chestnut-tanning-extract plant had been burned. These the newly organized Sylva Paperboard Company was able to convert into shipping-container board, with a daily production of 60 tons, plus 100 barrels of tanning extract. In 1941, the Sylva plant (now known as the Sylva Division of the Mead Corporation) expanded to a production of 125 tons of corrugating board and 200 barrels of tanning extract. The operation uses 210 cords of chestnut acid wood daily, purchased from farmers and other timber growers in principally Jackson, Swain, and Macon counties. It employs 350 workers and has an annual payroll of $800,000.[4]

Every twenty-four hours at Plymouth, where the Roanoke River nears Albemarle Sound, the North Carolina Pulp Company cooks 1,200 cords of pine and gum timber into 700 tons of pulp and squeezes and rolls it into 650 tons of stiff white or tough brown paper. "The Kraftsman"—the million-dollar pride of the Plymouth plant—has a rated capacity of 600 tons of brown paper board every day, and each of the other two machines is 100 tons a day.

The Ecusta Paper Corporation (now a part of Olin Industries), at Pisgah Forest in Transylvania County is remarkable in its use of a waste product, seed flax fiber, in manufacturing cigarette paper. Originally cigarette paper was made from discarded linen, of which there was obviously a limited supply in this country. In the search for a substitute, it was discovered that straw from the seed flax (from which linen is made)

---

[3] *Ibid.*, pp. 6–7, 35–36.
[4] *Ibid.*, pp. 11, 38.

was admirably suited. Furthermore, it was refuse from seeds which had been extracted for other industrial puposes. and it had been burned, at some expense. The flax straw now comes from a considerable distance, Minnesota and California, but three local factors make the Pisgah Forest location ideal for the location of such a paper mill: First, there is an ample labor supply; second, there is a constant supply of suitable water in the Davidson River; and perhaps most important, the great cigarette factories, the paper's ultimate destination, are close at hand.[5]

The manufacturing process is similar to that used for wood pulp. The flax is pressure cooked in great, revolving, spherical vessels, then placed in tubs where the fibers are separated and impurities removed. The entire process is repeated. The next step is to bleach the fiber with chemical reagents and wash the substance six times. The finished pulp is then charged into the beaters to receive the desired characteristics. Next, the milky fibers flow out on a continuous, fine wire-mesh screen, are suddenly snatched off by felts and then dried, and at the end of the machine pass onto a tremendous roll of snow-white cigarette paper about a hundred inches wide.

After the reels, or rolls, of paper are rewound and inspected, they are put in a machine which slits them into strips, much like ticker tape, and alternating strips are wound into bobbins. The standard bobbin is about three and one-half miles long—enough to roll 85,000 cigarettes.

In addition to cigarette paper, Ecusta has started the manufacture of other fine types of paper, including fine flax writing paper, light-weight printing paper, air mail sheets, text or Bible paper, and other types of paper in which lightness and opaqueness are required.

The Sonoco Products Company, Rockingham Division, at Rockingham is the only plant of its kind in the entire South and one of only thirteen in the United States. It is engaged in the manufacture of glassine and greaseproof paper, and unlike any of the other plants manufacturing these two grades of paper, the Sonoco plant also converts this paper into glassine bags of all descriptions. In addition to the bags, the plant, like the other plants, converts this paper into printed, waxed, and laminated papers.

This plant purchases virgin sulphite wood pulp from the Pacific Northwest, from Canada, and from Sweden. About eight tons of unbleached and bleached sulphite pulp are used each day, this type pulp being required for the grades of paper being manufactured.

The Riegel–Carolina Corporation at Acme is the youngest pulp and paper mill in the state, and ranks as one of the largest in the state. Products of this corporation are shipped throughout the United States and to many foreign countries.

---

[5] *Ibid.*, pp. 3–4.

Two other companies, the Carolina Paper Board Corporation at Charlotte and the Manchester Board and Paper Company at Roanoke Rapids, make paper-board boxes almost entirely from waste paper. And the American Cyanamid Company has announced plans to build a multi-million-dollar flakeboard operation at Farmville.

The five strictly pulp and paper mills mentioned above have a daily capacity of 2,380 tons of pulp. The chances are good for additional mills in North Carolina since the state has the capacity to supply raw materials in abundance, and in addition has an abundance of labor, plus unexcelled water for paper manufacture.

BIBLIOGRAPHY

DAMTOFT, W. J. Radio Talks on Forestry. Mimeographed. N.p.: Society of American Foresters, Southern Appalachian Section, [1927?].

MANGHAN, WILLIAM. *A Guide to Forestry Activities in North Carolina.* Society of American Foresters, Southern Appalachian Section, 1938.

North Carolina Employment Security Quarterly, VI (Winter, 1948).

"The Paper Industry in the Carolinas," *The Wachovia*, XXXVIII (March, 1946), 3–16.

WILLIAMS, C. E. *A Well Rounded-Out Paper-Making in Western North Carolina.* Canton, North Carolina: Champion Fiber Company, 1925. (Reprinted from *Manufacturer's Record*, March 29, 1923.)

Chapter 15

THE ELECTRIC PRODUCTS INDUSTRY

Before World War II the electrical industry was practically non-existent in North Carolina. According to the 1940 census, there were no electrical manufacturers in the state of any reportable size; in 1955 there were approximately 35 such industries throughout the state. One reason for this expansion is the increasing national population with an "exploding" consumer demand, which is opening up a tremendous market for electrical equipment. The population of the United States has increased by more than 16,000,000 from 1950 to July 1, 1956. This has affected all industries whether they make consumer goods or not. Industrial production is increasing at about 4 per cent a year, while use of electrical energy is increasing at about 6 per cent annually. This relationship is significant because it clearly indicates the trend toward greater use of electrical equipment, both consumer and industrial, hence larger markets for the electrical industry. In North Carolina the superabundance of labor supply, the accessibility and low importation cost of raw materials, and the availability of small towns free from extensive labor organization help to explain North Carolina's appeal to new industry. In addition, proximity to southern markets and the influx of other industries, plus the growth of well-established North Carolina manufacturers, have influenced the electrical industry's location in the state.

The size of this industry can be observed from North Carolina's position among the southern states. The 1955 figures compiled from the *Blue Book of Southern Progress* indicate that North Carolina ranks third in production of electrical goods with an output of $148,000,000, representing an increase of $81,000,000 since 1952; third in payrolls and profits with $65,000,000 paid out. In August, 1957, there were 18,900 employees with average weekly earnings of $69.08, or $13.00 above the average of all industrial workers, $56.20. There are twenty-nine cities in seventeen counties in North Carolina producing electrical products.

An amazing variety of products are produced by the electrical industry. Most plants are parts of larger companies such as Western Electric, General Electric, Westinghouse, Cornell-Dubilier, International Resistance Company, Globe-Union, and the Great Lakes Carbon Company. The majority of these branch plants are engaged in the manufacture or fabrication of one single product. Such items as radar equipment, firing systems for guided missiles, watt-hour–meter apparatus, vibrators, capacitors, resistors, lead-in wires for lamps, radio and television tubes, automobile and flashlight batteries, electrodes and other carbon and graphite products, electrical appliances, and insulated cable are among the products produced.

The economy of North Carolina is the greatest beneficiary of the electrical-products industry's expansion. Aside from bringing new sources of income to the people and the state, the electrical industry has paved the way for many new diversified industries to locate in North Carolina. Larger and more numerous payrolls mean more consumer purchasing power. New demands for goods, housing, recreation, education, and other facilities will become more evident as the industry grows.

BIBLIOGRAPHY

North Carolina Employment Security Commission Quarterly, XIII (Winter-Spring, 1954).

News and Observer (Raleigh, N. C.), December 9, 1954.

Blue Book of Southern Progress, 1955. Baltimore: Manufacturer's Record, 1955.

Chapter 16

THE STATE HIGHWAY SYSTEM[1]

History

Road building in North Carolina goes back to the time when the state was a wilderness being opened for colonization by the English crown. The first roads, of course, were the Indian trails beaten down for communicative purposes among the several tribes and between the villages in various areas from the sea to the mountains. After coming to North Carolina, the white man utilized the rivers and sounds of the coastal regions to move from place to place. Travel through dense forest lands was impracticable and unwise, and colonization was easiest near the coastline or navigable rivers where water and fish were plentiful. Note that the oldest cities in the state developed along the shores of Albemarle, Pamlico, and Currituck sounds many years before the piedmont and mountain areas opened. Settlement at Fayetteville was facilitated by the location and navigable length of the Cape Fear River.

Eventually the sound and river frontages were diminished by royal grants. Settlers who established themselves beyond the boundaries of water landings experienced the hardships of restricted transportation outlets, and as the westward movement increased, the demand for roads grew. The first effort in road building was poorly effected and did little to relieve the hardships of obstructed movement. The small population could do no more than cut away the brush and trees to widen a trail and permit the sunlight to come through to help keep it as dry as possible.

The lack of building materials, among other deterrents, delayed the construction of roadways. Asphalt, concrete, and crushed stone were unknown in those days, and in an effort to penetrate the marshy lands, the settlers adopted a device which had been employed since before the days of the Roman Empire: "Corduroy" roads were made by laying logs lengthwise on a trail and crossing them with saplings or boards. The crevices were filled in with small cuttings, or with sandy soil. The last such road was laid by the Highway Commission in 1922 between Elizabeth

---

[1]This chapter, with permission, draws heavily from Capus M. Waynick, *North Carolina Roads and their Builders* (Raleigh, Superior Stone Co., 1952). Mr. Waynick served as chairman of the North Carolina State Highway Commission from 1934 through 1937.

City and the Camden line in Pasquotank. Some residents in the coastal areas of the state still use the corduroy pattern for private and commercial roads.

The first resemblance of a road commission was created in the "County of Albemarle." Albemarle was subdivided into "precincts," and a board of justices from each precinct was to appoint supervisors for road construction and maintenance. These boards were charged with enforcing the law which required all able-bodied men to spend a specified length of time in road building and upkeep. This law was effective into the twentieth century.

Commercial ventures and social communication in the colony of North Carolina slowed to almost a standstill during the eighteenth century. Virginia and South Carolina enacted legislation to prohibit North Carolina's marketable goods from gaining access to the ocean from their ports. However, after its reversion to the status of a royal colony in 1729 after many years of proprietory administration, much of this intercolonial dispute was cleared up. The crown recognized a petition to do away with the Virginia restriction of the movement of North Carolina tobacco in its territory and a period of commercial progress followed for nearly fifty years.

Intercolonial roads were built in the years between 1700 and 1728. The boundary commission surveying the disputed line between North Carolina and Virginia in 1728 crossed several of these roads in Currituck County. It appears that the first of them ran from the head of navigation on the Perquimans River to Suffolk, Virginia. A second road came out of Currituck County to Norfolk and a third one joined the Roanoke River with points in Virginia.

Roads were also built within the state during this period. In the early years of the eighteenth century a short route was constructed running from the lower end of Albemarle Sound to the Scuppernong River. A road from Bath to New Bern was completed in 1722. Road building south of Albemarle Sound began after the Indian War of 1711–13 and after the clearing out of pirates who had remained near the shores until about 1718.

During the Indian War of 1711–13, a special "power money" tax was levied. After the conclusion of the war this tax remained in force, and the funds were employed to open roads to the Cape Fear settlements, which ran from New Bern to Wilmington. This is the first evidence of a general colony tax to be used for road construction. The first strand of the state's road web was woven.

The momentum of the westward movement picked up. By the middle of the eighteenth century the movement had accelerated at a great pace. After the Revolution was over, the state was divided into forty-eight counties. The population of the western half of the state was gaining rapidly and was nearly equal to that of the eastern half. With this west-ward movement sectionalism developed within the state which created a conflict in many fields of interest, among them road construction. The sectionalism grew from racial, religious, and economic differences. As we have seen, the eastern part of the state was richer, had larger agricultural holdings, and owned more slaves, all of which influenced political thought and action. And added to the dissension was the problem of emigration, the state constantly being bled of the manpower resources sorely needed for the development of its potentialities.

In 1815 Governor William Miller, in his address to the legislature, gave voice to a growing awareness in the state of the necessity of improv-ing transportation facilities. Archibald D. Murphey, state senator from Orange County, took the lead in the legislative assembly and offered a resolution "to provide more efficiently for the improvement of the inland navigation of the state." The word "navigation" was a catchword to ob-tain the support of eastern legislators. The resolution was carried, and a commission was created to study transportation conditions. Murphy was placed at the head of this commission, and he submitted a series of reports indicating the need for a statewide transportation network. He wisely claimed that the state would not progress internally without the develop-ment of marketing centers to which farmers could transport their products in an unobstructed passage.

Murphey's initiative and zeal attracted legislative support. He was appointed to a commission which had the power to carry out an engineer-ing survey purported to put his scheme into operation. The chairman of the commission, Peter Browne, sailed for England in 1818 to procure the services of a road engineer, and returned with Hamilton Fulton, an engi-neer of first-class skill who worked diligently to put Murphey's plan into operation. This plan called for an inland road system consisting of a few main state roads, a network of county roads, and a feeder-road system under private operation. Once again sectionalism defeated the effort: the dominant influence of the eastern part of the state refused to support the plan. After six years of trying to develop the road system, Fulton yielded to political pressure and resigned his job in 1825.

Sectionalism and poverty put an end to Murphey's dream of an im-proved roadway system. An economic depression hit the state in the 1830's and thousands of people sought brighter lands beyond North Carolina's boundaries.

The depression ended in 1833, and there was a revitalized interest in internal improvements, influenced to a great extent by the new steam locomotive. In December, 1838, an internal improvements convention was held in Raleigh. This convention made six proposals. Of the six, three concerned the financing of railroads in several sections of the state; two concerned navigable waterways; and one called for "a survey from Raleigh by Hillsboro to Greensboro with the view to a macadamized turnpike road, a company to build it, and subscription of two-fifths of the cost by the state." This convention was sincere in its resolutions, and submitted its recommendations to the General Assembly for consideration. The construction of rail lines spurted, but the building of roadways was tied up in a mass of legal enactments. It appeared that the state was depending on private enterprise to build and operate specified roads with or without state aid.

Railroads had started in the state more than a decade earlier, but by 1849 the high cost of construction and the limited lines lent merit to the building of plank roads, known as "farmer railroads." During the period from 1849 to 1860, the General Assembly granted eighty-four charters for plank roads. Only a small percentage of these roads were constructed, however—approximately five hundred miles of road were built at a cost of nearly $1,000,000. These included thirteen stretches completed and four partially built. Fayetteville, located at the head of navigation on the Cape Fear River and with poor prospects of railroad connections, built plank roads radiating in five different directions. The longest, the Fayetteville and Western road, went through Salem to Bethania, headed toward Mount Airy and the Virginia coal fields. This road, one hundred and twenty miles long, was chartered on the same day as the North Carolina Railroad. Among the last records of plank-road operation were those of 1864, when stretches of road were taken over for military purposes.

Most of the plank roads followed a general pattern, with local subscriptions frequently supplemented by state aid. Toll houses, costing around $300, were erected on right-of-way sites each ten or twelve miles, and toll collectors were paid around $150 a year. Many travelers devised methods of free travel by constructing cutoffs around the toll houses. Most of the roads paid well in the earlier years, some of them declaring dividends up to 10 or 12 per cent. Occasional repairs and rebuilding of stretches of road were undertaken, but many of the roads were abandoned in the early 1860's, the General Assembly providing that they be taken over by county commissioners and made free of tolls. Of the roads built, the Fayetteville and Western road was the most important.

Two interstate roads were constructed: one from Yanceyville to the Virginia line to meet the road from Danville; and the other from Rocky River, near Center, via Wadesboro to the South Carolina line, where it joined the Cheraw road. Another interstate road, from Asheville to Greenville, South Carolina, was partially constructed, and it became a military road in 1864.

Other plank roads constructed in the state were as follows: the Greenville and Raleigh road, completed to Wilson in 1853 but not extended to Raleigh; the Wilmington and Topsail road, twenty miles from Wilmington northeastward to near the New Hanover-Onslow County line; the Western Plank road from Charlotte to Lincolnton, completed in 1853; the Fayetteville and Southern road, 15 1/2 miles, to Lumber Bridge, open to traffic in 1852, entering Fayetteville on two streets, Gillespie and Winslow; the Fayetteville and Center road, from Fayetteville to the Pee Dee River (Yadkin), completed around 1853; the Fayetteville and Northern road, intended to reach Raleigh, built about ten miles to Kingbury and not extended to Raleigh; the Charlotte and Taylorsville road, opened in 1853–54 to a point a little beyond Davidson, not completed; the Salisbury to Statesville road, built eight or ten miles in 1852 and not completed; the Clinton to Warsaw road, opened in 1862. The Washington and Tarboro and the Haywood and Pittsboro roads, chartered in 1852, were built for only a few miles.

Turnpike construction finally got the attention of the state legislature in 1846. The legislature passed an enabling act allowing the construction of the Western Turnpike which was to run from Raleigh through Salisbury to the Georgia line in Cherokee County. It was intended that this roadway was to be built by the state under contract. It was planned as a toll road, however the cost was to be supported by the sale of Indian lands which had been acquired from the Cherokees. The Civil War ended this and other western turnpike projects.

Road construction in North Carolina remained in constant decline for two decades after 1865, and up-to-date interest in public-road construction did not begin until 1879. This was the year that the state legislature passed the Mecklenburg road law. The statute was intended to apply to the state as a whole but at the time of enactment was directed to Mecklenburg County alone. This law levied a property tax for the construction and maintenance of roads in Mecklenburg County. It further provided that all able-bodied males between the ages of eighteen and forty-five were to sacrifice four days a year in road-maintenance work. The administration of the law was charged to the township authorities.

The cry for internal improvements echoed and reverberated into the twentieth century. Men of foresight endeavored to blot out sectional prejudices and to align the forces of progress in order to build a modern road network to facilitate economic development. In 1899, progressive citizens of that area organized the Good Roads Association of Asheville and Buncombe County. This group was responsible for a macadam road which was constructed from Asheville to Vanderbilt's Village, and the organization inspired the formation of a similar statewide group.

The promoters of road-building interests came from a variety of sources. In the early years of the new century, the U. S. Department of Agriculture created the Office of Public Road Inquiries. This unit functioned as an educational organization to promote public consideration of road-construction improvements. Even the railroad companies of the South campaigned for a better road system. The Southern Railway sent a special train through the South displaying road-building equipment which made three stops in North Carolina—Salem, Asheville, and Raleigh. This excursion influenced community consideration of the execrable road situation, and provided the occasion for the progressive citizenry to join forces in mapping a plan to achieve internal improvements. Prominent men spoke on the matter. Note Charles B. Aycock's famous quotation: "We must bring the country people closer together by good roads, and then we can have good schools;" and State Senator Furnifold M. Simmons: "Educate the people and there is no power in the world that will keep them from building roads. Build roads and you cannot keep the people from being educated."

There were many others who made notable contributions to the development of modern North Carolina highways. From the University of North Carolina came three renowned geologists to lend leadership. Elisha Mitchell surveyed the east-west road to the Georgia line. J. A. Holmes constantly pleaded for road improvements and was the first secretary to the state Good Roads Association. Colonel Joseph Hyde Pratt also served as its secretary, and he enlisted Miss Hattie Berry of Chapel Hill to his cause.

Despite persuasion and prompting, there was actually little progress in highway construction during the years from 1900 through 1914. The year 1915 brought change. Through legislative sanction, and with the anticipation of federal aid, Governor Locke Craig set up the North Carolina State Highway Commission in 1915. This body was to consist of the governor, the state geologist, a professor of engineering from North Carolina State College, another from the University at Chapel Hill, and three appointees selected by the governor. The commission was allotted $10,000 a year and was charged as an advisory body to the counties.

Woodrow Wilson signed the first Federal Aid Act on July 11, 1916, and immediately the United States Bureau of Roads was established with authorization to allot money to all the states for road construction. This act stimulated the state legislatures to formulate and pass state highway statutes, and from 1916, the year the aid act became effective, to 1920, 15,944 miles of federal-aid roads were built in the United States, of which 7,600 miles were made of bituminous concrete, portland cement, and brick.

The North Carolina General Assembly moved quickly in 1917 to enact a law under which the State Highway Commission was authorized to accept federal aid and to dole it out to those counties agreeing to match the amount of federal contributions. Thus it did not obligate the state government to be responsible for raising the required funds but placed the obligation on the county governments.

In 1919 the State Highway Commission was reorganized and its authority greatly increased. The commission was headed by Frank Page, one of the greatest influences in the development of the state's present-day state highway system. Page was an honest and forward man. He had gained invaluable experience in road building while serving with the American Expeditionary Forces in France, and he was eager for the state to undertake highway construction and maintenance in order to create a road network which was not dependent on county participation and financial assistance. In connection with this idea, Page suggested that each county seat and each principal town be connected by state road arteries. This is often referred to as the "Chapel Hill Plan," backed by Pratt, Miss Berry, and associates.

Road construction in North Carolina accelerated in 1921, and the state divided into many excited and anxious groups. All agreed that the state was obligated to build and maintain a highway road system, however they wrangled on the details of construction and financing. Colonel T. L. Kirkpatrick of Charlotte founded the Wilmington-Charlotte Highway Association, which favored the building of a great highway from the sea to the Tennessee line. He asked for a state bond issue to arrange a $50,000,000 credit for road construction. At the time of this proposal, Governor Thomas W. Bickett was in office, and he vigorously opposed any plan which would put the state in debt for road construction. However, the next governor, Cameron Morrison, had committed himself in pre-election promises to the support of a state road program.

At the same time (1920) Miss Hattie Berry had taken over the secretaryship of the North Carolina Good Roads Association. Miss Berry was an outstanding spokesman and did much to develop public support for the roads program. Her ideas concerning financing differed from Colonel Kirkpatrick's: She advocated a 5,500-mile road network connecting the various county seats, as Frank Page proposed, the state paying half the costs and assuming maintenance responsibility and the program to be financed by automobile-license fees, an ad valorem tax, and a tax on gasoline.

Miss Berry and Colonel Kirkpatrick, recognizing a common interest, resolved their differences and joined forces to prepare a good-roads bill to be introduced in the General Assembly. The drafting committee was made up of Heriot Clarkson of Charlotte, Dr. L. B. Morse of Blowing Rock, T. L. Gwynn of Waynesville, John Sprunt Hill of Durham, and Miss Berry. This committee ignored Kirkpatrick's $50,000,000 bond proposal and prepared a draft which embraced most of the Berry ideas. However, in the end it was the Kirkpatrick financing plan which was accepted by the General Assembly in the roads act of 1921. This act also placed a one-cent tax on each gallon of gasoline purchased on the retail level; automobile license fees were greatly increased.

The final hurdle was accomplished and the way opened to begin the vast job of developing a modern state highway system. Within ninety days after the adjournment of the General Assembly, plans were laid out, equipment purchased, and personnel hired to carry out the enormous task. Succeeding legislatures were favorable to the highway program: the Assembly of 1923 authorized an additional $15,000,000 worth of bonds, in 1925 another $20,000,000 bond issue was approved, and in 1927 another $30,000,000 was sanctioned.

Frank Page resigned his position from the commission in 1929. He had done a magnificent job. In the five years from 1921 to 1926, more than 6,200 miles of new roads had been added to the system. This averaged over a thousand miles per year, which was a phenomenal rate.

In 1931 the state voted to take over the county and local roads from the county road commissions, and the state has supervised their maintenance since that date. At that time no other state in the Union had assumed such a task. In fact, North Carolina was the first state to assume absolute control of all rural public roads within its boundaries. As a matter of record, it may be noted that in 1931, when the state first took over the county roads, the total distance of these roads amounted to 45,091 miles. In ten years the mileage increased by 2,294, of which 1,585 miles were hard surfaced.

The economic crisis which affected the entire nation during the 1930's caused a slackening in road construction and maintenance in North Carolina. In 1935 the General Assembly was advised of the generally poor conditions of the roads due to improper care. It was also advised that numerous bridges over small streams needed replacing. The Highway Commission had been denied the privilege of continued construction during the crisis, and even maintenance had been restricted by budgetary appropriations. Considering the emergency situation, the legislature appropriated $3,000,000 to improve the condition of dangerous bridges. Later in the session the Assembly appropriated funds to maintain the roads adequately.

Construction and maintenance continued uninterrupted during the period from 1935 to 1948. The road mileage jumped from 58,000 to approximately 64,000. The major part of this construction was done at the request of the counties.

When Gregg Cherry took over the governorship of the state in January, 1945, demands for road improvements still came from all sections of the state. The governor favored a continued good-roads program, however he realized that the emphasis should be changed from major highway construction to the improvement of the rural roads. During his term of office, the highway commission pursued an energetic secondary-road-construction program. It accomplished a notable goal: more new mileage in the rural areas were put into operation than had been built during any previous administration. An enlightened rural population welcomed the conveniences of good roadways and the cry became louder for more of them. An improved secondary-road system became one of the main issues of the 1948 primary.

The next governor was another champion of secondary-road improvement. W. Kerr Scott, a man who knew the problems of the farm population, made a successful issue of rural roads and won the 1948 primary. He had to fight a somewhat hostile legislature to get financial backing for his proposed road program, and he had to get a referendum vote for the program. The election deciding the issue was held June 4, 1949, and of 100 counties in the state, only three voted against the issuance of $200,000,000 in bonds to finance the secondary-road-improvement program. These bonds were absorbed readily by the market at low interest rates. In a little more than three years after the referendum was held, the governor's program was approximately 94 per cent completed.

In accomplishing the secondary-road-improvement plans, the state set new national and world records in road paving. During the period from January 1, 1949 to June 30, 1953, 14,550 miles of paving were applied to the state's secondary roads.

Present Status of Roads

CURRENT MILEAGE.

The North Carolina Highway Commission reports that on January 1, 1957, there were 11,114 miles of state primary highways, of which 11,015 were hard surfaced.

Rural secondary mileage under state control was 56,498, and municipal mileage under state control was 2,619. These data do not include the Blue Ridge Parkway, military reservations, or nonsystem roads in national parks. The total mileage of these roads was 1,268 in 1955. The total existing mileage under state control on January 1, 1957, was 70,231. This was some 20,000 more miles than in any other state system. County roads are under state control in Alabama (six counties), Delaware, North Carolina, Virginia (all but two counties), and West Virginia.

Out of a total mileage of 70,231, as of January 1, 1957, 11,114 miles were classed as rural primary roads; 1,171 miles were municipal primary roads; 1,448 were municipal secondary roads; and 56,498 miles were rural secondary roads. All but 99 miles of the rural primary roads were hard surfaced, and all but two miles of the municipal primary streets were hard surfaced. Hard-surfaced rural secondary roads totaled 22,735 miles, and municipal secondary roads with hard surface totaled 1,127 miles. Thus of the 70,231 miles in the North Carolina Highway System, 36,046 miles were hard surfaced, as of January 1, 1957.

North Carolina has some 6,500 miles of municipal streets. About 84 per cent of municipal streets are surfaced.

The State Highway Commission.

The first highway commission was established before the independence of the colonies. This was the Albemarle Road Commission mentioned earlier. A board of justices of the peace was selected for each precinct within the county. This body had the responsibility for appointing road supervisors and enforcing the law which required all able-bodied men to work on the roads.

More than a hundred years passed after the Revolution before the state made an attempt to establish a commission to build and maintain a roadway system. In 1901, the General Assembly authorized the commissioner of agriculture and the state geologist to choose a third person as a highway commissioner. This group lasted only two years, but a pattern had been established. In 1909 the legislature provided $5,000 to increase the functions of the North Carolina Geological Board. This board was to advise the county and township authorities in the building and improvement of public roads. Under this enactment, the state was to furnish competent road engineers to assist the county and township authorities in locating improved road sites.

The State Highway Commission was established by legislative enactment in 1915. This commission had seven members, with the governor designated as the chairman. The functions of the 1915 commission were strictly advisory, and the state was not authorized to engage in actual construction of a highway system.

The 1915 commission lasted four years. In 1919 a law was passed creating an entirely new State Highway Commission, and the chairman of this organization was given the title of State Highway Commissioner. The act also provided for a membership of four, appointed by the governor.

A legislative act of 1921 again changed the structure of the Commission and greatly increased its power and authority. This law provided for a commission of nine members and a full-time chairman. It was this body, under the leadership of Frank Page, that began the enormous road-building job provided for by the first large bond issue.

In 1931 the size of the commission was reduced to six members and a full-time chairman, and in 1937 it was increased to ten members, and a chairman. It retained this size until 1953 when it was increased to fifteen members, including the chairman. The 1957 General Assembly reduced membership to seven, appointed from the state at large, and also provided for a director of highways.

Members of the Highway Commission are appointed by the governor to serve a specified period. They have usually been selected from districts and have functioned mainly as district commissioners. On the higher level they are to serve as a statewide policy-making body, meeting frequently with various county boards, city officials, and other groups to explain the state road laws in order to be well informed on state road conditions.

Specifically the duties of the commission include the administration of all matters relating to the function of the state in location, design, construction, maintenance, and operation of all public rural roads, bridges, and other rural traffic facilities in the state, including certain portions of city streets. Until July 1, 1957 the administration of the state prison system included the central prison, women's prison, prison industries, prison farms and canneries, and the many dispersed prison camps (dormitory units) all over the state. The 1957 legislature created a Prison Commission of seven members and separated the prison system from the highway commission, under which it had been placed in 1931. It is now a separate agency.

Future Requirements

The state's primary roads are becoming obsolete and inadequate for modern transportation vehicles. Automobile traffic has jumped considerably since these roads were planned and built. At the time of construction, no particular thought was given to the prospect that heavy freight vehicles would one day continually traverse the highways, and the burden placed on them necessitates constant maintenance care. Highway planning must be expanded to alleviate hazardous and overcrowded road conditions. Perhaps the outstanding need as of 1957 is the modernization of the primary roads of the state. It appears that this will be the policy of the new highway commission, which will spend some $390,000,000 of state and federal funds during the 1957–59 biennium in expanding the highway system.

BIBLIOGRAPHY

BROWN, C. K. *The State Highway System of North Carolina*. Chapel Hill: University of North Carolina Press, 1931.

CONNOR, R. D. W. *History of North Carolina, The Colonial and Revolutionary Periods, 1584–1783*. Vol. I. Chicago: Lewis Publishing Company, 1919.

HOBBS, S. H., JR. *North Carolina: Economic and Social*. Chapel Hill: University of North Carolina Press, 1930.

STARLING, R. B. "The Plank Road Movement in North Carolina," *North Carolina Historical Review*, XVI (January, 1939; April, 1939), 1–22, 147–93.

U. S. Department of Commerce, Bureau of Public Roads. *Annual Report, 1954*. Washington: U. S. Government Printing Office, 1955.

WAYNICK, C. M. *North Carolina Roads and Their Builders*. Raleigh: Superior Stone Company, 1952.

Chapter 17

Public Transportation[1]

The category of public transportation covers those individuals or private corporations engaged in public transportation service for both persons and property without the use of facilities furnished by the public. In the early days these carriers were wagon trains and stagecoaches. The law designated them as common carriers, granting to them certain franchises and at the same time imposing certain obligations to the public, such as an insurer's liability and reasonable rates to the public. It is interesting that in the framing of our federal Constitution that the carriage of intelligence, *i.e.*, sealed correspondence, was delegated to the federal government. However, the carriage of persons and property was left in the hands of individuals and private corporations.

In the mid-nineteenth century, railroads became our foremost common carriers and had a monopoly on all intercity transportation for almost a hundred years. In the 1930's, motor carriers began intercity transportation of persons and property and within less than a decade the short-haul passenger and package traffic left the railroads for the cheaper and more flexible service available by highway. With this influx of traffic, the motor carriers extended their operations and the average haul of traffic by motor carrier continued to lengthen.

Short-haul traffic was not profitable for the railroads and it was yielded without a struggle, yet the railroads have made many rate adjustments to retain their long-haul traffic, a necessity unheard of before the entrance of highway competition.

As a result of the highway competition, there were many advocates of removing regulation from all transportation companies. Regulatory legislation was not repealed, but rather the motor carriers providing public transportation service were placed under regulation. The primary object of the early regulations was not only to guarantee the public reasonable and nondiscriminatory rates but to protect the transportation system against noncompensatory rates which might threaten the financial stability of the railroad.[2]

---

[1] In the preparation of this section the author is deeply indebted to Mr. Parks M. Low, rate specialist, North Carolina Utilities Commission.

[2] C. McD. Davis, president of the Atlantic Coast Line Railroad of Wilmington, North Carolina, in addressing the New York Society of Security Analysts on February 25, 1955, said: "I am definitely not 'de regulation' minded, though I do think there is room for improvement in the present regulatory structure. In fact, I think a 'policeman' is definitely needed, not only to shield the railroad industry from outside influences, but also to shield one railroad from another in dangerous rate cutting practices."

Railroads
HISTORY.

Joseph C. Caldwell, first president of the University of North Carolina, is credited with being the first to promote a horse-drawn railroad system for North Carolina when in 1826 he urged that the state undertake the construction of such a railroad extending westward from Beaufort Harbor to Raleigh and thence bisecting the state to the Tennessee border.[3] Thus all of North Carolina except the southeastern portion would be within fifty miles of a railroad outlet, and all its farmers could market their produce without the necessity of the long wagon journeys to the coast which required several weeks away from home. Caldwell's idea did not take concrete form until 1848, when the first part of the proposed state steam railroad, known as the North Carolina Railroad, was built from Goldsboro via Greensboro to Charlotte. In 1854, the state began construction of the eastern extension from Goldsboro to Beaufort Harbor and a western extension from Salisbury toward the Tennessee Border. Earlier than this, however, Virginia interests began extending their lines, one (owned by Baltimore capitalists) from Petersburg to Weldon and ultimately to Wilmington, another from Portsmouth to Raleigh, and still a third from Richmond toward Greensboro. South Carolina interests began to tap resources of North Carolina by extending a railroad to Charlotte.

After the Civil War, the state's partially constructed line from Salisbury toward the Tennessee border became heavily indebted and of necessity was sold to the Richmond and Danville, a Virginia corporation. The North Carolina Railroad was leased to this same corporation, and with numerous extensions and leases, these lines became the Southern Railway, which today serves a greater portion of North Carolina than any other single railroad system.

The railroad extending southward from Petersburg, Virginia, to Wilmington, after acquiring numerous other lines and constructing extensions and cutoffs, became the Atlantic Coast Line, which is next in mileage within the state and serves most of the important cities in the eastern part of the state.

The railroad that extended southward from Portsmouth, Virginia, ultimately to reach Raleigh by a series of leases and extensions, became the Seaboard Air Line, which is third in mileage and serves many important cities, with an east-west line from Wilmington as far west as Rutherfordton that serves all important towns and cities along the North Carolina-South Carolina border. Incidentally, this line (Hamlet to Navassa) contains the longest stretch of track without a curve in the world.

By consolidating a number of railroads built by lumber companies to exploit the forests of North Carolina and by constructing a five-mile bridge

---

[3] *Numbers of Carlton, Address to the People of North Carolina on a Central Railroad through the State* (New York: G. Long, 1828) [ascribed to Joseph C. Caldwell].

across Albemarle Sound, the longest bridge over navigable water in the world, the Norfolk Southern system was formed. While its headquarters are in Virginia, 95 per cent of the Norfolk Southern's mileage is in North Carolina.

There are many short-line railroads in North Carolina which were originally constructed by lumber companies. After the communities along the line were developed and when the timber supply became exhausted, the railroads evolved into community enterprise.

PRESENT RAILROAD SYSTEMS.

Since 1920, the railroad mileage of North Carolina has declined, mainly because of changed economic conditions and the fact that the areas once served no longer need rail services. While there are eight counties in the state not served by railroads, should railroad service become necessary to such a county or community, any of the railroad systems would extend its lines or the community would project a railroad to the nearest railroad connection. With the evolution of the uniform rate structure, very little advantage is obtained in having a single railroad system handle traffic from origin to destination; and with nationwide agreements on car-service rules, uniform-class rates, and so on, the importance of being located on a certain railroad because of rate advantages has almost vanished. The important factor is railroad service.

There are five north-south railroad lines across North Carolina: (1) The Atlantic Coast Line with a double track, plus a network of alternate secondary main lines, serves Rocky Mount, Wilson, Fayetteville, etc. (2) The Seaboard, with a main line having centralized train control and passing tracks which permit double-track efficiency at single-track maintenance expense, serves Henderson, Raleigh, Sanford, Hamlet, etc., with a network of branch lines. (3) The Southern, with double-track main line, serves Reidsville, Greensboro, High Point, Thomasville, Lexington, Salisbury, Concord, Charlotte, Gastonia, etc., with many branches and secondary main lines. (4) The Norfolk and Western, Winston-Salem Southbound, a single-line freight railroad, goes from Roanoke southward through Winston-Salem, Lexington, and Albemarle to Wadesboro, where it connects with the Coast Line. (5) And the Clinchfield, crossing the state in the rugged mountain territory with a single-line track but having centralized train control, serves Marion, Bostic, Forest City, etc.

By the use of a combination of systems, several east–west lines are available: (1) the Norfolk Southern entering North Carolina in its northeast corner to Charlotte, directly serves Elizabeth City, Edenton, Plymouth, Washington, Greenville, Wilson, and Raleigh. (2) The Atlantic and East Carolina from Beaufort Harbor via New Bern and Kinston to Goldsboro (recently acquired by the Southern Railway), then Southern Railway to the Tennessee border, goes through Raleigh, Durham, Burlington, Greens-boro, Winston-Salem, Statesville, Hickory, Morganton, Marion, Ashe-ville, etc. (3) the Seaboard runs from Wilmington to Rutherfordton, serving Lumberton, Laurinburg, Rockingham, Wadesboro, Monroe, Charlotte, Shelby, and thence via Clinchfield to the Tennessee border. The railroads' most important service to the state is the transportation of freight, people preferring the flexibility of private automobile and the speed of airplane. However, at huge losses the railroads are still offering at all principal cities comfortable and expedited passenger service.

With the exception of the Norfolk and Western and a few short-line railroads, all trains are propelled by Diesel locomotive. Several of the railroads have purchased some roller-bearing freight cars and all are con-stantly striving to improve the efficiency of operation in order to offer railroad transportation to patrons in North Carolina for as little cost as possible.

During the calendar year of 1954, the railroads originated in North Carolina over twelve and one-half million tons of freight traffic and ter-minated approximately twice that amount. Individually, for every man, woman and child in North Carolina, the railroads originated approx-imately three tons of freight and terminated approximately six tons. This traffic does not include the freight handled by the vast fleets of motor trucks moving over the highways of North Carolina. See Table 74 for amounts of freight carried by and mileage for North Carolina railroads.

Motor-freight Carriers

When the legislative bodies decided to regulate the for-hire transporta-tion of property by motor carriers, they were confronted with an array of types of carriers so complex that simple or uniform rules were an im-possibility. There were general-commodity regular route carriers opera-ting over regular routes on regular schedules; contract carriers hauling traffic for only a few firms; movers of household goods rendering families changing their residences with complete house-to-house services; bulk-commodity haulers which furnished the container for the commodity handled; newspaper and film carriers operating on exacting schedules and making delivery through locked doors; carriers handling general com-modities when called upon over a wide area, and many others.

For this reason, the regulation of the motor-freight carriers has been most difficult. However, the legislative body formulating the statutes and the regulatory bodies administrating the motor-carrier acts have been very careful that individual rights are not invaded and that the economy of both motor-freight carriers and their users be not impaired by regula-tion.

The shippers and receivers of freight traffic in North Carolina have at disposal many varied and specialized motor-freight carriers. Should a need for motor-freight service arise and no carrier be authorized to provide such service, the regulatory body can authorize such service on an emergency basis subject to investigation and final adjudication.

In North Carolina, there are 455 regulated motor freight carriers operating 18,087 units of equipment. Carriers who are exempt from regulation operate 4,995 units of equipment. These latter carriers handle government traffic, farm commodities, forest products, or afford local deliveries and other traffic not readily regulated without adversely affecting the economy of the carrier or user.

Transportation Rates

In the early days of the railroads the principal traffic was passengers, mail, and express, the freight traffic consisting principally of merchandise moving to the general stores in less than carload quantities and an outbound movement of farm products—principally cotton, tobacco, and grain.

The freight rates were usually local rates of the railroad on a mileage basis, and when large systems such as the Southern were organized, each division had its own locals. As the markets of the farm products began to enlarge and forest products required a wide distribution over long distances, the railroads established joint through rates known as commodity rates on particular items. Water competition from water carriers was met at the ports. Due to the relatively high volume of freight traffic moving in southern territory, the class rates (rates for a group of commodities listed in a governing classification) were higher mile for mile than corresponding rates in the so-called official territory lying east of the Mississippi River and north of the Ohio River and the main line of Norfolk and Western Railway from Cincinnati to Norfolk via Roanoke, Lynchburg, Petersburg, and Suffolk. This difference was recognized by the Interstate Commerce Commission when it permitted the establishment of a scale of class rates substantially higher in the South than in northern territory. (However, prior to this the railroads had established a few commodity rates covering the movement of such traffic as lumber, cotton, factory products, manufactured tobacco, etc. which were comparable to the rates within the North and enabled a few southern manufacturers to compete with producers in other territories.)

After the establishment of a uniform Southwide system of class rates[4] in 1928, the southern railroads began to relate their commodity rates to

_____

[4] 100 ICC; 513; 100 ICC 301.

this system of rates, which resulted in many instances in a higher scale of rates from the South to the North than within the North.

In 1931, revised class rates between points in official territory[5] became effective. These rates were approximately 30 per cent lower than rates within the South. To compound this disparity, interterritorial rates were made on the basis of the southern class-rate scale. The state of North Carolina is in close proximity to the southern border of official territory and in many instances combination rates, *i.e.*, rates to Virginia points in official territory plus rates south thereof, were lower than the through rates.

After a thorough study of the situation, the North Carolina Commission in 1932 filed a complaint with the Interstate Commerce Commission attacking the interterritorial class rates to and from points in North Carolina. This protest brought some relief by reducing these rates slightly.[6] In making this small reduction, the Interstate Commerce Commission stated that more relief should have been granted and that it would encourage a further reduction throughout the South.

For many years the railroads in the South were able to provide lower commodity rates for southern manufacturers, but the disparity between northern and southern rates was a great deterrent to prospective manufacturers in the South, and as the industrialization of the South began to accelerate, any efforts to adjust commodity rates for these interests were blocked by the railroads in the North. This situation was intolerable to the South, which felt that it had not received fair treatment. Definite action was taken by the Southern Governors' Conference in 1937 when a complaint was filed with the Interstate Commerce Commission attacking rates on numerous commodities produced in the South and distributed in the North in competition with northern manufacturers. The rates on these commodities were made with relation to the northbound class rates, which were slightly lower than rates applied in southern territory and considerably less than class rates in northern territory. This proceeding was decided in 1939, and the result was a reduction of rates on a few commodities involved by ordering the classification rating reduced on traffic moving from the South to the North.[7]

However the real goal of the efforts of the Southern Governors Conference was attained by an investigation of class rates from, to, and between all points east of the Rocky Mountains which began in 1939.[8] A uniform system of class rates and classification ratings east of the Rockies

---

[5] 164 ICC 314; 171 ICC 481.

[6] 213 ICC 259.

[7] 235 ICC 255; 237 ICC 515.

[8] 262 ICC 447; 264 ICC 41; 268 ICC 577.

became effective on May 31, 1952. An investigation of class rates between points west of the Rockies, on the one hand, and points east of the Rockies on the other, is now pending before the Interstate Commerce Commission.

There still remain many commodity rates which were not affected by the class-rate cases, and a strenuous effort is being made to establish a uniform basis of commodity rates as well as class rates. This is a rather complex task in that there must be kept in mind many interdependent factors—possible effect of such a widespread revision on the financial condition of the railroads; on the movement of competing commodities; the location of industry, processing plants, raw materials, and markets.

Under Sections 62–131 of the *General Statutes*, the North Carolina Utilities Commission is delegated the duty of assisting citizens of North Carolina in their efforts to procure reasonable and nondiscriminatory interstate rates. Its able staff has for many years assisted the shippers and receivers of freight in North Carolina in the solution of freight-rate problems confronting the South.

When the investigation of class rates began in 1939, the unit cost (per car per mile) of transporting freight traffic in the South was higher than the corresponding unit cost in the North, and for many years this discrepancy was justified because of these higher costs. Since World War II, the unit cost of transporting freight traffic within the South is generally less than in the North, and also the railroads of the South are generally in better financial condition than any group in the country with the exception of those in the Pocahontas Region.

While the outlook for removing the freight-rate discrimination against the South is very bright, the adjustment cannot be accomplished by the efforts of the North Carolina Utilities Commission alone. It must receive full support from interested shippers and receivers. A very important factor in the South has been the ability of the southern shipper or receiver to operate his private truck and thus control the price of his transportation.[9]

---

[9] In North Carolina there are over 200,000 motor-truck units licensed for private use, exclusive of 88,000 vehicles licensed for farm use.

Bibliography

Annual reports of the North Carolina Utilities Commission. Raleigh.

Barringer, Rufus. History of the North Carolina Railroad. Manuscript, 1894. Papers of the North Carolina Historical Society at the University of North Carolina.

Brown, C. K. *A State Movement in Railroad Development.* Chapel Hill: University of North Carolina Press, 1927.

Hobbs, S. H., Jr. *North Carolina: Economic and Social.* Chapel Hill: University of North Carolina Press, 1930.

Johnson, Guion Griffis. *Ante-Bellum North Carolina.* Chapel Hill: University of North Carolina Press, 1937.

Numbers of Carlton, Address to the People of North Carolina on a Central Railroad through the State [ascribed to Joseph C. Caldwell]. New York: G. Long, 1828.

Waynick, C. M. *North Carolina Roads and their Builders.* Raleigh: Superior Stone Company, 1952.

Chapter 18

Intracoastal and Connecting Waterways

The Intracoastal Waterway is the official name for the series of connected water routes along the Atlantic and Gulf coasts of the United States between Boston, Massachusetts, and Rio Grande, Texas, that have been dredged and improved to provide an almost completely protected passage for small craft. These waterways extend for 3,000 miles.

At present, the two inland waterways extending from Boston to the Florida Keys on the Atlantic Coast and from Carabella, Florida, to Brownsville, Texas, on the Gulf coast have not been connected to form a through waterway. With the completion of the congressionally authorized Cross-Florida Barge Canal (one of the last major links to be constructed in the through waterway), small craft not suitable for ocean navigation will be able to travel from Trenton, New Jersey, to the Rio Grande completely by inland sounds, canals, and other improved waterways.

The main route of the Intracoastal Waterway as it enters North Carolina just north of the mouth of the North Landing River extends from its point of entrance 308 statute miles to the South Carolina boundary; however, if the Dismal Swamp Canal is included in the total waterway mileage for North Carolina, the state has approximately 350 miles of main-route inland waterways. In compiling total mileage of inland waterways in North Carolina, the total is somewhat smaller than might be expected because a large portion of the Dismal Swamp Canal route extending from the point of intersection of the two waterway routes via Pamlico Sound to Beaufort is classified as an "improved connecting channel."

Early History.

Before the arrival of the early settlers in the United States, the Indians used the coastal and inland waterways as arteries of communication. These inland sounds, bays, and rivers were prime factors in penetrating the interior and colonizing the coastal areas, since water travel at this time was the fastest and most convenient means for transportation of freight and passengers.

In certain areas along the coast where the bays and sounds were separated by narrow strips of land, the freight, passengers, and sometimes small ships were "hauled over" the barriers. The word "haulover" is still used today in areas where small strips of land separated the water route. In areas where the natural waterways were more widely separated, it became necessary for the small vessels to use the open seas at considerable hazards to the boats, crew, and cargo. Under these conditions it was evident that improvement and interconnection of the natural waterway would be necessary in order to exploit fully the potential of these inland seas.

The history of the Inland Waterway's construction goes back to 1643, when private companies completed a canal from Ipswich Bay to Gloucester Bay in Massachusetts. Exactly 120 years later, in 1763, George Washington had a survey made for the projected Dismal Swamp Canal for the state of Virginia in an attempt to link the series of rivers, sounds, and canals lying along the Atlantic Coast. The Dismal Swamp Canal was opened in 1820.

As early as 1790, Congress passed legislation covering improvements for navigation under the power delegated by the Constitution "to regulate commerce with foreign nations and among the several states and with Indian tribes." In 1837 Congress authorized a survey from the southern end of the Dismal Swamp in North Carolina to Winyah Bay in South Carolina to determine whether it was feasible to open a coastal route between Chesapeake Bay and Charleston, South Carolina. No further action was taken until 1875, when another survey was made between Norfolk, Virginia, and the Cape Fear River in North Carolina. Some minor work was done in 1886, but the real work on the waterway began only in 1911 when a ten-foot canal was built between the Neuse River and Beaufort Inlet. In 1932 the long stretch of waterway was completed between Norfolk, Virginia, and Wilmington, North Carolina, at a cost of over $14,000,000. From these early, small, and scattered beginnings, steps toward the realization of a complete waterway network have followed.

THE PRESENT WATERWAY IN NORTH CAROLINA.

In developing North Carolina's great water-transportation potential, the state has received federal aid through the Army Corps of Engineers, which has improved over 1,250 miles of waterways for navigation since the project was initiated in 1928. Excluding the work of the State Ports Authority, which has helped in developing deep-water harbors at Wilmington, Morehead City, and Cape Lookout in recent years, about $26,320,000 has been spent through federal aid in North Carolina to further develop the state's water transportation.

There are two routes by which the Inland Waterway enters North Carolina from Virginia: the Dismal Swamp Canal route and the Albemarle and Chesapeake Canal route. The Albemarle and Chesapeake Canal route, a sea-level path through the coastal sounds and marine marshes, follows the natural waterways of the North Landing River and Currituck Sound and other land cuts into Albemarle Sound to an intersection at a point about eight miles south of Wade Point at the mouth of the Pasquotank River. From this point the Inland Waterway continues southward via the Alligator River and a twenty-two-mile land cut into the Pungo River, across Pamlico Sound, and thence by other land cuts to Beaufort, North Carolina.

This route provides for: (1) a waterway twelve feet deep with widths varying from 90 feet in land cuts to three hundred feet in open waters; (2) the construction, operation, and maintenance of suitable bridges; (3) a tidal lock in Snows Cut near the Cape Fear River; (4) a channel twelve feet deep and ninety feet wide in New River between the waterway and the Atlantic Coast Line railroad bridge at Jacksonville; (5) a side channel 12 feet deep and a turning basin at Swansboro; (6) an entrance channel six feet deep at New River; (7) six mooring basins at various locations along the waterway; (8) a fourteen-foot channel at Masonboro Inlet; and (9) salt-water-intrusion preventative measures and improvement of drainage in the vicinity of Fairfield.

The Dismal Swamp route enters North Carolina through the Dismal Swamp Canal and follows natural waterways southward to the point of intersection with the main waterway about eight miles south of Wade Point near the mouth of the Pasquotank River. From this point it follows a more southeasterly route through Croatan and Pamlico sounds to a point of mergence with the main intracoastal route. This waterway has a controlling depth of nine feet.

There is also a third alternate route branching from the sound route through Core Sound and thence to Beaufort, North Carolina.

From Beaufort the waterway follows a southern route approximately paralleling the Atlantic Ocean, entering the Cape Fear River via Snows Cut about thirteen miles below Wilmington. The waterway leaves the Cape Fear River at Southport and again follows sounds and marshes to a point about three miles south of Little River, where it enters South Carolina.

CONNECTING WATERWAYS FOR SHALLOW-DRAFT VESSELS.

Connecting with the main Intracoastal Waterway in North Carolina are many miles of navigable waterways which serve as feeding and distributing arteries for an extensive and growing commerce within the state. These arterial waterways have been developed principally by the United States Army Engineers within the past twenty-five years.

Among these projects which serve local areas is Knobbs Creek. This channel, completed in 1931 at a cost of $80,500, provides a waterway ten feet deep from that depth in the Pasquotank River to Elizabeth City. The average annual commerce for the 1947–51 period was 21,675 tons and the commerce in 1951 was about 22,000 tons. The chief commodities handled were logs and petroleum products.

The Army engineers have constructed a channel in the Meherrin River, extending from Murfreesboro to the Chowan River, for a distance of about 10.5 miles. This channel was completed in 1938 at a cost of $47,700. The average annual tonnage of commodities, principally petroleum and pulpwood, transported on this channel during the 1947–51 period totaled 12,400 tons. In 1951 commerce totaled about 7,900 tons.

The Cashie River project provides for clearance of logs, snags, and other obstructions, three cut-off channels in areas of sharp bends, and a turning basin at Windsor. These improvements were completed in 1939 at the cost of about $40,400. In 1951 there were 13,000 tons of pulpwood and petroleum products transported over this waterway.

One of the largest projects in developing inland navigation was completed on the Roanoke River in 1941 at a cost of $404,600. This channel, 131 miles long, was completed to Palmyra Landing, 50 miles below Weldon, which is the practical limit for providing improvement for navigation by channel improvement. The average annual water-borne traffic for the 1947–51 period was 326,000 tons, mostly wood and petroleum products. In 1951 commerce transported over the Cashie River system increased 67,000 tons over the previous four-year-period average.

The Scuppernong River consists of a shallow-draft channel from the mouth of the river in Bull Bay to Cherry, a total distance of about 20 miles. Commerce on this river averaged about 32,000 tons during the 1947–51 period. In 1951, 86,100 tons were transported, including over 57,000 tons of gravel for road work.

The Pamlico and Tar River project consists of a shallow-draft channel of varying depths from the twelve-foot mark in Pamlico Sound to Little Falls near Rocky Mount, a total distance of 97 miles. The project was completed in 1939 at a cost of $674,700. Logs and petroleum products were the chief products transported on these rivers in the 1947–51 period. Commerce in 1951 totaled 39,700 tons.

Improvement in the Bay River area provides for a twelve-foot channel in the river to Vandermere, North Carolina. The project was completed in 1939 at a cost of $44,400. The average annual commerce for the 1947–51 period was 4,400 tons—principally fish, shellfish, petroleum products, poles, and rafted logs.

Other minor connecting bodies of water include Mackay Creek, which transported 325 tons, principally pulpwood and fish in 1951; Stumpy Point Bay, which transported 438 tons of commerce in 1951, mostly seafood;

Drum Inlet, an opening between Core Sound and the Atlantic Ocean, which transported some 198 tons of seafood in 1951; and the Shallotte River, twenty miles west of the mouth of the Cape Fear River; with an average annual water-borne traffic in the 1947–51 period of 396 tons, mostly seafood.

There are several other smaller improved channels classified as connecting bodies of water, but in recent years water-borne traffic on these projects has been practically nil. Among the rivers and creeks in this category are Newbegun Creek, Fishing Creek, Contentnea Creek, Black River, and the Waccamaw River.

IMPORTANCE OF THE WATERWAYS.

In 1941, the last normal prewar year, over 3,700,000 tons of freight were transported on the waterway south of Norfolk. The principal commodities transported were: sand, rock, gravel, slag—692,592 tons; pulpwood—597,517 tons; gasoline, fuel oil, and other petroleum products—492,160 tons; lumber, crossties, and other unprocessed wood products—396,555 tons; logs, piling, and other unprocessed forest products—276,266 tons; and fertilizer and fertilizer materials, including fish so used—190,747 tons. Other miscellaneous commodities totaled 1,074,393 tons, among which were sugar, fish, oysters, coal, iron, steel, tobacco, and automobiles.

Water-borne commerce on the waterway in North Carolina totaled 873,063 tons in 1947. Commodities which exceeded 25,000 tons were fertilizers, pulpwood, logs, petroleum, marine products, and gravel.

In 1951 the Intracoastal Waterway in North Carolina carried a total of 1,396,565 tons of commerce. Timber products, petroleum products, sand and gravel, fertilizer products, menhaden, vegetable food products, automobiles, grain, soybeans, and chemicals were included. With the exception of seafood, most of the commerce transported was in bulk quantities.

In addition to the large commercial traffic, the Intracoastal Waterway has also benefited many small-craft owners. In the last several years, there has been a marked increase in the number of pleasure craft plying the waterway en route to Florida, and also making return trips north. The many sounds, bays, rivers, and basins located along the waterway make North Carolina waters ideal for recreational use from distant interior points as well as for boats based at coastal harbors. The state, recognizing the potential income from these waterway vacationists, has prepared a waterway map and guide especially for these tourists. The waterway also serves the important fishing industry along the coast. Many shrimp, menhaden, and other commercial fishing craft make use of the sheltered route the year around, especially during stormy weather.

THE FUTURE.

At the present there is a movement to abandon one of the alternate Intracoastal Waterway routes leading into North Carolina from Virginia. Army engineers are studying and soon will report on the cost of operation of the two North Carolina routes, and probably will suggest that one be abandoned.

Because of periodic closures of the Dismal Swamp Canal, many boatmen fear that this route will be shut down. (Closure of the canal is brought about by the failure of Lake Drummond to supply it with sufficient water in dry weather.) This matter is of more importance to the state than might be suspected because these two waterway routes handle over 3,000 pleasure craft and freight boats each year.

At this moment, with the combined aid of the national and state governments, efforts are being made further to utilize North Carolina's excellent system of waterways for recreation and commerce. It is hoped that the initiation of the inland harbor program and other programs essential to this development will accomplish, in the near future, a waterway system that will mean to eastern North Carolina what the Blue Ridge Parkway means to the mountain areas in terms of commerce and tourists.

BIBLIOGRAPHY

COOPER, MORELY. *Cruising to Florida.* New York: McGraw-Hill, 1946.

The Corps of Engineers in North Carolina. U. S. Engineer Department. Washington: U. S. Government Printing Office, 1949.

The Intracoastal Waterway. U. S. Army Corps of Engineers. Washington: U. S. Government Printing Office, 1951.

The Intracoastal Waterway. Part I, Atlantic Section. U. S. Engineer Department. Washington: U. S. Government Printing Office, 1948.

Water Resources Development. U. S. Engineer Department. Atlanta: 1953.

Chapter 19

INCOME, WEALTH, AND RELATED FACTORS

Reports on North Carolina's wealth and income have appeared periodically over the last forty years or so, but it is only recently that much concern has been exhibited in these matters. While the state ranks no lower today than it has for a number of years, in the last few years there has developed statewide interest in improving its economic situation, spearheaded by Governor Luther H. Hodges. A foundation administered by the state but maintained by private subscription has been created to lend money to small industries, and an organization called the Research Triangle has been set up to use the research resources of Duke University, the University of North Carolina at Chapel Hill, and the State College of Agriculture and Engineering at Raleigh on matters of state economy. A tract of some four thousand acres located between Nelson and Lowes' Grove has recently been acquired for the major activities of the Research Triangle. Many other groups are trying to promote industrial development and the general economic well being of the state.

The 1955 session of the legislature provided for the appointment of the Tax Study Commission, partly to see whether taxation was a deterrent to industrial development. The Commission reported on November 10, 1956. The following paragraphs dealing with the economic situation in the state are from that report:

Among the facts found were the following pertinent ones which have been publicized by the press: Per capita income is quite low; a large portion of existing jobs require relatively low skills; many individual proprietorships, businesses, industries, farms and other economic institutions are faced with high costs and unsatisfactory profit margins; there is large net emigration of residents to other states, which persons have been educated at the expense of this state; the number of farm units is high and the average size is small; there are large numbers of marginal farm units; there is a large rural population subsisting on such relatively poor economic units that twenty per cent of the farmers are supplementing their income by off-the-farm employment for more than one hundred days per year; many farmers need additional opportunities to supplement their incomes and many need full time employment in other occupations; and the distribution of the total North Carolina population is such that there is a relatively high percentage of school age population, which places great pressure on the General Fund expenditures for public schools, in relation to the proportion of the population in the age groups from which General Fund Revenue receipts may be normally anticipated.

Of course, the Commission found economic facts of which everyone is justly proud. For instance, North Carolina is a leading state in the growth of flue cured tobacco and in the manufacture of cigarettes, it is foremost in the manufacture of wood furniture, it is a leading producer of hosiery, it is outstanding in most facets of the textile industry and, above all, it is the home of a multitude of people who are eager for job opportunities to provide employment and a chance to upgrade their skills. Experience has proven the labor force to be adaptable to ready training and productivity records have been excellent.

It was found that our pride has lulled us into complacency, however, and the state has reached a point in its economic history where it must take stock of its economic potential or seriously impair its possibility for obtaining a larger share of the nation's income. In fact, the state's economy may easily become stagnant or regress from its present position. It was found that some of the apparent increase in the economic progress of North Carolina is due to the gradual inflation that has taken place in the nation with the amount of dollar increase in North Carolina being smaller than the dollar increase in the nation as a whole. In other words some of our so-called economic improvement may be illusory. Of course, there has been steady long range improvement in this state and in the nation which has been principally due to a gradual increase in productivity. The real increase in productivity has not been sufficient to generate the economic activities necessary properly to sustain the buying power of the citizenry of this state at a desirable level, nor has it been sufficient to provide the future base for producing the amount of General Fund Revenues which can reasonably be expected to be necessary to finance the basic functions of state government at the level of quality apparently desired.

North Carolina was a leader in the early industrialization movement in the South. It has been one of the first twelve industrial states in the nation for several decades. Its industrialization was built around the processing of locally produced agricultural products. These manufacturing enterprises and agricultural pursuits stimulated the development of the services, trades and professions. There is evidence that the generative effect of industrialization has not kept pace with the increase in our population. Conditions necessitating reduced acreage allotments of the principal cash farm crop, tobacco, have placed a ceiling on the agricultural segment. Over 200,000 North Carolinians have indicated their availability for employment were the opportunity available. There are many persons engaged in agriculture, business and industry whose productive potential is only partially utilized in productive pursuits either because of the highly seasonal nature of their endeavors or because of the lack of proper job opportunities. The rate of industrial growth has fallen behind the rate of growth in the other Southeastern States and behind the rate of growth in the nation as a whole.

The need for further industrialization is widely accepted, but, whether or not one desires the immigration of industry and the local development of industry, further growth in the industrial segment of our economy is an absolute necessity because in the process of economic evolution the development of industry precedes and stimulates the secondary development in the service, trade and professional sectors. The economic stimulus provided by industrial payrolls and the purchasing power of the business itself rapidly affects the marketing and distribution businesses. Our business, civic, and political leaders face a challenge to encourage proper industrialization. The additional investment of capital within our borders would provide job opportunities for the people and this in turn would result in the creation of a healthier economic base. Unless our human resources are used to a far greater extent we cannot hope to lift ourselves by a tug on our economic boot straps . . . .

The similarity of the economic plight of indigenous industry and the agricultural economy out of which it grew has been pointed out above. More job opportunities for members of the rural family are needed so that the farm income of the family unit may be better supplemented. In the farming business there is real need to attract capital investment to reduce the labor input and increase the income of the farmers. There is real need for a mutual understanding between agriculture, business and industry. The cost-price squeeze in North Carolina and in North Carolina industry is serious. The continuous acreage cuts in cash crops increases the need for further industrialization. There is an ever-increasing need for better utilization of land and labor through diversification and further additions of capital in the farming sector of our economy.[1]

These tables show the main facts about income in North Carolina for the most recent years available: Table 75 (Personal Income in North Carolina in 1955) shows the total amount of income and the breakdown between farm and nonfarm income. This table shows selected components of nonfarm income. Table 76 (Total and Per Capita Income for North Carolina, 1929–55) shows the total amount of income for each year; the total per capita income for each year; the percentage comparison of North Carolina's per capita income with the national average for each year; and the difference in dollars between North Carolina's average income and the average for the United States. This table shows that North Carolina's total income has increased from $603,000,000 in 1932 to $5,371,000,000 in 1955. The per capita income has risen from $187 in 1932 to $1,236 in 1955. In 1930 and 1931 North Carolina's per capita income was only 42.8 per cent of the average for the United States. This figure has gradually increased since that time. It has stood at around two-thirds the national average for the last several years. The difference in income per capita in dollars between North Carolina and the national average was $163 in 1933 and $611 in 1955. In other words, the average amount of income per capita for the nation was $611 above the average of $1,236 in North Carolina in 1955.

Table 77, Personal Income Data by States and Regions, 1955, shows the total income for the United States for each geographic region and for each state in each geographic region. This table also shows the per capita income of each state and region; the percentage increase in total personal income from 1929–55; and the percentage increase in per capita income from 1929–55. It will be observed that North Carolina's per capita income in 1955 was $1,236, as compared with the national average of $1,847. Its rank in per capita income was forty-fourth among the states. The percentage increase in the total income of North Carolina from 1929–55 was 413, as compared with a national increase of 254 per cent. This was due largely to the low base from which North Carolina started in 1929. During the same period it had a 270 per cent increase in per capita income as compared with the national average of 163 per cent.

Table 78, Rank of North Carolina in Income and Related Factors, shows basic data on population, income, and related factors. This table is

---

[1]*Report of the Tax Study Commission of North Carolina*, Commission for the Study of the Tax Structure of the State (Raleigh, 1956), pp. 3–4, 5.

self-explanatory and needs no comment, except to state that it throws considerable light on why North Carolina's rank is low.

There is a high correlation between income and retail sales. States rank about the same in income and retail trade. We do not have recent data showing the amount of income by counties. Table 79 does show the amount of taxable retail sales in each county, the nontaxable retail sales, and the total amount of retail trade for the period of June 30, 1955, to June 30, 1956. Incidentally, it will be observed that about two-thirds of North Carolina's retail sales are taxable and one-third are nontaxable. It is understood, of course, that much retail trade crosses county lines.

A number of studies have been made on income in North Carolina. Among these are: (1) Conference on Economic and Social Factors in the Development of North Carolina, prepared by the School of Business Administration and the Institute for Research in Social Science, University of North Carolina, Chapel Hill, April 5, 1956; and (2) A Study of Per Capita Income in North Carolina, prepared by an Interinstitutional Committee of North Carolina State College at Raleigh and the University of North Carolina at Chapel Hill.

The following is a summary of some facts about income in North Carolina from the second report mentioned above:

INCOME OF NORTH CAROLINA FARM PEOPLE.

The incomes of North Carolina families are low compared with the incomes of families in most other states. In 1950, median net money income of families in North Carolina was $2,121, putting the state number forty-one among the forty-eight. This average income broke down thus:

Nonfarm families, $2,471—rank 39

Farm families, $1,304—rank 40

North Carolina ranks second in the nation in the average number of *persons per family* (4.07). The ratio of persons in the family under 15 years and over 70 years of age to those from 20 to 64 years of age is greater than in nonfarm states and is also greater in North Carolina farm families than in the average farm family in the United States.

North Carolina has *more farm people* than any other state, and ranks second in the total number of farms. Therefore the relatively low per-farm income and the relatively large number of farms are responsible in a large measure for the low per-capita income in North Carolina.

The amount of all *farm land per worker* is small (18.9 acres), but in comparison with other states, the monetary productivity of land per acre in North Carolina is high (ranks seventh). An increase in amount of land per worker will not materially raise incomes of farm families unless additional capital is added to facilitate more effective land use. While capital per worker is low on North Carolina farms, the return which may be expected from additional investment in agriculture is high in comparison with the return received for capital in many other uses.

Farm incomes per family are relatively high in the areas with the largest industrial development. The number of farmers employed in off-farm work increased 40 per cent between 1940 and 1950. North Carolina ranks first among the states both in number and percentage of farm fe-males working in nonfarm employment and third in the number of farm males working in nonfarm employment.

Reduction in labor required per unit of farm production has improved per capita farm income in recent years. Yields of corn, tobacco, and most feed crops have almost doubled in the last twenty years. Livestock income has increased 554 per cent since 1940. Crop income increased 341 per cent during the same period. The production of livestock provides fuller em-ployment throughout the year and tends to distribute and stabilize income.

The gap between income per farm person in North Carolina and in the United States has increased over time. This has been due, in a very large measure, to the high concentration of human labor in the traditional pattern of farming in North Carolina and the low capital investment per farm. About 53 per cent of the realized gross income per farm accrues to the family as realized net income. This is a higher percentage than for any other state in the United States because the family constitutes a large part of the labor force used in producing North Carolina farm products; thus a relatively small part of the receipts is paid to persons off the farm and a large percentage remains with the farm family.

The relative position of North Carolina in average realized net income per farm improved sharply from $1,690 (thirty-eighth) in 1949 to $2,091 (thirtieth) in 1954. Only six states in the United States enjoyed a higher percentage increase in realized gross income per farm from 1949 to 1954 than North Carolina's 30 per cent increase.

THE INCOMES OF NONFARM PEOPLE IN NORTH CAROLINA.

About two-thirds (1,100,000) of the labor force in North Carolina are employed in nonagricultural activities. In 1954, North Carolina ranked tenth among the states in total number of persons employed in manufac-turing (443,100).

The earnings of workers in manufacturing in North Carolina are low relative to the earnings of workers in other states. In average weekly earn-ings per worker in manufacturing ($47.88), North Carolina placed last in 1954. This represents a decrease from thirtieth position in 1949. With an increase of only 20 per cent in average weekly earnings from 1949 to 1954, the state ranked forty-eighth.

REASONS FOR LOW INDUSTRIAL INCOMES.

Nonagricultural employment in North Carolina is principally in the textile, furniture, and tobacco manufacturing and in the service industries.

Except for tobacco, most of the major industries located in North Carolina have large numbers of small plants. The small size of plants encourages competition but tends to keep prices and profits low and employment unstable.

Much of the work in North Carolina industry requires little skill, and females constitute a high proportion of the employed labor force.

The value productivity per worker in North Carolina industries is lower than that for workers in similar industries in most other states. This low productivity may be due to differences in the kinds of products produced, to less productive labor, or to less efficient design and equipment of plants than is found in other states. From a long-time viewpoint, industrial development in North Carolina will expand at a relatively high rate only if firms located in the state can produce and sell their products for greater profits than firms located in other states. To increase wages, the productivity of industrial labor in North Carolina must equal or exceed that of labor in other states.

Most of the major industrial products produced in North Carolina—clothing, furniture, and tobacco—are regarded as necessities. Consumption of these commodities does not change much in response to changes in income. Rather, consumption is closely related to the population. These industries, therefore, will expand at a lower rate in the future than industries that produce commodities whose consumption increases greatly with increases in income.

In addition to an expansion in food processing and textile and furniture manufacturing, North Carolina should encourage expansion in the production of paper, chemicals, electrical equipment, and machine tools. Also, every effort should be made to encourage the development of atomic sources of power in North Carolina. The development and location of low-priced power may alter the industrial map for the entire nation.

WEALTH IN NORTH CAROLINA.

The United States Department of Commerce formerly reported on true wealth by states, but these reports have been discontinued since 1922. It does report on the total national wealth. The *Statistical Abstract of the United States* for 1956 shows true wealth and reproducible tangible assets for several years, ending 1952, and, with these figures from both sources, we can approximate the true wealth of North Carolina for the year 1952. Reproducible tangible assets average about 80 per cent of the national wealth. In 1952 the reproducible tangible assets amounted to $968,000,000,000. From this it is estimated that the national wealth of the United States was $1,210,000,000,000. Since there is almost perfect correlation between income and wealth, it is easy to approximate the true wealth of North Carolina. We know that the state's income was 1.77

per cent of the national total. Applying this percentage to the national total, we get slightly more than $21,000,000,000 of true wealth. Total wealth refers to all structures, such as residential, nonresidential, mining, farm, institutional, and government; all equipment and reproducible tangible assets, such as inventories of livestock, crops, nonfarm and public; monetary gold and silver; and all land, both private and public. From data in 1956 *Statistical Abstract* it is seen that the total national wealth averages about four times the personal income for any particular year. If we multiply North Carolina's 1955 income of $5,371,000,000 by four, we arrive at almost the same figure, $21,000,000,000 as North Carolina's true wealth in that year. Thus we get approximately the same figure from two different approaches, although for periods three years apart.

See Tables 80 through 82 for assessed valuation on taxable property for selected years and Table 83 for cogent social and economic facts about the state of North Carolina.

BIBLIOGRAPHY

Conference on Economic and Social Factors in the Development of North Carolina. Unpublished. School of Business Advimistration and Institute for Research in Social Science, University of North Carolina, Chapel Hill, 1956.

Report of the Tax Study Commission of the State of North Carolina. Commission for the Study of the Revenue Structure of the State. Raleigh, 1956.

Statistics of Taxation, 1956. North Carolina Department of Revenue, North Carolina Department of Tax Research, and the State Board of Assessments. Raleigh, 1956.

Studies of Per Capita Income in North Carolina. Report of an Interinstitutional Committee of North Carolina State College, Raleigh, and the University of North Carolina, Chapel Hill. Unpublished. March, 1956.

U. S. Department of Commerce. Office of Business Economics. *Survey of Current Business*, XXXVI (August, 1956,).

_____. Bureau of the Census. *Statistical Abstract of the United States*. Seventy-seventh ed. Washington, U. S. Government Printing Office, 1956.

Chapter 20

LIFE INSURANCE

History

In 1894 there were one hundred and eleven insurance companies licensed to do business in the state, twenty-five of which were life insurance companies. The only four companies to be incorporated by the state of North Carolina were all fire insurance companies, and none of them exist today: The Carolina Insurance Company, the North Carolina Home Insurance Company, the Pamlico Insurance and Banking Company, and the North Carolina Insurance Company.[1] With the turn of the century a number of new companies were organized. The big majority of these have enjoyed steady and consistent growth and are now recognized as among the leaders in this section of the country.[2]

Since 1899, with the establishment of the office of the state insurance commissioner, the insurance business has developed to enormous proportions in all fields, including life, fire, fire and calualty, marine, and others. Growth was evident before 1899, and the office of Commissioner of Insurance was set up to prevent policyholders from being taken in by unscrupulous companies. Since that time the worth of this office has been demonstrated time and again. Before 1899 the companies were subject to supervision by the secretary of state.

NORTH CAROLINA INSURANCE DEPARTMENT.

The North Carolina Insurance Department, organized in 1899, has been headed by six commissioners of insurance: James B. Young, 1899–1921; Stacey Wade, 1921–1927; Dan C. Boney, 1927–1942; William P. Hodges, 1942–1949; Waldo C. Cheek, June, 1949, to October, 1953; and Charles F. Gold, who began his term in November, 1953.

This department has general supervision of the operation of insurance companies and their agents; building and loan associations; electrical inspectors; inspection of buildings within the fire limits of towns and cities; the insuring of state property; and investigation of suspicious fires. The commissioner is elected by the people and serves for a period of four years. He is a member of the Council of State.

---

[1] "How Insurance Has Made its Growth in the State," *The State*, VIII (February 22, 1941), p. 17.
[2] *Ibid.*

The department is charged also with the duty of making periodic examinations of the companies themselves, of checking investments of insurance companies, of approving all policy forms used in the state, and of approving all rates charged the insurance-buying public with the exception of life insurance and certain marine coverages which are exempt from rate-regulatory laws.

All agents must be licensed by the department and are subject to penalties of law for violations of the statutes governing their conduct. In order to write insurance in North Carolina, all agents except those selling travel or credit policies and employed by common carriers and lending institutions must take the department's examination. Approximately 46,000 agents were issued licenses for the year 1950.

The Department of Insurance also has supervision of the licensing of nonresident brokers, collection agencies, and lightning-rod salesmen, and in addition it has the duty of inspecting all state-owned properties.

The statutes require the commissioner of insurance to examine each domestic company, association, or order doing business in the state once every three years. A great number of companies domiciled in other states are licensed to do business in North Carolina. It has for many years been the practice to conduct official examinations of such insurers in cooperation with supervisory officials of a representative number of states.[3]

In 1948 fourteen home life insurance companies were in existence in North Carolina, and seven new ones have been chartered since that date (the first figure refers to insurance in force in 1954, the second to business in North Carolina, 1956): (1) Jefferson Standard Life Insurance Company, Greensboro, 1907, $1,324,440,513, ($1,680,052,823 on September 30, 1957); North Carolina business in 1956 was $415,403,571. (2) Durham Life Insurance Company, 1906, $251,079,471; North Carolina business in 1956 was $98,381,190. (3) Pilot Life Insurance Company, Greensboro, 1903, $929,000,000; North Carolina business in 1956 was $207,748,892. (4) North Carolina Mutual Life Insurance Company, Durham, 1898, $205,000,000; North Carolina business in 1956 was $21,751,438. (5) Security Life and Trust Company, Winston-Salem, 1920, $531,830,274; North Carolina business in 1956 was $286,444,679. (6) Home Security Life Insurance Company, Durham, 1916, $182,305,177; North Carolina business in 1956 was $118,030,851. (7) Occidental Life Insurance Company, Raleigh (moved to Raleigh from New Mexico in 1926) $165,291,092; North Carolina business in 1956 was $99,316,837. (8) Imperial Life Insurance Company, Asheville, 1905, $146,163,839; North Carolina business

---

[3]Waldo Cheek, "Insurance in North Carolina," *North Carolina Almanac, 1951–1952* (Raleigh: Almanac Publishing Co., 1951), pp. 407–9.

in 1956 was $81,409,054. (9) State Capital Life Insurance Company, Raleigh, 1936, $220,877,009; North Carolina business in 1956 was $157,361,804. (10) Southern Life Insurance Company, Greensboro, 1927, $127,710,292; North Carolina business in 1956 was $41,781,363. (11) Pyramid Life Insurance Company, Charlotte, 1931, $197,405,528; North Carolina business in 1956 was $14,320,583. (12) Winston Mutual Life Insurance Company, Winston-Salem, 1906, $12,056,716; North Carolina business in 1956 was $2,116,897. (13) Coastal Plain Life Insurance Company, Rocky Mount, 1947, $11,711,277; North Carolina business in 1956 was $1,903,588. (14) Charlotte Liberty Mutual Insurance Company, Charlotte, 1926, no total figures available; North Carolina business in 1956 was $200,500. Recently chartered companies are the Allied Life Insurance Company, 1954, and the Central Insurance Company, 1955, both of Charlotte; the Life Insurance Company of North Carolina, 1955, of Kinston; Carolina Home Life Insurance Company, Sir Walter Raleigh, Skyland Life, Sturdivant Life, and Sentinel Life.

See Tables 84 through 86 for further figures on North Carolina's insurance enterprises.

AMOUNT OF INSURANCE IN FORCE.

Group insurance, which started some forth years ago, covers groups of employees of the same employer at a low premium rate. Group insurance in 1940 amounted to $89,768,870 written by nineteen companies. The 1948–1949 biennial report of North Carolina insurance shows that there was in force as of December 31, 1949, a total of 1,565 group policies amounting to $701,924,583. The total for all group companies on December 31, 1956, was $2,119,535,000. The ordinary business of North Carolina companies on that date totaled $1,556,003,986. Industrial business of North Carolina companies totaled $709,113,966. Industrial business in North Carolina by companies in other states was $580,463,551. Ordinary business by companies in other states was $2,596,771,274. Total life insurance in North Carolina on December 31, 1956, was $7,572,147,312.

North Carolina companies engaged in industrial and group insurance come nearer to dominating the industrial insurance field than do the straight life insurance companies. This form of insurance consists of small policies for industrial workers, with weekly or monthly premium collections at a somewhat higher rate. This type of insurance appeals to the many industrial workers and wage-earners in North Carolina.

The following data show the development of the life insurance business in North Carolina:

In 1909: On December 31, 1909, there were 193,534 life insurance policies in force in the state amounting to $147,783,155. Premiums received totaled $4,909,699. Losses were $1,540,704.

In 1918: On December 31, 1918, there were 837,661 policies in force in the state which amounted to $362,279,080, an increase in the amount of insurance of 145.1 per cent. In premiums $11,361,062 were received, or an increase of 131.4 per cent over the 1909 figures.

In 1923: The total amount of life insurance in force in North Carolina on December 31, 1923, was $752,567,659, an increase over 1918 of 107.7 per cent. The number representing this insurance was 1,302,607. During the year premiums received reached $25,771,685, an increase over 1918 of 126.8 per cent.

In 1931: There were in force in North Carolina 1,696,984 life policies amounting to $1,306,199,335 in value, an increase of 73.5 per cent over 1923 figures.

In 1941: Life insurance in force in North Carolina on December 31, 1941, totaled $1,815,114,155 as represented by 2,814,211 policies. This was an increase of 38.9 per cent over the 1931 figure. The premiums received amounted to $51,097,260, or an increase of 26.4 per cent.

In 1945: There was in force $2,414,926,703 of life insurance on December 31, 1945, which was represented by 3,517,240 policies. This was an increase of 33 per cent over the 1941 figures.

In 1951: There were approximately 5,400,000 policies in force in the state with total life insurance in force of $4,557,952,361. This was an increase over the 1945 figures of 88.7 per cent. There was $918,040,531 of new insurance during 1951.

In 1954: The fourteen companies listed previously had admitted assets of $702,000,000 and total insurance in force amounted to approximately $4,591,000,000.

In 1956: The total of all companies doing business in North Carolina was $7,572,147,312. The amount of new business written that year was $1,742,192,268, an all-time high.

Definite trends can be seen in the growth of life insurance. After World War I there were some lean years in the insurance business and also in the early thirties, when many policies lapsed or were cancelled. In those years it was the privilege of borrowing on life insurance that saved many people.

At the end of 1954 North Carolina ranked fifteenth in the total amount of life insurance in force in the forty-eight states and the District of Columbia. It had $6,048,000,000 of life insurance in force, or 1.80 per cent of the total of $333,719,000,000 in force in the United States. In 1954 it ranked thirtieth in the amount of insurance in force per family with $4,900 (see Table 87). In 1951 North Carolina had fourteen domestic legal-reserve life insurance companies in the state, with an estimated insurance in force of $3,060,000,000. The estimated assets of these companies at the end of 1951 was $560,000,000.

According to the Institute of Life Insurance, at the end of 1955 North Carolina families owned 6,560,000 life insurance policies providing $6,760,000,000 worth of protection. (The amount on December 31, 1956, was $7,572,794,535.) There were 1,364,000 ordinary-life policies worth $3,698,000,000. An additional $1,161,000,000 worth of protection was owned in 3,678,000 industrial policies, and another $1,516,000,000 was in 555,000 group insurance policies. Credit life insurance totaled $385,000,000 under 964,000 individual policies and certificates.

In 1956 North Carolina had benefit payments of $32,716,298 to beneficiaries holding life-accident and health policies; $6,673,151 to holders of miscellaneous accident and health policies; $87,053 from fraternal policies; and $13,631,137 from hospital association accident and health policies. The total of all benefit payments was $53,107,640. The total of premiums paid amounted to $81,670,567.[4]

Thus one begins to see that insurance is big business. This chapter does not include other lines of insurance which involve huge sums of premiums. For instance there are hundreds of thousands of persons carrying hospital and medical-care insurance. There are the public employees who carry retirement insurance with the state and federal governments. Space does not permit a full presentation on all areas of insurance. In the field of life insurance North Carolina companies have shown phenomenal growth and North Carolina now holds high rank in this area.

BIBLIOGRAPHY

CHEEK, WALDO. "Industry in North Carolina," *North Carolina Almanac, 1951–1952*. Raleigh: 1951. Pp. 407–9.

"How Insurance Made Its Growth in the State," *The State*, VIII (February 22, 1941), 17.

North Carolina Business of Life Insurance Companies, year ending December 31, 1956. Raleigh: North Carolina Department of Insurance.

Unique Manual of Life Insurance. Cincinnati, Ohio: National Underwriter Company, 1952.

---

[4]Annual Report of the North Carolina Department of Insurance, 1956.

Chapter 21

Banks and Building and Loan Associations

Banking

For some years after the Civil War the state of North Carolina was very short of cash. The federal government had compounded the problem by placing a 10 per cent tax on state bank circulation, and in 1866 the General Assembly passed legislation enabling such banks as were still operating to close their doors. Further, legislation was passed permitting banks to take as security for loans liens on crops before they were even planted and on the products of mines and manufacturing before they were even produced. This was the origin of the crop-lien system, designed to help the state through this period of emergency, but still the basis of finance for the cash crops of the bulk of farm tenants.[1]

Just after the Civil War there were but five banks with a total capital of $395,000 in North Carolina. Business was transacted through barter, and the standard of value was an honest day's work. The economy of the state was still so depressed that the panic of 1873 could not touch it, however the depression of '93 was a blow and it took several years to recover in bank deposits, lost through bad business and bank failures. By this time the number of banks had increased to 120 and total capital to $32,552,894.[2]

The years from 1900 to 1933 were unusually difficult ones for American banking. During the first part of this era, the American economy was called upon to adjust from a relatively complacent peacetime basis to the status of a military economy, highly geared to the requirements of World War I. After the war, with the extension of cotton and tobacco acreage and the expansion of the manufacturing facilities to fabricate these raw materials, there came the expansion of bank credit in this state to finance these operations. With the postwar building boom and its concurrent demands on the lumber and furniture industries, an expansion of bank credit occurred to facilitate both the construction operations and the resulting expansion of the furniture industry. With the overstimulation of real estate operations, bank credit found its way into these temporarily profitable activities. The postwar expansion of the manufacturing, construction, and furniture

---

[1] A. H. Fries, "Finance in North America," *The Wachovia*, XIX (December, 1926), 3–5.
[2] S. H. Hobbs, Jr., *North Carolina, Economic and Social* (Chapel Hill: University of North Carolina Press, 1930), p. 151.

industries is indicated by the rapid expansion of bank resources in this state.[3] "In 1914 the total assets of North Carolina banks were $153,114,438 or $64.90 per capita. By 1928 bank assets had increased to $534,047,000 which amounted to $184 per capita."[4]

It is hard to establish a picture of the average bank in North Carolina because of the diversity of the state. One bank may be serving a cotton section and another may be located in a tourist area; one may be located in a textile-manufacturing town while another may be situated in a city which is primarily distributive in nature.

The greatest growth of banks came during the period from 1914 to 1923, when the total bank resources of the state grew from $153,114,438 in 1914 to $474,117,609 in 1923. But it is the comparatively small increase in the number of banks that is the most favorable aspect of this growth; during this ten-year period the number of banks expanded only one-fifth, while the average volume of business done by each bank increased threefold.

The growth was not the result of any outside influence, for North Carolina is distinctly not a financial center, nor does she possess any great commercial or jobbing center. The character of her banking is predominantly domestic. That North Carolina was awakening during this period can be seen by the fact that the rate of its banking growth was more than double that of the nation's even though that banking was largely domestic, and accomplished with an unusually small amount of operating capital.[5]

Yet the volume of North Carolina still lagged behind that of many states during this period. It is a phenomenon that despite the dimensions of its industrial development, the amount of capital in the state remained small. What is true of Forsyth, the state's leading industrial county, is true of the state as a whole. At the time that Forsyth's factory products were more than $200,000,000 a year, its bank capital was less than $5,000,000. Its total bank capital accumulated in sixty years was less than the checks she issued for tobacco stamps alone every two weeks. Many of the largest accounts in North Carolina have been in Richmond banks and elsewhere outside the state.

In the early thirties there was a large decrease in the number of banks in North Carolina. Depression-era failures account primarily for this, although banking consolidations were also responsible for a portion of the decline. The period from January, 1921, to March, 1933, saw 316 bank

---

[3] *Trends in North Carolina Banking, 1927–1937* (Raleigh: Research Committee of the North Carolina Bankers' Association, 1938), p. 9.

[4] *Ibid.*

[5] *University of North Carolina News Letter*, XI (November 26, 1924).

closures in the state, involving $133,790,000 in deposits. While North Caroline's bank mortality rate was not the largest in the nation or even in the South, it was considerably above the average for the country as a whole and for the South as a region.[6] See Table 88 for figures on the state's banking failures in this period.

On March 15, 1933, President Roosevelt declared what was termed a "banking holiday," and on June 30, 1933, the banks of North Carolina had on call deposits of $188,215,443.47. The banks of the entire nation started the wheels rolling to improve the over-all banking system as well as their own individual institutions.

The North Carolina state banking structure has been improved and strengthened on a scale fully commensurate with the scale of improvements wrought in the national banking system. Its state banks were once the creatures of a vicious piece of legislation under which a bank could be established, if the town in which it was to be located did not exceed a certain population, with a capital stock of only $10,000. It could open its doors for business when one-half of that amount had been paid in. Even more serious was the lack of limitation on the number of such banks. Anyone could establish a bank by simply raising the necessary $5,000. Consequently, in many places, banking fell into the hands of incapable and at times designing persons, who brought disaster or near disaster to many communities. This has been changed and quite a different standard now prevails. Under existing law, $25,000 is the minimum capital required for a bank, no matter how small the town. An even more important factor is that the commissioner of banks is vested with the irrevocable power of chartering new banks. The commissioner conducts a careful investigation to find out whether the community in question is already adequately served with banking facilities. If he finds that another institution is not necessary for the public interest, the charter is not issued.[7]

After the debacle of 1929, in an attempt to protect bank depositors and restore confidence in the banking system, the Banking Act of 1933 set up the Federal Deposit Insurance Corporation. The plan provided for the federal government to make an initial contribution to a guarantee fund, the participating banks to carry any losses over and above this amount. The aim of the plan was to set up a temporary guarantee of funds of each depositor up to $2,500, and also to set up a permanent guarantee system.[8] Under the permanent plan all funds of each depositor up to $10,000 are

---

[6] *Trends in North Carolina Banking, 1927–1937*, p. 17.

[7] R. C. Lawrence, "Changes in Our Banking Law," *The State*, XIII (May 19, 1945), 9, 17.

[8] R. M. Hanes, "New Insurance Plan for Depositors Begins to Operate January 1," *The State*, I (December 30, 1933), 1.

covered in full. The participating banks contribute to the permanent fund equal to one-half of 1 per cent of their total deposit liabilities. If and when the funds provided by these subscriptions are exhausted through failures of banks, additional assessments will be made in order to replenish the funds of the corporation. There is no limit to either the number or frequency of such assessments.

All members of the Federal Reserve System, which included all national banks and about 10 per cent of the state banks of the country, were required to join the F.D.I.C.[9] In order to participate in the F.D.I.C., all state banks not already members of the Federal Reserve System were required to join it by July 1, 1936, later extended to 1937. This proviso no longer exists, and any bank may become a member of the F.D.I.C. simply by meeting its requirements, regardless of Federal Reserve affiliation.

By 1887 the General Assembly had recognized the duty of the state to supervise banks. In that year banks operating in North Carolina were required to make reports to the state treasurer at least twice a year, and some limited authority was given the state treasurer to make special examinations to determine a bank's solvency. The first consolidated statement of the banks of the state was made by the state treasurer in 1887 and the total resources were slightly more than $3,000,000. Nine years later the resources had increased to about $19,000,000.

The banking laws were amended at the sessions of 1889, 1891, and 1893, giving the state treasurer more authority in the supervision of banks. At the session of 1899, the Corporation Commission was created, and the supervision of banks was placed under its jurisdiction. In 1903 the legislature gave the Corporation Commission authority to make rules governing banks, provided such rules were not inconsistent with the banking law, and in 1907 supervision was slightly extended and definite fees were provided to cover the cost of examination. In 1903 authority was also given the Corporation Commission to create a department for bank examination. Very few additional supervisory powers were given from 1907 to 1921.

In 1921 the General Assembly passed the first comprehensive legislation concerning the supervision and examination of banks, including discretionary powers to refuse bank charters. It provided for the establishment of a Banking Department within the Corporation Commission and the appointment of a chief state bank examiner. Again in 1927 the General Assembly put through the Liquidation Act, which provided for the liquidation of all closed banks through the Corporation Commission. In 1931 banking legislation was revised so that the powers and duties and authority

---

[9] *Ibid.*, pp. 1, 26.

formerly held by the Corporation Commission passed to the newly created post of Commissioner of Banks. In addition the Advisory Committee was set up, to consist of the state treasurer, the attorney general, two bankers, and one businessman. The Advisory Committee was superseded in 1939 by the State Banking Commission, which consisted of the state treasurer and the attorney general as ex officio members (the state treasurer as chairman) and five members appointed by the governor, four of them bankers and one of them a businessman who was not an executive officer of any bank; the appointive members served terms of four years.[10]

Since the depression of the thirties, the number of banks in North Carolina had undergone relatively minor changes until 1950. In 1934 there were 215 commercial banks in the state. Through consolidations the number gradually decreased. In 1943 there were 195 banks. By 1948 the number had increased to 198; two more in 1949 and twenty-five in 1950 brought the total to 225. By December 31, 1953, the number had increased to 226 parent banks with 270 branches. Of the 226 parent banks, 180 were state banks and the remainder national banks. Of the branches, 37 were affiliates of national banks and 233 were affiliates of state banks. Commissioner of Banks W. W. Jones reports that on September 26, 1956, there were 167 state banks with 283 branches. The number of national banks has changed little.

Among the factors involved in the increase in the number of banks and branches were the tremendous increase in deposits, the growing congestion in business districts where the original banks were established, the increase and shifts in population, the wider use of banking facilities reflected by a significant increase in the number of accounts, and the rising production and income levels. The gross national product in 1934 was $64,900,000,000, as compared with $279,800,000,000 in 1950, while the national income was $48,600,000,000 and $235,600,000,000 in the respective years. Meanwhile the total assets of North Carolina banks rose from $335,184,479 to $2,430,800,554.79 on December 31, 1953, and to $2,631,670,093 by September, 1956.

The increase in the number of banks in North Carolina, and for the nation as well, has been of such minor proportions relative to the increase in deposits that the size of the banks has steadily increased. In 1934 only 62 of the 215 banks in this state had deposits of over a million dollars, while in 1950, after the sharp increase in number in that year, 188 of the 225 banks had deposits in excess of that figure. By 1954 over 200 of the banks had deposits of more than a million dollars.

---

[10]G. P. Hood, "State Bank Supervision Since 1887 in North Carolina," *North Carolina Employment Security Commission Quarterly*, VII (Winter, 1949), 11–12.

Because of the effects of war on the American economy, 1943 was an abnormal year. Total deposits in North Carolina banks in 1943 amounted to $1,113,781,350, which represented an increase of 17.5 per cent over 1942 and a 61.8 per cent increase over 1941. The rate of increase in deposits in this state in 1943 was below the national 18.6 per cent rate of increase. Thus, for the first time since the recovery from the depression, North Carolina's rate of increase lagged behind the national rate, though the difference was not great. By 1943 the tide of war production reached its peak and areas more fully devoted to the production of war materials, with the consquently higher income levels, experienced a more marked increase in bank deposits. In view of the wartime shifts in industry, employment, and income within the country, the attainment and maintenance of the 1943 level in North Carolina is a substantial achievement. Certain states, because of the nature of their economy, have experienced absolute decreases in the volume of their production as labor was drained to the centers of war production.[11]

Until recent years, the curse of the South has been a nagging, chronic lack of capital. The total bank deposits in North Carolina in 1900, for instance, were only $16,000,000. This lack of capital persisted until it developed some sizable banks of its own. Fifty years ago a North Carolinian seeking to borrow as much as $100,000 had to go, hat in hand, to the big banks of the North. Under the state law no bank can lend a single borrower an amount larger than 10 per cent of that bank's capital and surplus stock.[12] This is one of the major reasons why business in the past has been retarded in North Carolina, although today there are several banks which can lend up to $2,000,000 to a single borrower. Also, many times that amount is lent where several borrowers combine to bring some type of industry to the state.

To keep the record of soundness intact, bank management in the state has added to reserves and capital funds as the deposit level has moved upward. The capital funds of North Carolina banks were increased by nearly $8,000,000 in 1947. Over $6,500,000 was added in 1945 and nearly $9,000,000 in 1946, a total of $23,500,000 in that three-year period. Banks in North Carolina have used over 75 per cent of their total net earnings during these years to strengthen their capital structure. This is highly important to both the banker and the public because with loans increasing and the holdings of United States government bonds declining, the volume of risk assets is growing. Good banking practice demands that bank funds be protected as fully as possible by adequate reserves and capital funds.

---

[11] *Trends in North Carolina Banking, 1943, passim.*
[12] *Winston-Salem Journal and Sentinel* (N. C.), June 13, 1924.

Banking in North Carolina now occupies, along with the state's industry and agriculture, a position of leadership in the South and in the nation. As the state continues to progress economically and to develop its many resources and capacities, banking will have the opportunity to do an even better job of serving and helping individuals, business, and industry.[13]

Other factors in the progress of North Carolina banking include the North Carolina Bankers Association, formed July 24, 1897. Its main publication is the magazine *The Tar Heel Banker*. By 1950 every bank in North Carolina was a member of the state association as well as a member of the American Bankers Association.[14] Also North Carolina was the first state in the Union to establish banking conferences, in 1937. These conferences were in the form of summer schools, where bankers could meet and be instructed by national authorities on all phases of better banking. This movement has spread over the entire nation. In 1948 eighteen such conferences were held, with some states joining others in promoting joint conferences, as South Carolina did with North Carolina.[15]

North Carolina has the largest Negro bank in the world—the Mechanics and Farmers Bank, with headquarters in Durham and a branch in Raleigh. This bank also sends "students" to attend banking schools at our universities.

The total bonded indebtedness for the various governmental units were: (1) the state on December 31, 1953, $306,841,000.00 (net indebtedness, however, amounted to $253,735,000.00. At the 1953 dates of examination state banks owned $32,188,000.00 or 10.5 per cent of this indebtedness); cities and towns on June 30, 1953, $173,056,695.76 (of which at the 1953 examination state banks owned $28,522,563.87, or 16.5 per cent); counties and districts on June 30, 1953, $162,260,794.93 (of which state banks owned $31,639,771.86, or 19.5 per cent). The total bonded indebtedness shown for the cities, towns, counties, and districts is in gross figures, sinking-fund figures for these political subdivisions not being available.

See Tables 89 through 94 for figures on the state's banking facilities and resources.

Building and Loan Associations

The building and loan idea is strictly American—Benjamin Franklin is credited with this plan for assisting people to become home owners, and it is probably the best plan yet devised for promoting home ownership among urban people. Attempts have been made to apply the plan to farm

---

[13] *University of North Carolina News Letter*, XXXV (March 16, 1949).

[14] Hood, *op. cit.*, p. 9.

[15] *Ibid.*, p. 10.

and rural home ownership, but there are obvious faults. The North Carolina legislature in 1915 passed an act that would allow farmers to organize and operate building and loan associations, but none has ever been organized. The time period is too short for farmers, and the nature of farm income is not compatible with weekly or monthly payments.

The building and loan plan has been remarkably successful in North Carolina, especially since it is a rural state and building and loan associations are strictly for urbanites. In fact, North Carolina ranks far higher among the states in building-and-loan-association assets per capita than in bank resources per capita. Some years ago, officials of the Federal Housing Administration were wondering why North Carolinians made such little use of their facilities. The answer lay in well-established local building and loan associations. The federal building and loan associations, which operate along the same lines as state-chartered associations, have also been successful. Table 95 shows the growth of North Carolina building and loan associations since they were placed under the supervision of the state insurance department in 1905.

During the year 1956 there was a total of $144,029,110 lent by 148 associations on 37,164 mortgages. Total mortgages held at the end of 1955 amounted to $393,402,595, or 87.2 per cent of total assets. The period of most rapid growth has been since 1945. From that year to the end of 1956 assets have increased from around $102,000,000 to nearly $508,373,000. Mortgage loans were $56,779,000 greater in 1955 than in 1954 and $50,000,000 more in 1953 than in 1952.

At the end of 1954 seventeen associations with assets of $23,581,790 were still lending on the serial plan. Ninety-two of the then 146 associations had their shares insured by the Federal Savings and Loan Insurance Corporation. Two associations were paying dividends of 2 1/2 per cent; 118 were paying 3 per cent; and 24 were paying more than 3 per cent.

Federal savings and loan associations began operation in North Carolina in 1934. Total assets of Federal savings and loan associations at the end of 1956 amounted to $321,233,382. Table 96 shows the growth of these associations.

Building and loan associations have played a tremendous role in promoting urban home ownership in North Carolina. The state-chartered associations in 1956 made 15,711 loans amounting to around $90,500,000 for construction or purchase of homes. Some 1,969 refinancing loans and 15,700 loans for other purposes were made, making a total of nearly $139,490,000 in loans in 1956. Stocks retired during the year amounted to more than $72,876,000. Assets of federal associations are nearly two-thirds the total of state associations. If federal loans are in line with state loans, then a total of some 25,000 construction and purchase loans to build or buy houses were made in 1956. The building and loan associations have played, and will continue to play, a big role in the promotion of urban home ownership and as a means of convenient, systematic savings.

Bibliography

Annual Report of the Commissioner of Banks of the State of North Carolina for the Year Ending December 31, 1953. Raleigh: 1954.

Assets and Liabilities of All Operating Banks, by State, June 30, 1954. Federal Deposit Insurance Corporation, Division of Research and Statistics. Washington: U. S. Government Printing Office, 1954.

Biennial Report of the North Carolina Insurance Department for the Years Ending December 31, 1951 and 1952; 1953, 1954 and 1956. Raleigh.

Fries, F. H. "Finance in North Carolina," *Wachovia,* XIX (December, 1926), 3–5.

Hobbs, S. H., Jr. *North Carolina: Economic and Social.* Chapel Hill: University of North Carolina Press, 1930.

Hood, G. P. "State Bank Supervision since 1887 in North Carolina," *North Carolina Employment Security Quarterly,* VII (Winter 1949), 11–12.

Winston-Salem Journal and Sentinel (N. C.), June 13, 1954.

Lawrence, R. C. "Changes in Our Banking Law," *The State,* XIII (May 19, 1945), 9, 17.

Trends in North Carolina Banking, 1927–1937. Raleigh: Research Committee of the North Carolina Bankers Association, 1938.

Trends in North Carolina Banking, 1943. Raleigh: Research Committee of the North Carolina Bankers Association, 1943.

Trends in North Carolina Banking, 1950. Raleigh: Research Committee of the North Carolina Bankers Association, 1950.

University of North Carolina News Letter, XI (November 26, 1924); XXXV (March 16, 1949).

Chapter 22

STATE GOVERNMENT, THE EXECUTIVE BUDGET,
AND THE TAX STRUCTURE

Background and Constitution

HISTORY.

In 1663 and 1665 Charles II granted charters to several lords proprietor for a described territory in the area of America which in the beginning was called Carolina. These lords proprietor in 1669 adopted fundamental constitutions prepared by John Locke as a model for the government of Carolina. About forty years later the territory was divided into North Carolina and South Carolina, and shortly thereafter the lords proprietor sold their interest to the Crown and North Carolina became a royal colony.

At Halifax on April 12, 1776, a date commemorated on its present state flag, North Carolina resolved against the tyranny of Great Britain and instructed its delegates to vote for independence, and on December 18, 1776, it adopted its first constitution.

North Carolina's first permanent capital was at New Bern, and the first capitol building was Tryon's Palace, completed shortly before the adoption of the first constitution. When the permanent seat of government was moved to Raleigh, a new capitol was built which was destroyed by fire on June 21, 1831. It was replaced by the present State Capitol, completed in 1840. The constitution provides that the seat of government of the state of North Carolina shall remain in the city of Raleigh.

The original constitution of the state was a relatively simple document, being little more than a statement of principles. When North Carolina was forced to change its constitution following the Civil War, rather than amend or revise the constitution of 1776 as former conventions had done, the convention which convened in Raleigh on January 14, 1868, rewrote the entire document, giving North Carolina its second and present constitution. This, of course, has been substantially changed by the amending process. The constitution itself provides for two methods of amendment. It may be amended by a convention of delegates elected by the people for that specific purpose or by the General Assembly's enacting specific amendments to be effective when and if they are ratified by popular vote of the people. Amendments have been adopted which were drafted by a convention, and many have been adopted which were submitted by the General Assembly.

The government of North Carolina provides for a constitutional democracy. One of the most important fundamental principles written into the new constitution was the creation for the first time in the state's history of an effective system of separation of powers.

LEGISLATIVE DEPARTMENT.

The legislative department consists of two branches, the Senate and the House of Representatives. The Senate is composed of 50 members who are elected by the people from districts containing one or more counties. These districts are theoretically designated by the General Assembly at its first session after each census enumeration (which occurs every ten years) and contain, as nearly as possible, an equal number of inhabitants. At the present time there are 33 senatorial districts from which the 50 senators are elected. The districts must remain unaltered until another census enumeration and must consist of contiguous territory. Each member of the Senate must be at least 25 years of age. He must have been a resident of the state for two years and of his district for one year prior to his election. The Lieutenant Governor, who is elected by the people of the state at the same time the Governor is elected, presides over the Senate. Under the rules of that body, he appoints all standing committees, but he has no vote on any matter unless there is a tie vote among the senators who are present and voting. All other officers of the Senate are elected by the members, including the important position of Speaker *pro tempore*. Under the constitution this officer succeeds to the lieutenant governorship and then to the governorship in case of vacancies in first the one and then both offices.

The House of Representatives is composed of 120 members. They are elected from the respective 100 counties of the state. One must be elected from each county and two or more from the larger counties. Each member of the House of Representatives must be at least 21 years of age and must be a resident of the county from which he is chosen for at least one year prior to his election. The members of the House of Representatives elect their Speaker from their own membership and choose all their other officers.

The two branches are required to meet every two years in regular session. Since 1957 the time for assembling is the first Wednesday after the first Monday in February next after their elections. Each branch sits upon its own adjournment from day to day and prepares bills to be enacted into laws. The two branches may jointly adjourn until any future day or to any other place. The length of the session is not restricted. The members of both branches are elected for two-year terms which commence at the time of their elections. They receive a compensation of $15.00 per day for each day of the session for a period not exceeding 120 days. The compensation for the presiding officers is $20.00 per day. There are provisions for certain per diem allowances. Similar compensation is provided for extra sessions for a period not exceeding 25 days.

All bills and resolutions passed and enacted into law must be read three times in each branch and be ratified and signed by the two presiding officers on the same day. In all cases where a tax is levied or the faith and credit of a governmental unit is pledged, the bill must be read three times and on separate days in each branch, and the ayes and noes on the second and third reading must be recorded in the journal. The action of the two branches is final in that the Governor has no veto power.

Executive Department.

The executive department consists of the Governor, Lieutenant Governor, Secretary of State, Auditor, Treasurer, Superintendent of Public Instruction, Attorney General, Commissioner of Agriculture, Commissioner of Labor, and Commissioner of Insurance. Each of these is elected by the people of the state for four-year terms. Their terms begin on the January 1 following their elections. Their salaries, which cannot be increased or decreased during the term for which they were elected, are fixed by the General Assembly. Each may succeed himself, with the exception of the Governor and Lieutenant Governor. The qualifications for each office are the same as for members of the House of Representatives, with the exception of the Governor and Lieutenant Governor. A candidate for the governorship must be at least 34 years of age, a citizen of the United States for five years, and a resident of the state for two years before his election in order to be eligible. Neither the Governor nor the Lieutenant-Governor may be elected to two successive terms.

The supreme executive power of the state is vested in the Governor. He is sworn in either in the presence of both branches of the General Assembly or before any justice of the state supreme court. He is required to live at the seat of government and is charged with giving to the General Assembly information on the affairs of the state as well as those recommendations that he deems proper. He is head of the military power of the state and may use that power when necessary for the proper enforcement of the law and for the protection of the lives and property of the citizens. He may call the legislature in special session by and with advice of the Council of State. The Council of State consists of every elective officer in the state government who is an officer of the executive department, with the exceptions of the Lieutenant Governor and the Attorney General. The Attorney General is the legal adviser to the executive department. The Lieutenant Governor is the presiding officer of the Senate and upon the absence or incapacity of the Governor, or in case of a vacancy in that office, he succeeds to the office of Governor. All other officers of the executive department enumerated here have duties prescribed by law. If the office of any of the officers is vacated by death, resignation, or otherwise, it is the duty of the Governor to appoint another until the disability is removed or a successor is elected and qualified.

In addition to the officers designated in the constitution, the legislature has from time to time created many departments and agencies of the state government, prescribing their powers and duties, for example the new Department of Administration created by the 1957 legislature. The population of the state has constantly increased, nearly doubling itself every forty years. There has been a constant demand for increased governmental services. Departments and agencies have been established to provide them. Arranged alphabetically, these are: the Department of the Adjutant General, the Department of Administration, the State Board of Agriculture, the State Board of Alcoholic Control, the Department of Archives and History, the Art Gallery, the Banking Commission, the Commission for the Blind, the Budget Bureau, the Burial Association Commission, the Department of Conservation and Development, the Board of Correction and Training, the State Board of Education, the State Board of Elections, the Employment Security Commission, the State Board of Health, the State Highway and Public Works Commission, the Board of Higher Education, the State Hospitals Board of Control, the State Industrial Commission, the Insurance Department, the Bureau of Investigation, the Laboratory of Hygiene, the State Library, the Local Government Commission, the Medical Care Commission, the Department of Motor Vehicles, the Parole Commission, the Personnel Department, the Probation Commission, the Board of Public Buildings and Grounds, the Department of Public Welfare, the Division of Purchase and Contract, the Recreation Commission, the Department of Revenue, the Rural Electrification Authority, the Tax Research Department, the Teachers' and State Employees' Retirement System, the Utilities Commission, the North Carolina Veterans Commission, and the Wildlife Resources Commission. The Governor appoints these board, commission, and department heads in accordance with the provisions of the act by which the posts were created.

JUDICIAL DEPARTMENT.

The judicial department consists of a court for the trial of impeachment, a supreme court, superior courts, courts of justices of the peace, and such other courts inferior to the supreme court as may be established by law.

The Court of Impeachment is the Senate. Its jurisdiction and power as such is solely to remove from office persons disqualified by malfeasance holding office in the state. To do this, a concurrence of two-thirds of the senators present is required. The court is presided over by the Lieutenant Governor, except when the Governor is impeached. and in such event it is presided over by the Chief Justice of the Supreme Court. All charges for impeachment are presented and prosecuted by the House of Representatives.

The Supreme Court consists of a chief justice and six associate justices. Each is elected by the people of the state for a term of eight years. Their salaries, which can be increased but not decreased during the terms for which the respective justices were elected, are determined by the legislature. All sessions of the court are held in Raleigh, and all decisions are by a majority of the justices. It has original jurisdiction of all claims against the state and appellate jurisdiction of all cases coming up for review from the lower courts through the superior courts.

The General Assembly is authorized to divide the state into a number of judicial divisions with judicial districts consisting of counties. One or more superior court judges (who must be resident in that district) is elected for each district. The number of judges and their compensation is determined by the legislature. Elected judges hold office for a term of eight years. It is required that there be a superior court in each county at least twice in each year. Before March 2, 1955, the state was divided into two judicial divisions, eastern and western, with ten districts in the east and eleven in the west. There were twenty-one resident judges, or one for each district. The 1953 legislature had authorized the Governor to appoint as many as twelve special superior court judges-at-large and not assigned to any district; not all were appointed. On March 2, 1955, the legislature reconstructed the judicial districts and judicial manpower, the first major change in forty-two years. This act calls for thirty-two regular judges, all elected by the people. The lines of judicial districts were redrawn and the number increased from twenty-one to thirty. Most districts are composed of more than one county and are assigned one judge. Four counties— Wake, Durham, Forsyth, and Buncombe—are assigned one judge each. Two others—Guilford and Mecklenburg—have two judges each. In each district a solicitor or prosecuting attorney is elected for a term of four years to prosecute all cases in the Superior Court for the violation of the criminal law.

Justices of the peace are judicial officers who are elected by the people or appointed by the General Assembly or by the Governor at his pleasure. They have jurisdiction over civil actions founded on contracts in which the sum demanded does not exceed two hundred dollars and in which the title to real estate is not in controversy. They also have jurisdiction in all criminal matters arising within their counties where the punishment cannot exceed a fine of fifty dollars or imprisonment for 30 days. Mayors' courts in incorporated cities and towns have the same jurisdiction as justices of the peace. Recorders' courts are established in counties, cities, and localities under general law, and by special act of the legislature, either with or without a vote of the people, as may be required by law.

Services and Growth of State Government

Since the completion and occupancy of the present State Capitol in 1840, the population of North Carolina has grown from 753,409 to far beyond the 1950 census figures of 4,061,929. This growth is reflected also in the growth of North Carolina's government. In 1840 the Capitol housed the personnel of state government, numbering 75 employees. Today there are more than 70,000 employees in departments and institutions, including highway and prison personnel and teachers and public school employees paid by the state. With a state appropriation of around four hundred million dollars (not including federal aid expenditure for highways, public welfare, agriculture, etc.) annually for the biennium 1957–59, state government has become North Carolina's biggest business. The increase in population indicated above increased the demand for governmental services in the fields of health, education, roads and other communications, and general public welfare. This resulted in the creation of the numerous boards, commissions, and departments enumerated in this chapter under the head of the Executive department.

North Carolina was one of the first states to recognize *public education* as a primary responsibility of the state rather than of its subdivisions, and in 1931 it established uniform minimum standards wholly supported from state revenues. This universal standard is now a nine-months school term. The state-supported minimum elementary school term was attended the first month of 1956–1957 by approximately 1,043,000 pupils. There were 36,014 teachers and principals employed at that date, and in 1955 there were 3,190 school buildings, representing an appraised value of $480,000,000. North Carolina's school-bus fleet, numbering 7,502 buses serving 1,650 schools in 1956, is the world's largest. The number of school children transported is more than 489,000 daily and will soon be half a million.

North Carolina was the first state to incorporate all its principal *highways* into a state-supported and administered system. At the beginning of 1957 the system included some 70,000 miles. Of these, 10,968 miles of primary roads and 22,074 miles of secondary roads were paved. There were 22,360 bridges and other structures, none of which bore tolls: where traffic is heavy and no bridge is available, the state operates free ferries. Investing the proceeds of a $200,000,000 bond issue voted by the people in 1949, the state paved approximately 12,000 miles of secondary roads and stabilized 15,000 miles for all-weather travel, to set a road-building record for a four-year period.

Great progress has been made in *public health*. Established health departments in all counties work in cooperation with the State Board of Health, which is responsible to the public for the administration of laws governing sanitation and curbing the spread of contagious diseases, and, in addition, conducting vigorous educational campaigns against preventable illnesses. The North Carolina Medical Care Commission was created in 1945 and given the responsibility of administering federal funds made available through the Hill-Burton Act and state monies appropriated for a hospital survey and hospital construction. From July 1, 1947, through 1955, the commission has approved 127 projects in 73 counties of the state. Of these, there are 72 local general hospitals located in 60 counties; 23 county health centers; 24 nurses' homes; and 8 state-owned projects. These projects, when all are completed, will add 4,332 new local general-hospital beds and 627 new beds in state-owned hospitals—a total of 4,959 new beds for patients. In the number of new beds constructed under the Hill-Burton program, North Carolina ranks second only to Texas.

The state's *public-welfare program* embraces public assistance through old-age assistance, aid to dependent children, aid to the permanently and totally disabled, medical aid, and general assistance, which are important to large numbers of citizens. In April, 1957, the average monthly grant for old-age assistance was $34.39; the monthly case load was 51,689. For aid to dependent children, an average of $67.37 per family per month was spent to help 21,453 families, or 63,973 children. In April, 1957, the program for aid to the permanently and totally disabled helped 14,603 cases; the monthly grant averaged $38.81. Funds come largely from the federal government. General assistance and nonfinancial services, payments for which are less in only two or three states, are administered by the Department of Public Welfare. The welfare program is carried out uniformly in each county of the state. Services are available to any citizen who seeks them from a public agency. The over-all program is directed toward rehabilitative, protective, and preventive services and toward helping people to help themselves.

Outstanding among the services provided by the state for its inhabitants are the regulatory services rendered by such agencies as the Department of Agriculture, the Insurance Department, Banking Department, Utilities Commission, and others. And also the safety programs promulgated by the Department of Motor Vehicles, the Industrial Commission, and the Department of Labor are worthy of mention and commendation.

Reorganization

North Carolina is generally recognized as one of the most progressive southern states, but the state has greatly outgrown its administrative structure. There has been no extensive administrative reorganization since 1868. The present constitution has been called a patchwork of essentials, and students of state government point out that true correlation can be achieved only by calling a constitutional convention to draft a modern constitution after a thorough study of the present constitution and the work of each individual state agency has been made.

Such thorough studies recommending complete administrative reorganization and consolidation were made in 1921 and 1931. Very few of the recommendations resulting from these studies were adopted at the time, though several changes growing directly or indirectly out of that of 1931 have been put into effect by acts of the General Assembly. Among these are the creation of the Consolidated University of North Carolina, the uniting of all schools for delinquent minors under the Board of Correction and Training, and the placing of all institutions for the care of the mentally disordered under the control of a single Board of Hospitals.

Harriet L. Herring, member of the First and Second Commission on Reorganization of State Government, makes this statement about the need for a radical reorganization:

During the 1930's and 1940's government functions and agencies grew rapidly all over the country and in North Carolina, making reorganization even more urgent. The General Assembly of 1953 authorized a commission to study and make recommendations with respect to the reorganization of agencies of the executive branch of state government in the interest of economy and efficiency. Since it was not a full time body, this commission made no effort to cover the whole field of state administration, but concentrated in a few areas. Some of these were the abolition of several semi-dormant agencies, the classification of over-lapping authority among others, and the merging of still others.

While most of the Commission's recommendations were enacted into law by the 1955 General Assembly, there were many areas untouched. Therefore, that legislature authorized a second such commission which in turn considered other areas of state administration for classification and improvement by the 1957 General Assembly. The most important change recommended by the Second Commission was the creation of a Department of Administration. This involved the consolidation of the budget and purchasing functions and the addition of new duties concerned with inventorying and controlling state's real property, planning for capital improvements, over long range planning to meet economic and population changes. Administrative analysis was also authorized, thus making it possible to effect many changes as needed without every detail being the subject of legislative action. The 1957 General Assembly accepted these recommendations along with many others, such as requiring more public responsibility of occupational licensing boards, clarifying and simplifying the building codes and coordinating the work of agencies in the field of water resources.

This gradual, even piece meal, approach is no real substitute for a thoroughgoing reorganization and a new Constitution. But North Carolina, along with most of the other states, has found an overhauling extremely difficult to achieve. And pending more fundamental revision, this method seems to remedy some of the most pressing needs in the administrative field of the state's government.[1]

---

[1]Prepared for the author by Harriet Herring, member of the Commission on the Reorganization of State Government.

Equally as pressing is the need for change in some legislative practices, particularly as related to local legislation by the General Assembly.

Experts in the field indicate as a major weakness in the present system of state government the fact that more than half of the laws enacted by the General Assembly, frequently with only a few members present, are local laws, a time-consuming arrangement, which could be eliminated by provision in the constitution prohibiting the legislature from passing any local or special act in any case where a general law can be made available. A further provision expressly delegating authority to boards of county commissioners and governing bodies of cities to create offices and fix powers, duties, and compensation within their jurisdictions would eliminate the introduction and passage of hundreds of local bills during each session of the General Assembly.

Students of government have also pointed out that for many years there has been a definite trend towards a centralization of authority on the state level, that while it is often necessary that the state prescribe reasonable minimum standards, it is not necessary for so many matters affecting governmental units and the general citizenry to be decided on the state level. They recommended that thorough study of this entire problem, especially of administrative affairs, be made and necessary safeguards enacted to insure keeping the responsibilities of government closer to the people.

A constitutional provision listing and designating departments for the major purposes and functions of government other than those headed by elective officials, each of these major departments to have a single executive head appointed by the Governor to serve at his will, would eliminate the mushrooming of boards, commissions, and agencies, thereby eliminating the duplication in services and cost and definitely fixing executive authority and responsibility.

A major portion of administrative reorganization could be accomplished by legislative changes: after a proper study, inactive agencies could be abolished, many could be regrouped and consolidated where there are overlapping functions or where the public interest would be better protected. The reports of the commissions authorized in 1953 and 1955 are along this line. The constitutional commission authorized by the 1957 General Assembly holds out some hope for more thoroughgoing improvement.

The Executive Budget: Its Purpose and How It Functions[2]

The state's financial affairs are administered under Executive Budget Act, by which the governor is designated Director of the Budget, with

---

[2]Reproduced by permission of R. E. Giles from "The Budget: Blueprint of Government," *Popular Government*, XXI (November, 1954), 7–12; Budget data for 1955–57 are from *Budget of the State of North Carolina for the Biennium, 1955–1957*, Advisory Budget Commission (Raleigh, 1955).

broad powers and responsibilities in the preparation of a comprehensive budget of all state revenues and expenditures and in the exercise of budget control over all state agencies after appropriations have been made by the General Assembly. To provide for close cooperation between the executive and the legislative branches of state government, and for a common understanding of mutual problems, the Executive Budget Act also makes provision for an Advisory Budget Commission. The commission is composed of six members, the chairman of the Appropriation and Finance Committees of the House and the chairman of the Appropriations and Finance Committees of the Senate who served during the previous legislative session, and two appointees named by the governor.

The Budget Commission works closely with the governor and his staff in the Budget Bureau in preparing the biennial state budget. While, strictly speaking, the budget recommendations which will be presented to the General Assembly at the next biennium will be the recommendations of the governor, with the right of the Advisory Budget Commission to concur or dissent, as a matter of practice the budget planning is customarily the joint effort of the Governor and the Advisory Budget Commission, and is presented to the General Assembly as such.

North Carolina's state budget law was originally enacted in 1925. The previous year, in his campaign for the governorship, Angus W. McLean had made the adoption of a budget law a successful major issue. In his first budget message under the new law, Governor McLean had this to say:

The enactment of the Executive Budget Act committed the State Government to the business principles which have crystalized from the experience of private enterprises. It made the Governor, as ex officio Director of the Budget, responsible for the conduct of the State's business in the manner of any other executive charged with the management of the affairs of a concern in which there is a general interest and ownership. As Director of the Budget, the Governor represents the people, but in a more particular sense he is the fiscal agent of the General Assembly, to supervise and carry out the various projects and activities it has authorized . . . In this great enterprise of the State, the people are the stockholders, the members of the General Assembly their voting trustees, the Governor the Chief Executive Officer.[3]

STATE GOVERNMENT IN REVIEW.

Beginning in the month of June or earlier in every even-numbered year, there takes place throughout the whole of state government what might be described as a special and particular self-examination. Every agency and every division and subdivision within every agency reviews its past performance, takes measure of its present duties and obligations, and charts the course of future accomplishment. These reviews take the form of detailed reports on the year's past expenditures: for salaries and wages, for supplies

---

[3] Giles, *op. cit.*, p. 7.

and materials, for postage and telephone, for printing and binding, for motor-vehicle operations, for lights and water, for repairs and alterations, for insurance and bonding, for equipment, and for additions and improvements to state-owned buildings. The chart for the future takes the form of detailed appropriation requests and explanations for the coming biennium.

Continuing in July, the Advisory Budget Commission with officials from the Budget Bureau visits state institutions and agencies throughout North Carolina. They inspect at first hand the physical properties which belong to the state and meet and become acquainted with the state officials who manage the properties and give leadership to the programs of state activities set in motion by previous sessions of the General Assembly.

In September officials and personnel meet in Raleigh with the Governor and the Advisory Budget Commission to explain, emphasize, and justify their programs and aspirations—in short, to give an account of their stewardship of the state's affairs.

The consideration of the needs of worthy functions of state government and the weighing of the requested appropriations against the expected revenues continue until the General Assembly convenes in early February. During this period the future program for North Carolina's state government is charted by the governor, together with the six members of the Advisory Budget Commission.

State Government Appropriations

North Carolina's state government is operated on three major funds: (1) the General Fund, (2) the Highway Fund, and (3) the Agriculture Fund (revenue for the Agriculture Fund is derived from a fertilizer tax, from the sale of licenses, permits and test-farm produce; and from various miscellaneous fees).

The state's budget of actual appropriations from the General Fund for the 1957–59 biennium totals $546,877,806, and this amount is divided among eight major divisions: legislative, judicial, executive and administrative, educational institutions, charitable and correctional institutions, state aid and obligations, pensions, and public schools. The biennium appropriation to the Highway Fund for 1957–59 was $259,101,225. Additional funds for construction may come from bond issues and from federal appropriations: federal appropriations for the biennium are estimated at $136,149,992. The estimated biennium appropriation to the Agriculture Fund was $2,491,718.

Table 97 shows the 1957–59 consolidated biennium appropriations for the major broad areas of service and the expected revenues for the same period.

North Carolina Tax Structure[4]

During the past quarter century the nation's total tax bill, including federal, state and local taxes, has increased from about 11 per cent of the national income to more than 27 per cent. The greatest increase, however, has been in federal taxes, which climbed from 4 per cent of the national income in 1929 to almost 21 per cent, while state and local taxes remained at about 7 per cent. Thus the sheer weight of total taxes has added to the difficulties of state and local taxation.

The increases in state and local taxes have resulted principally from the response of state and local governments to the demands of the people for greatly expanded functions and services at the state and local level. Through a myriad of organizations nationwide in their scope, minimum standards have been established. Thus, for example, all the states in the southeast provide public schools, higher education, mental hospitals, public welfare programs, charitable and correctional institutions, highways, and the administration of government. In some jurisdictions those essential services are performed at the state level, while in others the responsibility rests largely upon the local government. Those services cost money, generally in proportion to their value, and the cost is about the same in all jurisdictions irrespective of the level of government at which they are furnished, so that we get from government just about what we pay for.

Regardless of all their fancy labels and technical terms, all taxes are levied basically on what you own, what you earn, what you spend, or what you do. Taxes on what you own may be levied against real property, tangible or intangible personal property, or the privilege of giving it away during your lifetime or at your death. Taxes on what you earn are imposed by the federal Government and by many states as income taxes. Taxes on what you spend are generally classified as consumer taxes and in part include retail-sales taxes, special-commodity taxes, and excise taxes. Privilege license, corporate franchise, and occupational taxes are a charge on engaging in a business or activity.

Consumer taxes have increased from $9,000,000 collected by North Carolina and Mississippi in 1933 to two and a half billion dollars collected by 31 states and the District of Columbia in 1954. Similarly during that same period the tax on tobacco products has been greatly extended and is now levied in forty-three states and the District of Columbia with annual revenues of about $469,000,000.

In states where consumer taxes constitute the major source of revenue requirements, the need for taxes from industry is accordingly diminished.

---

[4]The author is indebted to Eugene Shaw, North Carolina commissioner of revenue, for the discussion on tax structure.

This has been a significant development in North Carolina's tax structure during the past twenty-five years.

To the individual citizen taxation is the means by which he makes his contribution to his government, but to business management it has a somewhat different aspect. It must be considered a business expense and like other expenses of operating a business must be taken into account in determining the profit element. Many studies have been made and numerous papers have been written on the subject of comparative taxation. But the subject is a nebulous one and realistic comparisons are extremely difficult. The source material and statistical information accompanying such studies may be informative, but the results are generally inconclusive.

PROPERTY TAXES.

There are no state taxes in North Carolina on property except intangible personal property. Ad valorem taxes are levied and collected by cities and counties at the local level, and there is wide variation in the methods, policies, and practices of local governments in respect to ad valorem taxation. Historically the differences arose from the fact that the state has never supervised the original assessment of privately owned properties and has left that function to the local governments. However, varying fiscal needs of local governments has perpetuated them. In some instances there is a relatively high basis for assessed valuation with a low rate and in other instances a low basis of assessed valuation and a high rate. Just as the assessed valuations vary, so also do percentages of assessed valuations to sound value vary. In some counties the assessed valuation may be as low as 30 to 35 per cent of sound value while in others it may run as high as 80 to 85 per cent.

In North Carolina the state's responsibility for schools greatly reduces the requirements and rates in different localities. Thus business and industrial organizations have found their property tax burden relatively lighter in North Carolina than in other states.

INTANGIBLES TAX.

The intangibles tax in North Carolina is levied at a state level, but the entire amount collected is distributed to local governments. Here again the burden of property taxes is lightened.

The principal intangibles taxes are as follows: (1) a tax at the rate of 10 cents per $100 on cash or bank deposits; and (2) the intangible tax on accounts receivable and evidences of debt, which is 25 cents per $100 as of December 31 of each year.

SALES AND USE TAXES.

North Carolina is one of the thirty-one states levying a sales and use tax. This levy is favorable to industry. Building materials are taxable and hence sales taxes must be taken into account in computing cost of construction or repair of manufacturing plants. Industries are required to pay sales and use taxes on tangible personal property which is not a part of its mill machinery; however, under North Carolina law, mill machinery, mill-machinery parts, and accessories are subject only to the wholesale rate of tax. The long-established interpretation and administration of this provision has been quite liberal, and perhaps more so than any of the southeastern states.

FRANCHISE TAXES.

The franchise tax (along with income taxes the most important state levy to concern business management) is a tax imposed on a corporation for the privilege of continuing annually its corporate existence. In North Caroline the bases of franchise tax are as follows: (1) capital, surplus and undivided profits; (2) assessed valuation of real and tangible personal property in this state and net value of intangibles; (3) actual investment in tangible property in this state.

All eleven southeastern states levy a corporate franchise tax with varying bases and rates. The bases are generally related to the issued and outstanding capital stock, surplus and undivided profits, and borrowed capital; but in Virginia it is based upon the authorized capital. The rates applicable to these bases vary from 70 cents per thousand in Kentucky to $2.50 per thousand in Alabama. The North Carolina rate of $1.50 is about the average. The only material change in its franchise tax for many years was made in 1937 when the rate was reduced from $1.75 to $1.50.

INCOME TAXES.

North Carolina levies an income tax at the rate of 6 per cent annually on the net income of corporations. The tax on a domestic corporation is based upon the entire net income, whereas the tax on a foreign corporation doing business in the state is based upon a proportion of the entire net income as determined by certain allocation formulas. For the corporation organized under the laws of North Carolina or a foreign corporation whose activities are confined entirely to the state, the determination of the amount of net income to which the rate is applied is a relatively simple matter. The proportion of net income of a foreign corporation domesticated in the state and doing a multistate business must be determined according to the allocation formula applicable to the type of business in which such corporation is engaged.

North Carolina's rate of 6 per cent has been in effect for many years and may be considered relatively high, since federal income taxes are not deductible in determining net income; however, other states have increased their rates in recent years or have made changes otherwise affecting the stability of corporate income taxes. For example, South Carolina increased its rate from 4 per cent to 5 1/2 per cent in 1955. Georgia reduced its rate from 5 1/2 per cent to 4 per cent but increased the net tax by disallowing federal income taxes as a deduction. The rate in Virginia was increased to 5 per cent several years ago. Tennessee has a rate of 3.75 per cent. Florida is the only state in the Southeast that does not levy a tax on net income; however it is noted for its wide variety of consumer taxes.

There are no bargain counters in state government, and sadly deluded is the industry that is lured into the snare of tax immunities or preferential treatment. Well-managed industry recognizes that its best interests are served by stable, honest, and efficient government and by sound fiscal policy, and it does not protest at carrying its share of the financial burden. While taxation is an important factor in considering plant location, there are many others equally important: availability of labor, desirable plant sites, accessibility to markets; adequate supply of water power, natural gas or other available fuels; and other considerations peculiar to certain types of manufacturing.

Tax Study Commission Proposals. The General Assembly of 1955 created, and the governor in turn appointed, the nine-member Commission for the Study of the Revenue Structure of the state. The Commission made numerous proposals for statutory revisions to remove tax inequities and modernize the state's tax structure and administration, and to these proposals the administration gave vigorous support. In 1957 the Budget Revenue Bill (SB 7), in addition to its normal function of presenting the recommendations of the Director of the Budget and Advisory Budget Commission on state revenue requirements for the biennium and changes in the tax laws, also served as the vehicle for presentation to the General Assembly of the statutory changes recommended by the Tax Study Commission. Following are some of the major changes proposed by that Commission and effected by SB 7 as enacted (Chapter 1340).

Income tax: The method of determining the proportion of the net income of corporations taxable by North Carolina was revised to (1) limit the levy of tax to corporate net income reasonably attributable to operations in North Carolina; (2) provide that corporations manufacturing, producing, selling, or dealing in tangible personality are to use the arithmetic average of ratios of property, payrolls, and sales in allocating their income for taxation in North Carolina; (3) eliminate the distinction based on whether the corporate taxpayer's principal business in this state is manufacturing or selling; (4) redefine the "sales" and "property" factors, define the "payrolls" factor, and eliminate the "cost of manufacturing" ratio; and (5) make special provision for income allocation by common carriers and telephone and telegraph companies. The Revenue Act was modified to follow the federal Internal Revenue Code of 1954 on several points, including (1) non-recognition of capital gain on sale of residence if the proceeds are used in the purchase of another residence; (2) reporting of income from installment sales as received; (3) tax treatment of income from annuities and pensions; (4) exclusion from the employee's gross income of the value of food and lodging furnished him solely for the convenience of his employer; and (5) availability of the optional standard deduction to all taxpayers, regardless of sources of income. Several other modifications were made in the individual income tax laws to the general advantage of the taxpayer including (1) exclusion of Social Security benefits from gross income; (2) increasing the maximum deduction allowed for medical expenses from $2,500 to $5,000; (3) exclusion from the gross income of an employee of the amount of premiums paid by his employer for group insurance for the employee's benefit; (4) deduction of up to $800 expenses for the care of an institutionalized dependent of the taxpayer; and (5) the use of the short-form return by all taxpayers, irrespective of income sources.

Franchise tax: The method of determining the franchise tax payable by corporations manufacturing, producing, or selling tangible personality was revised to (1) provide for the allocation to North Carolina of that proportion of a corporation's capital stock, surplus, and undivided profits represented by the arithmetic average of property, payrolls, and sales ratios; (2) eliminate the distinction based on whether the corporate taxpayer's principal business activity in this state is manufacturing or selling; and (3) redefine the "sales" and "property" factors, define the new "payrolls" factor, and eliminate the "cost of manufacturing" ratio.

Intangible tax: The state is now required to distribute to the counties and municipalities under the existing formula 100 per cent (rather than 80 per cent) of the net collections from the intangible personal property tax.

Gift tax: The gift tax provisions were modified to permit an annual exclusion of $3,000 (formerly $1,000) in gifts to any one donee.

Banks: In order to equalize the state tax impact on state and national banks, an excise tax measured by 4 1/2 per cent of the entire net income of all banks (state and national) was substituted for the share tax, franchise tax, income tax, intangible tax, and local ad valorem personal property tax previously paid by banks.

Savings and loan associations: Savings and loan associations are relieved of the share tax and income tax, and are subjected instead to (1) a privilege tax of 6 cents per $100 of the capital stock liability of the association, and (2) an excise tax of 6 per cent on the net income of the association less dividends on outstanding capital stock.

Miscellaneous: Amendments adopted in the course of legislative consideration of SB 7 (1) exempted from the retail sales tax sales of parts and accessories for farm machinery; and sales of broadcasting equipment and parts to commercial radio and television stations; (2) reduced the franchise tax on bus companies; (3) reduced the license taxes on indoor and outdoor movie theaters; and (4) reduced the gross premiums tax on domestic life insurance companies.

Sales tax: One feature of SB 7 which was not a product of the Tax Study Commission was a complete rewriting of the sales tax article. Schedule E. As rewritten, the article (1) permits the use of sales and use tax proceeds for "other necessary uses and purposes," in addition to support of the public schools; (2) codifies much of existing administrative practice and regulations; (3) relieves the Commissioner of Revenue and the Attorney General from the duty of following existing administrative interpretations, policies, and practices not cofidied; and (4) requires the retailer to pay over to the state his total sales tax collections (less a 3 per cent compensatory discount), rather than 3 per cent of his gross taxable sales.[5]

See Tables 98 through 102 for figures on the state's tax system.

---

[5] *Popular Government*, XXIV (September, 1957), 11–12.

BIBLIOGRAPHY

Book of the States. Chicago: Council of State Governments, published biennially.

Budget of the State of North Carolina for the Biennium, 1953–55; 1955–57; 1957–59; Advisory Budget Commission. Raleigh.

CHEEK, R. S. *A Preliminary Study of Government Management in North Carolina.* Office of the Governor. Raleigh, 1950.

Facts and Figures on Government Finance, 1954–1955. New York: The Tax Foundation, 1955.

GILES, R. E. "The Budget: Blueprint of Government," *Popular Government,* XXI (November, 1954), 7–12.

Handbook of North Carolina State Agencies. Chapel Hill: Institute of Government, University of North Carolina, 1955.

North Carolina Manual, 1955. Office of the Secretary of the State. Raleigh.

RANKIN, ROBERT S. *The Government and Administration of North Carolina.* New York: Thomas Y. Crowell Co., 1950.

Report of the Tax Study Commission of the State of North Carolina. Commission for the Study of the Revenue Structure of the State. Raleigh: 1956.

U. S. Bureau of the Census. *Compendium of State Government Finances.* Washington: U. S. Government Printing Office, published annually.

WAGER, P. W. *North Carolina: The State and Its Government.* New York: Oxford Book Company, 1947.

Chapter 23

County Government[1]

Introduction

North Carolina, along with all other states except Rhode Island, is divided into counties. The number stands at an even hundred. The counties vary in area (1950) from 180 square miles in Chowan to 990 square miles in Sampson, in population from 5,048 in Tyrrell to 197,052 in Mecklenburg, and in taxable wealth (1955) from $3,779,000 in Clay to $577,997,000 in Forsyth. The average county has an area of 487 square miles, a population of about 44,000, and taxable wealth of about $62,000,000 in 1955.

There have been no new counties established since 1911, and it is doubtful that any more will be formed. A network of good highways and the widespread use of automobiles have so reduced the barriers of distance that the need for a courthouse every few miles no longer exists. In fact there are more counties now than the need justifies. In 1950 there were thirty-four counties without a census-size town, and in 1953 there were seventeen counties with less than $10,000,000 of assessed valuation. The ten poorest counties averaged $6,002,000 in assessed valuation, whereas the ten richest counties had an average of $273,419,000. The consolidation of certain contiguous counties would be in the interest of economy and improved governmental services, but tradition and local pride will deter any movement in that direction.

Politically, a county has a dual nature. It is a "body politic" and a "body corporate." In the exercise of most of its functions it is simply an agency of the state set up for the convenience of local administration. It is created by the legislature to whose control it is subject. In most states the constitution imposes certain limitations upon the legislature, but in North Carolina counties may be created, changed, or abolished at the will of the legislature. A county is a body corporate but it is not a true municipal corporation. It possesses only such corporate powers and delegated authority as the legislature may wish to confer, and such power and

---

[1]The author is indebted to Paul W. Wager, professor of Political Science at the University of North Carolina, for revising this chapter on county government. It is a revision of a similar chapter in S. H. Hobbs, Jr., *North Carolina: Economic and Social* (Chapel Hill: University of North Carolina Press, 1930).

authority must be exercised in the way and for the purpose that the legislature enacts.[2] However a county enjoys a certain measure of local auton-
omy. It chooses its own officers and in many respects determines its own
policies. It is a quasi-corporation: it has a corporate existence, but its
powers are less than those of a full municipal corporation; it may exercise
its corporate powers only in the furtherance of governmental functions.
Unlike municipal corporations, counties are not ordinarily liable to civil
suit for the manner in which they exercise, or fail to exercise, their corporate powers.[3]

As in many states, the North Carolina county serves as a district for
choosing representatives to the legislature. In the lower house (1957) 84
counties have one representative each, 12 have two each, and four have
three each. Single counties and combinations of counties make up the
senatorial districts, each being entitled to one or two senators. There are
33 districts electing a total of 50 representatives to the upper house. The
county has thus been recognized as a political community and has been
made, as far as is practicable, a unit of representation.

The county in North Carolina and throughout the South as a whole
is relatively more important than in those states where the township figures prominently in the scheme of local government. North Carolina has
townships, but they have little political significance. They were introduced into the Carolinas during the Reconstruction regime, and for a few
years a full township organization was maintained. But that scheme of
government was a foreign institution and was never popular. Most of its
features were overthrown within a few years. The unit itself has remained,
but it is now nothing more than a magisterial district and a voting precinct. There is a diminishing need for a political unit smaller than the
county, and states in which the township is still of some importance are
considering its abolishment.

The absence of a township organization in the South increases the
importance of the county. It has become the unit of administration in
public education, public health, public welfare, law enforcement, library
service, and other fields of activity. There is a strong sense of county
citizenship, and in many instances the county-seat town is the trade and
culture center of the county. On first Mondays, when the commissioners
meet, and on court days, hundreds of people assemble at the county seat.
Within recent years several North Carolina counties have built new courthouses, most of them rather pretentious. One poor mountain county
erected a courthouse largely of native marble, and several other rural counties have put up courthouses costing at least a quarter of a million dollars.

[2]Dare v. Currituck, 95 N. C. 158.
[3]White v. Commissioners, 90 N. C. 439.

This strong sense of county pride and loyalty indicates that the North Carolina county is more than a mere administrative district. It is a political community, and every representative who goes to the General Assembly attempts to secure legislation for his particular county. Hundreds of these public-local bills, so-called, are enacted at each session of the legislature. The fact that legislation dealing with a single county does not interest the representatives from other counties makes it possible for much mischievous law to be enacted. Important changes are made in the personnel or governmental structure of a county at the whim of the representative and often without the knowledge and support of its citizens. Even when supported by local sentiment, these public-local acts are often inimical to the progress of the state. Equally vicious has been the practice of getting one's county exempted from the provisions of general statutes. Local legislation figured so prominently in one session of the General Assembly that the governor reprimanded the legislators for being "county-minded" rather than "state-minded."

However obstructive a provincial attitude may be to state progress, county consciousness may be conducive to the development of a county and its institutions. The constant comparison of one county with another on every conceivable score introduces a wholesome kind of rivalry and often stimulates the backward counties to overcome their deficiencies. The North Carolina county is often far more than a political unit; it is a social and economic unit of real vitality. This is not true of all the counties of the state, but it is true of part of them, particularly those in which the county-seat town is the trade center for the whole county.

County Political Organization

The constitution makes provision for the election of the following county officers: sheriff, clerk of superior court, coroner, treasurer, register of deeds, surveyor, and board of commissioners.[4] But the amendment of 1875 authorized the General Assembly "to modify, change, or abrogate" the sections in which some of these officers are mentioned.[5] Only the court officers—sheriff, clerk of superior court, and coroner—may therefore be considered constitutional officers. The constitution provides that in each county a sheriff, coroner, and clerk of superior court shall be elected by the qualified voters for a term of four years. The constitution refers to justices of the peace and indicates their jurisdiction but leaves the manner of selection to the General Assembly. The treasurer, register of deeds, surveyor, and commissioners are statutory officers, and the offices may be

---

[4] *North Carolina Constitution*, art. 7, sec. 1, and art. 4, secs. 16, 24.
[5] *Ibid.*, art. 7, sec. 14.

abolished at the will of the legislature. The duties of even the constitutional officers are fixed by statute.

In addition to the officers mentioned above, there are other officials or boards created by statute for all counties or for particular counties. Every county has an appointed county board of education with three or five members, which in turn chooses a county superintendent of schools. Every county either constitutes or is embraced within a public-health district. If a single county constitutes a district, there is a county board of health, which normally consists of the chairman of the county board of commissioners, the county superintendent of schools, and the mayor of the county-seat town, who serve ex officio, and two practicing physicians and a dentist of the county, who are named by the ex officio members. In a few instances the composition of the board, by special acts of the legislature, departs from this pattern. In the health districts embracing two or more counties, the membership of the board is expanded to include the ex officio representatives from each of the member counties. The health officer is named by the board.

There is in each county a board of public welfare of three members. One is named by the county board of commissioners, one by the state Board of Public Welfare, and the third member by the other two. The superintendent of public welfare is named by this board from a list of eligibles who have qualified under the state merit system. The case workers and other members of the staff are also selected under the merit system.

All counties are required to have a juvenile court. Except for two or three counties which have an independent judge for this court, the clerk of the Superior Court serves in this capacity. Practically all except the very smallest counties have established at least one inferior court, called either a recorder's court or a general county court. Usually it has only criminal jurisdiction. There is no uniform method of selecting the judge and the prosecuting attorney, but most often it is by popular election.

County Officers

THE BOARD OF COUNTY COMMISSIONERS.

The governing body of the county is the board of commissioners, which represents the county in its corporate capacity and corresponds to the board of directors of a business corporation. In general, county boards in the United States are of two kinds: large boards composed of representatives from the townships, and small boards elected from the county at large or from districts into which the county has been divided. North Carolina has the small board, which is generally conceded to be the preferable type. There are usually three or five members, and in most counties they are chosen at large.

The county board is sometimes referred to as the legislative branch of county government, but actually it has very little legislative power. It has no police power; it has no ordinance-making power; it has no more than a degree of discretion in the exercise of those powers which are conferred upon the county by the state. It is like a legislative body in that it has the power to levy taxes, but unlike a legislative body in that it expends its own appropriations. The county is little more than an agency of the state, and the work of the commissioners is mainly that of administering those functions which the state imposes upon the county. Thus the board is better considered an administrative body rather than a legislative body.

Ordinarily the term of a commissioner is two years, though an increasing number of counties are operating under special acts which provide for longer terms and rotation. A vacancy on the board of commissioners is filled by appointment by the clerk of superior court. There is no standard scale of compensation, but most counties pay mileage and from five to eight dollars per diem. A few counties pay each member of the board a nominal salary, and several pay the chairman a full salary. The board meets regularly on the first Monday of each month, and there are usually several special or adjourned meetings in the course of a year.

The constitution declares that "it shall be the duty of the commissioners to exercise a general supervision and control of the penal and charitable institutions, schools, roads, bridges, levying of taxes and finances of the county, as may be prescribed by law."[6] There has been a tendency, however, to delegate some of their duties and responsibilities to special boards. Hence each county now has a board of education, a board of elections, a board of health, and a board of public welfare. The board of commissioners has thus come to be primarily a fiscal board with a residuum of administrative duties.

The fiscal powers of the board include the preparation of the annual budget, determination of the tax rate, appropriation of county funds, selection of a county depository, and the power to make contracts, audit claims, and incur indebtedness. These powers are subject, however, to many limitations, constitutional or statutory. The state not only names a large number of functions which the county must support by taxation, but limits the tax which a county may levy to pay for these services. For instance, the county is required to provide and maintain a courthouse and a set of officers, hold court, maintain a jail, assess and list taxable property, take care of dependents, and perform many other services. Yet the state constitution limits the tax which the county may impose on

---

[6] *Ibid.*, art. 7, sec. 2.

property to 20 cents on a valuation of $100, except when the tax is levied for a special purpose and with the special approval of the General Assembly, which may be done by special or general act. This limitation does not apply to the tax levied for the support of the public schools for the constitutional term nor to levies for debt service. Since no county could perform all the other functions required of it from the proceds of such a meager levy, the legislature has by special acts authorized every county in the state to impose other specific levies. In 1953 every county in the state imposed one or more special levies for such purposes as public health, public welfare, support of a hospital, support of a library, and a variety of other purposes. The countywide tax that year ranged from 68 cents on a hundred dollars' valuation in Davie County to $2.50 in Greene County, the mean rate being $1.30. It should be recognized, of course, that there is wide variation among counties in the ratio of assessed value to true value; hence the tax rate alone is no true measure of tax burden. A tax cannot be levied for purposes other than to meet necessary expenses, either within or in excess of the constitutional limitation, except by a vote of the people under special legislative authority. It is left to the courts to determine what are necessary expenses.

The constitution of the state sets up no debt limitation for counties. There are, however, two important limitations in respect to the incurrence of debt. First, as we have seen, no debt may be incurred for other than a necessary purpose without a favorable vote of the people. When the court has once held that courthouses, jails, schoolhouses, homes for the indigent, and the like are necessary to the functioning of county government the legitimacy of the purpose may be assumed to have been established; the court does not pass on the necessity of a particular debt in one of these approved categories. Only when it has been proposed to incur debt for what at the time was a new purpose, such as an airport or a library, has the court held that a referendum was necessary. Second, no county may, without the approval of the voters, contract debts during any fiscal year or an amount exceeding two-thirds of the amount by which the outstanding indebtedness of that particular county shall have been reduced during the preceding year. The restriction does not apply to funding or refunding bonds or to limited borrowing in anticipation of the collection of taxes.

In addition to these constitutional limitations on the incurring of debt, there are important statutory requirements or limitations. Thus there are specified purposes for which bonds may be issued. All bonds must be of the serial type, and they must be matured within the expected life of the improvement for which they were issued.

Another important responsibility of the board is that of getting the taxables on the tax rolls. Real property is reassessed quadrennially, or at least is supposed to be, and in an assessment year the commissioners are required to set up machinery for that work. A county tax supervisor is appointed, and he, usually with the advice and consent of the commissioners, appoints one or more assessors in each township to assess the property in their respective townships. The county supervisor has general oversight of the work and endeavors to get uniform standards applied. The commissioners may indeed provide for the assessing to be done on a countywide basis, and in recent years several counties have employed expert appraisers from outside the county for the purpose. After the assessors have completed their work the commissioners meet as a board of equalization and review to hear complaints and adjust inequalities. Legally they have no right to change valuations, except to correct errors, at any other time.

Since the commissioners act for the county in its corporate capacity, they have control over all county property. It is their duty to erect and keep in repair the necessary county buildings, to purchase equipment for the various offices and departments, to let contracts, employ labor, and transact business in the name of the county. They may be sued for breach of contract but not ordinarily for damages resulting from bad judgment or negligence on the part of an official or county employee. At least the courts have consistently held that the county is not subject to tort liability when engaged in governmental, as distinguished from proprietary, functions.

Until 1931 an important responsibility of the board was the construction and maintenance of the public roads, but in that year the state relieved the counties of this historic and increasingly costly function.

Another ancient function has been the care of the poor. This responsibility was met, in a measure, by giving one of two forms of aid. If the person or family in distress had a place to live, then a cash dole or a grocery order might suffice; this was known as "outdoor relief." If the person had no relatives or friends who could provide him shelter, he was committed to the county home. This was known as "indoor relief." Both types of aid are still administered, but "outdoor relief" is now handled by trained case workers under the oversight of the board of public welfare. The availability of old-age assistance and of pensions for the blind and disabled under the Social Security program has gone far in depopulating the county homes. In fact, only about half the counties still maintain them. In these counties the board of commissioners still is responsible for the upkeep of the property, though the care of the inmates is supervised by the personnel of the welfare department.

None of the other boards in the county has the tax-levying power; hence each must come to the county commissioners for an appropriation. This means that the county commissioners set the limit of expenditures for every division or activity of the county government except for the services mandatory for the county to perform for the state, such as holding court. There are times when the appropriation for such services may have to be exceeded.

Although the board of commissioners has numerous and important powers, it lacks certain powers necessary to make its will effective. Since the board is the representative and guardian of the county, this is a serious lack. Except in a limited way, the board cannot regulate or control the activities of the elective officers. It may request reports from them, but it cannot compel them to comply. Even though there may be co-operation through courtesy, there is no real coordination. Each office is a separate entity and occupies the same status politically as the board itself. The commissioners are only nominally the head of the county. Only over their own appointees can they exert real control. With numerous elective officers, and fortunately they are not as numerous in North Carolina as in some states, it is impossible to fix responsibility.

An even greater weakness in county government has been the lack of an executive agent to act for the board when it is not in session. To overcome this deficiency a few counties have provided for the appointment of a county manager. In other counties the county auditor, or county accountant, as he is now called, has been granted a considerable degree of administrative authority and has become a key figure in county administration.

REGISTER OF DEEDS.

There is in each county a register of deeds elected by popular vote for a four-year term. His principal duty is to record all instruments delivered to him for registration after they have been probated by the clerk of superior court. Such instruments include deeds, mortgages, deeds of trust, liens, and other business contracts. In some counties the register of deeds acts as clerk to the board of county commissioners. In this capacity he rarely does more than perform such routine duties as writing up the minutes of the board meetings. His clerical duties at one time included the preparation of the tax roll, and that work is still done by the register of deeds in several counties. There is a tendency, however, to delegate this work to the tax supervisor or the county accountant. Finally, his duties include that of issuing marriage licenses.

CLERK OF SUPERIOR COURT.

The clerk of superior court is elected for a term of four years. In case of a vacancy the office is filled by the judge of the superior court. The duties of the clerk may be divided into three classes: first, those which he performs as an officer of the superior court; second, those which he performs as an independent judge; and third, various clerical duties which are in no way connected with court.[7]

As the secretarial officer of the superior court, he must be in regular attendance to issue writs, swear witnesses and jurors, assemble and assume custody of all papers connected with each case, keep a record of the court proceedings, and make out the bills of cost. Between terms of court he represents the court, which gives him jurisdiction to hear and decide all questions of practice and procedure, to enforce the orders of the court, and to render certain kinds of judgment. Practically all cases tried in the superior court are begun and ended by the clerk, who issues the original summons and the final execution.

In North Carolina the clerk of superior court is also judge of probate, in which capacity he is not a part of the superior court but an independent tribunal of original jurisdiction, and is called upon to approve or acknowledge all instruments for registry in the office of the register of deeds. He also has many duties in connection with the settlement of estates, such as to grant or revoke letters testamentary and of administration; to appoint and remove guardians; to audit the inventories, accounts, and final settlements of administrators, executors, and commissioners; and occasionally to act as trustee of an estate himself. He is responsible for the investment and safekeeping of fiduciary funds left in his hands. The clerk is also judge of special proceedings, that is, cases brought into court for settlement which do not involve a suit. Proceedings for dower, partition, and widow's allowance are examples of this kind of case. Finally, except in a few cases, the clerk is judge of the juvenile court.

Of his miscellaneous duties only a few need be mentioned. He issues commissions to justices of the peace and notaries public; issues hunters' licenses; commits convicted criminals to the penitentiary; assists in the examination of persons alleged to be insane; serves on the county board of pensions; and keeps a great variety of records. The clerk is usually a man of considerable ability, and there has been a tendency for the state to impose more and more duties upon him.

If there is an inferior court in the county, the clerk of superior court is often made the clerk of this lower court also.

Formerly it was the custom for the register of deeds and the clerk of superior court to be compensated with the fees of their offices, and a few counties may still adhere to this practice. Most counties, however, pay salaries to the incumbents of these offices.

---

[7]P. W. Wager, *County Government and Administration in North Carolina* (Chapel Hill: University of North Carolina Press, 1928), pp. 247–53.

COUNTY TREASURER.

Formerly every county had an elective county treasurer. In 1913 an act was passed by the General Assembly authorizing the board of commissioners in twenty or more counties to abolish at their discretion the office of county treasurer and appoint in lieu thereof one or more solvent banks or trust companies.[8] Since that date many other counties have secured special acts permitting them to take the same step. Now there are more than forty counties in which banks act as financial agents. Since the counties are now required to have a competent county accountant, there is little need for a treasurer. In 1927 the legislature authorized the county commissioners to designate some bank or banks as the official depository of the county funds even where there is a treasurer, and this is now the universal practice.[9]

SHERIFF.

The sheriff has always been a very important officer in North Carolina, usually enjoying more prestige than other officials. Not infrequently the position is gained and held because of political influence. The sheriff has been popularly elected since 1829, longer than any other county officer. He is practically independent of the county commissioners but may be removed for cause by the judge of the superior court. He is quite as much a state officer as a county officer.

The sheriff in this state has three types of duties. (1) He is the ministerial officer of the court and as such summons jurors and witnesses, serves warrants, opens and closes court, delivers prisoners to and from the courtroom, and preforms other related services. If there is an inferior court in the county, he and his deputies perform similar functions for it. (2) The sheriff is the principal peace officer of the county, and the maintenance of law and order is in his hands. He may make an arrest with or without a warrant and in making an arrest may use as much force as is necessary. In order to apprehend and capture felons, he may summon the *posse comitatus*, or power of the county, to his aid. In times of riot or serious disorder, he may call on the governor of the state for militia. The sheriff is not always an efficient police officer, both because he lacks the training to combat professional crime and because he is too prone to measure political effect to be aggressive in law enforcement when local people are involved. (3) The sheriff has the care and custody of the jail, and either appoints the jailer or serves himself. It is his responsibility to see that persons confined are secure from danger and reasonably comfortable. If a

---

[8] *Public Laws of the State of North Carolina*, 1913, chap. 142, and of the Extra Session, 1913, chap. 35.
[9] *Public Laws*, 1927, chap. 146, sec. 19.

prisoner escapes, the burden of proof rests upon the officer to show that the escape was not due to consent or negligence.

CORONER.

Like most other states, North Carolina still elects a coroner in each county, though the office could be dospensed with. The main function of the coroner is to investigate deaths which have occurred under unusual or mysterious circumstances, and, is it appears that there has been foul play, to conduct an inquest. This function could very well be preformed by the county physician or the county health officer, or even better, attached to the solicitor's office. Under the Medical Examiner Act which went into effect January 1, 1956, a county may retain the old coroner system or adopt the new plan; under the new plan a medical examiner may be appointed to act where medical knowledge is needed. He must be a physician. The office is not abolished. The only other duty of the coroner is to serve as sheriff when there is no sheriff or when the sheriff is disqualified by reason of the fact that he is a party to a proceeding in the court. If the office were abolished, the court could appoint a sheriff to act in such emergencies.

SURVEYOR.

The county surveyor is an officer of waning importance. Originally such an officer was chosen to survey lands that were transferred from the public domain to private ownership. Occasionally he was called upon to determine the boundaries of lands involved in a suit in court. The office is a relic of the past and might well be abolished. As a matter of fact there is often no candidate for the office.

Several county offices have developed in recent years which are more important than some of the long-established ones. Some of these are discussed in other chapters specifically treating the activities connected with these offices (e.g., school, health, and welfare officers) and will be but mentioned here.

AUDITOR.

Perhaps the most important officer in the county is the county accountant, or auditor. Since 1927 it has been mandatory for every county to have such an officer to serve as bookkeeper and budget officer. Since he is appointed for professional competence and the same person often continues in office for many years, the commissioners have tended to add constantly to his duties and responsibilities. Often he is tax supervisor, purchasing agent, and clerk to the board. In numerous counties his office has become almost that of a county manager, and in a half-dozen counties he is so designated. However, in Guilford County there is a county manager in addition to the county accountant.

COUNTY AGENT.

To promote better agricultural practices and to serve as a transmitter and interpreter of national and state agricultural services there has been established in each county the office of county agent. In most counties the work has so expanded that there is also an assistant agent and often a Negro agent, the latter to work exclusively among Negro farmers. Duplicating this staff of agricultural specialists to aid the farmers is a staff of women trained in home economics to aid and instruct the farm women. Thus there is in each county a home demonstrator, who may have both white and colored assistants. These men and women constitute a part of the Agricultural Extension Service of the State Agricultural College and the United States Department of Agriculture. Although they are considered county officers or employees, their salaries are paid jointly from federal, state, and local sources.

BOARD OF ELECTIONS.

Finally, the roster of county officials includes a county board of elections with three members, two from the majority party and one from the minority party. They are appointed by the state board of elections. This board is responsible for the establishment of election precincts, the appointment of registrars and judges, the issuance of certificates of elections, and other matters incident to honest and orderly elections. The members are paid per diem for the few days of work demanded.

Fiscal Administration

The efficiency of any business organization is dependent in a large measure upon unity in fiscal control; yet the business of the county, though grown to large proportions, has lacked this essential element. School boards and road boards formerly spent huge sums of money without detailed accounting to the board of commissioners. Frequently they spent far in excess of their appropriations, with the result that the commissioners had to issue bonds to cover the deficits. Moreover, serious deficits developed in the accounts over which the commissioners had immediate control.

The General Assembly of 1927 enacted legislation designed to improve the accounting systems and financial practices of the counties. The County Fiscal Control Act[10] may be summarized as follows: The commissioners of each county are required to appoint "some person of honesty and ability," who is experienced in modern methods of accounting, as county accountant. The duties of the accountant are to keep the financial records of the county, examine the accounts of each courthouse officer regularly, prepare the financial statements, and assist in the preparation of the budget. The act requires that every county operate on a budget basis,

---

[10] *Ibid.*, chap. 146.

and that no contract or agreement requiring the payment of money, or requisition for supplies or materials, be valid unless endorsed by the county accountant as follows: "Provision for the payment of the moneys to fall due under this agreement has been made by appropriation or by bonds or notes duly authorized." All claims must be presented to and approved by the county accountant, or by the board, in the event of his disapprobation, by entering on its minutes the reason therefor.

A companion act, known as the County Finance Act,[11] was designed to safeguard county credit by restricting the extent to which and the purpose for which debts may be incurred. A county is permitted to borrow for ordinary expenses in anticipation of taxes or other unrealized revenue of the current year up to 80 per cent of the amount of such uncollected revenue, provided such loan is repaid not later than 30 days after the close of the fiscal year. A county may borrow in anticipation of the receipt of the proceeds of a bond issue up to the amount of the issue, provided such loans are made payable within three years. Counties may issue bonds for any one of the purposes mentioned in the law provided they are serial bonds, the first installment of which is payable within three years after the date of issue, and provided they are entirely retired during the probable lifetime of the improvement for which they were issued. Funding bonds must mature within fifteen years and refunding bonds within twenty years.

Another provision of the Finance Act requires that all bonds issued under the provisions of the act be submitted to a vote of the people if as many as 15 per cent of the qualified voters request it. The act also sets up debt limitations. For school purposes the indebtedness must not exceed 5 per cent of the property valuation unless it was in excess of 4 per cent at the time the act was ratified, in which case the limit becomes 7 per cent. When a county assumes all local school indebtedness, the maximum becomes 8 per cent. For other than school purposes, the limits are also set at 5 and 7 per cent. These limitations do not apply to funding or refunding bonds.

The Local Government Commission was created in 1931 to establish further protection for the credit of the counties.[12] This state agency, unique to North Carolina, restrains the cities and counties from incurring debt unwisely but, when borrowing is justified, helps them to float their loans on favorable terms. No unit of local government may incur debt without first seeking the approval of the Local Government Commission. If this agency withholds its approval, then the note or bond may be floated

---

[11] *Ibid.*, chap. 81.
[12] *Public Laws*, 1931, chap. 202.

only after a favorable vote has been obtained in a popular referendum. If the commission gives its approval, it aids the local unit by advertising and selling the issue for it. Moreover, it requires the unit to submit each year for its approval the budget which the unit has set up for debt service, and approval will not be given unless the budget is adequate to meet all interest and principal payments that will fall due in that fiscal year. This virtual guarantee by a state agency that there will be no default makes it possible for local units to float their loans on very favorable terms.

New legislation has been enacted in the interest of better tax collecting. Except in possibly half a dozen counties, tax collection has been taken from the sheriff and placed in the hands of a separate tax collector. Sale of the tax lien for delinquency is held more promptly than formerly, and if the tax is still not paid. the tax-sale certificate may, after a few months, be foreclosed like a mortgage. While this last step is not taken as often or as promptly as might be, at least an effective procedure for forcing payment is available.

These tighter fiscal controls, imposed a quarter of a century ago, were prompted not only by the loose practices which prevailed but by the mounting debt that accompanied that road- and school-building era despite heavy taxes. In 1927 county and district taxes, including school taxes, amounted to over $45,000,000. Even so, the tax levies were not keeping up with expenditures, and on June 30, 1928, the counties of the state had a bonded indebtedness of $128,000,000. When the state took over the secondary roads in 1931 and most of the operating cost of the schools in 1933, the counties were able to reduce current expenditures and apply a considerable portion of their tax levies to the reduction of their debts. They could do this even with a lower tax rate. Gradually, however, the cost of county government has been creeping up again, not only because of the reduced purchasing power of the dollar but also because of more liberal expenditures for schools, libraries, welfare, health, and agricultural services. In 1955–56 the counties levied taxes to the amount of $32,402,000 for schools and $34,807,000 for other purposes. In thirty-eight counties in 1953–54 the tax rate for schools, despite the contributions from the state, exceeded the combined rate for all other purposes. Since World War II, the counties have found it also necessary to borrow heavily for capital improvements, mainly school buildings, until their indebtedness now has reached an all-time high. On June 30, 1954, the bonded debt of the counties was $171,268,000, and there was an additional district indebtedness of $9,988,000. The sheer size of the fiscal operations fully warrants all the controls that have been imposed.

New and Expanded Functions

It has been noted that the expenditures of county government have been mounting rapidly in recent years. While part of the increase can of course be attributed to a growing population, the principal explanation is to be found in new and expanded functions. Lately the increases have been tapering off.

Although the state has borne the minimum operating costs of the *public schools* since 1933, the funds provided by the state are never sufficient to meet fully all the current expense items which they are presumed to cover. The county levies must meet these deficits, pay for any extra features, and bear the additional cost of maintaining a standard that is in any respect above the minimum. Moreover, except for some assistance from two state bond issues, the counties have had to provide all school buildings and keep them in repair. Thus the tax levy for school support in most counties represents the largest single levy, and in many instances exceeds all other levies combined.

The largest single expenditure by the counties is not for schools, however, but for *public welfare*. Most of this money (76 to 80 per cent) comes from federal and state grants. Unlike the arrangement for the support of public education, by which the state pays for certain things and the county for other things, public-welfare expenditures are all set up in the county budget.

Public welfare in the modern sense is far broader and more adequate than the old-fashioned poor relief. It includes aid to the indigent, to the blind, to the permanently disabled, to mothers with dependent children, and to those in need of hospital care who are not financially able to provide it. These are roughly the categories for which federal and state money may be expended. Usually there are other persons in distress who do not fall into any of these categories. These may receive "general assistance." Whatever the class of dependency, the modern philosophy in respect to aid as well as the type of care is quite different from what it used to be. There is a more sensitive social conscience. Generally those in need are considered victims of misfortune rather than of their own indolence. Their needs are administered to by trained social workers, the effort always being to rehabilitate if possible and, failing this, to support with some degree of adequacy. Despite a generally rising level of living, the amount of dependency remains disturbingly high. It may be that the social cost of poverty is no greater relatively than at any other time in history, but that more of it is relieved through taxation. At any rate, even with generous federal and state assistance, it has become and is likely to remain a major item in the budgets of North Carolina counties.

Farm and home-demonstration work has been receiving an increasingly higher appropriation, though it remains a minor item in the total cost of county government. Also it may be expected to more than pay its way by strengthening the tax base.

A relatively new and always modest item of expenditure is *support of libraries*. In 1941 there were only 28 counties in the state with countywide library service, but in 1954 there were 92 counties with such service. North Carolina has more bookmobiles serving its rural areas than any other state—a total of 93 serving 91 counties.[13]

One of the most significant developments in North Carolina county government in recent decades has been the steady expansion of the *public health program* until now every county enjoys the benefits of a well-rounded public health service. Every county either constitutes or is embraced within one of the 77 public health districts which, together with three city districts, cover the state. As of a recent date, these units had on their staffs 57 health officers; 6 assistant health officers; 4 dentists; 32 supervising nurses, 406 staff nurses; 213 sanitarians, engineers, and veterinarians; 8 public health investigators; 16 health educators; and 287 clerks, bacteriologists, technicians, and mental-health specialists—a total of 1,031 full-time positions, filled. There were on that date 69 budgeted positions unfilled. The 1953–1954 budgets of the county and district units aggregated $4,601,195, about 70 per cent of which came from local taxes. The figure becomes $5,282,492 if the budgets of the three city units are included, with an even larger percentage of the support coming from local taxes. A mere listing of these positions and a glance at these budgets will indicate the sweep and volume of the public health program.

An even more recent development has been the construction of county hospitals and health centers under the stimulus of federal grants made available under the Hill-Burton Act. Between 1946 and 1953 no less than 158 projects were launched, and 96 were completed and in use by June 30, 1953. These structures, located in 83 counties, consisted of 72 hospitals, 44 health centers, 34 nurses' homes, and 8 state-owned buildings. The number of hospital beds in the state increased from 9,262 in 1946 to 13,742 in 1953. Many additions have been made since that date. The expansion and improved distribution of hospital beds and clinical facilities has not only brought hospital and medical treatment within reach of more of the rural population but the numerous health centers have increased the effectiveness of the public-health service in the prevention of disease.

Many services are combinations of state and local governments. Table 98 shows the growth of state and local taxes since 1928–29.

---

[13] *Twenty-Third Report of the North Carolina Library Commission, 1952–54* (Raleigh, 1954), p. 30.

Recommendations for the Improvement of County Government

County government is administered much more soundly today than it was a quarter of a century ago. However, much remains to be done if North Carolina is to have really efficient and effective county government, and some of the most obvious improvements needed in county government are listed here:

1. A few of the small, weak counties should be consolidated with adjoining counties.

2. There is need for improvement in the machinery of assessing and listing taxable property in order that property may be placed on the books with more completeness and equality.

3. Tax-sale certificates issued because of delinquency in the payment of taxes should be foreclosed with reasonable promptness.

4. The officers of treasurer, surveyor, and register of deeds should cease to be elective and be filled by appointment by the county commissioners. Often there will be no need for either a treasurer or a surveyor.

5. The office of coroner should be abolished and the functions of the office attached to the solicitor's office. The latter should be empowered to engage the services of an approved medical examiner when needed.

6. The number of justices of the peace should be drastically reduced and higher qualifications and more responsible reporting required of those retained. The receipt of a fee should not be contingent on a conviction.

7. The county board should be granted sufficient polic power outside city limits to regulate motels, trailer camps, etc.; set standards for subdivisions and drive-in theaters; and regulate or prevent other developments and practices that may imperil public safety.

BIBLIOGRAPHY

Biennial Report of the Local Government Commission, 1954. Local Government Commission. Raleigh.

BRANSON, E. C. and other. "County Government and County Affairs in North Carolina," *University of North Carolina Record*, No. 159 (October 1918), pp. 7–188.

General Statutes of North Carolina, I, II, III, 1943.

North Carolina Constitution, Articles 4 and 7.

Public Laws, Biennial Sessions of the Legislature since 1943.

Statistics of Taxation, 1954, North Carolina Department of Revenue, North Carolina Department of Tax Research, and State Board of Assessment. Raleigh: 1954.

Thirty-Fourth Biennial Report of the North Carolina State Board of Health, 1952–1954. Raleigh.

Twenty-Third Report of the North Carolina Library Commission, 1952–1954. Raleigh.

WAGER, P. W. *County Government and Administration in North Carolina.* Chapel Hill: University of North Carolina Press, 1928.

———. *North Carolina: The State and Its Government.* New York: Oxford Book Company, 1947.

Chapter 24

THE PAST IN PUBLIC EDUCATION

History

COLONIAL SCHOOLS.

During the colonial period in North Carolina the philosophy of those in authority was "that the great body of the people were to obey and not to govern, and that the social status of unborn generations was already fixed."[1] It is easy to understand why little educational progress was made and why many believed that education was unnecessary.

Even so in colonial times, many children received a somewhat "formal" education in the home. Some of these "home schools" grew into schools that enrolled students from miles around. Some families employed tutors from abroad or from the East. One of the chief contributors to colonial educational efforts was a Church of England organization known as the Society for the Propagation of the Gospel, which furnished money, books, and various kinds of materials to help provide educational opportunities for both white and Indian children. Some of the first teachers in the state were supported by the Society for the Propagation of the Gospel. It also furnished the books for many of the early libraries of the state.[2]

One of the first significant educational efforts made in North Carolina was the establishment of the apprentice system for the education of destitute orphans in 1695. The cost of this program was to be paid by the public. This system included a provision that required compulsory attendance, and provided that the orphans "be bound out to some one who would agree to teach them a trade and see that they learned to read and write."[3]

The first school of any note in North Carolina was established in Pasquotank in 1709 by the Rev. William Gordon. It was a very successful school because of the personal influence of its founder. Mr. Gordon later left Pasquotank and moved to Chowan, where he started another school

---

[1] E. W. Knight, *Public Education in North Carolina* (Boston and New York: Houghton, Mifflin Co., 1916), p. 3.

[2] R. D. W. Connor, *History of North Carolina, The Colonial and Revolutionary Period, 1584–1783* (Chicago, Lewis Publishing Co., 1919), I, 200.

[3] M. C. S. Noble, *A History of the Public Schools of North Carolina* (Chapel Hill: University of North Carolina Press, 1930), p. 5.

which was also quite successful. Another early North Carolina school was established by an Episcopal missionary, the Rev. Giles Remsford. Established in 1712 and called Marshburn's School, it failed to receive aid from the Society for the Propagation of the Gospel, as had been promised, and so went out of existence.

Governor Charles Eden, as early as 1716, promised that if the Society for the Propagation of the Gospel would continue to furnish teachers, the people would willingly pay their share of the money for the teacher's salaries. He was probably the first governor of the state to express faith in the public's willingness to give limited support to public education. Gabriel Johnson, in 1734, was the first governor to urge the General Assembly to make some provision for public education:

In all civilized Societys of men, it has always been looked upon as a matter of greatest consequence to their Peace and happiness, to polish the minds of young Persons with some degree of learning, and early to instill into them the Principles of virtue and religion, and that the Legislature has never yet taken the least care to erect one school, which deserves the name in this wide extended country, must in the judgment of all thinking men, be reckoned one of our greatest misfortunes.[4]

However it was 1745 before the legislature granted any aid for schools. At this session the town commissioners in Edenton were given the power to build a schoolhouse. It was to be paid for by money secured by the sale of town lots and by donations and subscriptions which the commissioners were authorized to receive. Fines collected from two sections of the law were to be used for erecting pounds, bridges, public wharfs, the market house, and the schoolhouse.[5] Twenty-five years later, in 1770, the people of Edenton had purchased two lots and had constructed a schoolhouse.

Nevertheless, progress was slow, and "in 1829 Joseph Caldwell, president of the University, declared that North Carolina was three centuries behind the other States in the education of her children, and that a great many people actually boasted of their ignorance of letters"[6] R. D. W. Connor reports that "a careful estimate, made in 1838, placed the number of illiterate children in the state between five and fifteen years of age, at 120,000; and that the United States Census of 1840 revealed to the world the humiliating fact that, after more than sixty years of independence, one-third of the adult white population of North Carolina could neither read nor write."[7]

The blame for the low status of education in the state before 1840 can be laid entirely at the doors of the legislature. The governors of the state

[4]W. L. Saunders (ed.), *The Colonial Records of North Carolina* (Raleigh: R. M. Hale, Printer to the State), IV, 227.
[5]Noble, *op. cit.*, p. 10.
[6]R. D. W. Connor, *Ante-Bellum Builders of North Carolina* (Greensboro: The College, 1914), p. 10.
[7]*Ibid.*

had been exceptionally able men, and all of them had tried to coerce the legislature into providing for public schools.[8] "In 1835, Governor Swain, in his last message, took a parting shot at the Legislature by declaring that the history of that body for fifty years would exhibit to posterity little more than the annual imposition of taxes, one-half of which was spent on the Legislature itself, and the other half on the train of officers who superintended the machinery of government. The establishment of schools for the convenient instruction of youth, and the development and improvement of our resources will seem scarcely to have been regarded as proper objects of legislative concern."[9]

Archibald D. Murphey was the state's first great advocate of public education. His famous plan for a system of public schools was submitted to the 1817 legislature, which received it with utter indifference. However many features of the plan were later incorporated into the basic structure for public education in North Carolina.[10]

The first substantial victory for public education came in 1825, when the legislature established the Literary Fund, the income from which was to be used for the support of the schools. It was greatly increased in 1836, when the surplus revenue of the federal government was distributed to the several states, and of her share North Carolina devoted $1,133,757.39 to the Literary Fund. This was sufficient to give a fair start to the first public school system, enacted by law in 1839, which gave legal sanction to much that had been advocated by Murphey in 1817. From 1840 to the outbreak of the Civil War, North Carolina enjoyed a period of leadership and progress not unlike that of the last fifty years or so.

1865–1900.

The Civil War came at a particularly unfortunate time for North Carolina, for the state had taken a great stride during the period just preceding it, especially in the fields of education and internal improvements. The effects of the war virtually destroyed the educational system, forcing the University to close its doors for a period of ten years. The legislature of 1869 re-enacted practically the same school law as that of 1839, but progress was slow until 1900. The position to which public education had been reduced may be judged from the fact that the total expenditure on public schools for the year 1899–1900 was only $1,062,304, or less than two dollars per child of school age in the state, and this had increased from $650,000 in 1885. The value of all public school property in the state in 1900 was only $1,000,000, or just 1 per cent of the value

[8] *Ibid.*, pp. 10–11, 30–34.
[9] *Ibid.*, p. 15.
[10] *Ibid.*, pp. 55–56.

of school property in 1929 and about one-fourth of 1 per cent of the present value. Not more than 2,000 pupils were enrolled in the thirty high schools then in existence.

1900–10[11]

When C. B. Aycock was inaugurated governor of the state in January, 1901, he declared that it would be his aim to aid the cause of education during his four years in office. Accordingly, he called a conference of the educational workers of the state, which he presided over himself. As a result of the conference an educational campaign was organized and "The Central Campaign Committee for the Promotion of Public Education in North Carolina" appointed. The work of this committee was to make campaigns for local taxation, for the consolidation of school districts, for building and equipping better schoolhouses, for longer school terms, for larger salaries of teachers, and for the collection and release to the newspapers of articles relating to the improvement of the public schools. It also called on ministers of the state to preach a sermon at least once a year on public education.

Educational rallies were held in every part of the state, and men of every calling worked in them. The press and the other agencies also lent their support to the movement, and at the close of the campaign in 1904 more than 350 rallies had been held in addition to the regular township meetings conducted by the county superintendents. A growth in sentiment for public education was everywhere noticeable. The legislative appropriation of $100,000 to be distributed to the counties was doubled. Aid was given to the establishment of rural libraries, and the old Literary Fund was reorganized and set aside on a permanent revolving basis to be used as a loan fund for building and improving schoolhouses. In 1907 the legislature authorized the establishment of rural schools, and the first annual appropriation of $45,000 was made as an aid in their maintenance.

1910–20.

This was a period of continued growth and improvement in all branches of education. Several pieces of legislation were enacted, the most important of which were the following:

In 1913 the legislature changed the method of distributing state aid for schools by requiring the counties to show that they had provided funds for a four-month school term before they might participate in the State's equalizing fund. The act was intended to lengthen the school term to as much as six months, and a statewide property tax of five cents was levied

----

[11]The historical account of progress in education from this point is based on materials compiled by the State Department of Public Instruction, especially from *State School Facts*, V (November, 1928), and for recent years, *ibid.*, XXIV (June, 1952), and the *North Carolina Public School Bulletin*, XIX (September, 1954).

for the purpose. This same legislature passed an improved compulsory-attendance act requiring all children between eight and twelve years of age to attend school for at least four months each year, while still a third law, passed in 1913, prohibited children under twelve from being employed in factories except as apprentices and only after having attended school for the required four months. The statewide law providing for the teaching of agriculture and domestic science in high schools was passed in the same year, and counties were permitted to issue schoolhouse bonds upon approval by a vote of the people.

In 1917 legislation was enacted to improve the training of teaching personnel. The act required that a state board of examiners be appointed to control the issuing of certificates to all persons employed in the public schools. The work of this board was transferred to the State Board of Education in 1921.

Probably the most far-reaching legislation enacted during the period was that of 1917, which provided for the extension of the school term to six months. This amendment to the constitution passed and first went into effect during the school year 1919–20.

1920 TO THE PRESENT.

In the period from 1920 to 1930 two outstanding school laws were passed:

1. The provision of the four special building funds totaling $17,500,000 which have enabled counties to borrow money from the state at a low rate of interest to erect school buildings.

2. The increasing of the State Equalization Fund. By increasing its aid to the public schools through this fund, the state has definitely assumed part of the responsibility for supporting these institutions. The General Assembly broke all precedents by making an annual appropriation of $3,250,000 for distribution during 1927–28 and 1928–29. The 1929 General Assembly doubled the equalization fund, making $6,500,000 available annually for the biennium 1929–31. This same General Assembly passed a new general school law that was vague and lacked the approval of the school people of the state. The rulings passed down by the attorney-general were liberal, however, and the 1929 law may be regarded as a step forward.

North Carolina's Rank in Public Education

The significant fact to consider is the accomplishment that North Carolina has made in public education in light of the income of the state, and the percentage of the public and private income that is invested in public education. Table 103 gives the standings of all the states in various criteria by which the excellence of a school system may be judged. Note that while North Carolina ranked forty-fourth in per capita income in 1954, it ranked seventh in the percentage of individual income and fifth in percentage of state resources devoted to public schools. Also, it ranked ninth in average daily attendance with 89.3 per cent; and with nearly the lowest per capita income, the state ranked twenty-second in the average annual salary paid the instructional staff, which indicates that North Carolina cares a good deal about public education.[12]

Since the depression era, expenditures for the schools have increased eight times. Value of public school property has risen from $100,000,000 to $450,000,000, and there were in 1954 10,000 more instructional personnel with total salary expenditures six times greater than during the 1933–34 period.[13]

A list of accomplishments since the early thirties would include:

1. A state retirement system covering all state employees, including public school personnel, 1949.

2. Institution of the twelve-year program to replace the eleven-year program, 1942.

3. A state-wide nine-months term, 1943.

4. A school-lunch program, 1943 (1,500 schools now participate).

5. Free textbooks to all children, grades 1–7, 1933, and in grades 1–8, 1945. A textbook-rental plan for high schools, 1937.

6. Special education for physically handicapped, 1947.

7. Provision for supervisors of instruction under State Board of Education, 1949.

8. Public-school insurance fund established, 1949.

9. Annual appropriation of $550,000 for school-health program, 1949.

10. Contribution by the state of $25,000,000 toward a school-building program, plus $75,000,000 statewide bonds voted and $250,000,000 through local bond issues.[14]

See Tables 103 through 107 for further data on the history and present status of North Carolina schools.

---

[12] *State School Facts*, XXVIII (August, 1956); *North Carolina Public School Bulletin*, XIX (September, 1954), pp. 1, 4.

[13] *Ibid.*, p. 1.

[14] *Ibid.*

Bibliography

Connor, R. D. W. *Ante-Bellum Builders of North Carolina.* Greensboro, North Carolina: The College, 1914.

———. *History of North Carolina, The Colonial and Revolutionary Period, 1584–1783.* Vol. I. Chicago: Lewis Publishing Company, 1919.

Knight, E. W. *Public Education in North Carolina.* Boston and New York: Houghton Mifflin Company, 1916.

Noble, M. C. S. *A History of the Public Schools of North Carolina.* Chapel Hill: University of North Carolina Press, 1930.

North Carolina Public School Bulletin, XIX (September, 1954).

Report of the Superintendent of Common Schools for the Year 1859 (Legislative Document No. 9). Raleigh: W. W. Holden, Printer to the State, 1860.

Saunders, W. L. (ed.). *The Colonial Records of North Carolina.* Vol. IV. Raleigh: P. M. Hale, Printer to the State, 1886.

State School Facts, V (November 1, 1928); XXIV (June 1952).

Chapter 25

Public Education Today

State Participation

State support of schools was accepted as a principle in North Carolina many years before adequate legislation insured implementation of this principle on a statewide basis. In 1933 the General Assembly enacted legislation creating the State School Commission to administer the state school system. The school term was extended to eight months, and all existing ad valorem taxes on property for school purposes were abolished. Certain districts, by vote of the people and approval of the State School Commission, were permitted to levy a property tax for school services beyond those supported by the state.

Succeeding legislatures readopted the School Machinery Act until 1939, when it was made permanent. Each two years appropriations have been made to carry out provisions of the act. Provision was made in 1935 for all fines, forfeitures, penalties, dog taxes, and other funds, except those of the state, to be delegated to the schools for maintenance of plant and for payment of fixed charges. The General Assembly by increased appropriations and legislative enactment provided in 1941 for the addition of the twelfth year (effective in 1942) to the school program. In 1943 the legislature provided for a nine-month term, at the same time making that the maximum for which the state would provide funds.

State Board of Education.

To administer the state school system in cooperation with the Department of Public Instruction, the constitution of North Carolina, as amended in 1945, provides for a State Board of Education composed of thirteen persons, as follows: (a) three ex officio members including the lieutenant governor (elected as chairman of the board), the state treasurer, and the superintendent of public instruction as secretary; and (b) ten members appointed by the governor and confirmed by the General Assembly in joint session, with two appointed from the state at large and one each from eight educational districts as determined by the General Assembly. Appointments, subsequent to the first one, are made every two years for overlapping terms of eight years, in a 3-2, 3-2 order.

The state board is empowered to (1) administer the state appropriations for instructional services, instructional materials such as textbooks and libraries, plant operation, vocational education, transportation, and other operational costs; (2) make rules and regulations for certification of teachers, principals, supervisors, and superintendents; (3) make rules and regulations on census and attendance; (4) devise financial records and reports; (5) approve powers for local administrative units' actions; (6) manage the state's permanent school fund; (7) determine the school centers and attendance areas; and (8) administer federal funds for vocational education.

Authority is vested in the board to make all rules and regulations necessary to carry out the prupose and intent of the law. Executive functions of the board are carried out by the state superintendent, who is responsible for instructional policies, and by the controller, who is responsible for managing fiscal affairs. In accordance with the law, regular board meetings are held each month. Special meetings may be called by the state superintendent, who is secretary, with the approval of the chairman. A majority of the board constitutes a quorum for transacting business.

State Superintendent of Public Instruction.

The constitution provides that the state superintendent of public instruction be the administrative head of the public school system and secretary of the Board of Education. In addition he is a member of the Council of State, an ex officio member of the State Board of Education, ex officio chairman of the Board of Trustees of East Carolina College, and an ex officio member of the Board of Trustees of the Consolidated University of North Carolina.

Generally, the state superintendent looks after the interests of the schools, directing their operations and enforcing laws and regulations pertaining to them. He is a liaison agent between state and local educational authorities; he is required to report biennially to the governor on the state of the school system in anticipation of the new session of the General Assembly.

Specifically the state superintendent (1) approves a program of studies for standard high schools; (2) prepares a course of study for the elementary schools; (3) approves building plans for school buildings; and (4) serves as executive officer of the state board with regard to vocational education.

In implementing the constitutional provisions of 1945, which created a State Board of Education and state superintendent of public instruction, the General Assembly of 1945 provided, in effect, for two executive officers of the state board. The constitutional amendment, which recognized the necessity of centralizing responsibility and of placing authority for the several functions relating to schools in a single source, replaced the five agencies existing in 1943 with the single newly created board. In contrast, in violation of the unitary intention of the amendment, the implementing law as set up by the General Assembly in sections 8 and 9 calls for a procedure and course of action based on a division of authority in that it creates both the superintendent of public instruction, with jurisdiction in matters of educational policy, and the controller, with jurisdiction in financial affairs. This division of authority may prove a source of trouble in the event these two officials do not maintain common understanding and friendly cooperation in carrying out their several duties for public education.

STATE STAFF AND SERVICES.

An assistant state superintendent and administrative assistants act for the state superintendent in his absence and perform such duties as he may direct. Additional professional staff is organized by divisions, each of which is responsible to one or both of the executive officers of the board. There are fifteen of these divisions, with duties and responsibilities clearly defined. It is through these divisions and their personnel that the state administers its program to the county and city administrative units throughout the state.

1. The *Division of Elementary and Secondary Education* provides services as follows: inspection and accreditation of schools; general supervisory assistance in the improvement of instruction; preparation of curriculum bulletins and other publications for use of teachers and other school personnel; and assistance in such other areas as surveys, evaluations, safety, and adult education.

2. The *Division of Negro Education*, provided for by law, renders special assistance to Negro schools, including inspection and rating, supervision, improvement of teacher training in cooperation with colleges for the Negro race, and in race relations.

3. The *Division of Professional Service*, provided for by law, has charge of the administration of the rules and regulations of the State Board of Education with regard to certification of teachers; issues all teachers' certificates; rates teachers employed each year as to certificate held and teaching experience; and coordinates the work of the department with that of the various institutions of higher learning in the field of teacher education.

4. The *Division of Publications* edits, compiles, and prepares materials to be printed, and distributes bulletins, forms, etc. to local units and individuals; serves as the purchasing agency for all other divisions except Plant Operation, Textbooks, Transportation, and a part of Auditing and Accounting; and distributes mail and supplies to all divisions.

5. The *Division of Health and Physical Education* is concerned with health instruction, physical education, safety, healthful environment, mental hygiene, and health services in public schools.

6. The *Division of Research and Statistics*, organized since 1953, is concerned with planning and directing a research program for the Department of Public Instruction and the State Board of Education.

7. The *Division of Textbooks* has charge of purchasing and distributing free basic textbooks and of the rental system for high school books and approved supplementary readers in the elementary schools.

8. The *Division of Teacher Allotment and General Control* has the responsibility of applying the rules of the state board governing allotment of teachers and allots funds to be expended for the object of general control in local budgets.

9. The *Division of Auditing and Accounting* is concerned with a continuous auditing of expenditures by local units from the State Nine Months' School Fund and is charged with the accounting of all funds, state and federal, under the control of the State Board of Education.

10. The *Division of Plant Operation* has charge of plant operation, which includes janitors' wages and supplies, fuel, water, power, and telephone.

11. The *Division of Transportation* administers the school-bus transportation system. Through this division, more than 7,000 buses are operated, replaced, maintained, and routed.

12. The *Division of Vocational Education* administers the program of vocational education, which includes vocational agriculture, home economics, trades and industries, distributive occupations, guidance, vocational rehabilitation, veterans' related training, school-lunch program, and certain phases of training under the G. I. Bill.

13. The *Division of Insurance* has the responsibility for administering the public-school insurance fund which the General Assembly authorized in 1949 to insure school property of participating units.

14. The *Division of Special Education*, created in 1947, has the responsibility for the promotion, operation, and supervision of special courses of instruction for the handicapped, the crippled, and others requiring special types of instruction.

15. The *Division of School Planning* is responsible for the expenditure of the funds raised for school construction. It surveys local schools and determines needs and aids in the equitable distribution of the funds among the three races for which schools are maintained.

Local Participation

The public schools of North Carolina are administered through 100 county administrative units and 74 city administrative units. In the 100 county units in 1953–54 there were in existence 784 school districts for whites and 398 districts for Negroes. The number of school districts per county ranges from 2 to 22 for whites, and from 1 to 12 for Negroes for the 97 counties having such districts. Seven county and 12 city administrative units had an average daily attendance of 1,500 or less. In the same year six county units and one city administrative unit had an average daily attendance of from 1,5000 to 20,000.

COUNTY BOARD OF EDUCATION.

County boards of education, the governing authorities for county units, consist of from three to seven members. Sixty-six of the hundred county units have five-member boards. County boards of education members are nominated by party primaries or conventions and are approved by the General Assembly for terms of two, four, or six years. Should the General Assembly fail to elect or appoint board members, the State Board of Education, by law, fills vacancies. The term of office of each member begins on the first Monday of May of the year in which he is elected and continues until his successor is elected, and qualified. Boards must meet at least four times a year and may elect to meet monthly and for other special meetings as the school business may require.

A county board of education is a corporate body, and as such it may hold school property belonging to the county, and it is capable of purchasing and holding real property and personal property, of building and repairing schoolhouses, of selling and transferring these for school purposes, and of prosecuting and defending suits for or against the corporation. In addition to providing school buildings, it drafts county school budgets, considers educational policy, and appoints the county superintendent.

COUNTY SUPERINTENDENT OF SCHOOLS.

The superintendent is appointed by the county board of education for a two-year term, subject to the approval of the state superintendent and the State Board of Education. He must be a graduate of a four-year standard college, hold a superintendent's certificate, have had three years of experience in school work in the past ten years, and present a doctor's certificate that he is free from any contagious disease.

The county superintendent's salary is determined in accordance with a state standard salary schedule fixed and determined by the state board. However, his salary may be supplemented from local funds by authority of the county board.

CITY SCHOOLS.

The governing administrative authorities in city schools are boards of trustees. A vast majority of these boards have either five, six, or seven members; one has three; and 14 have more than seven members. Members of boards of trustees are named either by election by popular vote, by appointment, or by a combination of the two, except for four boards reported as self-perpetuating. A few boards of trustees, due to legislative enactments, have certain powers that are not common to all boards of trustees or to county boards.

CITY SUPERINTENDENT OF SCHOOLS.

The superintendent of a city unit is appointed for a two-year term by its board of trustees, subject to the approval of the state board and the state superintendent. He serves as the administrative officer and ex officio secretary of the board of trustees. Superintendents of city units must meet the same qualifications as county superintendents.

POWERS AND DUTIES OF CITY AND COUNTY SUPERINTENDENTS.

The general powers and duties of county and city superintendents may be summarized as follows: (1) accounting for finances (records and reports); (2) making records and reports to the public; (3) taking census and directing attendance service; (4) preparing budget estimates; (5) directing storage, repair, and distribution of textbooks; (6) directing storage and distribution of supplies; fuel, etc.; (7) supervising transportation activities; (8) directing maintenance and operation of school plants; (9) directing library service; (10) directing operation of school lunch programs; (11) directing health services; (12) securing and assigning the instructional personnel; (13) evaluating educational services involving testing, promotion, and efficiency of instruction; (14) allocating responsibility; (15) planning and implementing the educational program including reorganization, expansion, and facilities; (16) planning and administering the extracurricular program; (17) planning and administering the community program.

Instructional Personnel

Because of the changeover from a plan of organization calling for seven primary grades and four secondary grades to a plan based on eight primary grades and four secondary years in 1942-43, there has been an increase of the number of elementary teachers and a compensatory decrease in the number of high school teachers. The increased average daily attendance and the slight change downward in the basis of teacher allotment have brought a marked increase in the number of teachers in recent years. Yet this increase is not sufficient to maintain a proper teacher-pupil ratio in view of the tremendously increasing enrollments in the schools (see below). Table 108 gives figures on the increases in the instructional staff.

The number of elementary-school principals, both white and Negro, tends to increase as the school enrollments rise, whereas the number of high school principals in accordance with the number of high schools tends to remain constant (see Table 109).

In 1949 the General Assembly created a new position—supervisors of public instruction—and made provision for paying their salaries from state funds. The state board in 1953–54 allotted funds for paying the salaries of 260 persons so employed—176 white and 84 Negro. Several of the larger city units provided for the employment of additional supervisors to give attention to specific subjects areas.

TRAINING OF INSTRUCTIONAL PERSONNEL.

The 6,368 white teachers, principals, and supervisors employed in the 72 city administrative units during 1951–52 were slightly better trained than those employed for service in the 100 county units. This fact can best be expressed in percentages: 96.6 per cent of city personnel held Class A and Graduate Certificates, whereas 87,7 per cent of the instructional personnel in county units held such certificates. Stating the situation another way, 3.4 per cent of city teaching personnel for white schools had training less than college graduation, whereas 12.3 per cent of county teachers were in this group.

All except 171 of the 8,033 Negro instructional personnel employed in all units during 1951–52 held the highest types of certificates issued— Graduate and Class A. There were 816 persons with Graduate certificates and 7,046 with Class A certificates, or 97.9 per cent of the total teachers employed. As with white teachers, Negro teachers employed in city administrative units were better trained than those employed in county units.

SALARIES OF INSTRUCTIONAL PERSONNEL.

Table 110 shows in full detail the average salaries and the rise therein over the period 1944–54 paid teachers and principals from both state and local funds, and Table 111 gives the number of persons and average salaries paid from state funds. Briefly, the average salary for teachers, of both races and for both elementary and high school, rose from $1,297.33 in 1944 to $3,199.14 in 1954 (see also Fig. 16). For principals and supervisors it rose from $2,225.74 to $5,023.08. Vocational teachers' salaries, including travel allowance, climbed from $2,114.29 to $4,255.00 over the same period, the total number of teachers rose from 23,095 to 28,576 and principals from 1,328 to 1,555. Their jobs having been greated in 1949, supervisors increased from 225 to 260.

Public School Problems

The most serious and pressing of the many problems facing education in North Carolina today are: (1) increasing school enrollments; (2) inadequate supply of property trained teachers; and (3) insufficient school plants to house pupils for the present and for the foreseeable future. A close look into these three problem areas will show the rapid growth of the ststewide school system in North Carolina and at the same time at least indicate something of the rate of future growth and development.

INCREASING SCHOOL ENROLLMENT.

Since 1944–45 there has been a rather steady increase in average daily attendance. Table 112 shows a total average attendance in 1944–45 of

Fig. 16.   Average Annual Salaries of Teachers
1934-1954

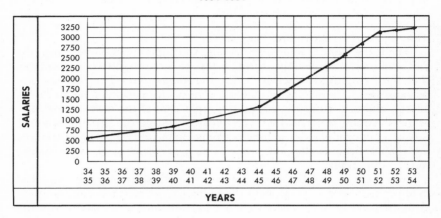

713,146 as compared with a total average attendance of 874,165 in 1953–54. But these average daily attendance figures are but one way of showing the growth of schools in North Carolina. North Carolina's characteristic high birth rate, an ever increasing belief in the "magic" of education, enforcement of existing attendance laws, and increasing difficulty in securing employment will not only increase school enrollments but will also hold a more even pattern in both average daily membership and average daily attendance.

Fig. 17.   Pupil Enrollment, Grades 1–12
1941-1961

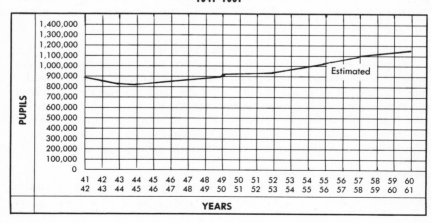

Paradoxically, at the same time another great problem is the tremendous drop-out rate, in which only roughly a third of those who enter the first grade finish high school in twelve years. See Table 113.

Fig. 18. High School Graduates
1946-1956

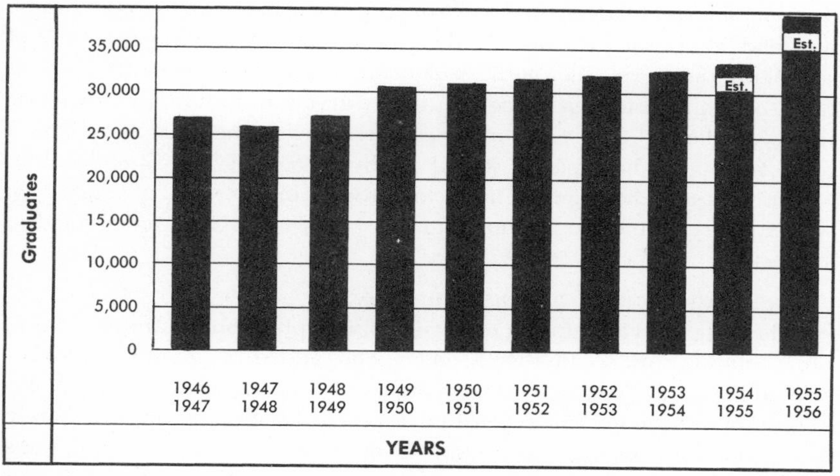

INSUFFICIENT TEACHERS.

As a result of this increased enrollment and, even more, as a result of the low salary scale and deline in social position among the teaching profession, the relative number of young people entering the field is dropping alarmingly, and people who have taught for years are being forced to find better compensation in other lines. This means that often those who remain in the classroom must handle classes much too large for optimum teaching.

NEED FOR INCREASED SCHOOL PLANTS.

Adequate school housing facilities is one of the most pressing problems facing school authorities and the people of the state. In recent years the construction of schools has shown a rapid increase, but the tremendous building program that has taken place since 1949 has accomplished only partial and temporary relief. Certain areas of the state have fared better in solving their school-construction problems than others. Though the need for buildings is statewide, there are areas or districts where the need is greater and the ability to meet it more limited than in other areas. A special report presented to the Advisory Budget Commission in 1954 claimed that approximately $194,000,000 would be required to provide adequate school housing.

The erection of school buildings and the care of school property are responsibilities of county boards of education in county units and of city boards of trustees in city units. Construction is financed from funds raised by bond issues, borrowed money, tax levies, gifts, and state grants. In 1949 the General Assembly appropriated $25,000,000 to aid local units to construct, improve, and repair school-plant facilities. An additional $25,000,000 was made available through a bond issue. In October, 1953, a second bond issue provided another $50,000,000 for the improvement of school buildings, yet still another $68,000,000 would be necessary to meet fully the requirements in school housing. Surveys of building needs made in 1953 indicated that 7,401 more classrooms were needed, as well as a total of 2,580 other special school facilities. *State School Facts* (March, 1957) gives the shortage of instruction rooms in 1957–58 as 2,328 even with 1,424 scheduled for completion in 1956–57, and 1,291 completed in 1955–56.

FINANCING THE SCHOOL-BUILDING PROGRAM.

The state fund amounting to $100,000,000, plus county and city bond issues totaling close to another $100,000,000, added to the monies appropriated for capital outlay by the counties still is not enough to provide for minimum needs now. The federal government has poured approximately $3,000,000 into school construction in areas where federal installations have caused abnormal increases in population. From the percentage of its income that it invests in public education, North Carolina can be expected to continue its efforts to improve its school situation. Possibilities of other sources of revenue in the form of new or additional taxes or outside aid from the federal government may be further investigated. It appears that the needs will be greater before they become less.

BIBLIOGRAPHY

Education Differences Among the States. Washington: National Education Association of the United States. March, 1954.

Education in North Carolina Today and Tomorrow. Report of the State Education Commission, 1949. Raleigh, North Carolina: The Graphic Press, n. d.

GREEN, C. S. (comp.). Conservation and Development in North Carolina. Mimeographed, 2 vols. Conservation Congress Report, Raleigh: 1952.

Legal Status of the School Superintendent. Washington: National Education Association of the United States, Research Bulletin XXIX (October, 1951).

North Carolina Public Schools. State Department of Public Instruction, Biennial Report. Raleigh: 1952.

Public School Laws of North Carolina, Cumulative Supplement, 1943–1953. Raleigh: State Superintendent of Public Instruction.

Public School Revenues 1949–1950. Washington: National Education Association of the United States, Research Bulletin XXX (December, 1952).

Schools and the 1950 Census. Washington: National Education Association of the United States, Research Bulletin XXIX (December, 1951).

State School Facts, XXIV (September, 1952); XXV (May, 1953 and June, 1953); XXVI (June, 1954); XXVII (February, 1955).

Summary of 1953 Legislation. Chapel Hill: Institute of Government, The University of North Carolina, 1953.

Chapter 26

HIGHER EDUCATION

Enrollment Trends

Since 1900 the number of students attending colleges and universities in the state has increased almost tenfold. The enrollment of students in institutions of higher learning in 1900 was 4,698, and in 1957 it was 53,727. In recent times the enrollment has jumped from 18,929 in 1930 to the 1957 figure, an increase of 184 per cent. The rates of increase compare favorably with the rates for the nation as a whole.

Enrollment has grown in both public and private institutions, but the larger part of the increase has been in the publicly supported schools. At the turn of the century, enrollments in privately supported institutions were more than 50 per cent greater than in the state-supported ones. As late as 1940 the private colleges and universities had more students, but by October 1, 1956, enrollments in public institutions were 28,228, compared with 25,499 in the private schools. The figures in Table 114 present the data on enrollments in North Carolina since 1900, from a total of 4,698 to 49,202 in 1955–1956. As indicated above, this figure had increased by 4,525 for the fall term 1956. While the great bulk of this growth in college and university enrollment has been in the undergraduate years, there has been a significant increase in the number of students enrolled in graduate programs. In 1900 there were only 56 graduate students enrolled in the entire state. By 1930 this figure had risen to 592; and by 1950 there was almost a fivefold increase over the 1930 figure to 2,380. The increase for North Carolina was roughly comparable to the increase in the nation as a whole. In the modern world of science and technology, the growth of facilities for graduate instruction along with facilities for professional training in such areas as medicine, constitutes one of the major resources in the development of the state.[1]

---

[1] *Higher Education in the Forty-Eight States* (Chicago: The Council of State Government, 1952), p. 178, Table 5A. The following table refers to numbers of graduate students in the given years.

	1900	1910	1920	1930	1940	1950
North Carolina	56	113	104	592	1,025	2,380
United States	5,831	9,371	15,260	51,064	103,276	223,786

The growth of teacher-training institutions and of junior colleges, while considerable, has not been so great as that of other institutions. Both teachers' colleges and junior colleges had a period of rapid growth from 1920 to 1940, but between 1940 and 1950 the rate of growth slowed down.[2]

In North Carolina, as elsewhere, the post-World War II period was one of great fluctuation in college and university enrollments. The peak year was 1947-48, when the enrollment of veterans was at its highest, and total enrollment was 47,071. There was a decline through 1951-52, and then an upswing that appears to be continuing. Enrollment for 1956-57 was 53,727. Tables 115 and 116 present the postwar enrollments by years and the enrollment by institutions for 1954-55 and 1955-56.[3]

Between 1930 and 1950 the colleges and universities located in North Carolina increased their expenditures for educational and general expenses from $6,568,000 to $35,799,000. The increase for publicly controlled institutions was from $3,560,000 to $20,336,000; for privately controlled schools the increase was from $3,009,000 to $15,464,000. The rate of increase was slightly greater for the publicly controlled institutions.[4] The current expenditure is far beyond the 1950 figure but exact data are not at hand.

Notwithstanding the increases of recent years in enrollments and expenditures, North Carolina does not stand high among the states in the proportion of its young people who go to college, both as compared with other southern states and with the nation as a whole (see Table 117).

This situation may be measured in two ways. First, there are data available on the proportion of the total population enrolled in colleges for specified years. The latest year for which such data are available is 1949-50. In that year, North Carolina ranked forty-seventh in the proportion of its population in college, with one North Carolinian enrolled in college for every 95.1 persons living in the state. For the nation as a whole, there was one college student for every 60.6 persons. The low rank

---

[2]*Ibid.*, p. 181, Table 6A, and p. 184, Table 7A.

	1900	1910	1920	1930	1940	1950
Teachers' colleges	1,413	1,649	1,600	2,925	5,139	5,387
Junior colleges	—	—	90	1,815	4,356	4,973

[3]These figures in Table 115 vary slightly from those given on these pages because of method and time of enumeration.

[3]*Higher Education in the Forty-Eight States*, pp. 194-95, Table 11.

	1930	1940	1950
North Carolina, total	$ 6,568,000	$ 12,612,000	$ 35,799,000
Public	3,560,000	6,174,000	20,336,000
Private	3,009,000	6,438,000	15,464,000
United States	$352,283,000	$517,043,000	$1,692,858,000

of North Carolina in 1949–50 represented a decline from ten years previously, when the state ranked thirty-sixth in the nation. This low rank relative to other states both in and out of the South is not due to the Negro population. Counting whites alone for 1949–50, North Carolina's position remains the same.

The situation is not changed materially if the proportion of the college-age population (eighteen to twenty-one) actually in college be taken as the measure. In 1949–50, 16 per cent of the college-age population of North Carolina was enrolled in college. Only one state, Mississippi, had a smaller percentage. Two states—South Carolina and New Jersey—have the same percentage as North Carolina.

Despite the fact that a relatively low proportion of North Carolinians go to college, this proportion has been increasing. On this basis alone, the prospect is for continuing increases in college enrollments in the state. To this must be added two additional factors. First, the number of high school graduates is increasing. And, second, the high birth rates of the 1940's, continuing into the 1950's, have produced increased numbers of young people in the population of the state. Within very few years, these young people will be of college age. North Carolina is confronted, therefore, with future increases in college enrollments of considerable size. The Committee on Higher Education, established by the General Assembly of 1953 to survey the facilities and future needs of the state, estimated in 1955 that the enrollment would be almost doubled by 1970. The Commission further brought back the report that (1) unwarranted duplication of programs, (2) divergent and sometimes conflicting educational policies, (3) differing systems of accounting which made comparisons among institutions difficult, (4) and the lack of an authority to lay over-all plans for the entire system were causing the state to receive insufficient return from its investment in its entire system of higher education. The commission's principal recommendation was the establishment of a State Board of Higher Education, charged with the responsibility of coordinating the system and making plans projected into the future to meet the anticipated tremendous increase in enrollment. Specifically the commission recommended:

1. That there be created a State Board of Higher Education for North Carolina. (Such a board was provided for by the 1955 legislature.)

2. That the Board consist of nine citizens of the State who shall be appointed by the Governor and confirmed by the General Assembly for overlapping terms of six years, the terms of three members to expire every two years, the members of the Board to serve without compensation except for allowances for per diem and travel expenses.

3. That the Board serve as a coordinating agency for State-supported institutions of higher education.

4. That the Board determine the general functions and activities of such institutions and the types of degrees to be granted to the end that uneconomical practices may be eliminated.

5. That the Board make at least one inspection of the facilities of each institution each biennium.

6. That the Board, after holding hearings on the budget requests of such institutions, make such recommendations to the Director of the Budget and the Advisory Budget Commission as it deems necessary for the most efficient operation of each institution.

7. That the institutions be represented and heard, if they so desire, at the budget hearings before the Advisory Budget Commission.

8. That the General Assembly make appropriations to such institutions.

9. That the Board have the power to grant approval of the quarterly requisitions of allotments from appropriations, or such modifications of them as it may deem necessary to make, subject to the approval of the Director of the Budget who is to be notified of any such action.

10. That the Board have the power to adopt a revised budget for each institution, after consultation with the officers of that institution, so as to adjust such budgets to any reduction of appropriations by the Director of the Budget in order to prevent an overdraft or deficit as is now permitted by law.

11. That the Board have the power to grant approval of requests from each institution for transfers and changes as between objects and items in the budget of the institution making the request, subject to the approval of the Director of the Budget who is to be notified of any such action.

12. That the Board prescribe uniform practices and policies for the institutions.

13. That the Board engage in study and planning directed toward the development of a unified program of State-supported higher education.

14. That the Board have authority to appoint and fix the salary of a full-time Executive Secretary subject to the approval of the Governor.

15. That the boards of trustees of the respective institutions continue to control such institutions as at present, subject to the action of the State Board of Higher Education within the limits of its jurisdiction.[5]

North Carolina Universities and Colleges

North Carolina was the second state in the Union to charter a state university and the first to put its university into operation. The University of North Carolina was chartered in 1789 and opened its doors to students in 1795. Today (1957) there are 59 colleges and universities in the state. In this respect only seven others outrank it—New York, 145; California,

---

[5] *Popular Government*, XXI (March, 1955), 11.

139; Texas, 120; Pennsylvania, 111; Illinois, 109; Massachusetts, 91; and Ohio, 78. North Carolina has more colleges and universities for Negroes than any other state in the Union. Enrollment in these institutions in October, 1956, numbered 8,579.

SENIOR COLLEGES.

1. Agricultural and Technical College of North Carolina; Greensboro; 1891; Negro.
2. Appalachian State Teachers College; Boone; 1903.
3. Atlantic Christian College; Wilson; 1902; Christian.
4. Barber-Scotia College; Concord; 1867; Negro, women.
5. Belmont Abbey; Belmont; 1878; men; Roman Catholic.
6. Bennett College; Greensboro; 1873; Negro, women; Methodist Episcopal.
7. Black Mountain College; Black Mountain; 1933; nondenominational.
8. Catawba College; Salisbury; 1851; Evangelical and Reformed.
9. Davidson College; Davidson; 1836; men; Presbyterian.
10. Duke University; Durham; 1838; Methodist.
    Engineering, 1939; Religion, 1926; Graduate School of Arts and Sciences, 1926; Medicine and Hospital, 1930; Nursing, 1930; Woman's College, 1930; Graduate School of Forestry, 1938.
11. East Carolina College; Greenville; 1907.
12. Elizabeth City State Teachers College; Elizabeth City; 1892; Negro.
13. Elon College; Elon College; 1889; Congregational Christian.
14. Fayetteville State Teachers College; Fayetteville; 1877; Negro.
15. Flora MacDonald College; Red Springs; 1896; women; Baptist.
16. Greensboro College; Greensboro; 1838; women; Methodist.
17. Guilford College; Guilford College; 1889; Friends.
18. High Point College; High Point; 1924; Methodist.
19. Johnson C. Smith University; Charlotte; 1867; Negro; nondenominational.
20. Lenoir-Rhyne College; Hickory; 1891; Lutheran.
21. Livingston College; Salisbury; 1879; Negro.
22. Meredith College; Raleigh; 1899; women; Baptist.
23. Montreat College; Montreat; 1916; women; Presbyterian.
24. North Carolina College; Durham; 1910; Negro.
25. North Carolina State College; Raleigh; 1889.
    School of Textiles, 1925; School of Education, 1928; School of Design, 1948; School of Forestry, 1950; unit of the Consolidated University of North Carolina, 1932.
26. Pembroke State College; Pembroke; 1887; Indian.
27. Pfeiffer College; Misenheimer; 1885; Methodist.
28. Queens College; Charlotte; 1857; women; Presbyterian.

29. St. Augustine's College; Raleigh; 1867; Negro; Episcopal.
30. Salem College; Winston-Salem; 1872; women; Moravian.
31. Shaw University; Raleigh; 1865; Negro; Baptist.
    School of Medicine, 1882; School of Law, 1888; School of Religion, 1933.
32. University of North Carolina; Chapel Hill; 1795.
    Law, 1845; Graduate School, 1876; Medicine, 1879; Pharmacy, 1880; Education, 1913; Business Administration, 1919; Library Science, 1931; General College, 1935; Arts and Sciences, 1935; Public Health, 1936; Social Work, 1937; Journalism, 1949; Nursing, 1949; Dentistry, 1949; became part of the Consolidated University of North Carolina, 1932.
33. Wake Forest College; Winston-Salem; 1834; Baptist.
    Law, 1894; Medicine, 1902; Business Administration, 1949.
34. Western Carolina Teachers College; Cullowhee; 1889.
35. Winston-Salem Teachers College; Winston-Salem; 1892; Negro
36. Woman's College of the University of North Carolina; Greensboro; 1891; women.
    Arts and Sciences, 1891; Music, 1922; Graduate, 1942; Education, 1948; Home Economics, 1949; became part of the Consolidated University of North Carolina, 1932.

JUNIOR COLLEGES.
1. Asheville-Biltmore College; Asheville; 1927.
2. Brevard College; Brevard; 1853; Methodist.
3. Campbell College; Buie's Creek; 1926; Baptist.
4. Carver Junior College; Charlotte; 1949; Negro.
5. Charlotte College; Charlotte; 1946; municipal (evening instruction only).
6. Chowan College; Murfreesboro; 1948; Baptist.
7. Gardner-Webb College; Boiling-Springs; 1905; Baptist.
8. Immanuel Lutheran College; Greensboro; 1903; Negro; Lutheran.
9. Lees-McRae College; Banner Elk; 1900; Presbyterian.
10. Louisburg College; Louisburg; 1787; Methodist.
11. Mars Hill College; Mars Hill; 1856; Baptist.
12. Mitchell College; Statesville; 1852; Presbyterian.
13. Oak Ridge Military Institute; Oak Ridge; 1852; men; nondenominational.
14. Peace College; Raleigh; 1872; women; Presbyterian.
15. Pineland College and Edwards Military Institute; Salemburg; 1875; nondenominational.
16. Presbyterian Junior College; 1929; men; Presbyterian.

17. Sacred Heart; Belmont; 1892; women; Roman Catholic.
18. St. Genevieve-of-the-Pines Junior College; Asheville; 1908; women; Roman Catholic.
19. St. Mary's School and Junior College; Raleigh; 1842; women; Episcopal.
20. Warren Wilson College; Swannanoa; 1894; Presbyterian.
21. Wilmington College; Wilmington; 1947; municipal.
22. Wingate Junior College; Wingate; 1896; Baptist.

BIBLIOGRAPHY

BOGUE, J. P. (ed.). *American Junior Colleges*. 3d ed. Washington: American Council on Education, 1952.

GRAY, GORDON. *The President's Report, 1948–1953, a Five-year Report from President Gray to his Excellency, William B. Umstead and the Members of the Board of Trustees of the University of North Carolina.*

Higher Education in the Forty-Eight States. Chicago: The Council of State Government, 1952.

HURT, H. W. (ed.). *The College Blue Book*. 6th ed. Yonkers-on-Hudson, New York: Christian E. Burckel, 1950.

IRWIN, MARY (ed.). *American Universities and Colleges*. 6th ed. Washington: American Council on Education, 1952.

North Carolina Public School Bulletin, XIX (March, 1955).

Popular Government, XXI (March, 1955).

State School Facts, XXVII (March, 1955); XXVIII (February, 1956); XXIX (February, 1957).

Chapter 27

ADULT EDUCATION[1]

History

The adult-education program in North Carolina began in November, 1915, with a volunteer movement called "Moonlight School Month" for the teaching of adult illiterates. There were about a thousand classes throughout the state, with an estimated enrollment of ten thousand, all aiming to obtain some grasp of reading and writing. As might be anticipated, however, only about half were able to complete the course, none with marked proficiency.

The General Assembly tried to remedy the innate problems involved in a volunteer movement operating over such a short period and provided an annual appropriation of $25,000 for teaching adult illiterates. Community schools were organized in thirty counties. These schools were similar to the Moonlight Schools in that classes were usually held at night, but in place of volunteers, paid teachers carried out the program. These community schools became a part of the public school system during 1919–20 and more than fifteen thousand adult students were enrolled in sixty-six counties of the state.

Progress on the state level declined, however, because of the depression. It remained to the Federal Emergency Relief Administration in 1933 to bring back the program of adult education on a statewide basis. The 1930 census revealed 236,261 absolute illiterates and 500,000 near illiterates in the state, and under such programs as the Civil Works Administration and the Works Progress Administration, thousands of adult illiterates had available as instructors hundreds of unemployed teachers.

The various emergency programs were taken over by the Works Progress Administration in 1935, which began its education program in 1936. It was a tentative three-year program based on the interests of the students; literacy was regarded more as a means toward obtaining command of a field with more pertinence to the student than the mere ability to read and write alone. Generally, the three-year program worked within the broad areas of literacy, nursery schools, parent education, general

---

[1]The author is indebted to student A. H. Young for assistance in the preparation of this chapter. Introductory material is based largely on *State School Facts*, XIII (February, 1941).

adult education, leisure-time activities, workers' education, and vocational education.

In 1937 the General Assembly enacted a law making adult education part of the public school system and provided an annual appropriation of $25,000. Of this appropriation, $20,000 was offered to those counties and cities wishing to participate, on a fifty-fifty basis. In 1938 closer community and professional relationships were initiated for adult education. The philosophy and purpose of the program for adults centered around their problems; and action was based upon the fact that the students learned best by doing and that their major interests were jobs, self and home improvement, community relationships, and recreation.

In 1939 the General Assembly increased the annual appropriation to $30,000. Twenty-eight counties and cities participated in the state-aid funds on a fifty-fifty basis. The statewide program included the following major phases: literacy, family-life education, safety education, and general adult education (health and civic education; business education; crafts, occupational information and guidance; and leisure-time activities both for home and family groups and for each phase of the program). The program was continued until 1942, when it died for lack of financial support by the legislature.

Today, in every community throughout the state, there are numerous agencies in addition to schools, colleges, and universities that directly or indirectly influence thought or change behavior; to that extent they are adult-educational institutions of various types. In addition, there are other groups working toward an informed citizenry: churches of all denominations; labor unions; fraternal orders; civic and patriotic organizations; state, county, and city units; medical and dental societies; the Farm Bureau; the Grange; radio; television; driver-safety education and prison-camp educational programs; business and merchant associations; folklore groups and others.

General Education

AGRICULTURAL EXTENSION SERVICE.

The statewide Cooperative Extension Service, the name "cooperative" being attached to the Agricultural Extension Service from the fact that the cost of this tax-supported adult-education program is shared by the federal, state, and county governments, provides educational opportunities to adults through its program of extension work in agriculture and home economics. The administration of the service is located at North Carolina's land-grant agricultural college, the State College of Agriculture and Engineering of the University of North Carolina, at Raleigh. Under the director of extension there are the agricultural field workers, called agricultural agents, and home-demonstration agents to carry the latest in farm and home improvements to the people.

The agricultural and home demonstration agents and local community leaders are trained by subject-matter specialists of North Carolina State College. They are concerned with marketing, animal husbandry, dairying, poultry, clothing, canning, housing, community organization, family living, and recreation. The selection, preparation, and preservation of food; the provision of proper clothing for all members of the family; home decoration; sanitation; household budgeting; and child care and training are an important part of the program of the extension service. Every county in the state is served. These agents were under the general supervision of the state extension director and his assistants, and the regional directors. In one way or another they touch the lives of practically the entire farm population of the state.

COMMUNITY COLLEGES FOR ADULTS.

The community colleges in North Carolina provide an opportunity for adults to acquire new knowledge, learn new skills, and reconsider old attitudes, but there is an urgent need for additional courses for adults in the present community colleges of the state, and there is also an immediate need for an increased number of such colleges. At present they include only Asheville-Biltmore College, Charlotte College, Greensboro Evening College, Wilmington College, and a few others. In general they strive (1) to provide adults with the opportunity to improve their competence in their chosen vocation; or to train for a new vocation, or to attain cultural self-improvement; and (2) to cooperate with business, industry, the professions, and community agencies in establishing training programs designed to increase the efficiency of their personnel. Adults who are not eligible for college credit may enroll for adult courses. At Wilmington College, for example, while there are no educational prerequisites and no credit is given toward graduation or for transfer, an adult student may take, among others, courses in advertising, atomic energy, business law, building estimating, clothing construction, dairy-product merchandising, driver training, electrical estimating, first aid, food handling, human relations, selling, textiles, and health.

COLLEGE AND UNIVERSITY EXTENSION FOR ADULTS.

Through college and university extension services, unlimited education opportunities are placed within reach of all individuals who have the ability and the will to learn. The public institutions of higher learning conduct extension courses for adults beyond high school age—those with a high school education or its equivalent. The objectives of the adult-education service are both cultural and vocational: it provides for adult students who are deficient in the usual prerequisites for advanced courses but who are able to do advanced work, and it also enables professional

persons and others to pursue specialized lines of study. The curricula of
extension courses are usually academic subjects of the colleges of arts and
sciences, courses in commerce and business, engineering, agriculture, and
industrial subjects. However, many additional subjects are offered, including teacher training, applied social science, writing, literature, and
art appreciation. They are designed for groups containing such cross
sections as teachers, social workers, businessmen, doctors, dentists, ac-
countants, housewives, clubwomen, and others.

The University of North Carolina's extension activities in 1952-53,
a typical year, served an estimated total of more than 500,000 individuals,
more than 31,000 of them directly. The activities included service to art-
extension groups, adult discussion groups, adult-education programs in
prison camps, audio-visual education, community drama, continuating
education in public health, English instruction, folklore councils, high
school athletic associations, the Institute of Opera, postgraduate medical
courses, recreation, school relations, short courses, conferences, and the
University of North Carolina News Letter.

Classes under the University of North Carolina's extension service
were organized at twelve centers in 1953-54—Charlotte, Lincolnton,
Monroe, Warsaw, Asheville, Greensboro, Fayetteville, Morganton, Pembroke, Wilson, Greenville, and Gastonia. There were a total of 977 regis-
trations by 752 adults. Twenty-seven credit courses and two noncredit
courses were offered by twelve instructors representing the departments
of Education, Public Health Nursing, Social Work, Religion, Sociology,
Psychology, and Physical Education.

In addition, the central University extension office at Chapel Hill
included: adult-discussion groups, the adult film project, a southern
regional institute on hospital recreation, the Institute of Opera with the
Grass Roots Opera, a leadership-training workshop, an economic education workshop, and the study of adult-education programs in North
Carolina prison camps. Educational television began on January 8, 1955,
with all three units of the Consolidated University participating.

North Carolina State College had 3,688 enrollments in short courses
in 1952–53: more than 1,800 in extension classes, over 1,500 in correspondence courses, and 160 at the Gastonia Technical Institute. The total
enrollment in the extension activities of the college—correspondence
courses, short courses, conferences, extension courses, technical institutes,
and driver-training school—was close to 7,500.

The short courses were in the fields of agriculture, forestry, engineering, education, textiles, and general studies. A total of eighty-nine extension courses were conducted in fourteen communities, and 1,521 adult
students were registered for these courses. College-credit courses were

conducted jointly by faculty from Chapel Hill and Raleigh for 412 soldiers at Fort Bragg. More than 250 adults were enrolled in the driver-training school for professional motor-transportation drivers. Night adult extension classes were offered at High Point, Greensboro, Durham, Fort Bragg, Cherry Point, Greenville, Morehead City, Raleigh, Gastonia, Winston-Salem, and Burlington.

Correspondence courses are of special advantage to adults in isolated areas and to handicapped persons. The extension correspondence-teaching program is administered by the University of North Carolina at Chapel Hill, North Carolina State College at Raleigh, and several other educational institutions. At the University, a total of more than 150 courses is offered. The service is statewide (in fact worldwide), and since 1920 more than 20,000 adult students have been enrolled. In 1952–53 some 1,330 were enrolled for 1,700 correspondence courses from 98 counties in North Carolina, from 34 states, and from the District of Columbia. In the same year, 262 members of the armed forces were enrolled in the U. S. Armed Forces Institute. Fifty-six aliens were enrolled for citizenship courses. At North Carolina State College, in 1951–52, there was an enrollment of more than 1,800 students in over a hundred courses in such areas as architecture, agriculture, education, engineering, textiles, and general studies.

PUBLIC LIBRARIES.

Through the public libraries of the state, the possibility of self-education is open to the people in all communities. By providing reading materials and guidance, libraries hope to stimulate the desire among adults for greater knowledge through exhibits, reading lists, group meetings, films, and other audiovisual aids which the library can make available. The adults of North Carolina have access to reliable information throughout the state through an effective statewide public-library service, coordinated with other educational services and agencies. State aid, beginning in 1914, meant that counties with countywide library service have increased from 28 to 92 and counties with bookmobile service have increased from 0 to 91.

The library service includes the interlibrary-loan program, the public-library film program, traveling bookmobiles, and special library services. Facilities are available for interlibrary loans of special collections in areas of 75,000 or more population. Public libraries in Asheville, Charlotte, Durham, Gastonia, Greensboro, Raleigh, Salisbury, and Winston-Salem have developed special statewide resources. Subjects include textiles, gardening and horticulture, art, family life, home, architecture, vocational and technical manuals, business industries, and books by and about the Negro.

The public-library film program is also statewide, and it was developed in cooperation with the Bureau of Visual Education at the University of North Carolina. The counties and regions participating include Buncombe, Cabarrus, Caldwell, Durham, Forsyth, Gaston, Haywood, Nantahala region, Scotland, and Wake.

Traveling bookmobiles operate in ninety-one counties. These libraries on wheels take books and other materials to people of all ages across the state from the isolated mountain areas of the west to the Outer Banks. North Carolina is unique in the degree to which it has developed this perambulating facility.

Special services and workshops are also provided by libraries and their personnel, including cooperation with Home Demonstration Clubs, Parent-Teacher Associations, civic clubs, and other organizations. Reading materials are furnished to patients in hospitals; bookmobiles take books to inmates of prison camps, and branches are located in industrial centers. Story hours and book reviews are presented on radio and television. Several in-service–training workshops to emphasize public-library service in the community have been held.

RECREATION.

The philosophy of the state of North Carolina is that recreation has changed in its function and increased in its educational significance for adults. In this age of industrial organization and high specialization for the majority of people, recreation has become important to adults as a means of creative living. Accordingly, the recreation program in the state includes games and sports, arts and crafts, dancing, social activities, nature and outing activities, and many services. Parks, school areas and buildings, and other suitable facilities are maintained for recreational use. Various community programs provide recreation for school, industrial, and other adult groups. Agencies such as the Young Men's and Young Women's Christian Associations, Boy Scouts, churches, private clubs, fraternal organizations, sports organizations, and commercial agencies contribute to the adult recreation program, and state colleges and universities, libraries, and many county, state, and federal agencies assist.

The North Carolina Recreation Commission, the first such state commission in America, is continuously planning recreation for all citizens through wholesome activities, based primarily on the local level. The commission promotes a wide use of natural resources, including national and state parks and forests, hunting and fishing preserves, and recreational parkways. It stimulates and stresses the values of camping and attempts to bring camping opportunities to adults. It makes inventories of the state's available play lots, neighborhood playgrounds, play fields, reservations, community recreation centers, athletic areas, materials, and special-interest facilities. It stimulates athletics, sports, and games through wholesome competition and cooperative activities; promotes play days and festivals, tournaments and leagues; and encourages community singing, choruses, choirs, orchestras, and individual musical talents.

Visits to see North Carolina mountains, coastline, sandhills, and historical places of interest, along with the opportunities for hunting, fishing, and camping, are a vital part of the program for adult education.

HEALTH EDUCATION.

The aim of health education for adults in North Carolina is to help the individual understand his own personal health problems and the health problems of the entire state.

The individual's most direct health education is through personal experience with physicians or clinics, home visits by nurses, or inspections by sanitarians. Too few people are reached by this method and such experiences generally relate to only specific problems; the education received is confined to a small segment of a broad health field. Organized classes in health education provide valuable instruction on health practices. These classes are conducted on such subjects as nutrition, home nursing, first aid, accident prevention, infant and prenatal care. Enrollments are limited to persons or groups motivated by personal experience to obtain health information in a specific field, and to persons having time to attend regular classroom sessions.

Many adults are reached through extensive use of newspapers, posters, pamphlets, radio, motion pictures, and other audiovisual aids. Local leaders in some communities study individual and community health problems. The technical guidance of professional medical, nursing, and sanitary personnel of both official and voluntary health agencies are utilized.

The community health-education program is the task of health educators, of which the state Board of Health in Raleigh has a staff to assist in the statewide program. These people are located in communities and teacher-training institutions. In-service training is given teachers, school administrators, local health departments, and college students prospectively in these fields.

The School of Public Health at the University of North Carolina conducts the Continuation Education in Health project. The purpose of the activity is to raise the level of understanding of community health problems through a program of refresher courses, workshops, institutes, and conferences on specific public-health topics and problems for public-health workers; other officials concerned with public health; and business, trade, professional, and other groups whose work or interests are important to the statewide public-health program.

Health-education activities under the School of Public Health, assisted by the W. K. Kellogg Foundation, and carried on by the Continuation Education project for both professional public-health people and laymen include conferences on health-education field experience, public-health nursing, recruitment and training of sanitation personnel, radiological health, communicable diseases, nursing apprenticeship, insect and rodent control, industrial hygiene, health of school-age children, counseling, records, training, and others. Joint activities to expand techniques for evaluation of community health programs and programs on school health, dental health, care of premature infants, and home safety are being undertaken to make the health-education program of more value.

Education in Government.

The Institute of Government, located at Chapel Hill, is now an integral part of the Greater University of North Carolina, although originally it was an independent agency. Now as then through the cooperation of the directors and through representation on the official Board of the Institute of Government, the Extension Division, and other University administrative units, it coordinates its activities to render maximum service to the adults of the state.

The Institute of Government unites public officials, private citizens, and teachers (all adults) and students of civics and government (many of whom are adults) in a systematic effort to meet definite and practical needs in North Carolina. The aims and objectives are (1) to bridge the gap between government as it is taught in the schools and as it is practiced in city halls and county courthouses and in the state capitol; (2) to provide the machinery for putting the people in touch with their government and keeping them in touch with it; (3) to coordinate government machinery in overlapping governmental units and eliminate useless friction and waste; (4) to bridge the gap in knowledge and experience between outgoing and incoming public officials and cut down the lost time, motion, and money involved in a rotating governmental personnel; and (5) to build a demonstration laboratory and clearinghouse of governmental information.

Little information about government has been set down in books, and this small amount is scattered through constitutions, statutes, decisions, and administrative rulings. Much information about government is in the methods, practices, and experiences of officials in 100 counties, 300 cities and towns, and 80 or more state departments and agencies. Accordingly, the Institute's staff members go from city to city, county to county, state department to state department, collecting, comparing, and classifying these laws and practices in books and in action. The results of these cooperative studies are set forth in guidebooks, programs, and supplementary texts; taught in institutes; demonstrated in laboratories; and transmitted through the clearinghouse of information to the officials, citizens, and teachers and students of civics and government in the cities and counties and the state of North Carolina.

Vocational Education

APPRENTICESHIP.

North Carolina's system of apprenticeship is under the state Department of Labor. An apprentice is a worker who learns, according to a written agreement, a recognized skilled trade requiring two or more years of work experience on the job, supplemented by appropriate related trade instruction.

Apprenticeship by custom and tradition is normally for persons between 17 and 22 years of age. However, economic conditions and national security, as well as the employment needs of particular industries, determine the age groups for apprentices. During World War II, at the time of industrial expansion, the average age of apprentices rose to as high as 26 years. This resulted in part from the large number of veterans employed as apprentices, the majority of whom were in the older age brackets. Apprenticeship has become a training institution for adults as well as youths. The Servicemen's Readjustment Act of 1944 and the Vocational Rehabilitation Act (Public Law 16, 78th Congress) provided apprenticeship training opportunities for veterans of World War II. This latter act was extended by Congress to cover veterans with service-connected disability suffered since the start of the conflict in Korea.

The North Carolina system is designed to give the apprentice reasonably continuous employment, pay him a reasonable wage, train him thoroughly in all branches of the trade, and have his work experience supplemented with related technical instruction. The chief aim is to make the oncoming generation of skilled workers completely and thoroughly competent in every part of their trade and to provide the workers with practical experience on the job and theoretical knowledge associated with the job.

Under the apprenticeship training program there are opportunities for training in approximately 300 skilled occupations under 90 trade classifications. The apprentices become part of the work force at the beginning of their training. They produce as they learn and earn while learning. Their wages increase as they advance from one period of their apprenticeship to the next.

At the end of September, 1953, there were 3,493 apprentices in training in programs throughout the state, and for the most part these were adults. The apprentices in training and the registered programs are well distributed throughout the trades.

VETERANS' FARMER TRAINING.

The Veterans' Farmer-Training Program in North Carolina was organized in 1946 to meet the needs of thousands of young men returning to the farm from military service after World War II. North Carolina's basic industry is agriculture: one-third of the population engages in farming. Therefore, the training of these persons who are to farm is of vital concern to the state. The program is operated, under contract with the Veterans' Administration, by the State Board of Education through the Division of Vocational Education of the state Department of Public Instruction.

In 1946 there were 455 departments of vocational agriculture in the schools of eighty-nine counties of the state. Most of the departments were equipped to offer agricultural training, and qualified teachers of agriculture were available to direct the program in local communities. Classes were organized, whether vocational agriculture departments existed or not, in 98 of the 100 counties of the state in 1946. By December, 1952, 49,020 veterans had been enrolled for agricultural training. The peak year was 1950, when 26,273 veterans received instruction. In December, 1953, the Vocational Agricultural Education out-of-school program included 574 departments, with an enrollment of 13,588 persons in adult classes.

The primary objectives of the program were (1) to establish the trainee in farming, and (2) to teach him to farm successfully. These were attained through instruction in these areas: planning and managing the farm business; producing and marketing crops and livestock economically; buying, operating, and maintaining farm machinery and equipment; repairing and constructing farm buildings; conserving farm resources; producing and conserving food for home use; and keeping farm records and accounts. "Learning by doing" was a basic principle of the program. Trainees applied on the farm what was taught in the classroom; they learned and gained confidence through solving farm problems and doing farm jobs.

VOCATIONAL EDUCATION FOR ADULTS.

The vocational-education program operates under the direction of the Vocational Education Division of the State Department of Public Instruction. For more than thirty-five years the service has been extended to schools, industry, agriculture, and business. While the majority of classes are for high school students, a large number of younger adults benefit from the instruction.

The types of vocational education include vocational agricultural, vocational home economics, trade and industrial, and distributive. In the years 1956–57, there were 628 agricultural, 556 home economics, 180 trade and industrial, and 82 distributive centers in operation, and the total enrollment for the 901 high schools was 230,847. For the 724 rural high schools the enrollment was 153,147, and for 177 urban high schools, 77,707. Approximately 20 per cent of the high school enrollees go to college.

Vocational agricultural education provides one of the best means of equipping farm boys and their parents with the necessary knowledge and skills to operate farms. The specific objectives of the program are to enable each student to make a beginning and advance in farming, produce farm commodities efficiently, market farm products advantageously, manage a farm business, conserve soil and other natural resources, and maintain a favorable social and economic environment.

Vocational home economics education teaches such aspects of homemaking as how to plan an adequate diet, how to budget the family income wisely, how to conserve food, how to take care of home furnishings and clothing, how to care for the sick, and how to market.

The program of trade and industrial education helps provide a welltrained labor force to North Carolina's rapidly growing industries and increases the state's earning capacity. Trade extension or evening classes offered in comprehensive high schools are designed to supplement the skills of employed workers, or to prepare them for better jobs. Apprenticeship training offers students technical training to make them capable craftsmen. The part-time, or diversified occupations, plan provides training in a variety of skilled occupations; under this plan students spend half a day in school and half a day in a shop or office. Practical-nurse education for adults trains women for the care of the convalescent, subacutely, and chronically ill patients.

Distributive education is extension training for adults who are regularly employed workers, supervisors, and managers of distributive businesses.

BIBLIOGRAPHY

BRUNNER, E. DES. "The Cooperative Extension Service of the U. S. Department of Agriculture," in *Handbook of Adult Education in the United States*, ed. M. L. Ely. New York: Institute of Adult Education, Teachers College, Columbia University, 1948.

Catalogues, 1952–53. Asheville-Biltmore College, Charlotte College, Greensboro Evening College, and Wilmington College.

COATES, ALBERT. "The Institute of Government," in R. M. Grumman, *University Extension in Action*. Chapel Hill: University of North Carolina Press, 1947.

Community Recreation in North Carolina. North Carolina Recreation Commission. Raleigh, 1952.

Correspondence and Extension Instruction. University of North Carolina Extension Bulletin. Chapel Hill, 1952–53.

Dewberry, Mayhew. "Adult Health Education," in *Handbook of Adult Education in the United States*, ed. M. L. Ely. New York: Institute of Adult Education, Teachers College, Columbia University, 1948.

Ely, M. L., ed. *Handbook of Adult Education in the United States*. New York: Institute of Adult Education, Teachers College, Columbia University, 1948.

Fourth Biennial Report of the North Carolina Recreation Commission. North Carolina Recreation Commission, Publication No. 10. Raleigh: January, 1953.

Grumman, R. M. *Report of the University of North Carolina Extension Division, 1952–1953*. Chapel Hill: University of North Carolina Extension Division.

———. *University Extension in Action*. Chapel Hill: University of North Carolina Press, 1947.

Hurlburt, A. S. *Community College Study*. Office of the Superintendent of Public Education, Educational Publication No. 285. Raleigh: 1952.

Manual of the North Carolina Apprenticeship System. North Carolina Department of Labor. Raleigh: 1952.

Mathews, M. V. "The Public Library and Adult Education," in *Handbook of Adult Education in the United States*, ed. M. L. Ely. New York: Institute of Adult Education, Teachers College, Columbia University, 1948.

Proceedings. National University Extension Association. Bloomington, Indiana: Indiana University, 1944.

Ruggles, E. S. *Report of the Extension Division, North Carolina State College of Agriculture and Engineering, 1952–1953*. Raleigh: North Carolina State College of Agriculture and Engineering.

State School Facts, XIII (February, 1941).

Twenty-Second Report of the North Carolina Library Commission, 1950–1952. Raleigh.

U. S. Department of Agriculture. *Joint Committee Report on Extension Programs*. Washington: U. S. Government Printing Office, 1948.

U. S. Department of Labor. *National Apprenticeship Program*. Washington: U. S. Government Printing Office, 1952.

University of North Carolina News Letter, XXIX (March, 1953).

Chapter 28

LIBRARY RESOURCES[1]

Today over 95 per cent of the state's four million four hundred thousand citizens have access to library service through a system of school, college, special, and public libraries. Statistics from 2,490 library systems for the fiscal year 1953–54 showed a total collection of 11,268,224 books. This figure represents 2,163 schools with 4,958,642 volumes; 54 college and university libraries with 3,382,904 volumes; eight special libraries with 267,493 volumes; 265 public libraries with 2,659,185 volumes. All figures from the special libraries are supplied voluntarily and consequently many have no reporting system established. Statistics from public libraries include reports from municipal, branch, county, and regional libraries.

Approximately three-fourths of the 11,000,000 books available to North Carolinians are used almost exclusively by those attached to the institutions owning them. However, the interlibrary loan system gives the people of the state access to a wealth of library materials.

One of the questions asked by both business and industry before selecting new site locations is about library resources. They may have their own technical libraries, but they want to know what supplementary materials may be anticipated for employees and what facilities are available for employees' families.

Libraries today are going far beyond the printed page in providing information for their patrons. Films, recordings, exhibits, lectures, and discussion groups have all been included in the modern library. New library buildings have made special provision for these new media and older buildings have been renovated to accommodate an expanded library-service program.

In each field of library service there have been special factors contributing to its development. The following summaries indicate the current status of libraries and also outline briefly some of the highlights in library development in North Carolina.

PUBLIC SCHOOL LIBRARIES.

As early as 1858 the idea of school libraries was fostered through the office of the state superintendent of public instruction. The Civil War and

---

[1] The author is indebted to Elizabeth H. Hughey, secretary and director of the North Carolina Library Commission, for help in preparing this chapter.

its aftermath took its toll on all educational ventures, and it was not until 1898 that a strong movement began for the establishment of school libraries. The lack of library materials was so great that in 1901 the state superintendent of public instruction, with the Literary and Historical Association of North Carolina as the prime mover in seeing the necessary legislation enacted, appealed to the General Assembly for funds to purchase books for school libraries. An amount of $2,500 was appropriated to be allocated to the "thirty-dollar libraries," so called because they were financed on a matching basis of $10 from each school, $10 from its county, and $10 from the state. The General Assembly of 1903 increased the amount of aid to $3,750. Succeeding reports have shown continuous growth in school libraries and in state support. The state school reports for 1906 showed 117,900 volumes in the rural school libraries with an expenditure of $11,176, of which $3,750 came from state funds. Direct appropriation of state funds for school libraries began in 1931 with the sum of $25,000 or five cents per child. The 1953–54 report from the office of the state school library adviser showed the phenomenal growth of school libraries in the state, with 2,163 school libraries reporting a total book collection of 4,958,642 and a total expenditure of $1,422,094, including $810,328 from the state textbook rental and the state school library allotment funds. This averages 4.92 books per pupil and an expenditure of $1.41 per pupil enrolled in North Carolina schools.

As the book collections grew and more state funds were invested, the need for some type of library organization became apparent. In 1911 the secretary of the North Carolina Library Commission (established by the General Assembly in 1909) was requested to prepare a school-library handbook. This appears to be the first such handbook published by a state department of education. Since 1911 many other school-library publications have been issued by the North Carolina Department of Public Instruction.

The rapid growth of school libraries brought a need for professional guidance. The North Carolina Library Commission shared its field worker with the schools, but the need for such assistance was soon beyond the limited help one field worker could give, and in 1930, through funds from the General Education Board and the Rockefeller Foundation, the state Department of Public Instruction employed a trained school librarian as a member of its own staff, thus placing the responsibility for supervising school libraries in this department. Five years later, after the special funds were no longer available, the North Carolina General Assembly provided funds in the budget of the Department of Public Instruction for the establishment of the Office of the State School Library Adviser on a permanent basis.

From its beginning this office has aided in developing, improving, and promoting school-library services in all the public schools of North Carolina. Annual lists of books recommended for school libraries have been prepared. A plan was worked out in which the Division of Textbooks sells library books to the schools on a nonprofit basis. A newsletter packet of materials is sent at regular intervals to all school libraries. In visits to schools, concrete suggestions for improving the library are given and libraries are evaluated. Assistance is given in planning and equipping school-library rooms, in cooperating with schools in improving classroom work through the use of books, in formulating certification and accreditation standards, and in liaison activities with many allied agencies. In 1953 the position of Assistant State School Library Adviser was created to help meet the demands for professional and technical advice.

Today a school library is a requirement for an accredited school in North Carolina. As school libraries developed, the need for trained personnel became more and more apparent. The University answered the first call in 1904 with courses in library science for both public and school librarians. The School of Library Science was organized in 1931. As early as 1903, however, the University began to supply books to teachers and debaters, and in 1912–13 it organized the North Carolina High School Debating Society, which stimulated school libraries by pointing up the need for books and periodicals. The Woman's College in Greensboro offered a year of library training from 1928 to 1933.

Not to be overlooked in school-library development was the help of the federal government through the Works Progress Administration during the thirties. Auxiliary to the continuous state appropriations, approximately 1,200 library aides from the WPA library program helped in some thousand schools in North Carolina.

There is much to be done for many schools are still without adequate library services, however. The problem of personnel continues to be serious. Although there are over 1,200 school librarians with some library training, there are still more than 900 school libraries in North Carolina without any professional guidance. Some administrative units are employing local school-library supervisors to ease the shortage. In 1954, twenty-two administrative units had school-library supervisors.

There is keen interest among pupils, teachers, parents, and administrators for improving school-library service. This is continually being demonstrated through requests to the Department of Public Instruction for workshops and conferences on the use of the library, through evaluation of library facilities and book collections, and through consultations in the planning of bigger and better school libraries.

COLLEGE AND UNIVERSITY LIBRARIES.

The birth of the college and university library in North Carolina came with the establishment of the University of North Carolina in 1795. Reports indicate there were more college libraries in the state than any other type prior to 1900. Quite naturally, then, it was the college librarians who led in the organization of the North Carolina Library Association in 1904. Mrs. Annie Smith Ross, librarian of the Charlotte Carnegie Library, issued the call and was the association's first president. This organization gave the college librarians an immediate feeling of strength and unity.

The status of the college library soon became that of a department of the integrated teaching program. There was created the need for more professional personnel, which in turn helped promote the first course in librarianship at the University in Chapel Hill. With the direction of professional librarians, book collections grew rapidly and physical facilities were improved to take care of the expanding service.

The periods immediately following the two world wars were marked with many changes in the college-library field. Emphasis on research has been notable and the expansion of subject interests and staffs has been continuous. Also following each war there was a building boom. Since World War II there have been eight new college libraries completed in the state—four state supported, four privately operated. Two more new buildings are now under construction. Five libraries have had new additions.

Research needs resulted in the establishment of a Library of Congress card catalogue at the University of North Carolina, which has since been expanded into a union catalogue listing holdings of many major libraries of the country. There is a daily exchange service between Duke University at Durham and the University at Chapel Hill. Each library has an index of the other's holdings. Outstanding departmental libraries and special collections are provided through the strong college and university libraries now existing in this state.

There were 336 full-time staff members, 172 of them from the twelve state-supported institutions, at the 54 junior and senior college and university libraries reporting in 1953–54. These 54 libraries had a total operating expenditure of $1,990,668, with $1,075,955 coming from state funds. This was equivalent to $47.28 per student enrolled in state colleges and universities. For the privately endowed and denominational institutions, the per capita expenditure per enrollment was $43.39.

All the libraries in the institutions of higher learning participate in an interlibrary loan system. The smaller units are more regularly on the borrowing end of the loans, but in some instances they too have special material which may be needed by other libraries. These libraries also cooperate with the North Carolina Library Commission in making books available on interlibrary loan to public libraries and to citizens in areas not yet served by any library.

The book stock in the college or university libraries is distributed as follows: state institutions—1,353,024 volumes, or 59 per student; private and denominational institutions—2,128,391 volumes, or 100 per student.

SPECIAL LIBRARIES.

Special libraries reporting in 1953–54 included two medical, one industrial, one church, one army, and three state library agencies. Total book stock was 267,493, and total expenditures were $122,412.63. Of these totals, the three state library agencies reported a stock of 179,418 books and a total expenditure of $86,715.55.

The state libraries have specific functions designated by law. The State Library has as its primary duty the maintenance of a general reference library for the use of state agencies and citizens of the state. The Supreme Court Library provides law-library service for members of the supreme court and the members of the North Carolina State Bar as its primary function. The Library Commission, the library-extension agency for the state, is responsible for promoting and assisting in the development of public-library service throughout the state and for providing direct library service to those people in areas where there is no public-library service. The state's need for direct service is now limited to the 5 per cent of the population residing in Ashe, Alexander, Brunswick, Jones, Madison, Montgomery, Polk, and Robeson counties.

The State Library and the Library Commission are financed by appropriations made by the General Assembly to each specific agency. The Supreme Court Library is financed by appropriations from the General Fund for the use of the supreme court and supplementary funds from fees collected by the supreme court.

The General Assembly of 1955 passed an act to merge the State Library and the Library Commission, effective July 1, 1956, on a recommendation from the Commission on Reorganization of State Government after a thorough study and report on the existing services and facilities had been made by the Institute of Government. The immediate result of the merger was the combining of the two book and magazine collections, the reference services, the catalogue departments, and clerical activities. This reduced duplication and allowed for materials in more subject areas. A union catalogue of both collections and the holdings of other state departments is being made. The combined libraries were named the North Carolina State Library and are governed by a board of eight members, six appointed by the governor and two ex officio, the superintendent of public instruction and the librarian of the University of North Carolina.

PUBLIC LIBRARIES.

As early as 1695, the Rev. Thomas Bray planted the idea of public-library service in North Carolina when he was appointed as the Bishop of London's Commissary in Maryland. One of the provisions of his acceptance wat the promise of books for the colonies. North Carolina received some of those books, and even though they were in a parish, they were free to all "inhabitants of Beaufort Precinct." Parish libraries were followed by a series of subscription and society libraries.

After the Civil War little attention could be given to any public-service agencies, but the demands for public education toward the end of the nineteenth century at last focused attention on the public library, which seemed the only answer to the need to provide continuing education. The term "public library" now applies to municipal, county, regional, and branch libraries.

The state's first public library, supported by city taxes, was established in Durham in 1897. Others followed, and by 1910 there were fifteen free public libraries. The early libraries were developed on purely local initiative. A benefactor, a literary or civic organization, or a group of interested citizens was responsible for library establishment. Ten cities received grants totaling $166,445 from Andrew Carnegie for library development from 1896 to 1923.

The need for a state agency to aid and promote development of public library service was recognized by the North Carolina Library Association in April, 1906. Members of the Association worked tirelessly with the General Assembly of 1907 and 1909 to secure such an agency, and in 1909 the North Carolina Library Commission was established. The commission was authorized to give assistance, advice, and counsel to all libraries and to all persons interested in the selection of books, cataloguing, maintenance, and other details of library management. It was further authorized to aid in organizing new libraries and improving existing ones, and to establish and maintain traveling or other libraries. Traveling libraries were boxes containing between 35 and 40 books and were fitted with shelves so they could be used as bookcases. They were really the forerunners of the current bookmobiles. To aid the traveling libraries, the Federation of Women's Clubs gave all the books from its traveling collections to the Library Commission, and the federation has continued to exert strong efforts in public-library development.

The Library Commission took leadership in securing the necessary laws for establishment and maintenance of public libraries, and has continued to secure changes to keep library laws in line with county and municipal fiscal acts and with changing trends in library needs.

The North Carolina Library Association continued its support and cooperation in all areas of public-library development, and in the early twenties it emphasized and extended services to all citizens of the counties. Durham County was the first to use a bookmobile to serve people beyond the city limits. That first bookmobile was a gift of the Kiwanis Club of Durham to the city library and was christened "Miss Kiwanis."

In November, 1927, the association passed a resolution for a "library campaign for the education and promotion of library growth in North Carolina." From this grew the Citizens' Library Movement, which worked diligently for better libraries, including sponsoring a campaign to secure state aid to the Public Libraries Fund, and in 1941 the General Assembly appropriated $100,000 for each year of the biennium to "improve, stimulate, increase and equalize public library service to the people of the whole state." The Library Commission was authorized to administer the fund.

In the meantime, the association had given the commission a book-mobile to be used for demonstration purposes, and the WPA library program in North Carolina had in operation twelve demonstration book-mobiles. By the time state aid became available, most of the people in the seventy-two counties without countywide library service were eager to have their counties qualify for service.

State aid has provided constant stimulus to public-library development and finance in North Carolina. Library income per capita has increased from 10 cents in 1941 to 51 cents in 1954, and county and city funds have increased at a greater ratio than state aid. Service has been extended from 57 per cent of the population to over 95 per cent of the population. Counties with bookmobile service have increased from 12 to 91. Counties with countywide service have increased from 28 to 92. Eight do not have countywide service and three of the eight have no public library at all within their borders. Book stock has not increased proportionately. More people reading more books have worn them out so fast that the gain is slight—from one-third to a little over three-fifths book per capita.

Since public-library service has been spread over most of the state, more emphasis is now being placed on improving the service. More books and other library materials and personnel to administer them are urgently needed. Book stock need s to be increased to approximately eight million volumes to serve all the people. While 350 full-time and 210 part-time employees are now employed in the public libraries, there is a need for 500 full-time and 250 part-time employees to give more nearly adequate service. These needs translated into dollars and cents would require an annual public-library income of $6,000,000.

This figure does not include any capital outlay for housing of libraries. North Carolinians have made a good start to better library housing since the release of building materials following World War II. Over $2,000,000 from private sources and bond elections have paid for twenty new library buildings, six library units in new county or community buildings, and eleven renovations and additions. Twelve more buildings are now in the blueprint or building stage.

The development of more public libraries in the state has reduced the need for the traveling-library service from the commission. Emphasis has shifted from the general collection to more specific subject areas. Books are maintained in the general collection to serve the people without public libraries and to supplement book resources in expanding services in the public libraries, but a constantly increasing use of the Library Commission collection is to answer specific reference requests. Twelve public libraries, with a state-aid supplement, are building up special-subject collections in designated areas and are making the books available throughout the state through interlibrary loans. An adult-film program has been established cooperatively by the Bureau of Visual Education (Extension Division, University of North Carolina), the North Carolina Library Commission, and public libraries in the state.

THE LIBRARY SERVICES ACT.

The Library Services Act passed in 1956 by the second session of the 84th Congress is designed "to promote the further extension by the several states of public library service to rural areas without such services or with inadequate services."

In essence the Library Services Act[2] authorizes the appropriation by the Congress of $7,500,000 per year for five years. From the funds appropriated each state may receive an allotment of $40,000, plus "such part of the remainder of such funds as the rural population of the state bears to the rural population of the United States."

The Library Services Act will do much to promote library facilities in the rural areas of North Carolina.

Table 118 gives statistics on the public libraries of the state in 1953–1954.

BIBLIOGRAPHY

Biennial reports published by the North Carolina Library Commission, 1910–1957. Raleigh.

North Carolina Libraries, XIII (November, 1954).

Report of the School Library Adviser, 1953–1954. North Carolina Department of Public Instruction. Raleigh.

---

[2] Public Law 597, 84th Congress, Chapter 407, 2nd session. (All 70 Stat. 293).

Chapter 29

At the State Level

HISTORY.

In the 1870's Dr. Thomas Fanning Wood of Wilmington, editor of the *North Carolina State Medical Journal*, through his articles in this publication, stimulated an interest in some sort of state health program. Largely as a result of his efforts, the General Assembly in 1877 created the North Carolina State Board of Health, with an annual appropriation of $100. Two years later the board was reconstructed to consist of nine members—six appointed by the governor, three elected by the North Carolina Medical Society. Appropriations were raised to $200.

Under the provisions of this law, each county was to organize its own health board. These boards were to be composed of the mayor of the county seat and all regularly practicing physicians within the county. The machinery was set up in such a way that local agencies, receiving advice and other nonfinancial aids from the state board, could deal with problems as they arose in the community.

The state board was to be an integrating, unifying body in that it would serve as a liaison between the various county boards. Because of the small appropriations, the state board was necessarily limited in its operations. A large part of its funds were spent for the publication of public-information pamphlets to bring about a public consciousness of health and sanitation. The necessity for safe drinking water, disinfection and proper disposal of sewage and many other practical problems relating to such diseases as diphtheria, dysentery, typhoid, and smallpox were discussed in articles submitted by members of the board and interested physicians over the state. Meanwhile, surveys were undertaken to find out about varied health facilities, especially school sanitation. The results of these surveys were published in an effort to stimulate public interest. But, as indicated by the failure of the public to cooperate with a law passed in 1881 requiring the reporting of vital statistics at annual tax-listing time, the state Board of Health faced a tremendous task in educating the citizenry to accept and cooperate with public-health efforts.

The continued publication of essays and articles during the next few years gradually increased public understanding of the new service, but only after the smallpox and yellow-fever epidemics of the eighties proved the value of the board and its recommendations did the public become genuinely interested. Working with a more substantial appropriation of $2,000, the state board was able to extend its operations considerably. When "La Grippe," or the "grip" epidemic, seriously affected eighty-six of the hundred counties in 1890, the people found that they had a well-geared organization upon which to depend.

As the volume of work became larger and as demands upon the local boards became heavier it became necessary to remodel the county-level units into stronger, more compact bodies. New legislation provided for a county sanitary committee composed of the county commissioners and two physicians. Under the new system it was hoped that the appointed physicians would be salaried, or at least compensated in some way by the county governments, and thus would be encouraged to devote more time to public health.

It must be remembered that county government in North Carolina at this time was in a raw, unbalanced stage of development. Many of the counties were nebulous, decentralized population areas with no need for governmental complexity. And of the counties in these areas that had any sort of functional, county-level government, many considered a public-health program something of a luxury.

Thus, there was developing in the state a situation which saw the state health movement outrunning the progress of local government. Services were being demanded of the State Board of Health from areas where no local channel existed through which this service could flow. As a result, North Carolina for a long period of time contained within its borders some of the most advanced public-health counties in the nation and at the same time some of the most backward. In 1911, following a new shake-up in county-level organization, four counties began employing full-time county health officers. One of these, Guilford County, was the first county in the United States to begin operation of such a program. But in the same year there were counties in North Carolina which did not have a single resident physician. Many of these counties found it more practical to combine with other counties to form a single health area served by one health board. This practice greatly improved public-health work in some of the smaller counties.

As the county governments became more stable, county health departments enjoyed a parallel development; and in a manner proportional to local demand for public-health services, strong county governments supported strong public-health departments. Meanwhile, the central state organization, receiving favorable support in the legislature, was able itself to broaden both its capacity and its responsibility.

A fairly reliable yardstick for measuring the growth of the state organization during the years that followed is the amount of money appropriated by the General Assembly for its use. Appropriations for the year 1911 totaled $22,500. Two years later this support was raised to $40,500.

These figures demonstrate that North Carolina was rapidly expanding her public-health program, but the figures are only a part of the financial picture. Not shown here are the funds received from outside sources amounting to $166,131 in 1920, a sum nearly equaling the amount appropriated by the state. These funds swelled the total amount available to the State Board of Health for the year to $343,284. Also to be considered is the fact that at this time the General Assembly appropriated $25,000 to the state Laboratory of Hygiene, a division of the state health system, to which may be added $13,699 collected by this division from the counties for services rendered. Thus the total funds available to public-health operations in the state for the year 1920 amounted to nearly $400,000.

Except for the depression years, the General Assembly continued to supply its state health organization with ever increasing amounts of money. With this new money, the state continued to improve its existing services and open new facilities where the demand was great enough. The principal difficulty arising in many cases seemed to be the lack of clear-cut lines or divisions within the over-all state structure, and as new services were created the lines of authority in many cases began to overlap.

To facilitate the placement of new services and to clarify lines of authority, the General Assembly of 1931 passed an act that completely reorganized the fundamental divisions of the state board. The new divisions were set down in this manner: administration, laboratories, oral hygiene, preventative medicine, county health work and epidemiology, and sanitary engineering. These divisions were set up somewhat tentatively, and from time to time various changes were made, both in the departments of the state board and in the subdivisions of the departments. But until the sweeping program that was set up in 1949 and launched the following year, the fundamental structure of the organization remained the same.

The reorganization of the State Board of Health which took place in 1950 fixed the number of divisions at six, placed a director at the head of each, and designated the subdivisions as sections. The increase of over 200 per cent in the health budget of 1949 enabled the board to accelerate greatly the process of expanding the services already carried on by the various divisions and subdivisions, and by March 1 of that year public-health services had been extended to all of the hundred counties. Pamlico came into the program on July 1, 1949, as the last.

ORGANIZATION OF THE PUBLIC-HEALTH PROGRAM.

The enormous amount of work accomplished by the Board of Public Health is carried on in six large divisions broken down into subdivisions.

1. The *Personal Health Division* has five subdivisions or sections, each of which deals with a specific problem or group of related problems: maternal and child health, crippled children, heart-disease control, cancer control, and nutrition.

Thus the Maternal and Child Health Section concentrates most of its energies on lowering the infant-mortality rate, with emphasis on prenatal care, infant care and well-baby clinics, and a highly developed program for the finding and care of premature infants.

The Crippled Children Section examines about 12,000 children each year and recommends the best possible course of correction for each child: therapeutic, surgical, or mechanical or a combination of the three.

The Cancer-Control Section operates in much the same way as the Crippled Children Section in that its services are primarily for certain age groups (women past 35 and men past 40) and also in that it recommends medical attention but does not sponsor it.

2. The *Local Health Division* of the State Board of Health concerns itself largely with the major task of administering in various ways the county divisions. Each year it distributes equitably state and federal funds to the respective local health departments. It also advises and assists these departments in calculating their expenses for the coming year and aids in the planning of modern health departments, each of which has its own facilities and its own particular problems.

3. The *Division of Epidemiology* performs services that are vitally important to the North Carolina public. One of the most publicized of these services, directed by the Tuberculosis Control Section, is the mass chest X-ray program which during the 1950–52 period photographed over a quarter-million people throughout the state.

Under the same division is the Industrial Hygiene Section, the principal service of which is the inspection of the so-called "dusty trade" industries of the state. These include industries engaged in rock cutting, rock crushing, and asbestos manufacture. Their services to these firms are for the most part analyses of working conditions (analyzing air samples) and advice on possible changes and improvements. However, they will sponsor, upon request by the managements, chest X-rays for the workers involved.

The Public-Health Statistics Section, which was for a long time one of the most neglected features of the Epidemiology Department as well as of the entire state health program, has increased its scope of operations tremendously since 1949. For example: in 1940 the national Bureau of the Census reported that only 86 per cent of the infants born in North Carolina (during a test period) had birth certificates on file with the Bureau of Vital Statistics. In 1950 a similar report indicated that 96 per cent of the infants (born during the second test period) had birth certificates on file with the Bureau of Vital Statistics. Important in this improvement has been consolidation. Whereas 1,500 local registrars once were employed by the various city and county governments throughout the state, only 611 were employed in 1950. This number is still much too high for efficiency, but there is reason to believe that in time the number will at least approach the ideal situation of one registrar per county, or only 100 registrars for the whole state.

The Venereal Disease Control Section, because its success throughout the state has reduced the need for its services, has been turned over almost entirely to the county health departments (see page 265).

4. The *Sanitary Engineering Division* of the State Board of Health is probably the division with which the average citizen of North Carolina is most familiar. The Engineering Section, with its staff of eight engineers, is primarily a consultative organization. Engineers, municipal and state officials, and industrial officials engaged in laying out water and sewage systems rely on them for suggestions pertaining to building sites and methods of construction. Once the plants are running, the Engineering Section often is consulted on maintenance problems.

Industrial-waste studies, which have been carried on for the most part with federal funds, have been invaluable in helping industries solve their waste-disposal problems. Working with the State Stream Sanitation Committee and the other state organizations, the Engineering Section has been of assistance to industries interested in establishing plants in North Carolina.

See pages 267-68 for an account of the pest-control program and the inspection of all public establishments carried on in cooperation with the Sanitary Engineering Division.

5. Working closely with other divisions of the State Board of Health is the *State Laboratory of Hygiene* which, during the 1950–52 period, made almost a million laboratory examinations of various types, from examinations of water specimens (both for real estate developments and for industrial supplies) to autopsies of animals suspected of having rabies.

6. One of the less-publicized services of the State Board of Health is the *Oral Hygiene Division*, which every two years visits some 1,000 public schools, examines approximately 162,000 children, and performs a quarter of a million dental corrections. Children whose families are financially unable to provide them with dental care are given this attention by the department's staff dentists. Other children found to have certain mouth conditions are, of course, referred to their local dentists.

There are, in addition to these divisions of the State Board of Health, twenty-two sister organizations (some state, others federal), whose job it is to improve the public health in North Carolina. Among these are the North Carolina Division of the American Cancer Society, the State Tuberculosis Sanatoria Board, the North Carolina Medical Care Commission, the North Carolina Mental Health Council, the Executive Committee of the North Carolina Public Health Association, the Advisory Committee of the North Carolina Recreation Commission, the North Carolina Commission for the Blind, the North Carolina Eugenics Board, the North Carolina Resource-Use Education Commission, and the Governor's Committee on Interstate Co-operation.

MEDICAL CARE COMMISSION.

During the last decade, aided by federal funds made available by the Hill-Burton Act, North Carolina has tremendously increased her local hospitals and clinics. Only Texas has built more. The North Carolina Medical Care Commission, established March 21, 1945, has administered this vast program, and its report of March 1, 1957, gives this history of the enterprise:

> In 1947, there were approximately 8,019 local general hospital beds in North Carolina, or 2.4 beds per 1,000 population. There are now existing or authorized 13,980 acceptable local general hospital beds in North Carolina, or 3.3 beds per 1,000 population. This comparison does not give a reliable indication of actual progress, however, since many of the original beds were obsolete and were in buildings unacceptable for expansion and had to be abandoned. In all, North Carolina has built or contracted to build 6,567 new hospital beds since July 1, 1947, of which 727 are patient beds in State-owned hospitals with the balance of 5,730 located in local general hospitals; 30 in a rehabilitation hospital in Charlotte; and 80 in a chronic disease hospital unit in High Point. In addition to the expenditure of the Medical Care Commission, the State has supplied more than $40 million to state-owned hospitals for new facilities. [1]

See Table 119 for statistics on hospital construction.

At the Local Level[2]

INTRODUCTION.

Ever since 1911, when Guilford County became one of the first three counties in the United States to establish a full-time operating county health department, North Carolina has led progress in full-time local health services.

---

[1] *Summary of Activities, July 1, 1945, to March 1, 1957*, Medical Care Commission press release. March 1, 1957.

[2] The author is indebted to W. P. Richardson, M. D., professor of Preventive Medicine, University of North Carolina School of Medicine, for the preparation of this section.

The year beginning July 1, 1947, was particularly significant in the history of this progress for two reasons. First, it marked the first time every one of the state's one hundred counties had made appropriations for full-time local health service under a cooperative program with the State Board of Health; and, second, the 1947 legislature, by approving an increase of $80,000 in funds for aid to local health departments, making a total of $1,150,000 for local health agencies, provided for the first time for substantial state participation in the costs of local health services. In past years the state participation had been little more than a token. The burden of expansion and increased operating costs of the past decade had been met by local and federal funds. The assumption by the state of its economic responsibility for the maintenance of adequate local health services will give a tremendous boost to the health program.

Local public health services in North Carolina are the responsibility of the city or county, and are administered legally under the authority of city, county, or district boards of health through cooperative agreements with the State Board of Health. These agreements require the local board to maintain certain standards for its personnel and program, and require the State Board of Health to participate in the cost of operation of the local department through the allocation of state and federal funds which are appropriated to it for this purpose.

Fifty-three counties operate separate health departments—although, because of a shortage of health officers, several of these are served by the health officer of an adjoining county—and the remaining 47 counties are organized into 18 district departments. Three cities—Asheville, Charlotte, and Rocky Mount—operate separate city health departments, while the health activities of the other cities are consolidated with those of the respective counties. See Fig. 19 for the organization of the public-health program in one North Carolina county.

There is a generally accepted minimum standard of adequacy for appropriations for field health departments, and it is interesting to compare the situation in North Carolina with this standard. A minimum appropriation of $1.50 per capita has been accepted as necessary. Although the diminished value of the dollar and the increased responsibilities of health departments have made even this standard inadequate, expenditures for local health services in North Carolina fall below even this minimum.

SERVICES OFFERED.

The services made available by the local health departments may be considered under six heads: (1) preventable disease control; (2) maternal and child health; (3) school health; (4) sanitation; (5) health information; and (6) special services. While all local health departments strive to

Fig. 19. Public Health Organization in a North Carolina County

(Guilford, the first county in the U. S. to have a full-time public health department)

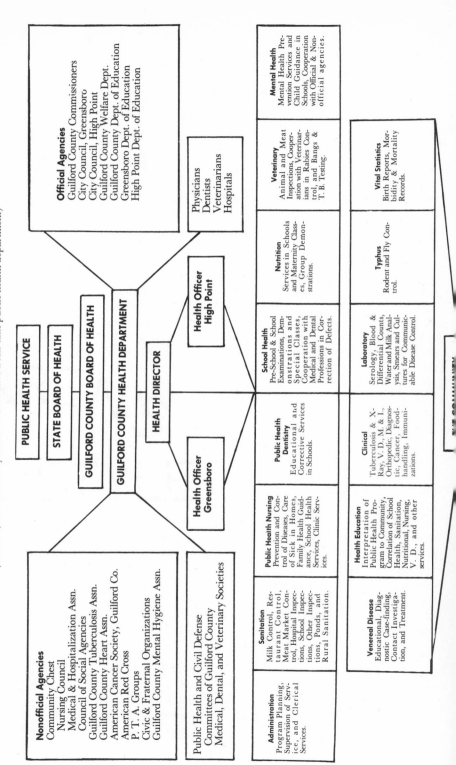

render the services described below, the services in a number of areas are spread very thinly, due partly to inadequate appropriations and partly to the scarcity of qualified personnel.

1. Communicable Disease Control. One of the earliest public health functions was the investigation of contagious or infectious diseases, the imposition of quarantine restrictions and the development of programs of control. Modern scientific discoveries have added tremendously to the effectiveness of these efforts. Sanitation of water and milk supplies has made typhoid fever a rare disease, smallpox has been all but eliminated by vaccination, and effective immunizing agents against diphtheria and whooping cough open up the possibility that these diseases may be reduced to negligible proportions. Tests have been developed which increase the accuracy of the diagnosis of many of these diseases, and the use of the new drugs and antibiotics in the treatment of these diseases is robbing them of much of their menace.

There are special programs against venereal diseases and tuberculosis. Regular clinics are held for the diagnosis of venereal diseases, the instruction of patients, the examination of contacts, and the treatment of gonorrhea and the less common venereal diseases. Syphilis usually is not treated locally. The patients are referred to a modern hospital or center where they receive good care and the most modern type of treatment, which usually cures them in ten days to two weeks. Two of these hospitals are maintained by the State Board of Health, one in Durham and the other in Charlotte.

The health department's services in the tuberculosis program are in the conduct of diagnostic programs, and the supervision of families in which tuberculosis has been found.

Many departments have their own X-ray units and carry on an active program of examination of family contacts, referred patients, those requesting examination on account of systems, special employment groups (teachers, industrial groups, food handlers, etc.), and sometimes the general public. In addition to this regular program most counties either have had or plan to have a comprehensive mass survey of the population over fifteen years of age, carried out cooperatively by the Bureau of Tuberculosis of the State Board of Health and the local health department.

2. Maternal and Child Health. Protection of the health of mothers of infants and small children is a major concern of the health department, and a large proportion of its activities are directly or indirectly related to this objective. Nurses visit expectant mothers and mothers of infants and small children in their homes for the purpose of giving help in the many problems they face—helping detect the need for medical care, and referring those needing care to their physicians. Clinics or medical

conferences are held at which those who may not be able to consult their physicians may secure medical examination and advice. Mothers and children who are ill, or who need medical treatment beyond general supervision, are referred to their own physicians.

Two special programs are carried on in the interest of maternal health. The first is the training and supervision of midwives. Just a few years ago as many as a third of North Carolina mothers were delivered by midwives. While the percentage today is down to 13 per cent, giving them the kind of training and supervision needed to make them safe attendants of the mothers who must call on them is still an important responsibility. The other program is that of planned-parenthood advice, which is provided to those mothers requesting it or to those who need it for health reasons. This service is a normal part of the maternal-health program.

Special services are maintained for crippled children. In cooperation with the Vocational Department of Public Instruction, monthly clinics are held at convenient points in the state for the examination and treatment of children up to the age of twenty-one with orthopedic and crippling conditions. Children from counties in which clinics are not held may be referred to the nearest clinic by their own health departments. Needed hospitalization and medical care beyond that provided at the clinics is available.

The greatest single cause of death during the first year of life is prematurity. It accounts for about a third of all infant deaths. Recently the State Board of Health's Bureau of Maternity and Infancy launched a special program in cooperation with the North Carolina Academy of Pediatrics to cut down on deaths from this cause. Cooperating hospitals in six cities from Asheville to Wilmington have completed or are planning specially designed and equipped premature nurseries, to be staffed by specially trained nurses.

3. School Health. For many years the State Board of Health and the State Department of Public Instruction have cooperated in developing a common philosophy and a coordinated program regarding health instruction in the schools. This joint concern extends down to the local county, where health and educational personnel plan jointly for the total health program of the schools. Health education and the operation of the school plant are the responsibility of the schools, while the medical nursing services provided by the school are the responsibility of the health department, but all are welded into one coordinated program through joint cooperative effort.

The specific plan of health services differs from county to county, but the following services are general:

A. Inspection and screening examination of pupils. Often the teachers participate in this by keeping health records of their pupils and inspecting them periodically for evidence that all may not be well with their health. Those who seem to have health problems are referred for a more careful check to the school nurse or physician. In other schools health department nurses and physicians regularly examine children in certain selected grades. In either case, those needing attention are referred to their own physicians or to appropriate medical clinics for care.

B. Immunizations. Since state laws require immunization against diphtheria, whooping cough, and smallpox, it is customary to require a certificate of immunization for admission to school, and to offer booster shots—or in some cases original vaccinations—at the school.

C. Inspections of physical plant. The health department periodically inspects the school plant's facilities in all items related to health, but especially water, sewage disposal, and lunchroom. The department makes recommendations regarding needed improvements.

D. Oral hygiene. Through the Division of Oral Hygiene of the State Board of Health, dentists with special training are made available regularly to carry on oral health programs in the schools. These programs include instruction in the care of the mouth and the teeth, cleaning and a limited number of dental corrections. Because of the inability to secure the needed number of dentists, these programs are not as extensive as is desirable.

E. Defect correction. Health departments do not have the funds or facilities for correction of the physical defects of school children (exceptions are the crippled children's program and the oral-hygiene program noted above). The department is active in developing special programs for this purpose for those who cannot secure needed care through their own physicians. Parent-Teacher associations, service clubs and other community groups, physicians and hospitals, and county departments of welfare, and—for eye defects—the State Commission for the Blind cooperate in this effort.

4. Sanitation. The sanitation program is a many-sided one. Although such strictly public installations as municipal water and sewage systems are supervised by the State Board of Health, the local department assumes responsibility for supervision of water and sewage-disposal facilities at schools and other institutions not served by public facilities. The State Board of Health provides assistance in water and sewage disposal installations at private homes and enforces those regulations passed by the local board of health regarding privies and septic tanks.

In addition to water and sewage sanitation, supervision is given to food handling and processing establishments and to dairies and milk plants. The responsibility for dairies and plants is shared with the State Department of Agriculture, but most of the routine inspections and bacteriological tests are made by the local health department.

Retail food-handling establishments, chicken-processing plants, abattoirs, meat markets and frozen locker plants are inspected and graded regularly, and cards showing a rating of A, B, or C are prominently posted for the information and protection of the public.

Other services in relation to sanitation include activities for the control of mosquitoes and flies, inspection of swimming pools where authorized by local regulations, sanitary supervision of hotels, tourist camps, hospitals and similar institutions, and rat-control programs. These programs are determined on the basis of need in the particular community.

5. Health Information. The health department makes sound health information available to citizens in a variety of ways. It distributes authoritative literature on health projects. It cooperates with the schools in providing materials and information for pupils. It makes use of radio, newspapers, educational films and group meetings of various kinds. All members of the health department staff participate in these activities. However, an increasing number of departments are employing specially trained health educators to augment and strengthen educational activities, especially through work with community groups and organizations in studying or remedying their particular health problems.

6. Special Services. There are certain special activities which are carried out by State Board of Health personnel and are available in only a limited number of centers in the state. The local health department can provide information regarding these and, where indicated, refer individuals to them. Of special interest are services in the fields of mental health, nutrition, and cancer control. A limited number of mental health clinics are held in the state, and a variety of helpful literature is available. Nutrition education programs are provided by nutritionists of the State Board of Health, who come into the local communities at the request of the health department. In addition, a consulting dietitian is available to assist large institutions in their food and dietary problems.

A number of cancer-detection centers and several cancer diagnostic-management centers are in operation in the state. Any individual forty years of age or over, or any younger person with suggestive symptoms, may go to a diagnostic center, but only those persons suspected of having cancer are referred to the diagnostic-management center.

See Tables 120 and 121 for figures on the reduction of preventable illnesses and deaths within the state, 1921 to 1953, and the increase in local health services (both in number of counties participating and in expenditures) from 1911 to 1953.

BIBLIOGRAPHY

The Health Bulletin, XXXVIII (May, 1923); XXXVIII (July, 1923); L (January, 1935); LXI (January, 1946); LXIII (December, 1948); LXVIII (June, 1953). North Carolina State Board of Health. Raleigh.

The Thirty-Fourth Biennial Report of the North Carolina State Board of Health, 1950–1952. Raleigh.

Chapter 30

PUBLIC WELFARE[1]

HISTORY.

Public welfare has a long and commendable record in the state. When the citizens of North Carolina were called upon to rewrite the constitution in 1868, they provided a basis for improving social conditions. In 1869 the General Assembly set up the Board of Public Charities to supervise charitable, penal, and correctional institutions in accordance with the recommendations of the report of the Committee on Punishment, Penal Institutions, and Public Charities.[2]

The early work done by the Board of Public Charities was in the form of alleviating penal injustices; investigating conditions in jails, almshouses, and so on; and determining the number of insane persons in the counties. The first *Annual Report* (1870) listed $21.00 as expenses incurred by that time. Dr. G. W. Blacknall, a member and special agent of this first board, reported that from 400 to 500 insane persons were confined in jails and county poorhouses, or were being kept at home without proper medical treatment.

Very little is known about the activities of the Board of Public Charities between 1871 and 1889, since no records were kept. However, in 1889, information regarding welfare in the state emerges in the board's reports dealing with juvenile offenders, mismanagement in county homes, county jails, workhouses, etc. The board strongly advocated separation of juvenile offenders from hardened criminals. From this time on, historical records show that a great many resolutions initiated by the board were later enacted into law to improve social and economic conditions in all areas throughout the state, not all of these improvements being confined to the realm of public welfare. The *Annual Report* of the board's work between 1897 and 1898 indicated progress. In the 1870's it had been reported that there were about 250 insane persons crowded into one 224-bed hospital. By 1898 there were three sizable hospitals for 1,537 patients.[3]

---

[1]The author is indebted to Elizabeth Fink of the North Carolina Department of Public Welfare for assistance in the preparation of this chapter.

[2]Laurence Aydlett, "The North Carolina State Board of Public Welfare," *The North Carolina Historical Review*, XXIV (January, 1947), 2.

[3]*Ibid.*, pp. 12–13.

By this time North Carolina was coming into the "limelight of national attention." Other states began communicating with North Carolina to learn how its program operated. Also some progress had been made in care and training of the deaf, dumb, and blind children of the state.

From 1900 to the present, North Carolina has continued to strive for better services for its citizens. Around 1900 the board began to work for a parole system in the penitentiary. In 1903 the first private child-placing agency came into being; it was called the North Carolina Children's Home Society and was located at Greensboro. The year 1907 brought the Stonewall Jackson Manual Training and Industrial School and the North Carolina Sanatorium for Treatment of Tuberculosis. Also, at the board's recommendation, a law was passed requiring school attendance for deaf and blind children. In 1909 pressure from the board brought about a law abolishing hanging as the method of death for condemned prisoners and substituting the electric chair. The first legislation pertaining to Negro delinquents was passed. In 1911 a school for the state's feeble-minded children was opened. Other recommendations of the board that became actualities were the beginning of the recording of vital statistics in 1912 and the creation in 1913 of the State Conference for Social Service and of the State Mental Hygiene Society.[4]

The last session of the Board of Public Charities as such met on April 2, 1917. It needed reorganization, for its responsibilities had been extended. The legislature of 1917 passed an act creating the North Carolina State Board of Charities and Public Welfare to replace the old board, and membership on the board was increased from five to seven members. Under the leadership of A. W. McAlister, Col. W. A. Blaire, Clarence Poe, E. C. Branson, and others, great strides were made in the reorganization of the system. The Board employed the first Commissioner of Public Welfare, Roland F. Beasley, later succeeded by Mrs. Kate Burr Johnson. The old county boards of visitors were reorganized as the official county boards of charities and public welfare. The law allowed the county welfare board to be appointed by the board of county commissioners.[5]

The Mandatory Act of 1919 required organization of every county in the state for public-welfare services and the employment of a superintendent in counties with a population of 25,000 people or more, later amended to 32,000 people.[6] The election of a superintendent was optional in counties with less than 32,000 population, but in counties where the

[4] All information by date has been taken from respective copies of annual and biennial reports of the North Carolina Board of Public Charities.

[5] Aydlett, op. cit., p. 19.

[6] S. H. Hobbs, Jr., North Carolina: Economic and Social (Chapel Hill: University of North Carolina Press, 1930), p. 296.

commissioners failed to elect one, the superintendent of schools was called upon to serve as ex officio superintendent of public welfare.[7]

In mentioning the changes in the spirit of public welfare work taking place all over the nation as well as in North Carolina, the *Biennial Report* of 1920–22 said: "Chief among these [changes] is the emphasis which is now being laid upon the idea of preventive vs. relief and palliation as the most important aspect of social work."[8]

On January 1, 1925 (by which time 57 counties had organized welfare departments, 46 with full-time superintendents), with the aid of a $30,000 grant from the Laura Spelman-Rockefeller Memorial Fund, the board established its Division of Work Among Negroes, the first in the South. Its objectives were: first, a comprehensive study of Negro life with its social problems; and then the development programs to stimulate co-operative self-help efforts among the Negroes.[9]

During the depression years, many of the staff of the state board served on the Governor's Council on Unemployment and Relief. The Emergency Relief Administration, which had taken care of many of the economic and unemployment problems of the state during the depression period, was liquidated in December, 1935. A federal grant of $225,000 was given to the State Board of Charities and Public Welfare to assume certain duties formerly handled by ERA, and herein began federal aid to public welfare.

After the Social Security Act was passed by Congress in 1935, North Carolina began to take advantage of its provisions. The administration of the public-assistance categories of old-age assistance and aid to dependent children was allotted to the state board by the General Assembly of 1937. Also the program of child-welfare services began to expand greatly in 1936.

In 1944 Mrs. W. T. Bost, who had succeeded as commissioner in 1930, resigned, to be succeeded in turn by Dr. Ellen Winston, the present commissioner.

In 1945 the legislature made far-reaching changes in laws pertaining to child welfare, services to old people, etc. It also changed the name of the state welfare agency again—this time to North Carolina State Board of Public Welfare, thus reflecting the latest concept of social service as truly public welfare and not as charity.

Currently, the North Carolina public-welfare program is headed by a State Board of Public Welfare composed of seven appointed members,

---

[7] *Ibid.*

[8] *Biennial Report of the North Carolina Board of Charities and Public Welfare, 1920–1922,* p. 9.

[9] *Biennial Report, 1924–1926,* p. 100.

one of whom must be a woman. The work of this state board is channeled through five divisions and ten special services. Each county has a county welfare department headed by a county welfare board. Membership on a county welfare board is limited to three persons (five members in Guilford County); one member is appointed by the state board, another by the board of county commissioners, and a third member by the first two members.

Money for the state welfare program comes from three sources: federal, state, and county. Funds for the fiscal year 1956 totaled almost $48,000,000 for all welfare purposes—65 per cent from the federal government, 14 per cent from state funds, and 21 per cent from county funds.

PUBLIC ASSISTANCE.

The three public-assistance programs which are administered by the State Board of Public Welfare are old-age assistance, aid to dependent children, and aid to the permanently and totally disabled. All three programs are financed jointly from federal, state, and county funds. Table 122 shows expenditures and source of funds under each category for the fiscal year 1956. Table 123 gives the picture in North Carolina as compared with the nation as a whole.

To receive old-age assistance, the individual must be 65 years of age or over, must be in need because he lacks basic necessities of life, must have resided in North Carolina for the past year, and must not live in a public institution or be a patient in a mental or tuberculosis hospital. In April, 1957, the number of recipients of old-age assistance in North Carolina was 51,689 with an average monthly payment of $34.39. The United States average was $55.00 in July.

The aid-to-dependent children program provides financial assistance to needy children under eighteen years of age who have been deprived of parental care and support because of the death, incapacity, or continued absence from home of one or both parents. As of April, 1957, there were 63,973 children receiving aid under this program, with an average monthly grant of $17.35 per person. This number represented 21,435 families; the average grant to each family was $67.37 per month. The national average was $96.37 in March of 1957.

The category of aid to the permanently and totally disabled provides financial help for many who previously received general assistance paid for wholly from county funds. A person is eligible for assistance under the aid to the permanently and totally disabled program if he is between the ages of eighteen and sixty-five, resides in North Carolina, is not an inmate of a public institution, is permanently and totally disabled, and is in need. The number of such persons receiving aid in April, 1957, was 14,603; the average monthly grant was $38.81. The United States average was $58.79 in March, 1957.

In addition to administering the three public-assistance programs, county departments of public welfare give help through general assistance. This fund, which is provided entirely by county tax levy and receives no federal or state subsidy, gives financial assistance to needy persons who are not eligible for public assistance. For the most part, general assistance goes to emergency cases which result from some sudden disaster. County welfare departments also perform for clients a wide variety of preventive, protective, and rehabilitative services which are nonfinancial in nature. Table 124 shows the scope and number of nonfinancial services which were performed by the one hundred county departments of public welfare in 1957.

INSTITUTIONAL AND PROTECTIVE SERVICES.

This area of responsibility of the State Board of Public Welfare takes charge of inspecting state and local institutions of a charitable or penal nature; it sets about raising their standards and fosters the expanding of homes for the aged. Any new jail or city lockup must be approved by the state board. All boarding homes for the aged caring for two or more persons receiving services or assistance from a county welfare department must be inspected and licensed by the state board.

CHILD WELFARE.

The state Board of Public Welfare, through its staff of child-welfare specialists, carries a variety of functions in this area. It sets standards for and licenses child-caring institutions, day-care facilities, foster homes, private child-placing agencies, and maternity homes. It also gives consultant help to all public and private agencies in improving their services to children. These emphasize services to children in their own homes, including the use of substitute homemakers when mothers are temporarily out of the picture, adoption, foster-family care, group care, and work with the juvenile courts. The superintendent of public welfare in each county serves as chief probation officer for the juvenile court of the county.

PSYCHOLOGICAL SERVICES.

Clinical psychologists on the staff of the state Board of Public Welfare work closely with the counties in giving psychological examinations to clients and suggesting appropriate programs of action. These services are available to every person in North Carolina. The psychologists hold clinics regularly in county welfare departments. Children are examined to determine suitability for adoption, placement in boarding homes, or placement in training school. Frequently the clinical psychologist examines children who are involved in school problems or who are referred by juvenile courts. These examinations serve not only to help in the placement of children but also to provide parents and adults with information that will help them to work with the children.

OTHER SERVICES.

In addition to the services outlined above, the staff of the state board renders a number of other specialized services. Among them are field service, research and statistics, licensing of fund-raising, publications and information, community services, and legal services.

Field service is the liaison between the state office and county welfare departments. The ten field representatives of the state board visit North Carolina's one hundred counties and work on policies and problems with the local welfare staffs and welfare boards to strengthen over-all administration of the public-welfare program.

The research and statistics service has the responsibility of collecting, editing, tabulating, publishing, and interpreting information on the total public-welfare program in North Carolina. County departments of public welfare submit reports periodically on services rendered, turnover in cases, amounts of assistance provided, and individuals and families served. Information of general interest is published monthly in *Public Welfare Statistics*. In addition, research bulletins on special topics are published by this division.

Agencies and organizations that ask the public to donate money for philanthropic purposes are investigated and licensed by the state board. The names of all organizations meeting requirements of the state solicitation law, as well as those to which licenses are refused, are made known to the public. Individuals who solicit from the public must obtain a license through the state Board of Public Welfare.

The publications and information service provides selective presentation of information about public welfare at both the state and local levels. Publicity assistance to welfare projects on both state and county levels is handled through this office. It also publishes the quarterly *Public Welfare News* and information booklets on various aspects of North Carolina's public-welfare program.

The aim of the community-services unit is to bring better service to North Carolinians through cooperative work with existing organizations and agencies. This unit attempts stimulation of community planning and action for the purpose of strengthening family life, protection of children, and prevention of juvenile delinquency. It provides leadership and guidance in developing and utilizing community resources to meet the needs of children and families as a supplement to the services of the public-welfare program.

The staff attorney of the state board provides needed legal services to the board and is available for consultation on legal matters with county departments of public welfare and with other county officials. Because of the many public-welfare laws, it is necessary to have a specialist in this field. Areas handled by the staff attorney include, among others, special attention to the lien law, the adoption law, the reciprocal support of dependents law, and work with juvenile and domestic-relations courts.

RECENT EMPHASES AND ACCOMPLISHMENTS.

A number of state laws have been enacted during the past ten years which strengthen the state board's responsibilities for the protection of children, for the better provision for older people, for the inspection of county and city jails, for the protection of children being adopted as well as for the other parties to the adoptive process, and for improving administrative procedure. At the same time the federal Social Security Act has been amended with resultant major changes in the scope and financing of the state's public-welfare program. The state board recognizes that a sound welfare program is based on sound legislation.

Perhaps the contribution of greatest importance in public welfare administration during the past decade have been these: (1) clarifying the underlying purposes of public welfare in the thinking of the citizens and leadership of the state; (2) enlisting the cooperation of many interested persons and agencies to share in the achievement of these purposes; (3) strengthening the administration of North Carolina's state-supervised and county-administered public-welfare program; (4) vitalizing and enlarging the program of services and aid to children through every means available—federal, state, and county—public and private; and placing increased emphasis upon preventive and rehabilitative services that help people to help themselves.

BIBLIOGRAPHY

Annual reports and biennial reports of the North Carolina Board of Public Charities. Raleigh.

AYDLETT, LAURENCE. "The North Carolina State Board of Public Welfare," *The North Carolina Historical Review*, XXIV (January 1947), 1–33.

Biennial Report of the North Carolina State Board of Charities and Public Welfare, December 1, 1920 to June 30, 1922. Raleigh.

Biennial Report of the North Carolina State Board of Charities and Public Welfare, July 1, 1924 to June 30, 1926. Raleigh.

HOBBS, S. H., Jr. *North Carolina: Economic and Social.* Chapel Hill: University of North Carolina Press, 1930.

Public Welfare in North Carolina. North Carolina Resource Bulletin Series. Raleigh: 1949.

The State Board of Public Welfare issues each month a report on all public welfare in North Carolina, summaries and by counties.

Public Welfare News. Fortieth Anniversary Special Issue. Forty Years of Public Welfare Progress. North Carolina State Board of Public Welfare. November 1957. Raleigh.

Table 1. Value of Mineral Production by Year

YEAR	VALUE OF OUTPUT
1900	$ 1,604,078
1910	2,848,446
1920	8,117,916
1927	12,569,433
1947	16,386,000
1948	18,231,000
1949	19,755,000
1950	26,343,000
1951	29,648,000

Source: Compiled, U. S. Department of the Interior, Bureau of Mines, *Minerals Yearbook* (Washington: U. S. Government Printing Office) for the years in question.

Table 2. Mineral Production in North Carolina, 1953 and 1954[a]

MINERAL	1953 Mineral tons (unless otherwise stated)	1953 VALUE	1954 Short tons (unless otherwise stated)	1954 VALUE
Abrasive stones	b	$ 16,150	587[c]	$ 12,125[c]
Clays	1,466,232	2,534,908	1,872,541	2,519,721
Copper, pounds			360	106
Feldspar, crude, long tons	268,042	3,290,495	230,744	2,220,707
Gold, troy ounces			214	7,490
Lead			4	1,049
Mica: scrap and flake	56,834	1,428,793	61,049	1,457,122
sheet, pounds	619,895	1,308,494	479,221	1,787,197
Sand and gravel	6,910,982	4,992,991	7,441,200	5,508,284
Silver, troy ounces			438[d]	396[d]
Stone	9,317,390[e]	14,424,323[e]	10,133,728	15,625,331
Talc and pyrophyllite, crude	119,341	578,239	112,704	388,428
Tungsten, concentrate 60 per cent wo[c] basis	2,074	f	2,538	f
Undistributed: asbestos, beryllium concentrate, columbium-tantalum concentrate, lithium minerals, manganiferous ore, millstones (1954); olivine, quartz, stone (crushed and dimension marble) (1953); tungsten concentrate, vermiculite, and minerals whose value must be concealed for particular years indicated by footnote f in appropriate column		9,876,773[g]		12,122,942
Total		38,451,000[g]		41,651,000

Source: J. R. Thoenen and Jasper L. Stuckey, *The Mineral Industry of North Carolina*, U. S. Department of the Interior, Bureau of Mines (Washington: U. S. Government Printing Office, 1954), p. 2.

[a]Production as measured by mine shipments, sales, or marketable production (including consumption by producers).

[b]Weight not recorded.

[c]Grinding pebbles and tube-mill liners only.

[d]Final figure; supersedes preliminary figure given in commodity chapter.

[e]Excludes certain stone, value for which is included with "undistributed."

[f]Value included with "undistributed."

[g]Revised figure.

Table 3. Gross Area by Broad Use Class, Northern Coastal Plain, 1955

Class of use	Area	
	Thousand acres	Per cent
Forest land:		
Commercial	4,140.4	46.6
Noncommercial:		
Productive-reserved	0.4	*
Unproductive	261.4	2.9
Total	4,402.2	49.5
Nonforest land:		
Agriculture	1,929.5	21.7
Marsh	205.1	2.3
Urban and other[a]	208.4	2.4
Total	2,343.0	26.4
Total land area	6,745.2	75.9
Total water area[b]	2,145.7	24.1
All classes	8,890.9	100.0

Source: James F. McCormack, *Forest Statistics for the Northern Plain of North Carolina, 1955*, U. S. Department of Agriculture Forest Service in cooperation with the North Carolina Department of Conservation and Development, Forest Survey Release No. 45 (Asheville, 1955), p. 9.

[a]Includes urban, suburban residential, and rural industrial areas, rights of way, cemeteries, schools, etc.

[b]Census water area reported in 1950 plus 3,200 acres of census water created since 1950. Also includes 32,400 acres of water according to Survey standards but defined by the Bureau of the Census as land area.

*Less than 0.05 per cent.

Table 4. Gross Area by Broad Use Class, Southern Coastal Plain, 1955

Class of use	Area	
	Thousand acres	Per cent
Forest land:		
Commercial	5,388.9	63.4
Noncommercial:		
Reserved from commercial use	4.9	0.1
Unproductive for timber use	86.0	1.0
Total forest	5,479.8	64.5
Nonforest land:		
Agriculture	2,510.5	29.5
Marsh	77.1	0.9
Urban and other[a]	287.2	3.4
Total nonforest	2,874.8	33.8
Total land area	8,354.6	98.3
Total water area[b]	142.7	1.7
All classes	8,497.3	100.0

Source: McCormack, *Forest Statistics for the Southern Coastal Plain of North Carolina, 1952*, U. S. Department of Agriculture, Forest Service, Forest Survey Release No. 41, p. 8.

[a]Includes urban, suburban residential, and rural industrial areas, rights of way, cemeteries, schools, etc.

[b]Includes 33,200 acres of water according to Survey standards of area classification but defined by the Bureau of the Census as land.

Table 5.   Gross Area by Broad Use Class, Piedmont Area, 1956

Class of use	Area	
	Thousand acres	Per cent
Forest land:		
Commercial	5,821.1	54.7
Noncommercial:		
Productive-reserved	15.9	0.2
Unproductive	4.5	*
Total forest	8,841.5	54.9
Nonforest land:		
Agriculture	4,194.0	39.4
Urban and other[a]	497.9	4.7
Total nonforest	4,691.9	44.1
Total land area	10,533.4	99.0
Total water area[b]	105.3	1.0
All classes	10,638.7	100.0

Source: McCormack, *Forest Statistics for the Piedmont of North Carolina, 1956*, U. S. Department of Agriculture, Forest Service, Forest Survey Release No. 48, p. 8.

[a]Includes urban, suburban, residential, and rural industrial areas, rights of way, cemeteries, schools, etc.

[b]Includes 48,600 acres of census water reported in 1950 plus 14,000 acres of census water created since 1950. Also includes 42,700 acres of water according to survey standards but defined by the Bureau of the Census as land area.

*Less than 0.5 per cent.

Table 6.   Gross Area by Broad Use Class, Mountain Region, 1955

Class of use	Area	
	Thousand acres	Per cent
Forest land:		
Commercial	3,991.0	69.9
Noncommercial:		
Productive-reserved	319.3	5.6
Unproductive	41.9	0.7
Total forest	4,352.2	76.2
Nonforest land:		
Agriculture	1,124.8	19.7
Urban and other[a]	157.7	2.8
Total nonforest	1,282.5	22.5
Total land area	5,634.7	98.7
Total water area[b]	74.1	1.3
All classes	5,708.6	100.0

Source: McCormack, *Forest Statistics for the Mountain Region of North Carolina, 1956*, U. S. Department of Agriculture, Forest Service, Forest Survey Bulletin 46, p. 11.

[a]Includes urban residential, rural industrial areas, rights of way, cemeteries, schools, etc.

[b]Includes 45,400 acres of census water reported in 1950 and 200 acres created since 1950, plus 28,500 acres of water in small streams and lakes which is defined by the Bureau of the Census as land area.

Table 7. Ownership of Commercial Forest Land

Class of ownership	Commercial forest land	
	Thousand acres	Per cent
Public land		
National forest	1,046.6	5.4
Indian	52.1	0.3
Other federal	231.5	1.2
Total federal	1,330.2	6.9
State	253.0	1.3
County and municipal	35.6	0.2
Total public	1,618.8	8.4
Private land		
Farm	13,268.7	68.6
Other	4,453.9	23.0
Total private	17,722.6	91.6
All classes	19,341.4	100.0

Source: Robert W. Larson, *North Carolina's Timber Supply, 1955*, U. S. Department of Agriculture Forest Service, Southeastern Forest Experiment Station, Forest Survey Release No. 49 (Asheville, 1957).

Table 8. Net Volume of Forest Type and Stand-Size Class, North Carolina, 1955 (in million board feet)

Forest type	Large sawtimber stands	Small sawtimber stands	Pole-timber stands	Seedling and sapling stands	Poorly stocked stands and unstocked areas	All stands
Softwood types:						
Longleaf pine	60.6	318.5	226.8	35.3	10.2	651.4
Loblolly pine	4,939.1	7,285.9	1,098.5	225.3	13.8	13,562.6
Shortleaf pine	512.5	3,475.2	411.3	41.0	1.8	4,441.8
Pond pine	380.0	1,590.4	355.9	228.8	43.1	2,598.2
Virginia pine	22.1	827.5	164.3	32.5	0.7	1,047.1
White pine	623.6	214.8	36.1	0.7	6.1	881.3
Spruce-fir	117.4	—	1.9	—	6.0	125.3
Total	6,655.3	13,712.3	2,294.8	563.6	81.7	23,307.7
Hardwood types:						
Oak-pine	1,518.3	1,628.3	698.2	297.5	3.9	4,146.2
Oak-hickory:						
Upland hdwds.	5,620.4	3,102.4	1,805.0	353.7	51.1	10,932.6
Scrub oak	—	—	—	33.9	24.8	58.7
Oak-gum-cypress	6,933.6	3,326.9	916.5	459.6	51.7	11,688.3
Maple-beech-birch	525.9	200.3	60.9	9.9	—	797.0
Total	14,598.2	8,257.9	3,480.6	1,154.6	131.5	27,622.8
All types	21,253.5	21,970.2	5,775.4	1,718.2	213.2	50,930.5
Per cent	41.7	43.1	11.4	3.4	0.4	100.0

Source: See Table 7.

Table 9. Average Annual Volume of Timber Cut by Tree-Size Class and Species Group, North Carolina, 1955

1. SAWTIMBER (in million board feet)

Tree-Size Class	Softwoods		Soft hardwoods	Hard hardwoods	All species
	Pine	Other			
Small sawtimber	932.0	36.5	66.5	108.3	1,143.3
Large sawtimber	480.7	85.8	237.5	198.6	1,002.6
All trees	1,412.7	122.3	304.0	306.9	2,145.9

2. GROWING STOCK (in thousand cords)

Pole trees	932	32	233	238	1,435
Small sawtimber	2,651	89	196	323	3,259
Large sawtimber	1,080	155	555	480	2,270
All trees	4,663	276	984	1,041	6,964

3. GROWING STOCK (in million board feet)

Pole trees	59.3	2.3	15.3	15.8	92.7
Small sawtimber	197.8	7.6	15.1	24.8	245.3
Large sawtimber	89.1	14.5	45.4	39.1	188.1
All trees	346.2	24.4	75.8	79.7	526.1

Source: See Table 7.

Table 10. Commercial Forest Area by Forest Type and Stand-Size Class (in thousand acres)

Forest type	Large sawtimber stands	Small sawtimber stands	Pole-timber stands	Seedling and sapling stands	Poorly stocked stands and unstocked areas	All stands
Softwood types:						
Longleaf pine	8.2	97.5	343.4	184.1	39.1	672.3
Loblolly pine	552.1	1,355.4	1,079.7	509.4	32.9	3,529.5
Shortleaf pine	78.7	729.7	732.6	189.8	18.3	1,749.1
Pond pine	75.1	340.2	379.7	569.9	91.0	1,455.9
Virginia pine	3.7	188.4	397.6	210.7	35.3	835.7
White pine	65.4	64.4	44.9	26.8	4.3	205.8
Spruce-fir	5.1	—	5.6	—	3.5	14.2
Total	788.3	2,775.6	2,983.5	1,690.7	224.4	8,462.5
Hardwood types:						
Oak-pine	234.9	436.3	776.6	547.3	32.0	2,027.1
Oak-hickory:						
Upland hdwds.	1,118.8	1,028.1	2,129.6	782.7	149.1	5,208.3
Scrub oak	—	—	—	70.9	133.3	204.2
Oak-gum-cypress	944.1	699.1	723.2	721.6	110.7	3,198.7
Maple-beech-birch	85.7	56.9	72.4	25.6	—	240.6
Total	2,383.5	2,220.4	3,701.8	2,148.1	425.1	10,878.9
All types	3,171.8	4,996.0	6,685.3	3,838.8	649.5	19,341.4
Per cent	16.4	25.8	34.6	19.8	3.4	100.0

Source: See Table 7.

Table 11.   Forest Facts for North Carolina, 1953

Total forest land, acres (rank 9th)	19,513,000
Commercial forest land, all ownership	18,976,000
Federal forests, acres	1,304,000
National forests, acres	999,000
Other	305,000
State, county, municipal, acres	279,000
Private forests, acres	17,393,000
Farm	13,590,000
Wood-using industries	2,584,000
Other	1,219,000
Live sawtimber, million board feet	44,152
Softwood	22,450
Hardwood	21,693
Net annual growth, live sawtimber, 1952, million board feet (rank 3rd)	2,951
Softwood	1,606
Hardwood	1,345
Net annual cut, 1952, million board feet (rank 4th)	2,381
Softwood	1,542
Hardwood	840
Growing stock, 1953. Min. 5 inches breast high, millions of cubic feet (rank 5th)	13,642
Softwood	6,379
Hardwood	7,263
Net annual growth, 1952, millions of cubic feet (rank 2nd)	802
Softwood	416
Hardwood	386
Net annual cut, 1952, millions of cubic feet	647
Softwood	415
Hardwood	232

Source: U. S. Bureau of the Census, *Statistical Abstract of the United States*, 77th Annual Edition (Washington: Government Printing Office, 1956).

Table 12. Average Temperature by Regions

Region	Spring	Summer	Autumn	Winter	Year
Coastal Plain	60	77	63	44	62
Piedmont Plateau	59	77	60	42	60
Mountain	54	71	56	38	55
For the state[a]	58	75	60	42	59

Compiled by the author from U. S. Weather Bureau reports.
[a]Unweighted averages.

Table 13. Average Precipitation in North Carolina, by Regions

Region	Spring	Summer	Autumn	Winter	Year
Coastal Plain	10.9	17.4	9.6	10.4	48.4
Piedmont Plateau	11.4	16.0	8.9	11.0	47.2
Mountain	13.4	16.6	10.7	13.5	54.1
For the state[a]	11.9	17.0	9.7	11.6	49.4

Compiled by the author from U. S. Weather Bureau reports.
[a]Unweighted averages.

Table 14. Hydroelectric Power in North Carolina, 1951

RIVER BASIN	INSTALLED CAPACITY—KW.		RESERVOIR STORAGE FOR POWER USE—AC.–FT.	
	EXISTING[a]	UNDEVELOPED	EXISTING[b]	UNDEVELOPED
Roanoke	8,884	207,000	0	37,000
Tar	1,600	11,500	0	271,000
Neuse	1,835	41,200	1,000	62,000
Cape Fear	10,268	172,100	2,000	492,000
Yadkin-Pee-Dee	226,099	344,700	558,000	2,680,000
Santee-Catawba	166,875	115,000	406,000	1,477,000
Broad	17,213	91,000	14,000	804,000
Tennessee, Hiwassee	528,539	242,600	1,867,000	381,000
Total	961,313	1,225,100	2,848,000	6,204,000

Source: Federal Power Commission Regional Office, Atlanta, Georgia.
[a]Includes electric utility plant and industrial establishments.
[b]At site.

Note: 1956 hydroelectric capacity was approximately 1,310,000 kilowatts due to additions to TVA and a new plant at Roanoke Rapids.

Table 15. Principal Rivers and Developed Power, 1956

RIVERS	KILOWATT
Hiwassee	192,100[a]
Little Tennessee and tributaries	658,835
Pigeon	108,000
Catawba	160,000
Roanoke	100,000
Yadkin	222,000
Total six rivers	1,280,935
Total all hydroelectric production (approximately)	1,310,000

Compiled by the author.
[a]Includes Appalachia Dam, with powerhouse in Tennessee.

Table 16. Electric Power Generating Plants in North Carolina, 1954–55[a]

Owner	Name of plant	Capacity (kw.) Hydro	Capacity (kw.) Steam	Total
Carolina Aluminum Company	Yadkin Narrows	81,200		
	Yadkin Falls	20,300		
	High Rock	33,000		
Aluminum Company of America	Cheoah	110,000		
	Santeetlah	45,000		
Total, hydro		289,500		289,500
Carolina Power and Light Company	Cape Fear		102,000	
	Elk Mountain		12,000	
	Goldsboro		165,000	
	Wilmington		213,000	
	Lumberton		180,000	
Total, steam			672,000	672,000
Note: Moncure Addition, 1956			140,000	
	Blewett	24,600		
	Buckhorn	2,900		
	Carbonton	1,000		
	Eury	600		
	Lockville	1,000		
	Marshall	3,000		
	Tillery	62,000		
	Walters	108,000		
	Weaver	2,500		
Total, hydro		205,600		
Total, all generation				877,600
Note: Carolina Power and Light Company purchases from other 161,000 kw. capacity				
Duke Power Company	Eno		30,000	
	Dan River		140,000	
	Buck		443,000	
	River Bend		631,000	
	Cliffside		210,000	
	Mount Holly		31,400	
Total, steam			1,485,400	
	Bridgewater	20,000		
	Rhodhiss	25,500		
	Oxford	36,000		
	Lookout	18,720		
	Mt. Island	60,000		
	Carters Falls	180		
	Gunpowder #1 & #2	500		
	Idols	1,411		
	Lake Tahoma	240		
	Little River	500		
	Mt. Airy #1 & #2	608		
	Pilot Mountain	500		

(Continued on next page)

285

Table 16 (continued)

Owner	Name of plant	Capacity (kw.)		Total
		Hydro	Steam	
Duke Power Company (continued)	Spencer Mountain	640		
	Turner	5,500		
	Tuxedo	5,000		
	Walnut Cove	544		
Total, hydro		175,843		
Total, all generation				1,661,243
Nantahala Power Company	Tennessee Creek	10,800		
	Bear Creek	9,000		
	Cedar Cliff	6,375		
	Tuckasegee	3,000		
	Queens Creek	1,440		
	Nantahala	43,200		
	Mission	1,800		
	Thorpe	21,600		
	Franklin	1,040		
	Bryson City	980		
Total, hydro		99,235		99,235
Virginia Electric and Power Company	Roanoke Rapids	3,600[b]		
	Nags Head (diesel)		1,200	
Total				4,800
Minor Companies				
Carolina Mountain Power Company		3,600		
Dillsboro and Sylva Electric Company	Dillsboro	225		3,825
Pamlico Power and Light Company	Englehard (diesel)		960	960
Municipally operated plants Steam	Greenville		15,000	
	Kinston		18,500	
	Rocky Mount		30,000	
	Wilson		27,500	
	Washington		8,250	
Total, steam			99,250	
Diesel	Belhaven		514	
	Farmville		3,000	
	New Bern		6,000	
	Tarboro		6,000	
	Southport		625	
	Windsor		425	
Total, diesel			16,564	
Total, all municipal				115,841
Tennessee Valley Authority	Chatuge, 1 unit	10,000		
	Appalachia, 2 units	75,000		
	Hiwassee, 2 units	117,100		
	Fontana, 3 units	202,500		
Total, hydro		404,600		

[a]Data for Duke Power Company, Carolina Power and Light Company, Carolina Aluminum Company, Nantahala Power Company, Virginia Electric and Power Company were supplied by respective companies and are for dates December 31, 1954 to May 5, 1955. These are the major public utilities.

[b]Enlarged to 100,000 kilowatts in 1956.

Table 17. Accumulative Progress Report, Rural Electric Distribution Coverage

YEAR	Total miles constructed	Total consumers connected	Estimated farms connected	PERCENTAGE FARMS ELECTRIFIED IN N. C.	IN U. S.
Jan. 1, 1935			9,672	3.2	10.9
Dec. 31, 1935	1,884		11,558	3.8	11.6
July, 1936	3,135	19,419	15,558	5.1	12.3
July, 1938	8,889	51,000	45,000	14.3	19.1
July, 1939	12,293	70,362	59,580	18.6	22.1
July, 1940	21,195	116,743	72,000	25.9	30.4
July, 1944	28,686	157,060	98,500	35.4	42.2
July, 1945	30,400	175,882	112,000	39.0	44.7
July, 1947	39,394	240,534	148,000	51.5	61.0
July, 1949	58,277	367,323	202,000	70.3	78.2
July, 1950	65,350	417,518	225,000	78.0	
July, 1952	72,673	481,113	260,811	90.4	88.1
July, 1954	77,095	530,476	279,685	96.9	92.3
July, 1956	80,284	569,495	257,500	96.1	94.2

Source: *Report of the North Carolina Rural Electrification Authority, 1956* (Raleigh, N. C.).

Table 18. Rural Electrification in North Carolina by Agencies, July 1, 1956[*]

AGENCY	Miles of rural electric distribution power lines			
	Completed and in operation	Under construction	Authorized but not under construction	Total miles
Electric utility companies	35,933.27	64.02	120.97	36,118.26
Electric membership corporations	40,302.64	152.30	590.00	41,044.94
Municipalities	3,909.77	0.00	4.50	3,914.27
Public institutions	139.10	1.00	.50	140.60
Totals	80,284.78	217.32	715.97	81,218.07

AGENCY	Consumers on above miles of line			
	Completed lines in operation	To be connected to lines under construction	Authorized but not under construction	Total consumers
Electric utility companies	337,168	178	824	338,170
Electric membership corporations	180,866	777	3,411	185,054
Municipalities	48,780	4	31	48,815
Public institutions	2,681	3	3	2,687
Totals	569,495	962	4,269	574,726

[*]As reported to the North Carolina Rural Electrification Authority by the cooperating electric agencies.

Table 19. Grand Total, All Power, 1955[a]

	Hydro kw.	Steam, diesel kw.
Aluminum Company of America	289,500	
Carolina Power and Light Company	205,600[b]	672,000
Duke Power Company	175,843	1,485,400[c]
Nantahala Power Company	99,230	
Virginia Electric and Power Company	3,600[d]	1,200
Municipal and minor companies		116,999
Tennessee Valley Authority	404,600	
Total	1,178,373	2,275,599
Grand total, all power		3,453,972

Compiled by the author.

[a]Exclusive of minor industrial power.

[b]Carolina Power and Light Company is making extensive additions, including a 150,000-kilowatt steam plant at Moncure.

[c]Duke Power Company plans to add 350,000 kilowatts in North and South Carolina at a cost of $51,000,000.

[d]Add approximately 100,000 kilowatts for the Roanoke Rapids plant completed in 1956; several steam stations are under construction.

Table 20.   Production of Electric Energy in the Southeast, 1954
(thousands of kilowatt hours)

	Electric utilities, 1954	Industrial establishments, 1954[a]	Total, 1954
United States	471,609,103	73,036,381	544,645,484
Alabama	15,797,640	1,435,958	17,233,598
Florida	8,738,653	1,269,621	10,008,274
Georgia	6,952,921	1,167,272	8,120,193
Mississippi	3,164,271	547,855	3,712,126
North Carolina	12,410,854	2,326,228	14,737,082
South Carolina	5,420,511	978,747	6,399,258
Tennessee	17,195,062	794,962	17,990,024
Total	69,679,912	8,520,643	78,200,555

Source: Federal Power Commission Regional Office, Atlanta, Georgia.

[a]Extended to represent total industrial production of electric energy from reported date accounting for some 85 per cent coverage, principally Carolina Aluminum Company. North Carolina leads the nation in power developed and consumed by industrial establishments.

Table 21. Growth of Electric Power in North Carolina, 1902–55

YEAR	Total installed hydro, kw.	Total installed steam, kw.	Output kw.-hr.	Per cent output hydro
1902			8,351,000	
1920	248,000	320,000	733,000,000	93.0
1928	617,000	426,000	2,245,000,000	88.6
1949	979,948	945,000	10,250,000,000	48.2
1952	979,948	1,277,000	12,000,000,000	25.0
1955	1,178,373[a]	2,275,373	15,000,000,000	est. 20.0

Compiled by the author.

[a]Includes aluminum and other nonutility, approximately 325,000 kilowatts; hydro-electric output averages about 2,326,000,000 kilowatt hours.

Note: Add 100,000 kilowatts hydroelectric at Roanoke Rapids completed in early 1956.

Table 22. Ranking of the States in Value of Fish Production, 1880, 1908, 1940, 1950

1880		1908		1940		1950	
STATE	VALUE, (thousands of dollars)	STATE	VALUE, (thousands of dollars)	STATE	VALUE, (thousands of dollars)	STATE	VALUE, (thousands of dollars)
Massachusetts	$7,960	Massachusetts	$7,095	California	$20,159	California	$81,605
Maryland	5,222	Virginia	4,716	Massachusetts	15,756	Massachusetts	40,767
New York	3,918	New York	4,594	Washington	6,676	Louisiana	23,645
New Jersey	3,104	Washington	3,513	Florida	5,005	Washington	19,070
Virginia	2,997	Florida	3,389	Louisiana	4,952	Virginia	16,119
Maine	2,743	Maryland	3,306	Virginia	4,858	New York	15,905
California	1,861	Maine	3,257	New York	4,392	Florida	15,704
Delaware	998	New Jersey	3,069	New Jersey	2,957	Maine	14,689
Connecticut	933	Connecticut	2,982	Oregon	2,742	Texas	11,265
North Carolina	846	California	1,970	Maine	2,606	New Jersey	10,201
Michigan	716	North Carolina	1,776	Maryland	2,599	Maryland	8,888
Rhode Island	697	Rhode Island	1,752	Michigan	2,022	Oregon	7,151
Florida	643	Louisiana	1,569	North Carolina	1,865	North Carolina	6,800
Oregon	605	Michigan	1,473	Ohio	1,349	Michigan	4,116[a]
Ohio	518	Illinois	1,436	Wisconsin	1,138	Georgia	3,584
Washington	418	Oregon	1,356	Connecticut	1,060	Ohio	3,464[a]
Louisiana	393	Wisconsin	1,067	Texas	993	Mississippi	3,371
Pennsylvania	320	Ohio	840	Rhode Island	956	Delaware	3,141
Wisconsin	253	Georgia	701	Mississippi	623	South Carolina	2,810
South Carolina	212	Mississippi	556	Alabama	562	Rhode Island	2,788
New Hampshire	177	Delaware	541	Delaware	475	Alabama	2,122
Texas	128	Pennsylvania	513	Georgia	381	Connecticut	2,114
Georgia	120	Texas	446	Minnesota	312	Wisconsin	2,919
Alabama	119	Alabama	387	Illinois	297	Pennsylvania	713[a]
Illinois	60	South Carolina	288	Pennsylvania	266	Minnesota	458[a]
Indiana	32	Indiana	223	South Carolina	266	Illinois	266[a]
Mississippi	22	Minnesota	192	New Hampshire	105	New Hampshire	219
Minnesota	5	New Hampshire	53	Indiana	65	Indiana	2[a]

Source: H. F. Taylor, "Marine Resources in North Carolina," in C. H. Green, comp., Conservation and Development in North Carolina (mimeographed; Raleigh, Conservation Congress, 1952), II, 214. Note: The value of North Carolina's 1953 fish production was $8,265,000.

[a]Great Lakes states, 1949; all other states, 1950.

Table 23. Kind, Quantity, and Value of Fish Taken in North Carolina Waters, July 1, 1954, to June 30, 1956

KIND OF FISH	PRICE (CENTS) PER LB.	NO. LBS.	VALUE TO FISHERMEN
Herring	1	25,062,932	$ 250,629
Blue fish	12	753,271	90,393
Bow fin	6	9,039	542
Butters	10	104,295	10,430
Carp	3	797,256	23,918
Catfish	8	2,056,000	164,506
Croakers	6	5,030,025	301,802
Black drum	6	58,858	3,531
Red drum	10	324,386	32,438
Eels (common)	5	167,880	8,394
Flounders	12	2,268,755	272,251
Star butters	8	1,055,800	84,464
Hickory shad	6	508,912	30,535
King mackerel	20	13,992	2,798
Sea mullet	7	3,266,364	228,680
Mullet	10	3,654,571	365,457
Hog fish	3	588,511	17,655
Pike	13	1,400	182
Pompano	30	7,693	2,308
Porgy or bream	7	113,631	7,954
Sea bass	11	101,230	11,135
Shad	25	1,404,964	351,241
Sheephead	8	22,212	1,777
Snapper (red)	20	41,954	8,391
Spanish mackerel	15	516,567	77,485
Spot	10	2,578,614	357,861
Striped bass	15	1,516,717	227,508
Sturgeon	20	20,611	4,122
Suckers	7	825	58
Sunfish	3	2,500	75
Swell fish	3	436,768	13,103
Trout (gray)	10	3,539,124	353,912
Trout (spotted)	30	869,424	260,827
White perch	8	2,339,858	187,189
Yellow perch	7	91,092	6,376
Total food fin fish		60,326,862	$3,759,927
Menhaden		482,148,569 Number of fish	$4,045,821
Oysters		244,381 bu., tubs, 5 pk.	672,048
Clams		22,092 bu.	59,648
Soft shell crabs		20,062 dz.	30,093
Escallops		18,766 gals.	75,064
Hard crabs		14,713,680 lbs.	441,410
Shrimp		10,530,881 lbs. (heads off)	4,212,352
Total value of shellfish			$5,490,615
Total value of water products			$13,296,363

Source: *Sixteenth Biennial Report of the North Carolina Department of Conservation and Development* (Raleigh, 1956), pp. 17-18.

Table 24. The Areas of the State Compared in Selected Items

	Tidewater	Upper Coastal Plain	Piedmont	Mountain
Per cent of state's population, 1950	11.00	26.54	52.65	9.81
Per cent of state's total land area, 1950	21.20	28.20	37.10	13.50
Land area, square miles, approx.	10,450	13,750	18,265	6,678
Population per square mile, 1950	65.3	79.1	112.0	70.1
Per cent of land area in farms, 1950	37.2	72.4	72.3	52.1
Per cent of farms operated by tenants, 1950	31.9	55.1	29.2	10.7
Per cent of state's taxed retail sales, 1955-56	9.6	20.8	61.8	7.8
Per cent of state's individual net taxable income, 1952	6.64	16.65	70.70	6.10
Per cent of state's real and personal property listed for taxation, 1953-54	7.6	18.6	67.2	6.6

Compiled. U. S. Bureau of the Census. *U. S. Census of Population: 1950*, Vol. II. *Characteristics of the Population*. Part 33, North Carolina, Chap. A (Washington: U. S. Government Printing Office, 1952); *U. S. Census of Agriculture*, Vol. I. *County and State Economic Area*, Part 16, North Carolina; *Statistics of Taxation, 1954* (Raleigh: North Carolina Department of Tax Research and State Board of Assessments, 1954).

Table 25. Growth of Population in North Carolina Before 1790

1584-1657	First attempts to establish settlements
1657	First permanent settlements
1675	4,000 estimated population
1701	5,000 ″ ″
1707	7,000 ″ ″
1715	11,200 estimated, including 3,700 slaves
1729	35,000 ″
1740	Scotch-Irish began coming from Pennsylvania
1745	Germans coming in from Pennsylvania and Virginia
1747	Scotch Highlanders settling in Cape Fear country
1754	90,000 estimated population, including 20,000 slaves
1760	130,000 ″ ″
1774	260,000 ″ ″
1786	350,000 ″ ″
1790	393,751
	White 288,204
	Negro 105,441
	Other 106
	Per cent white, 73.2

Compiled. *How North Carolina Grew*, North Carolina Writers' Program, Works Progress Administration, sponsored by the North Carolina Historical Commission (Raleigh: The News and Observer, 1941).

Table 26. Population by Decades, with Rank and Percentage Increase, North Carolina, 1790–1950

Year	Inhabitants	Rank in Population	Per cent Increase
1790	393,751	3	
1800	478,103	4	21.4
1810	555,500	4	16.2
1820	638,829	4	15.0
1830	737,987	5	15.5
1840	753,419	7	2.1
1850	869,039	10	15.3
1860	992,622	12	14.2
1870	1,071,361	14	7.9
1880	1,399,750	15	30.7
1890	1,617,949	16	15.6
1900	1,893,810	15	17.1
1910	2,206,287	16	16.5
1920	2,559,123	14	16.0
1930	3,170,287	12	23.9
1940	3,571,623	11	12.7
1950	4,061,929	10	13.7
1956 (mid)	4,423,000	10	8.9

Source: *U. S. Census of Population*, 1950, Vol. I. *Number of Inhabitants*, Part 33, North Carolina, Chap. A, p. 7, Table 1; U. S. Bureau of the Census, *Population Estimates for 1956* (November 18, 1956), Series P-25, No. 148.

Table 27. North Carolina Population by Color and Age, 1900 to 1950

COLOR AND AGE	POPULATION					
	1900	1910	1920	1930	1940	1950
White						
Total	1,263,603	1,500,511	1,783,779	2,234,958	2,567,635	2,983,121
0-14	511,920	593,301	708,804	830,292	804,845	907,769
15-64	703,441	849,998	999,638	1,314,314	1,645,096	1,899,830
65 & up	46,369	55,962	73,675	89,177	117,694	175,522
Nonwhite						
Total	630,207	705,776	775,344	935,318	1,003,998	1,078,808
0-14	270,481	300,355	324,503	370,268	356,374	403,954
15-64	336,954	381,277	424,253	537,692	608,768	625,079
65 & up	19,779	21,726	25,041	26,494	38,846	49,775

	PERCENTAGE					
	1900	1910	1920	1930	1940	1950
White						
Total	100.0	100.0	100.0	100.0	100.0	100.0
0-14	40.5	39.5	39.7	37.1	31.3	30.4
15-64	55.7	56.6	56.1	58.8	64.1	63.7
65 & up	3.7	3.7	4.1	4.0	4.6	5.9
Nonwhite						
Total	100.0	100.0	100.0	100.0	100.0	100.0
0-14	42.8	42.5	41.9	39.6	35.5	37.4
15-64	53.5	54.0	54.7	57.5	60.7	57.9
65 & up	3.2	3.1	3.2	2.8	3.8	4.6

Source: *U. S. Census of Population: 1950*, Vol. II, *Characteristics of the Population*, Part 33, North Carolina, Chap. B, p. 43, Table 16.

Table 28.   Urban and Rural Population of North Carolina, 1790 to 1950[*]

CENSUS DATE	POPULATION	Increase over preceding census	
		Number	Per cent
1950 (April 1)	4,061,929	490,306	13.7
1940 (April 1)	3,571,623	401,347	12.7
1930 (April 1)	3,170,276	611,153	23.9
1920 (Jan. 1)	2,559,123	352,836	16.0
1910 (April 1)	2,206,287	312,477	16.5
1900 (June 1)	1,893,810	275,861	17.1
1890 (June 1)	1,617,949	218,199	15.6
1880 (June 1)	1,399,750	328,389	30.7
1870 (June 1)	1,071,361	78,739	7.9
1860 (June 1)	992,622	123,583	14.2
1850 (June 1)	869,039	115,620	15.3
1840 (June 1)	753,419	15,432	2.1
1830 (June 1)	737,987	99,158	15.5
1820 (Aug. 7)	638,829	83,329	15.0
1810 (Aug. 6)	555,500	77,397	16.2
1800 (Aug. 4)	478,103	84,352	21.4
1790 (Aug. 2)	393,751		

Year	URBAN TERRITORY				RURAL TERRITORY			Per cent of Total	
	Number of urban places	Population	Increase over preceding census		Population	Increase over preceding census		Urban	Rural
			Number	Per cent		Number	Per cent		
1950 (Apr. 1)[a]	107	1,368,101			2,693,828			33.7	66.3
1950 (Apr. 1)	88	1,238,193	264,018	27.1	2,823,736	226,288	8.7	30.5	69.5
1940 (Apr. 1)	76	974,175	164,328	20.3	2,597,448	237,019	10.0	27.3	72.7
1930 (Apr. 1)	68	809,847	319,477	65.2	2,360,429	291,676	14.1	25.5	74.5
1920 (Jan. 1)	55	490,370	171,896	54.0	2,068,753	180,940	9.6	19.2	80.8
1910 (Apr. 1)	40	318,474	131,684	70.5	1,887,813	180,793	10.6	14.4	85.6
1900 (June 1)	28	186,790	71,031	61.4	1,707,020	204,830	13.6	9.9	90.1
1890 (June 1)	18	115,757	60,643	110.0	1,502,190	157,556	11.7	7.2	92.8
1880 (June 1)	9	55,116	18,898	52.2	1,344,634	309,491	29.9	3.9	96.1
1870 (June 1)	5	36,218	11,664	47.5	1,035,143	67,075	6.9	3.4	96.6
1860 (June 1)	4	24,554	3,445	16.3	968,068	120,138	14.2	2.5	97.5
1850 (June 1)	4	21,109	7,799	58.6	847,930	107,821	14.6	2.4	97.6
1840 (June 1)	3	13,310	2,855	27.3	740,109	12,577	1.7	1.8	98.2
1830 (June 1)	3	10,455	-2,047	-16.4	727,532	101,205	16.2	1.4	98.6
1820 (Aug. 7)	4	12,502	12,502		626,372	70,827	12.8	2.0	98.0
1810 (Aug. 6)					555,500	77,397	16.2		100.0
1800 (Aug. 4)					478,103	84,352	21.4		100.0
1790 (Aug. 2)					393,751				100.0

Source: *U. S. Census of Population: 1950*, Vol. II, *Characteristics of the Population*, Part 33, p. 7, Table 1.

[*]For description of new and old definitions, see text. Minus sign (-) denotes decrease. Per cent not shown where base is less than 100.

[a]New definition: see text; includes 31,135 persons in urban territory outside of urban places.

Table 29. Chief Population Facts for North Carolina, 1950

COUNTY	NUMBER	Per cent increase, 1940-50	PER CENT BY RESIDENCE			MEDIAN AGE (YEARS)	Per cent nonwhite	PER SQUARE MILE	Land area, square miles
			Urban	Rural nonfarm	Rural farm				
Alamance	71,220	24.0	41.5	40.4	18.1	26.6	18.5	164	434
Alexander	14,554	8.2		36.1	63.9	24.0	7.1	57	255
Alleghany	8,155	-2.2		21.4	78.6	26.8	3.3	35	230
Anson	26,781	-5.8	12.7	39.5	47.8	23.0	48.6	50	533
Ashe	21,878	-3.5		19.2	80.8	23.8	1.3	51	427
Avery	13,352	-1.5		36.7	63.3	22.0	1.5	54	247
Beaufort	37,134	1.9	32.9	27.4	39.7	24.9	37.3	45	831
Bertie	26,439	0.9		36.4	63.6	21.8	59.8	38	693
Bladen	29,703	9.4		40.6	59.4	20.5	41.2	34	879
Brunswick	19,238	12.3		48.1	51.9	22.6	36.6	22	873
Buncombe	124,403	14.4	47.0	37.2	15.8	29.1	12.3	193	646
Burke	45,518	17.9	24.3	55.5	20.2	25.5	7.5	90	506
Cabarrus	63,783	7.4	66.0	19.9	14.0	26.5	15.3	177	360
Caldwell	43,352	21.1	18.2	54.2	27.6	23.2	6.9	91	476
Camden	5,223	-4.0		57.0	43.0	26.1	38.7	22	239
Carteret	23,059	26.1	36.2	52.2	11.5	27.1	12.6	43	532
Caswell	20,870	4.2		25.3	74.7	20.9	47.6	48	435
Catawba	61,794	19.6	33.7	42.6	23.7	25.2	9.1	152	406
Chatham	25,392	2.7	9.8	38.6	51.5	25.5	32.1	36	707
Cherokee	18,294	-2.8		46.7	53.3	23.4	1.7	40	454
Chowan	12,540	8.4	35.6	15.6	48.8	24.0	43.6	70	180
Clay	6,006	-6.2		27.9	72.1	23.9	1.1	28	213
Cleveland	64,357	10.9	35.3	24.6	40.1	24.1	21.9	138	466
Columbus	50,621	10.9	8.4	32.4	59.3	21.3	33.9	54	939
Craven	48,823	56.0	32.4	46.5	21.2	23.9	32.4	67	725
Cumberland	96,006	61.8	39.7	44.4	15.8	23.4	28.0	145	661
Currituck	6,201	-7.6		53.7	46.3	29.4	32.0	23	273
Dare	5,405	-10.5		98.6	1.4	30.8	7.0	14	388
Davidson	62,244	16.6	39.7	38.3	21.9	25.8	10.3	114	548
Davie	15,420	3.4		56.1	43.9	26.3	14.0	58	264
Duplin	41,074	3.4		34.3	65.7	22.5	37.0	50	822
Durham	101,639	26.7	72.2	20.2	7.6	27.2	33.3	340	299
Edgecombe	51,634	5.0	40.7	17.1	42.3	23.3	51.9	101	511
Forsyth	146,135	15.5	65.8	25.0	9.3	27.9	28.4	345	424
Franklin	31,341	3.2	8.1	25.0	66.9	23.3	45.6	63	494
Gaston	110,836	26.6	55.2	35.2	9.5	25.1	13.4	310	358
Gates	9,555	-5.0		39.3	60.7	24.3	52.6	28	343
Graham	6,886	7.3		47.1	52.9	22.2	3.2	24	289
Granville	31,793	8.3	21.0	26.4	52.6	24.7	46.7	59	543
Greene	18,024	-2.8		17.4	82.6	20.4	46.5	67	269
Guilford	191,057	24.1	66.0	23.1	10.8	27.3	19.5	293	651
Halifax	58,377	3.3	24.1	30.1	45.9	22.0	56.6	81	722
Harnett	47,605	7.6	20.3	30.2	49.5	22.9	26.3	79	606
Haywood	37,631	8.1	27.1	39.9	33.0	25.1	2.2	69	543
Henderson	30,921	18.7	19.7	44.9	35.4	28.9	6.7	81	382
Hertford	21,453	10.9	16.7	35.8	47.5	23.4	60.0	60	356
Hoke	15,756	5.5		37.3	62.7	21.2	60.6	38	414
Hyde	6,479	-17.6		58.4	41.6	26.7	42.2	10	634
Iredell	56,303	11.7	42.7	24.9	32.4	26.3	17.8	95	591
Jackson	19,261	-0.5		42.3	57.7	23.4	7.6	39	496
Johnston	65,906	3.3	12.5	28.7	58.8	22.8	21.7	83	795
Jones	11,004	0.7		30.8	69.2	21.2	45.4	24	467

(Continued on next page)

295

Table 29 (Continued)

COUNTY	NUMBER	Per cent increase, 1940-50	PER CENT BY RESIDENCE			MEDIAN AGE (YEARS)	Per cent nonwhite	PER SQUARE MILE	Land area, square miles
			Urban	Rural nonfarm	Rural farm				
Lee	23,522	25.5	42.6	22.3	35.1	25.0	26.0	92	255
Lenoir	45,953	11.5	39.9	20.0	40.1	24.4	43.1	118	391
Lincoln	27,459	13.5	19.7	36.7	43.6	24.2	12.7	89	308
McDowell	25,720	11.8	21.9	48.3	29.8	24.2	5.6	58	442
Macon	16,174	1.9		37.0	63.0	24.5	2.2	31	517
Madison	20,522	−8.9		27.8	72.2	23.2	0.9	45	456
Martin	27,938	7.0	17.8	24.8	57.4	20.7	50.4	58	481
Mecklenburg	197,052	29.8	71.5	21.1	7.4	27.8	25.4	364	542
Mitchell	15,143	−5.2		39.4	60.6	23.7	0.3	69	220
Montgomery	17,260	6.0		66.5	33.5	25.3	22.9	35	488
Moore	33,129	7.0	12.9	51.1	36.0	25.3	26.9	49	672
Nash	59,919	7.8	24.7	24.0	51.3	23.0	42.4	109	552
New Hanover	63,272	32.0	71.2	26.1	2.7	28.3	31.4	326	194
Northampton	28,432	0.5		36.9	63.1	22.0	64.2	53	540
Onslow	42,047	134.4	18.2	56.2	25.6	21.9	15.9	56	756
Orange	34,435	49.3	26.7	44.9	28.5	23.9	25.1	87	398
Pamlico	9,993	3.0		71.3	28.7	24.0	34.6	29	341
Pasquotank	24,347	18.4	52.1	34.3	13.6	26.2	38.2	106	229
Pender	18,423	4.0		41.8	58.2	22.3	48.3	21	857
Perquimans	9,602	−1.7		59.4	40.6	25.8	47.8	37	261
Person	24,361	−2.7	17.7	22.3	60.0	23.2	36.2	61	400
Pitt	63,789	4.2	30.8	21.8	47.4	22.7	46.3	97	656
Polk	11,627	−2.1		55.9	44.1	26.3	13.0	50	234
Randolph	50,804	14.0	15.2	53.8	31.1	26.2	8.5	63	801
Richmond	39,597	7.6	34.3	44.0	21.7	24.2	30.5	83	477
Robeson	87,769	14.2	10.5	35.2	54.4	20.4	57.3	93	944
Rockingham	64,816	11.9	38.5	29.6	31.9	26.0	20.1	113	572
Rowan	75,410	9.0	41.1	40.0	18.9	27.1	17.1	146	517
Rutherford	46,356	1.7	33.4	30.9	35.6	25.2	12.3	82	566
Sampson	49,780	4.9	8.9	23.8	67.3	22.4	36.8	52	963
Scotland	26,336	13.4	27.1	35.8	37.1	21.7	47.8	83	317
Stanly	37,130	13.1	31.8	38.9	29.3	26.2	11.4	93	399
Stokes	21,520	−5.0		26.1	73.9	24.3	9.0	47	459
Surry	45,593	9.1	28.4	30.2	41.4	24.5	5.7	85	537
Swain	9,921	−18.5		46.6	53.4	22.2	15.6	19	530
Transylvania	15,194	24.1	25.7	43.0	31.3	24.1	4.9	40	379
Tyrrell	5,048	−9.1		56.2	43.8	25.1	41.4	13	399
Union	42,034	7.5	24.1	20.1	55.8	24.0	22.6	65	643
Vance	32,101	7.1	34.3	26.4	39.3	24.5	45.5	119	269
Wake	136,450	24.6	53.1	25.1	21.8	26.4	29.3	158	866
Warren	23,539	1.7		27.6	72.4	21.1	66.4	53	445
Washington	13,180	7.0	34.0	28.9	37.1	23.7	43.6	39	336
Watauga	18,342	1.3	16.2	19.6	64.2	23.0	1.2	57	320
Wayne	64,267	10.2	39.2	23.0	37.8	25.3	42.2	116	555
Wilkes	45,243	5.2	9.7	39.4	50.9	23.2	6.0	59	765
Wilson	54,506	8.5	42.2	16.3	41.5	23.7	40.4	146	373
Yadkin	22,133	7.1		34.5	65.5	25.2	5.0	66	335
Yancey	16,306	−5.2		26.8	73.2	22.8	1.1	62	311
State	4,061,929	13.7	33.7	32.4	33.9	25.0	26.6	82.7	49,097,000

Source: *U. S. Census of Population: 1950.* Vol. II, *Characteristics of the Population,* Part 33, North Carolina, chap. B, p. 35, Table 12.

Table 30. Estimates of Net Migration to North Carolina by Color and Sex for each Decade, 1900-1950

(Minus sign indicates a net loss of population)

	1900 1910	1910 1920	1920 1930	1930 1940	1940 1950	1900 1950
Total	−82,578	−76,382	−9,908	−87,138	−208,753	−464,759
White	−54,749	−47,220	5,755	−27,187	−81,464	−204,865
Male	−28,763	−21,436	−288	−13,541	−27,828	−91,856
Female	−25,986	−25,784	6,043	−13,646	−53,636	−113,009
Negroes	−27,829	−29,162	−15,663	−59,951	−127,289	−259,894
Male	−14,794	−13,046	−7,908	−22,060	−61,162	−118,970
Female	−13,035	−16,116	−7,755	−37,891	−66,127	−140,924

Source: James J. Maslowski, North Carolina Migration, 1870-1950 (unpublished doctoral dissertation, University of North Carolina, 1953).

Table 31. Total Population by Race, Race Ratios and Race Gains, North Carolina, 1790-1950

YEAR	TOTAL POPULATION[a]	TOTAL WHITE POPULATION	TOTAL NEGRO POPULATION	PER CENT OF TOTAL POPULATION WHITE	PER CENT INCREASE White	PER CENT INCREASE Negro
1790	393,751	288,204	105,499	73.2		
1800	478,103	337,764	140,339	70.7	17.2	33.2
1810	555,500	376,410	179,090	67.8	11.4	27.5
1820	638,829	419,200	219,629	65.6	11.4	22.7
1830	737,987	472,843	265,144	64.1	12.8	20.7
1840	753,419	484,700	268,549	64.4	2.5	1.3
1850	869,039	553,028	316,008	63.6	14.1	17.7
1860	992,622	629,942	361,522	63.5	13.9	14.4
1870	1,071,361	678,470	391,650	63.2	7.7	8.3
1880	1,399,750	867,242	531,277	62.0	28.7	35.7
1890	1,617,949	1,055,382	561,018	65.2	21.7	5.6
1900	1,893,810	1,263,603	624,469	66.7	19.7	11.3
1910	2,206,287	1,500,511	697,843	68.0	18.8	11.7
1920	2,559,123	1,783,779	763,407	69.7	18.9	9.5
1930	3,170,276	2,226,160	918,647	70.2	24.8	20.3
1940	3,571,623	2,567,635	981,298	71.9	15.3	6.8
1950	4,061,929	2,983,121	1,047,353	73.4	16.2	7.7

Source: *U. S. Census of Population, 1950*, Vol. I. *Number of Inhabitants*, Part 33, North Carolina, Chap. A, p. 7, Table 1. Percentages have been calculated by the author.

[a]Total population includes 31,445 individuals of other races.

297

Table 32. Population in Groups of Places According to Size, 1950

Types of area and size of place	Number of places	Population	Per cent of total population	Per cent of total
The state		4,061,929	100.0	
Urban, total	a	1,368,101	33.7	100.0
Within urbanized areas		517,367	12.7	37.8
Central cities, total	6	486,232	12.0	35.5
Cities of 100,000 to 250,000	1	134,042	3.3	9.8
Cities of 50,000 to 100,000	5	352,190	8.7	25.7
Urban fringes, total		31,135	0.8	2.3
Incorporated places under 1,000	1	882		0.1
Unincorporated territory		30,253	0.7	2.2
Outside urbanized area	101	850,734	20.9	62.2
Places of 25,000 to 50,000	5	175,876	4.3	12.9
Places of 10,000 to 25,000	20	318,782	7.8	23.3
Places of 5,000 to 10,000	27	181,158	4.5	13.2
Places of 2,500 to 5,000	49	174,918	4.3	12.8
Rural, total		2,693,828	66.3	100.0
Places under 2,500	415	334,929	8.2	12.4
Places of 2,000 to 2,500	29	65,069	1.6	2.4
Places of 1,500 to 2,000	36	63,284	1.6	2.3
Places of 1,000 to 1,500	71	87,116	2.1	3.2
Places under 1,000	279	119,460	2.9	4.4
Other rural territory		2,358,899	58.1	87.6
Urbanized areas, total	6	517,367	12.7	100.0
Areas of 100,000 to 250,000	1	140,930	3.5	27.2
Areas of 50,000 to 100,000	5	376,437	9.3	72.8

Source: *U. S. Census of Population, 1950.* Vol. II, Part A-33, p. 7, Table 1.

[a]There were 107 places of 2,500 or more.

Table 33. Number and Percentages of Urban, Rural Nonfarm and Rural Population, by Race, North Carolina, 1950

Classification	Total[a]		White		Negro	
	Number	Per cent	Number	Per cent of total population	Number	Per cent of total population
Total	4,030,474	100.0	2,983,121	100.0	1,047,353	100.0
Urban	1,367,429	33.9	1,005,744	33.7	361,685	35.5
Rural nonfarm	1,310,839	32.5	1,042,381	34.9	268,458	25.6
Rural farm	1,352,206	33.5	934,996	31.3	417,210	39.8

Source: *U. S. Census of Population, 1950*, Vol. II, Part A-33,. p. 16, Table 25.
[a]Other races not included: 31,455.

Table 34. Percentage of Employed Workers of Each Race, by Type of Occupation Group, Urban and Rural, in North Carolina, 1950

MAJOR OCCUPATION GROUP	URBAN		RURAL NONFARM		RURAL FARM	
	White	Nonwhite	White	Nonwhite	White	Nonwhite
Professional, technical and kindred workers	10.2	5.8	6.4	3.8	2.2	1.0
Farmers and farm managers	0.4	0.3	2.3	3.2	47.3	47.3
Managers, officials and proprietors, except farm	12.0	1.9	8.7	1.3	2.4	0.2
Clerical and kindred workers	14.1	1.8	7.3	0.7	2.6	0.1
Sales workers	11.0	1.3	7.6	0.9	2.5	0.2
Craftsmen, foremen and kindred workers	13.6	6.6	17.0	5.6	5.8	1.0
Operators and kindred workers	29.0	23.5	35.7	20.4	13.9	4.2
Private household workers	0.6	21.6	0.7	16.7	0.3	3.3
Service workers, except private household	5.4	18.1	4.2	8.7	1.3	1.2
Farm laborers, unpaid family workers		0.1	0.5	1.6	12.2	24.0
Farm laborers, except unpaid, and farm foremen	0.2	1.1	2.8	14.6	4.9	11.5
Laborers, except farm and mine	2.2	16.6	5.3	20.6	2.9	4.3
Occupation not reported	1.2	1.3	1.6	1.8	1.6	1.7

Source: *U. S. Census of Population: 1950*, Vol. II, Part A-33, p. 46, Table 25.

Table 35. Farms, Acreage and Value, 1954

Farms	Number	267,906
Approximate land area	Acres	31,422,080
Proportion to farms	Per cent	58.1
Land to farms	Acres	18,260,346
Average size of farm	Acres	68.2
Value of land and buildings		
Average per farm	dollars	8,105
Average per acre	dollars	128.13
Land in farms according to use		
Cropland harvested	farms reporting	245,703
	acres	5,504,204
1 to 9 acres	farms reporting	77,423
10 to 19 acres	farms reporting	67,558
20 to 29 acres	farms reporting	45,838
30 to 49 acres	farms reporting	35,529
50 to 99 acres	farms reporting	15,013
100 to 199 acres	farms reporting	3,360
200 acres and over	farms reporting	982
Cropland used only for pasture	farms reporting	68,703
	acres	702,345

Source: *U. S. Census of Agriculture, 1954*, Vol. I, Part 16, p. 3, Table 1.

Table 36. Number of Farms by Size, 1954

SIZE	NO. OF FARMS
Under 10 acres	34,479
Under 3 acres	5,391
3 to 9 acres	29,088
10 to 29 acres	76,672
30 to 49 acres	49,329
50 to 69 acres	31,778
70 to 99 acres	27,612
100 to 139 acres	20,168
140 to 179 acres	9,826
180 to 219 acres	5,702
220 to 259 acres	3,282
260 to 499 acres	6,458
500 to 999 acres	1,905
1000 acres and over	695

Source: *U. S. Census of Agriculture, 1954*, Vol. I, Part 16, p. 4, Table 4.

Table 37. Farms by Color and Tenure, 1950, 1954

	1950	1954
All operators	288,508	267,818
Full owners	142,085	129,237
Part owners	35,422	41,429
Managers	516	564
All tenants	110,485	96,586
Proportion of tenancy, percentage	38.3	36.1
Cash tenants	4,341	3,870
Share-cash tenants	1,462	1,785
Share tenants	38,805	36,051
Croppers	57,457	48,825
Other and unspecified tenants	8,420	6,055
All white operators	215,956	201,819
Full owners	127,105	115,116
Part owners	26.888	32,927
Managers	495	523
All tenants	61,468	53,253
Proportion of tenancy, percentage	28.5	26.4
Cash tenants	3,083	2,800
Share-cash tenants	861	1,275
Share tenants	24,671	22,960
Croppers	26,939	21,723
Other and unspecified tenants	55,914	4,495
All nonwhite operators	72,552	65,999
Full owners	14,980	14,123
Part owners	8,534	8,502
Managers	21	41
All tenants	49,017	43,333
Proportion of tenancy, percentage	67.6	65.6
Cash tenants	1,258	1,070
Share-cash tenants	601	510
Share tenants	14,134	13,091
Croppers	30,518	27,102
Other and unspecified tenants	2,506	1,560

Source: *U. S. Census of Agriculture, 1954*, Vol. I, Part 16, pp. 10–11, Table 3.

Table 38. Farm Operators by Color, Residence, Days of Off-Farm Work, 1950, 1954

		1950	1954
Operators by color:			
White	Number	215,956	200,998
Negro and other nonwhite	Number	72,552	66,908
Residence:			
Residing on farm operated	Operators reporting	268,365	247,808
Not residing on farm operated	Operators reporting	9,431	11,526
Operators not reporting residence	Number	10,712	8,572
Off-farm work:			
Working off their farm, total	Operators reporting	97,109	110,766
1 to 49 days	Operators reporting	23,353	27,897
50 to 99 days	Operators reporting	13,773	15,567
100 days or more	Operators reporting	59,983	67,242
100 to 199 days	Operators reporting	14,537	15,837
200 days and over	Operators reporting	45,446	51,405
Operators not working off their farm	Number	183,045	156,249
Operators not reporting	Number	8,319	863

Source: *U. S. Census of Agriculture: 1954*, Vol. I, Part 16, p. 30, Table 5.

Table 39.   Income from Crops and Livestock, Showing Principal Cash Crops, 1939-55

1. INCOME FROM CROPS AND LIVESTOCK

	1939	1953	1954	1955
Crops	$184,875,000	$672,000,000	$708,098,000	$712,502,000
Livestock	34,600,000	212,000,000	223,379,000	222,963,000
Total all farming	219,475,000	884,000,000	931,477,000	935,465,000
Acreage harvested	6,171,000	6,490,000	5,951,000	5,820,000

2. PRINCIPAL CASH CROPS

	1939	1953	1954	1955
Tobacco	$125,340,000	$452,000,000	$497,287,000	$533,701,000
Poultry	11,386,000	95,228,000	94,587,000	99,484,000
Cotton	25,861,000	84,000,000	76,604,000	58,488,000
Peanuts	10,495,800	31,000,000	31,695,000	26,271,000
Corn	3,022,000	10,549,000	9,942,000	10,335,000

Source: *Facts about North Carolina*, North Carolina Department of Conservation and Development (Raleigh, 1956), p. 4.

Table 40.   Total Gross and Realized Net Income per Farm, North Carolina and United States, 1949-55

1. GROSS INCOME (INCLUDES ALL CASH PLUS FAMILY LIVING)

	1949	1950	1951	1952	1953	1954	1955
North Carolina	$3,055	$3,327	$3,925	$3,930	$3,844	$3,960	$4,026
United States	5,518	5,684	6,714	6,853	6,703	6,561	6,588

2. NET INCOME (GROSS INCOME MINUS PRODUCTION EXPENSES)

	1949	1950	1951	1952	1953	1954	1955
North Carolina	$1,690	$1,899	$2,259	$2,215	$1,984	$2,037	$2,028
United States	2,389	2,276	2,682	2,660	2,649	2,357	2,268

Source: *The Farm Income Situation*, U. S. Department of Agriculture, Agricultural Marketing Service (September 17, 1956), pp. 12-13, Tables 1 and 2.

Note: Thus it is derived that farm expenses per farm are much lower in North Carolina than in the nation as a whole. Its net farm income per farm is not much below the national average.

Table 41. Realized Gross Income and Net Income, North Carolina Farmers, 1949-54

	(Millions of dollars)			
	1949	1951	1953	1954
Cash receipts from farm marketing	726.2	955.0	905.2	927.8
Government payments	7.6	8.0	3.9	6.1
Value of home consumption	139.5	153.4	145.9	139.2
Gross rental value of farm dwellings	46.4	50.2	58.4	53.3
Realized gross farm income	919.6	1,166.6	1,113.5	1,126.4
Farm production expenses	410.8	495.3	528.1	531.9
Realized net farm income	508.8	671.3	585.4	594.5
Net change in farm inventories	−20.7	36.3	−15.8	−17.6
Total net farm income	488.1	707.5	569.6	577.0

Source: *The Farm Income Situation*, U. S. D. A., Agricultural Marketing Service (December 16, 1955), p. 29, Table 10.

Note: Home consumption by North Carolina farmers in 1955 amounted to $136,064,000; livestock and products accounted for $75,319,000 and crops for $60,745,000.

Table 42. Total Farm Income and Production Expenses, North Carolina, 1929-55

Year	Realized gross income[a] (millions of dollars)	Production expenses (millions of dollars)	Realized net income (millions of dollars)
1929	349	153	196
1939	331	134	197
1949	920	411	509
1950	1,002	430	572
1951	1,167	496	671
1952	1,147	527	620
1953	1,110	537	573
1954	1,126	547	579
1955	1,135	563	572

Source: *Monthly Review* (December, 1956). Published by the Federal Reserve Bank of Richmond from data supplied by the U. S. Department of Agriculture.

[a]Includes family living from farm.

Table 43. Cash Farm Income by States, 1954

1. Total and per farm income from marketing, 1954

Rank	State	Total Cash Sales (000)	Cash Sales Per Farm	Rank	State	Total Cash Sales (000)	Cash Sales Per Farm
1	Arizona	$ 364,786	$35,035	25	New York	$ 816,854	$6,536
2	California	2,491,208	18,162	26	Oregon	383,901	6,417
3	New Jersey	336,826	13,561	27	Utah	144,476	5,976
4	Nevada	41,807	13,443	28	Wisconsin	992,538	5,888
5	Delaware	93,708	12,582	29	Texas	1,894,159	5,713
6	Iowa	2,347,221	11,554	30	Vermont	106,215	5,578
7	Connecticut	171,983	11,012	31	Ohio	1,080,531	5,420
8	Montana	367,978	10,488	32	Pennsylvania	748,860	5,098
9	Illinois	1,956,148	10,018	33	New Hampshire	67,405	5,033
10	Wyoming	125,693	9,964	34	Maine	147,676	4,864
11	Nebraska	1,067,634	9,961	35	Missouri	1,036,398	4,505
12	Rhode Island	25,378	9,768	36	Michigan	659,155	4,236
13	Florida	546,863	9,607	37	Oklahoma	527,911	3,711
14	Colorado	426,866	9,366	38	North Carolina	926,491	3,211
15	Massachusetts	192,329	8,656	39	Virginia	453,813	3,005
16	Washington	563,816	8,075	40	Arkansas	540,961	2,965
17	Idaho	322,417	8,003	41	Louisiana	362,164	2,916
18	South Dakota	530,928	7,990	42	Georgia	566,353	2,858
19	New Mexico	186,600	7,907	43	Kentucky	555,572	2,543
20	Kansas	952,547	7,249	44	South Carolina	315,094	2,261
21	Minnesota	1,231,126	6,874	45	Mississippi	520,060	2,069
22	Indiana	1,136,251	6,819	46	Tennessee	453,323	1,957
23	Maryland	245,411	6,797	47	Alabama	377,277	1,784
24	North Dakota	428,022	6,544	48	West Virginia	123,140	1,512

2. Total and per farm income from sale of livestock and products, 1954

Rank	State	Total Cash Livestock (000)	Livestock Sales Per Farm	Rank	State	Total Cash Livestock (000)	Livestock Sales Per Farm
1	Nevada	$ 36,139	$11,620	25	Pennsylvania	$573,495	$3,904
2	Arizona	103,090	9,901	26	Kansas	503,452	3,832
3	Delaware	70,179	9,422	27	Ohio	703,747	3,530
4	Iowa	1,891,210	9,309	28	Idaho	138,274	3,432
5	New Jersey	216,726	8,726	29	Maine	100,528	3,311
6	Wyoming	100,204	7,943	30	Missouri	737,313	3,205
7	Connecticut	114,437	7,329	31	Oregon	166,624	2,785
8	Nebraska	737,912	6,884	32	Washington	178,099	2,551
9	Rhode Island	17,625	6,784	33	Michigan	394,925	2,538
10	California	894,517	6,521	34	Texas	799,364	2,411
11	Colorado	278,359	6,107	35	Florida	127,343	2,237
12	Illinois	1,170,636	5,995	36	North Dakota	141,261	2,160
13	Massachusetts	128,103	5,765	37	Oklahoma	290,770	2,044
14	South Dakota	348,776	5,248	38	Virginia	257,814	1,707
15	Wisconsin	870,197	5,162	39	Georgia	263,270	1,328
16	Vermont	93,409	4,905	40	West Virginia	94,835	1,164
17	Minnesota	855,192	4,755	41	Kentucky	253,774	1,161
18	New York	574,274	4,595	42	Arkansas	171,748	941
19	Indiana	761,028	4,567	43	Tennessee	212,430	917
20	Maryland	164,461	4,555	44	Louisiana	111,729	900
21	Montana	156,358	4,456	45	Alabama	165,492	782
22	Utah	107,513	4,447	46	North Carolina	216,440	750
23	New Mexico	101,344	4,294	47	South Carolina	87,919	631
24	New Jersey	216,726	4,188	48	Mississippi	145,041	577

(Continued on next page)

304

Table 43 (Continued)

3. Total and per farm income from sale of crops, 1954

Rank	State	Total Cash Sales Crops (000)	Crop Sales Per Farm	Rank	State	Total Cash Sales Crops (000)	Crop Sales Per Farm
1	Arizona	$ 261,696	$25,134	25	Minnesota	$375,934	$2,099
2	California	1,596,691	11,640	26	Wyoming	25,489	2,021
3	Florida	419,520	7,370	27	Arkansas	369,213	2,056
4	Montana	211,620	6,032	28	Louisiana	250,435	2,017
5	Washington	385,717	5,524	29	New York	242,580	1,941
6	New Jersey	120,100	4,835	30	Ohio	376,784	1,890
7	Idaho	184,143	4,571	31	Nevada	5,663	1,822
8	North Dakota	286,761	4,384	32	Michigan	264,230	1,698
9	Illinois	785,512	4,023	33	Oklahoma	237,141	1,667
10	Connecticut	57,546	3,685	34	South Carolina	227,175	1,630
11	Oregon	217,277	3,632	35	Maine	47,148	1,553
12	New Mexico	85,256	3,613	36	Georgia	303,083	1,529
13	Kansas	449,095	3,418	36	Utah	36,963	1,529
14	Texas	1,094,795	3,301	38	Mississippi	375,019	1,492
15	Colorado	148,507	3,258	39	Kentucky	301,798	1,381
16	Delaware	23,529	3,159	40	Missouri	299,085	1,300
17	Nebraska	329,722	3,076	41	Virginia	195,999	1,298
18	Rhode Island	7,753	2,984	42	Pennsylvania	175,365	1,194
19	Massachusetts	64,226	2,890	43	Tennessee	240,893	1,040
20	South Dakota	182,152	2,741	44	Alabama	211,785	1,001
21	North Carolina	710,051	2,461	45	New Hampshire	11,318	845
22	Indiana	375,223	2,252	46	Wisconsin	122,341	726
23	Iowa	456,011	2,245	47	Vermont	12,806	672
24	Maryland	80,950	2,242	48	West Virginia	28,305	348

Sources: *The Farm Income Situation*, (March, 1955); *University of North Carolina News Letter*, XLI (March 16, 1955).

Table 44. Agricultural Trends in North Carolina, 1850–1954

Year	No. Farms	Avg. Size Farm	No. all Cattle	Working Oxen	Milk Cows	Other Cattle, Calves	No. Mules	No. Horses	No. Hogs	No. Sheep	Bu. Corn	Bu. Wheat	Bu. Oats	Tons Hay	Bales Cotton	Pounds Tobacco
1850	56,963	369	694,000	37,309					1,813,000	595,000						11,984,000
1867					204,000	293,000	33,000	99,000	1,160,000	329,000	21,657,000	3,415,000	3,479,000	179,000	91,000	
1900											32,100,000	7,968,000	3,614,000	282,000	477,000	
1901					214,000	356,000										
1909								192,000								
1920																434,000,000
1927					303,000	210,000	279,000		849,000	77,000	53,626,000	7,494,000	5,733,000	761,000	861,000	
1928																651,000,000
1950																
1951											67,611,000			1,209,000	542,000	
1953								64,000								
1954	267,906	68.2	948,341		598,704	598,704	(236,800)		1,419,458	45,811	42,613,000	6,110,000	13,467,000		366,711	831,500,000

Compiled from H. R. Smedes *Agricultural Graphics: North Carolina and the United States, 1866–1922* (Chapel Hill: University of North Carolina. 1923) and *U. S. Census of Agriculture* for 1850, 1950, and 1954.

Table 45. Cash Receipts by North Carolina Farmers, 1954–55

1. Cash receipts from marketings by months, 1955

	TOTAL	LIVESTOCK	CROPS
January	$ 30,022	$ 16,865	$ 13,157
February	22,514	16,008	6,506
March	24,583	17,518	7,065
April	25,124	17,930	7,194
May	27,886	19,602	8,284
June	35,471	19,891	15,580
July	27,614	18,202	9,412
August	91,949	19,406	72,543
September	255,616	20,612	235,004
October	227,475	20,283	207,192
November	119,067	18,649	110,418
December	48,144	17,997	30,147
Total	935,465	222,963	712,502

2. Cash receipts by commodities, 1954 and 1955

COMMODITY	1954	1955
Livestock and products	$223,379	$222,963
Dairy products	54,417	56,555
Eggs	44,073	45,727
Broilers	37,903	43,209
Hogs	50,043	40,365
Cattle and calves	21,600	24,625
Turkeys	6,657	5,671
Chickens	5,460	4,417
Other 49	3,226	2,394
Crops	708,098	712,502
Field crops:		
Tobacco	497,287	533,701
Cotton lint	68,509	53,656
Peanuts	31,695	26,271
Soybeans	13,892	10,590
Corn	9,942	10,335
Wheat	9,134	8,592
Potatoes	6,118	5,780
Cottonseed	8,095	4,832
Oats	4,722	4,175
Sweet potatoes	4,100	3,756
Hay	2,600	2,646
Snap beans	2,699	2,565
Cucumbers	2,546	2,324
Lespedeza seed	2,592	2,080
Sorghum grain	1,096	1,370
Sweet corn	1,163	1,050
Green peppers	1,469	708
Watermelons	899	650
Tomatoes	654	602
Barley	539	408
Other	7,076	6,850
Fruits and nuts:		
Apples	3,476	579
Strawberries	1,061	494
Peaches	2,494	
Other	665	536
Other products:		
Forest	15,065	19,236
Greenhouses and nursery	8,510	8,716
All commodities	931,477	935,465

Source: *Farm Income Situation*, (September 17, 1956), pp. 40–41, Table 14; pp. 58–9, Table 19.

Table 46. Food Processing in North Carolina, 1954

	Canned seafoods	Canned fruits, vegetables	Pickles, sauces
Number establishments	6	10	7
All employees	149	146	496
Payroll	$262,000	$ 409,000	$ 969,000
Value added by manufacture	465,000	707,000	1,793,000
Cost of materials	507,000	1,269,000	2,965,000
Value of shipments	972,000	1,976,000	4,758,000
Capital expenditure	160,000	141,000	21,000

Extracted from U. S. Bureau of the Census, *U. S. Census of Manufactures, 1954*, State Bulletin MC-132, North Carolina (Washington: U. S. Government Printing Office, 1956) pp. 132–36, Table 4.

Table 47. North Carolina's Industrial Progress since 1899

	1899	1919	1927	1947	1953
Wage earners	72,422	157,659	204,767	381,480	446,265
Wages paid	$14,051,784	$126,753,000	$158,287,197	$758,895,000	$1,201,031,000
Value of output	86,274,083	943,808,000	1,154,617,636	4,200,000,000[a]	6,121,000,000[b]
Value added by mfg.	40,419,859[c]	416,902,000[c]	592,531,353[c]	1,646,000,000[c]	2,274,000,000[c]

[a]Estimated by the author.
[b]*Blue Book of Southern Progress*, 1955 (Baltimore, Manufacturers' Record, 1955), p. 109.
[c]*U. S. Census of Manufactures* for the years shown.

Table 48. Trends in Industry in North Carolina, 1939–55

	1939	1953	1954	1955
Textiles	$ 549,700,000	$2,819,000,000	$2,430,000,000	$2,675,000,000
Tobacco	538,400,000	1,661,000,000	1,580,000,000	1,623,000,000
Food	69,200,000	496,000,000	590,000,000	439,000,000
Furniture	58,800,000	332,000,000	295,000,000	326,000,000
Lumber	45,800,000	271,000,000	254,000,000	262,000,000
Electrical Machinery		162,000,000	148,000,000	192,000,000
Chemicals	50,700,000	197,000,000	192,000,000	191,000,000
Apparel	19,000,000	125,000,000	128,000,000	176,000,000
Paper Pulp	26,000,000	194,000,000	192,000,000	175,000,000
Rubber	1,000,000	18,000,000	15,000,000	53,000,000
Others	62,700,000	324,000,000	297,000,000	370,000,000
Total	$1,421,300,000	$6,599,000,000	$6,121,000,000	$6,482,000,000
Employees	270,210	464,000	441,000	470,000

Source: *Facts about North Carolina*, p. 3.

Table 49. General Statistics of Manufacture for the State, 1954

Item	Unit of measure	1954	1947	% change 1947-54
Number of establishments, total	Number	6,645	5,321	+25
1-19 employees	do	4,365	3,311	(1)
20-99 employees	do	1,486	1,218	+19
100 or more employees	do	904	792	+14
All employees				
Number	Thousands	430	381.4	+12
Payroll	Million dollars	1,157.4	758.8	+52
Value added by manufacture	do	2,210.4	1,646.0	+34
Capital expenditures, new	do	129.6	137.6	− 5

Compiled. *U. S. Census of Manufactures, 1954*, State Bulletin MC–132, p. 4, Table 3; p. 11, Table 7.

Table 50. General Statistics for the State, by Major Industry Groups, 1954

Major industry group	Size of establishments				All employees		Value added by manufacture (000)	Capital expenditures (000)
	Total no. of establishments	1-19 employees	20-99 employees	100 or more employees	Number	Payroll ($1,000)		
All industries total	6,653	4,294	1,454	905	426,830	$1,151,799	$2,197,461	$130,056
Food and kindred products	845	547	242	56	24,737	72,949	154,001	10,334
Tobacco manufactures	58	1	15	42	26,146	77,086	390,064	11,494
Textile mill products	1,023	217	317	489	214,559	545,191	829,131	43,524
Apparel and related products	208	63	82	63	26,827	54,266	88,413	2,342
Lumber and wood products	2,485	2,139	302	44	32,258	62,729	100,063	5,975
Furniture and fixtures	429	218	121	90	31,809	86,884	139,698	4,323
Pulp, paper and products	67	20	28	19	9,721	38,880	91,424	7,438
Printing and publishing	430	347	72	11	7,506	27,333	45,428	1,775
Chemicals and products	217	136	68	13	11,496	43,721	103,854	10,177
Leather and leather products	35	23	7	5	1,383	3,988	5,755	152
Stone, clay, and glass products	235	151	71	13	6,975	19,943	33,964	3,722
Primary metal products	40	23	15	2	2,205	8,175	13,487	946
Fabricated metal products	136	96	26	14	4,949	17,546	32,743	2,376
Machinery, except electrical	211	142	54	15	6,362	22,255	36,589	2,047
Transportation equipment	58	41	11	6	4,929	18,829	39,336	630
Instruments and related products	17	15		2	789	2,654	4,350	151
Miscellaneous manufactures	104	85	17	2	1,720	4,194	7,241	1,966

Source: *U. S. Census of Manufactures, 1954*, State Bulletin MC–132.

Table 51. General Industrial Statistics, by Counties, 1954

County	Total no. of estab- lishments	All employees number	All employees payroll (000)	Value added by manufacture (000)	Capital expendi- tures, new
Alamance	153	18,639	$ 56,980	$ 104,532	$ 3,716
Alexander	38	1,027	2,408	3,309	322
Alleghany	9	509	839	1,070	38
Anson	57	1,552	3,732	5,352	166
Ashe	34	540	1,032	1,723	158
Avery	17	336	612	1,150	*
Beaufort	60	1,028	2,080	3,754	267
Bertie	49	895	1,949	3,361	214
Bladen	68	802	1,682	2,879	535
Brunswick	30	485	1,213	2,547	189
Buncombe	163	11,071	35,391	54,838	6,909
Burke	102	8,291	22,096	36,168	3,278
Cabarrus	63	22,239	55,136	76,384	1,764
Caldwell	83	9,041	23,396	39,351	1,034
Camden	6	14	20	74	4
Carteret	39	973	2,458	3,292	280
Caswell	16	200	551	681	*
Catawba	288	15,568	36,353	59,972	3,765
Chatham	99	3,302	8,190	13,795	1,149
Cherokee	25	910	1,968	2,377	187
Chowan	15	423	913	1,293	128
Clay	5	94	153	165	9
Cleveland	76	7,995	20,363	28,396	1,587
Columbus	51	2,189	4,930	13,972	1,628
Craven	62	1,762	4,333	6,857	692
Cumberland	75	4,187	10,031	16,813	751
Currituck	11	116	254	345	4
Dare	8	89	256	99	80
Davidson	181	13,424	34,000	52,842	2,449
Davie	34	1,923	4,804	7,532	489
Duplin	48	1,138	2,637	5,260	169
Durham	122	13,076	39,598	144,539	7,320
Edgecombe	53	2,446	6,143	10,442	526
Forsyth	187	29,930	96,515	303,756	18,956
Franklin	41	1,236	2,858	3,425	166
Gaston	219	27,192	68,685	115,165	7,307
Gates	23	213	358	719	43
Graham	9	237	655	927	49
Granville	40	1,382	2,970	4,973	222
Green	9	58	110	193	13
Guilford	509	37,380	104,332	169,106	8,190
Halifax	85	5,713	14,075	23,244	1,607
Harnett	56	2,632	5,773	9,071	418
Haywood	35	4,961	20,930	48,436	4,750
Henderson	49	2,348	6,221	9,641	603
Hertford	38	1,030	2,274	3,704	294
Hoke	12	1,062	2,811	4,984	49
Hyde	9	82	141	227	7
Iredell	132	9,349	23,626	37,397	2,003
Jackson	18	*	*	*	*

(Continued on next page)

Table 51 (Continued)

County	Total no. of establishments	All employees		Value added by manufacture (000)	Capital expenditures, new
		number	payroll (000)		
Johnston	66	2,531	5,356	8,294	319
Jones	12	143	253	560	29
Lee	89	3,472	8,434	14,420	1,237
Lenoir	51	4,278	14,388	40,312	3,356
Lincoln	61	3,061	6,714	9,697	272
McDowell	51	5,026	13,276	23,811	1,078
Macon	26	369	833	1,486	93
Madison	15	154	328	712	30
Martin	39	907	1,946	3,324	85
Mecklenburg	385	21,635	68,387	128,740	5,589
Mitchell	26	590	1,083	1,891	48
Montgomery	97	3,302	6,651	10,597	279
Moore	89	2,657	6,648	10,925	221
Nash	67	3,905	9,647	21,510	811
New Hanover	101	5,129	13,832	25,820	1,405
Northampton	33	638	1,274	2,018	130
Onslow	13	150	345	550	29
Orange	38	1,631	3,699	6,921	252
Pamlico	16	*	*	*	*
Pasquotank	47	1,538	3,488	5,531	496
Pender	32	434	774	1,330	66
Perquimans	20	198	334	631	58
Person	34	2,125	4,961	7,405	524
Pitt	56	2,141	4,825	7,805	383
Polk	6	842	1,943	2,710	58
Randolph	200	11,807	31,566	51,826	2,252
Richmond	54	4,349	12,130	17,760	1,478
Robeson	67	2,983	7,213	10,579	576
Rockingham	83	10,075	28,137	91,743	1,631
Rowan	111	7,838	19,627	29,633	1,631
Rutherford	80	7,216	17,924	30,544	2,309
Sampson	71	1,440	2,625	4,650	275
Scotland	30	2,851	6,716	10,326	1,203
Stanly	64	6,976	18,273	30,305	1,464
Stokes	24	479	951	1,629	79
Surry	107	8,255	20,686	30,626	766
Swain	13	362	968	1,746	40
Transylvania	27	2,901	10,687	24,899	898
Tyrrell	6	127	188	122	16
Union	55	2,113	4,361	9,021	664
Vance	28	2,571	6,038	9,650	480
Wake	167	6,045	17,009	25,885	9,403
Warren	34	612	1,099	1,720	137
Washington	18	*	*	*	*
Watauga	15	172	460	1,237	94
Wayne	70	2,728	6,476	10,174	323
Wilkes	100	3,205	5,564	9,995	484
Wilson	63	2,552	6,267	10,735	635
Yadkin	39	248	462	692	53
Yancey	16	739	1,961	2,924	*

Source: *U. S. Census of Manufactures, 1954*, State Bulletin MC-132, p. 4, Table 3.

*Detailed figures have been withheld from publication in order (a) to avoid disclosing figures for individual companies or (b) to permit checking of data for smaller counties.

Table 52. Leading North Carolina Industries, 1954

Industry	No. plants	Output	Per cent
Textiles	1,100	$2,430,000,000	40.0
Tobacco	100	1,580,000,000	25.8
Food	900	590,000,000	9.6
Furniture	400	295,000,000	4.8
Lumber	2,900	254,000,000	4.0
Chemicals	200	192,000,000	3.0
Paper	100	192,000,000	3.0
Electrical machinery	*	148,000,000	2.0
Apparel	200	124,000,000	2.0
Machinery	300	69,000,000	1.0
Printing	600	61,000,000	1.0
Stone, etc.	200	57,000,000	.9
Fabricated metals	200	45,000,000	.7
Primary metals	100	28,000,000	.5
Transportation	100	18,000,000	.3
Rubber	*	15,000,000	.2
Miscellaneous	100	11,000,000	.1
Leather	*	9,000,000	.1
Instruments	*	3,000,000	.04
All manufacturing totals	7,500	$6,121,000,000	100.0

Source: *Blue Book of Southern Progress*, 1955, p. 74.

*Too few for tabulation.

Table 53. Manufacturing Situation, by States and Regions, 1947–54

	MANUFACTURING EMPLOYEES			VALUE ADDED BY MANUFACTURE		
	Number 1954	Change 1947-1954	Rate of change 1947-1954	Rate of increase 1947-1954	Value added per employee 1954	Rate of increase value added per employee
United States	15,683,317	1,380,562	9.7	57.1	$7,445	43.2
Northeast	5,984,320	146,726	2.5	44.2	7,146	40.7
Maine	103,860	3,742	3.7	30.9	5,510	28.4
New Hampshire	75,818	1,066	1.4	30.9	5,616	36.8
Vermont	35,901	1,015	2.9	44.1	6,009	40.0
Massachusetts	679,919	-38,150	-5.3	29.1	6,375	36.4
Rhode Island	120,316	-27,066	-18.4	2.7	5,624	25.8
Connecticut	413,833	13,878	3.5	51.2	6,931	27.3
New York	1,910,904	137,766	7.8	46.5	7,405	36.0
New Jersey	784,188	45,153	6.1	49.7	7,991	41.1
Pennsylvania	1,425,032	-16,665	1.2	43.5	6,975	45.2
Delaware	39,067	4,329	12.5	93.4	9,062	72.0
Maryland	255,627	26,972	11.8	65.4	7,372	48.0
Dist. Columbia	20,224	2,409	13.5	59.5	7,815	40.5
West Virginia	119,631	-7,723	6.1	43.3	7,955	52.6
Southeast	2,253,365	304,327	15.6	56.1	6,029	35.0
Virginia	241,832	25,325	11.7	56.2	6,787	39.9
North Carolina	426,830	45,392	11.9	33.5	5,148	19.3
South Carolina	218,141	29,381	15.6	30.1	4,734	12.6
Georgia	302,754	52,796	21.1	56.9	5,267	29.6
Florida	122,900	44,235	56.2	124.5	6,394	43.7
Kentucky	146,824	17,271	13.3	65.7	8,387	46.2
Tennessee	261,220	38,920	17.5	74.6	6,425	48.6
Alabama	216,476	10,237	5.0	50.2	6,086	43.1
Mississippi	91,373	14,020	18.1	54.4	5,109	30.7
Arkansas	78,555	12,753	19.4	70.7	5,813	43.0
Louisiana	146,460	13,997	10.6	70.4	8,074	54.1
Southwest	534,845	161,466	43.2	102.4	8,268	41.3
Oklahoma	79,698	24,257	43.8	74.5	7,471	21.4
Texas	414,113	117,059	39.4	103.1	8,471	45.7
New Mexico	14,984	8,288	123.8	295.4	8,479	76.7
Arizona	26,050	11,862	83.6	128.3	7,347	24.4
Middle West	5,207,611	235,768	4.7	56.8	8,067	49.7
Ohio	1,270,157	75,894	6.4	59.7	7,994	50.1
Indiana	582,945	34,685	6.3	55.4	7,916	46.1
Illinois	1,183,381	-2,753	-0.2	44.3	8,147	44.6
Michigan	1,009,059	33,578	3.4	68.0	8,655	62.4
Wisconsin	426,005	7,331	1.8	46.4	7,779	43.9
Minnesota	203,993	22,473	12.4	57.1	7,867	39.8
Iowa	161,707	21,310	15.2	81.7	7,539	57.8
Missouri	370,364	43,250	13.2	68.2	7,363	48.6
Northwest	341,139	86,620	34.0	81.0	7,721	35.1
North Dakota	5,625	416	8.0	25.4	6,448	14.1
South Dakota	11,570	1,305	12.7	52.2	6,763	35.1
Nebraska	56,923	9,909	21.1	53.6	7,032	26.9
Kansas	125,956	50,851	67.7	116.2	7,954	28.9
Montana	18,899	3,061	19.3	55.5	7,472	30.3
Idaho	23,819	6,912	40.9	67.6	7,719	19.0
Wyoming	6,144	537	9.6	44.2	8,207	31.6
Colorado	63,154	9,083	16.8	74.9	7,466	40.8
Utah	29,049	4,546	18.6	110.5	9,278	77.5
Far West	1,362,037	445,655	48.6	104.0	8,330	37.3
Nevada	6,046	3,379	126.7	244.7	9,855	52.1
Washington	194,758	50,506	35.0	81.7	8,160	34.7
Oregon	134,883	29,292	27.7	52.2	7,616	19.1
California	1,026,350	362,478	54.6	117.0	8,448	40.4

Compiled. *U. S. Census of Manufactures, 1954,* from all state bulletins.

Table 54. Changing Proportion of North Carolina's Manufacturing Employees in Major Industry Groups, 1947–54

	Proportion of State's Total Manufacturing Employees		Per cent Change in Number of Employees
	1947	1954	1947–1954
Food and kindred products[a]	4.4	5.8	48.0
Tobacco manufacturing	8.5	6.1	−19.4
Textile mill products	55.2	50.3	2.0
Apparel and related products	4.3	6.3	61.2
Lumber and wood products[a]	8.2	7.6	3.8
Furniture and fixtures	7.3	7.5	14.2
Pulp and paper products	2.1	2.3	23.7
Printing and publishing	1.4	1.8	41.7
Chemicals and products	2.5	2.7	21.1
Leather and leather products	0.4	0.3	−14.8
Stone, clay and glass	1.5	1.6	24.3
Primary metal products	0.5	0.5	6.8
Fabricated metal products	0.7	1.2	77.7
Machinery, except electrical	1.0	1.5	60.9
Transportation equipment	0.3	1.2	300.4
Instruments and related products[b]		0.2	
Miscellaneous manufactures	0.2	0.4	77.5

Compiled. *U. S. Census of Manufactures, 1954*, State Bulletin MC-132.
[a]Not strictly comparable.
[b]Data withheld.

Table 55. Value Added per Manufacturing Worker, South Only, 1954

Rank	State	Value added per manufacturing worker
1	Kentucky	$8,387
2	Louisiana	8,074
3	Virginia	6,787
4	Tennessee	6,425
5	Florida	6,394
6	Alabama	6,086
7	Arkansas	5,813
8	Georgia	5,267
9	North Carolina	5,148
10	Mississippi	5,109
11	South Carolina	4,734
	Southeast	6,029
	United States	7,445

Compiled. *U. S. Census of Manufactures, 1954*, from all state bulletins.

Table 56. Employment, Hours, and Earnings in Nonagricultural Industries per Month July, 1956

Industry	Total employ-ment (000)	Average weekly earnings	Average weekly hours	Average hourly earnings
ALL NONAGRICULTURAL INDUSTRIES	1030.9	—	—	—
Manufacturing	450.6	$53.18	39.1	$1.36
Durable goods	122.4	54.40	40.9	1.33
Nondurable goods	328.2	52.99	38.4	1.38
Nonmanufacturing	580.3	—	—	—
Primary metal industries	2.6	82.06	42.3	1.94
Machinery (except electrical)	8.8	64.22	43.1	1.49
Fabricated metal products	5.1	61.80	41.2	1.50
Lumber and timber basic products	38.5	47.72	40.1	1.19
Sawmills and planing mills	27.2	45.94	39.6	1.16
Millwork, plywood, etc.	5.5	47.97	41.0	1.17
Wooden containers	1.7	—	—	—
Furniture and finished lumber products	36.1	52.45	41.3	1.27
Household furniture, mattress and bedsprings	32.4	52.32	41.2	1.27
Stone, clay and glass products	8.2	52.63	42.1	1.25
Other durable goods[a]	23.1	63.92	40.2	1.59
Textile mill products	225.1	50.41	37.9	1.33
Yarn and thread mills	50.9	46.48	38.1	1.22
Broadwoven fabrics	99.1	52.52	38.9	1.35
Knitting mills	61.1	50.26	35.9	1.40
Full fashioned hosiery	22.3	55.90	36.3	1.54
Seamless hosiery	29.7	46.42	34.9	1.33
Apparel and other finished products	22.4	43.50	37.5	1.16
Men's and boys' garments	9.9	42.78	37.2	1.15
Food and kindred products	24.1	49.56	42.0	1.18
Bakery products	—	—	—	—
Beverage industries	4.8	49.92	48.0	1.04
Tobacco manufacturers	23.5	64.55	39.6	1.63
Cigarettes	14.7	71.05	40.6	1.75
Stemmeries and redrying plants	6.6	52.33	38.2	1.37
Paper and allied products	10.0	83.82	41.7	2.01
Pulp, paper and paperboard mills	7.4	96.50	42.7	2.26
Printing, publishing and allied industries	8.6	73.54	38.3	1.92
Chemicals and allied products	11.8	69.19	40.7	1.70
Other nondurable goods[b]	2.7	74.25	45.0	1.65
Mining	4.0	62.44	44.6	1.40
Non-metallic mining	3.3	59.00	44.7	1.32
Transportation and public utilities	61.7	—	—	—
Transportation (except railroads)	27.4	—	—	—
Public utilities	18.7	69.56	39.3	1.77
Trades[c]	206.1	53.28	41.3	1.29
Wholesale	49.3	68.39	41.7	1.64
Retail	156.8	48.09	41.1	1.17
Retail general merchandise	32.7	33.98	35.4	.96
Department stores	15.4	39.35	36.1	1.09
Limited price variety stores	8.7	19.15	30.4	.63
Retail food stores	29.6	46.98	40.5	1.16
Grocery stores	22.8	42.71	37.8	1.13
Finance, insurance and real estate	33.8	71.03	—	—
Service	92.9	—	—	—
Hotels and rooming houses	6.4	24.54	46.3	.53
Personal services	24.5	—	—	—
Laundries and dry cleaners	14.6	28.97	40.8	.71
Government	129.1	—	—	—
Contract construction	52.7	—	—	—

Source: *Labor and Industry*, N. C. Department of Labor, XXIII (July, 1956), 2.

[a]Includes transportation; electrical machinery; instruments; and miscellaneous manufacturing industries.

[b]Includes leather and leather products and petroleum products.

[c]Excludes eating and drinking places.

Table 57. Cotton System Spinning Activity in the Southeast, 1955

	Spindles in place	Bales of cotton consumed
United States	22,273	8,841,000
Alabama	1,765	1,053,000
Georgia	3,164	1,757,000
North Carolina	5,994	2,511,000
South Carolina	6,382	2,355,000
Tennessee	517	191,000
Total	17,822	7,677,000

Source: *Statistical Abstract*, 1956, p. 818.

Table 58. Employment Data for the United States and Selected States Employing More than 50,000 in the Manufacturing of Textile Products, 1951

State	Employment in March, 1951	Per cent of nation's employment in textiles	Gross wages, first quarter
United States	1,317,960		$978,850,000
North Carolina	243,610	18.5	159,246,000
Pennsylvania	152,268	11.6	114,007,000
South Carolina	140,385	10.7	98,148,000
Georgia	115,042	8.7	75,347,000
Massachusetts	110,983	8.4	93,382,000
New York	92,580	7.0	77,917,000
Rhode Island	57,478	4.4	47,099,000
New Jersey	57,317	4.3	57,062,000
Alabama	56,032	4.3	38,192,000

Source: *North Carolina Employment Security Quarterly*, X (Summer-Fall, 1952), 73.

Table 59. Basic Textile Data for North Carolina, 1951

Type of production	Number of reporting units	Average monthly employment in 1951	Total wages in 1951
Scouring and combing	5	85	$ 178,425
Yarn and thread mills	791	60,525	148,945,050
Broad-woven fabric mills	663	105,175	283,218,700
Narrow fabrics	76	1,305	3,375,300
Knitting mills (inc. hosiery)	1,814	57,060	137,059,100
Dyeing and finishing	102	5,905	16,706,600
Carpets, rugs, linoleum, etc.	36	315	527,350
Miscellaneous textile goods	117	2,205	5,510,625
Total	3,604	232,575	$595,521,100

Source: *North Carolina Employment Security Quarterly*, X (Summer-Fall, 1952), 72.

Table 60. Wage and Employment Data for the 22 Counties Having 2,500 or More Textile Workers, North Carolina, 1951

County	Number of reporting firms	Average monthly employment	Total payrolls
Gaston	83	27,677	$ 69,641,300
Cabarrus	22	22,804	57,641,598
Guilford	59	19,939	57,801,576
Alamance	77	13,641	36,784,704
Catawba	97	9,504	21,467,963
Forsyth	20	7,779	19,580,824
Randolph	46	7,608	20,776,299
Cleveland	30	6,843	16,602,298
Rowan	16	6,514	15,653,947
Rockingham	11	6,321	16,768,451
Rutherford	14	6,243	16,498,437
Surry	50	5,723	14,984,032
Davidson	32	5,551	19,935,343
Iredell	17	5,514	14,756,426
Stanly	11	5,299	12,359,486
Richmond	10	4,297	11,704,858
Burke	31	4,270	10,416,761
Halifax	4	3,864	9,499,070
Buncombe	20	3,771	9,993,184
Durham	11	3,574	10,828,578
McDowell	19	3,033	7,877,302
Lincoln	17	3,011	6,785,568
Total	697	182,780	$478,358,005

Source: See Table 59.

Table 61. The Textile Industry in North Carolina, 1954

	No. estab.	All employees	Payroll (000)	Value added by manufacture (000)	Cost of materials (000)	Value of shipments (000)
Thread mills	13	2,646	$6,672	$12,179	$30,695	$42,875
Knit-fabric mills	31	2,250	6,375	12,555	43,986	56,541
Full-fashioned hosiery	165	22,396	65,013	97,909		
Furniture textiles except wood	39	7,430	22,763	37,017	55,569	92,586
Narrow fabrics	27	1,808	4,848	8,002	7,804	15,806
Woolen and worsted	10	4,978	15,845	21,864	42,417	64,282
Synthetic broad-woven tabrics	53	22,145	64,325	97,514	175,220	272,734
Cotton broad-woven fabrics	101	69,186	178,194	266,339	389,866	656,206
Other textile mills[a]	584	81,720	181,156	275,752	n. a.	n. a.
Total, all mills	1,023	214,559	545,191	829,131	n. a.	n. a.

Compiled from *U. S. Census of Manufactures, 1954*, Advanced reports, Bulletin MC-22-1 (November, 1956), Table 1; Bulletin MC-22-2.3 (July, 1956), Table 2; Bulletin MC-22-2.4 (July, 1956), Table 2; Bulletin MC-22-2.5 (August, 1956), Table 2; Bulletin MC-22-2.6 (August, 1956), MC-22-2.7 (August, 1956), Table 2; Bulletin MC-22-3.2 (June, 1956), Table 2; Bulletin MC-22-3.3 (July, 1956), Table 2.

[a]Data not available for other classifications.

N. a. = not available.

Table 62. General Statistics, Cotton, Rayon and Related Manufactures, North Carolina, 1954

Industry	No. estabs.	No. employees	Payroll (000)	Paid workers	Wages (000)	Value added by manufacture (000)	Cost of materials (000)	Value shipments (000)	Value shipments, 1947 (000)
Yarn throwing mills	24	2,298	$6,525	2,061	$5,198	$12,222	$17,309	$29,532	*
Thread mills	13	2,648	6,673	2,404	5,609	12,179	30,696	42,876	$5,371
Yarn mills, cotton	181	46,706	102,987	44,702	92,552	151,736	303,824	455,560	*
Cotton broad woven fabrics	102	69,280	178,417	65,833	161,735	266,671	389,884	656,555	315,090
Synthetic broad woven fabrics	53	22,146	64,325	20,552	56,231	97,514	175,220	272,735	80,235
Narrow fabrics	27	1,808	4,848	1,666	4,156	8,002	7,804	15,806	4,572
Finishing textiles except wood	39	7,578	22,658	6,560	17,147	36,884	55,703	92,587	22,694

Source: *U. S. Census of Manufactures, 1954*, Advanced reports, Industry Bulletin MC-22B, Cotton, Rayon, and Related Manufactures, pp. 6-7, Table 2.

*Data not released.

Table 63. Consumption of Raw Cotton, Running Bales, by Region, 1954

	Total all industries	Yarn mills	Cotton broad woven fabrics	All other
North Carolina	2,383,736	1,031,671	1,285,142	66,923
South Carolina	2,277,764	77,882	2,134,546	65,336
Georgia	1,685,078	355,494	1,249,531	80,053
Alabama	993,231		767,776	225,455
New England	467,460	37,386	393,750	36,324
United States	8,530,113	1,746,015	6,419,974	334,124

Source: *U. S. Census of Manufactures, 1954*, Advanced reports, Industry Bulletin, MC-22B, p. 26, Table 7B.

Table 64. Production of Flue-cured Tobacco, 1953-54

Type No.	Acreage harvested		Production (thousand pounds)		Value of production (thousand dollars)	
	1953	1954	1953	1954	1953	1954
11	258,000	266,000	261,870	297,920	$116,794	$157,004
12	331,000	334,000	450,160	477,620	260,643	264,124
13	85,000	86,000	120,275	113,950	69,639	61,875
Total	674,000	686,000	832,305	889,490	447,076	483,003

Source: *North Carolina Farm Report*, North Carolina Department of Agriculture, No. 184 (Raleigh, 1955). p. 4.

Table 65. General Statistics for the Tobacco Stemming and Redrying Industry by Regions and States, 1954

Region and state	Estab-lish-ments, number	All employees		Production workers		Value added by manufacture (090)	Cost of materials etc. (000)	Value of shipments (000)
		Number	Payroll (000)	Number	Wages (000)			
United States								
Total	133	18,846	$43,278	16,857	$32,983	$65,378	$977,833	$1,043,212
Northeast	16	761	1,851	711	1,485	2,210	14,275	16,486
East North:								
Central	7	376	783	339	695	1,628	2,932	4,560
South Atlantic	76	14,555	33,156	12,943	24,876	49,705	768,551	818,257
Virginia	19	4,303	9,376	3,864	7,186	13,877	205,915	219,792
North Carolina	49	9,501	22,355	8,342	16,368	33,740	545,930	579,671
East South								
Central	34	3,152	7,487	2,863	5,925	11,834	192,074	203,908

Source: *U. S. Census of Manufactures, 1954*, Advanced reports, Bulletin MC-21-1.2 (April, 1956), Table 1.

Table 66. The Growth of the Tobacco Industry in North Carolina, 1899–1953

	Number of estab-lishments	Number of wage earners	Wages	Taxes	Raw material, fuel, power	Value of output	Value added by manufacture
1953	100[a]	20,956	$58,548,000	$822,618,000[a]		$1,580,000,000[a]	$385,481,000
1947	69	16,798	54,475,000	741,214,473[c]			257,986,000
1927	21	15,976	12,545,075	204,473,505[b]	$124,712,918	413,274,114	288,561,196
1914	33	10,467	2,984,000	12,151,000	24,310,000	57,861,000	33,551,000
1899	96	6,583	907,000		4,312,000	13,851,000	9,539,000

Source: Unless otherwise indicated, the table is compiled from the reports of the Bureau of the Census and the Commissioner of Internal Revenue, by calendar year.

[a]*Blue Book of Southern Progress*, 1954, p. 29.

[b]Federal taxes only for the previous fiscal year.

[c]Fiscal year ending June 30, 1947.

[d]Fiscal year ending June 30, 1954.

Note: The value added by manufacture in 1954 was $390,064,000.

Table 67. Internal Revenue Collections from the Tobacco Industry, 1900–54

Year	North Carolina	United States
1900	$ 5,000,000	$ 59,000,000
1910	5,000,000	57,000,000
1920	108,000,000	295,000,000
1930	256,000,000	450,000,000
1940	332,000,000	608,000,000
1950	701,000,000	1,328,000,000
1954	$822,618,000	$1,580,229,000

Compiled. Annual Reports of the United States Commissioner of Internal Revenue, U. S. Treasury Department, Internal Revenue Service (Washington: Government Printing Office).

Table 68. Amount and Percentage of Total State Corporate Income Tax
Paid by Tobacco Industry, 1948-52

Year	Amount	Per cent of total
1948	$5,660,386	14.0
1950	6,747,060	17.1
1952	7,297,626	20.6

Source: *Statistics of Taxation*, 1954, p. 97.

Table 69. Total Cigarette Production and Consumption in the United States, 1900-54

Year	Production (billions)	U. S. Consumption (billions)
1900	3.2	—
1914	16.8	—
1927	99.8	—
1935-39 av.	164.2	157.0
1940-44 av.	255.9	223.5
1945	332.2	267.2
1946	350.0	321.7
1947	369.7	335.4
1948	386.8	348.5
1949	385.0	351.8
1950	392.0	360.2
1951	418.8	379.7
1952	435.5	394.1
1953	423.1	386.8
1954	401.9	368.6

Source: *The Tobacco Situation*, U. S. Department of Agriculture, Agriculture Marketing Service (June 10, 1955).

Table 70. General Statistics for the Cigarette Industry, by Region
and Selected States, 1954

Region and state	Number of establishments	All Employees		Production and Related Workers		Value added by manufacture (000)	Cost of materials, fuel, electricity and contract work (000)	Value of products shipped[a] (000)
		Number (average for the year)	Salaries and wages, total (000)	Number (average for the year)	Wages, total (000)			
United States Total	18	29,958	$103,694	27,666	$91,021	$677,207	$963,488	$1,640,695
South Atlantic	9	22,437	76,159	20,679	66,795	514,724	754,029	1,268,753
Virginia	5	8,271	28,413	7,598	24,771	177,451	261,080	438,531
North Carolina	4	14,166	47,746	13,081	42,024	337,273	492,949	830,222
All other states	9	7,521	27,535	6,987	24,226	162,483	209,459	371,942

Source: *U. S. Census of Manufactures, 1954*, Advanced reports, Bulletin MC-21-1.1 (December, 1955), p. 3, Table 2.

[a]Does not include excise tax payments.

Note: The per capita consumption of tobacco products by persons 14 years of age and over in the United States in 1955 in pounds of tobacco was: cigars, 1.22; cigarettes, 9.83; smoking tobacco, 0.40; chewing tobacco, 0.40; and snuff, 0.32 (*Statistical Abstract of the United States*, 1956, p. 815).

Table 71. Production of Cigars and Chewing-Snuff in North Carolina, 1900–50

Year	Cigars	Chewing-snuff
1900	$ 51,309.79	$ 4,798,526.80
1910	41,478.45	5,728,317.66
1920	208,754.51	21,637,787.40
1930	26,103.88	23,100,937.41
1940	76,523.78	22,484,147.75
1950	141,869.73	14,762,680.30

Source: Annual Reports of the Commissioner of Internal Revenue.

Table 72. Lumber and Timber Basic Products, 1954

	Number estab-lishments	All employees	Value added by manufacture	Cost of materials	Value of shipments
Logging camps and contractors	519	2,486	$ 6,694,000	$ 4,579,000	$ 11,273,000
Sawmills and planing mills	1,712	19,650	58,839,000	75,876,000	134,816,000
Veneer mills	47	2,163	7,011,000	7,749,000	14,760,000
Cooperage stock mills	12	310	819,000	1,147,000	1,966,000

Extracted from *U. S. Census of Manufactures, 1954*, State Bulletin MC-132, p. 3, Table 4.
Note: The census also reports one shingle mill and five excelsior mills, but no other data.

Table 73. Furniture Industry in North Carolina, 1954

	Number estab-lishments	Employees	Wages	Value added by manufacture	Cost of materials	Value of shipments
Wood, household furniture	153	22,082	$58,073,000	$ 92,565,000	$ 86,634,000	$179,199,000
Upholstered house-hold furniture	160	7,060	20,126,000	34,029,000	36,036,000	70,065,000
Wood office furniture	6	1,034	2,699,000	4,722,000	3,498,000	8,221,000
Public building furniture	14	1,465	3,963,000	6,358,000	5,650,000	12,008,000
Partitions, fixtures	14	292	1,188,000	2,054,000	1,045,000	3,100,000
Total[a]	347	31,933	$86,049,000	$139,728,000	$132,863,000	$272,594,000

Compiled from *U. S. Census of Manufactures*, 1954, Advanced reports, Bulletin MC-25-1.4 (August, 1956), page 3, Table 2; Bulletin MC-25-2 (September, 1956) page 6, Table 1; Bulletin MC-25-1.2 (August, 1956), page 4, Table 2.

[a]Minor classifications not reported by states include 82 additional establishments, for which 15 to 20 per cent must be added to totals.

Table 74.   Railroads in North Carolina in 1954

	Miles in North Carolina	North Carolina tonnage	
		Originated	Terminated
Class I			
Atlantic & Danville	20	17,001	8,007
Atlantic Coast Line	996	2,348,230	3,700,455
Clinchfield	117	354,219	550,228
Louisville & Nashville	13	29,419	20,127
Norfolk & Western	112	160,197	450,779
Norfolk Southern	555	2,033,423	2,392,044
Piedmont & Northern	86	n. a.	n. a.
Seaboard Air Line	630	2,643,439	3,335,648
Southern Railway	1,296	4,086,002	10,010,651
Total Class I	3,765	11,671,930	20,467,939
Class II			
Aberdeen & Rockfish	45	106,818	138,407
Atlantic & East Carolina	97	152,851	659,222
Cape Fear Railways	10	17,612	144,694
Carolina & Northwestern	156	228,785	1,270,017
Durham & Southern	59	84,163	228,986
HPT& D Railway	34	40,296	232,306
Laurinburg & Southern	28	25,688	91,259
Tallulah Falls	14	6,428	19,452
Virginia & Car. Southern	55	38,920	269,937
Winston-Salem Southbound	98	48,662	257,017
Total Class II	596	750,223	3,311,297
Class III			
Alexander Railroad	19	18,186	67,616
Atlantic & Western	24	21,225	64,593
Beaufort & Morehead	3	67,302	21,620
Black Mountain Railway	13	33,673	19,127
Cliffside	4	1,961	24,335
Carolina Southern	22	17,697	28,459
East Carolina	29	19,109	32,375
Graham County	12	13,410	8,233
Rockingham Railroad	20	4,365	34,423
State University	10	9,241	62,512
Warrenton Railroad	3	34,289	11,400
Total Class III	159	240,458	374,693
Grand Total	4,520	12,662,611	24,153,929

Source: North Carolina Utilities Commission.

N. a. = Not available.

Table 75. Personal Income in North Carolina, 1955

Total Income	$5,371,000,000
Farm Income	676,000,000
Nonfarm Income	4,695,000,000
Selected Components	
Government Income Disbursements	974,000,000
Wages and Salary Disbursements	
Manufacturing	1,342,000,000
Trade and Services	872,000,000
Contract Construction	160,000,000
Mining	13,000,000

Compiled. *Survey of Current Business*, U. S. Department of Commerce, Office of Business Economics, XXXVI (August, 1956), pp. 10, 12, Tables 1 and 3.

Table 76. Total and Per Capita Income for North Carolina, 1929-55

Year	Total income (000,000)	Total per capita income	Per cent of national average	Difference between U. S. and N. C. per capita income in dollars
1929	$1,048	$ 334	45.4	$371
1930	929	293	42.8	341
1931	789	248	42.8	286
1932	603	187	46.3	204
1933	678	207	55.7	163
1934	809	245	60.2	167
1935	894	269	58.7	190
1936	986	295	55.4	237
1937	1,088	321	55.6	249
1938	1,018	296	56.8	220
1939	1,111	316	57.1	231
1940	1,171	328	55.0	259
1941	1,533	426	57.7	293
1942	2,063	575	60.0	350
1943	2,515	691	58.8	436
1944	2,779	765	61.3	448
1945	2,892	821	63.3	437
1946	3,198	858	65.9	413
1947	3,372	894	66.2	437
1948	3,621	944	64.9	485
1949	3,596	919	64.9	465
1950	4,108	1,009	65.8	493
1951	4,613	1,114	66.0	538
1952	4,768	1,149	64.4	586
1953	4,885	1,165	64.2	612
1954	4,959	1,173	67.2	588
1955	5,371	1,236	67.0	611

Compiled. *Survey of Current Business*, U. S. Department of Commerce, XXXVI (August, 1956), p. 11, and previous issues, 1929 to 1955.

Table 77.   Personal Income Data by States and Regions, 1955

State and region	Total income millions of dollars	Per capita income	Per cent increase in total personal income 1929-55	Per cent increase in per capita income 1929-55
Continental United States	$303,391	$1,847	254	163
New England	20,075	2,087	182	138
Connecticut	5,497	2,499	235	143
Maine	1,443	1,593	201	165
Massachusetts	10,010	2,097	159	130
New Hampshire	958	1,732	198	151
Rhode Island	1,599	1,957	168	125
Vermont	568	1,535	152	145
Middle East	80,273	2,100	184	122
Delaware	980	2,513	308	147
District of Columbia	1,992	2,324	224	83
Maryland	5,463	1,991	334	156
New Jersey	12,304	2,311	231	148
New York	36,255	2,263	157	95
Pennsylvania	20,724	1,902	175	145
West Virginia	2,555	1,288	222	179
Southeast	43,758	1,292	376	257
Alabama	3,674	1,181	329	265
Arkansas	1,913	1,062	239	248
Florida	5,923	1,654	687	217
Georgia	4,882	1,333	381	281
Kentucky	3,728	1,238	265	217
Louisiana	3,910	1,333	352	221
Mississippi	2,018	946	254	232
NORTH CAROLINA	5,371	1,236	413	270
South Carolina	2,557	1,108	444	310
Tennessee	4,288	1,256	337	233
Virginia	5,494	1,535	421	253
Southwest	20,166	1,581	374	234
Arizona	1,588	1,577	525	167
New Mexico	1,134	1,430	563	251
Oklahoma	3,328	1,506	209	232
Texas	14,116	1,614	413	238
Central	86,999	1,992	242	165
Illinois	20,988	2,257	188	136
Indiana	8,201	1,894	316	209
Iowa	4,213	1,577	197	173
Michigan	15,632	2,134	311	169
Minnesota	5,394	1,691	250	183
Missouri	7,560	1,800	232	187
Ohio	18,442	2,062	256	164
Wisconsin	6,569	1,774	228	160
Northwest	13,841	1,595	249	194
Colorado	2,729	1,764	325	177
Idaho	895	1,462	298	191
Kansas	3,393	1,647	240	208
Montana	1,160	1,844	272	210
Nebraska	2,147	1,540	165	161
North Dakota	882	1,372	249	266
South Dakota	850	1,245	195	199
Utah	1,238	1,553	336	178
Wyoming	547	1,753	262	159
Far West	38,279	2,189	418	141
California	29,438	2,271	435	128
Nevada	572	2,434	624	177
Oregon	3,090	1,834	378	169
Washington	5,179	1,987	344	165

Source: Survey of Current Business, U. S. Department of Commerce, (August, 1956), pp. 10, 11, Tables 1 and 2.

Table 78.   Rank of North Carolina in Income and Related Factors

	Year	Figure	Rank
Population			
Total population	1954	4,225,000	11
Total Negro population	1950	1,047,350	2
Total farm population	1950	1,380,805	1
Average family size	1950	4.07	2
Labor force			
No. employees in nonagricultural			
establishments	1954	991,900	13
No. employees in manufacturing			
establishments	1954	433,100	10
No. employees in wholesale and			
retail establishments	1954	199,700	16
Income			
Total personal income	1955	$5,371,000,000	18
Per cent increase in total personal			
income	1929-55	413	8
Per family personal income	1954	$4,843	35
Per capita income	1955	$1,236	44
Manufacturing			
Average weekly earnings of all workers	1954	$47.88	48
(Rank in 1949—30)			
Per cent increase in average			
weekly earnings	1949-54	20	48
Average hourly earnings	1954	$1.25	46
Total value added by manufacturing	1953	$5,096,000,000	44
Per cent increase in value added			
by manufacturing	1947-53	38.1	44
Farming			
Per cent of personal income derived			
from agriculture	1954	12.7	10
Cash receipts from farm marketing	1954	$928,000,000	12
Realized gross income per farm	1954	$3,962	40
Per cent increase in realized gross			
income per farm	1949-54	29.69	7
Realized net income per farm	1954	$2,091	30
(Rank in 1949—38, with $1,690)			
Per cent realized net income per farm			
of realized gross income per farm	1954	52.78	1
Retail Sales			
Total retail sales	1954	$3,000,000,000	16
Retail sales per capita	1954	$698	45
Special features of business and			
** farming structure**			
Output value of textile manufacturing	1953	$2,800,000,000	1
Output value of tobacco manufacturing	1953	$1,600,000,000	1
Output value of furniture manufacturing	1953	$322,000,000	1
Per cent of females in labor force	1950	30.7	15
Per cent of employed persons engaged			
in manufacturing durable goods	1950	7.4	30
Per cent of employed persons engaged in			
professional and related services	1950	6.7	46
Per cent of persons 25 yrs. of age or			
older who have completed high school	1950	20.8	48
Number of farms	1954	267,906	2

(Continued on next page)

Table 78 (continued)

	Year	Figure	Rank
Special features of business and farming structure (continued)			
Average size of farm in acres	1954	68.2	48
Acres of cropland per farm dweller	1950	5.1	47
Acres of cropland per male farm resident 14 yrs. of age or older	1950	18.9	48
Cash receipts from crops	1954	$706,000,000	4
Cash receipts from tobacco	1954	$449,758,657	1
Cash receipts from livestock products	1954	$221,974,000	22

Source: Studies of Per Capita Income in North Carolina. A Report by an Inter-institutional Committee of North Carolina State College and the University of North Carolina (Chapel Hill, March, 1956, mimeographed).

Table 79. Gross Retail Sales Reported, Both Taxable and Nontaxable, by Counties, 1955-56

Counties	Retail sales taxable	Retail sales nontaxable	Total retail sales reported
Alamance	$ 51,319,652	$23,399,445	$ 74,719,097
Alexander	5,250,253	2,548,811	7,799,064
Alleghany	3,564,925	1,829,933	5,394,858
Anson	8,713,666	5,710,335	14,424,001
Ashe	4,795,780	3,175,039	7,970,819
Avery	2,224,483	1,594,379	3,818,862
Beaufort	16,643,871	9,134,386	25,778,257
Bertie	6,725,018	3,226,267	9,951,285
Bladen	9,861,596	4,950,354	14,811,950
Brunswick	3,754,552	2,049,111	5,803,663
Buncombe	91,299,699	48,381,550	139,681,249
Burke	18,610,547	8,958,201	27,568,748
Cabarrus	41,151,192	20,712,580	61,863,772
Caldwell	21,237,279	9,466,018	30,703,297
Camden	497,702	520,350	1,018,052
Carteret	14,182,462	8,565,356	22,747,818
Caswell	2,413,501	2,299,824	4,713,325
Catawba	49,084,446	24,413,669	73,498,115
Chatham	12,010,554	12,648,741	24,659,295
Cherokee	5,826,244	3,874,337	9,700,581
Chowan	5,532,737	2,768,759	8,301,496
Clay	950,657	917,561	1,868,218
Cleveland	30,161,022	16,136,017	46,297,039
Columbus	21,792,155	9,294,621	31,086,776
Craven	33,037,102	16,025,497	49,062,599
Cumberland	77,410,664	33,600,918	111,011,582
Currituck	1,240,541	1,569,737	2,810,278
Dare	4,329,837	1,087,106	5,416,943
Davidson	40,521,440	20,379,657	60,901,097
Davie	5,705,134	3,576,489	9,281,623
Duplin	12,956,097	6,474,604	19,430,701
Durham	78,775,800	40,421,175	119,196,975
Edgecombe	22,449,627	13,867,624	36,317,251
Forsyth	136,618,116	55,431,629	192,049,745
Franklin	8,693,151	5,775,423	14,468,574
Gaston	59,404,251	34,963,534	94,367,785
Gates	1,774,636	1,188,115	2,962,751
Graham	1,972,724	1,149,775	3,122,499
Granville	10,245,581	6,255,566	16,501,147
Greene	3,148,783	1,685,174	4,833,957
Guilford	192,969,327	86,693,717	279,663,044
Halifax	26,879,526	16,323,295	43,202,821
Harnett	22,241,242	13,351,247	35,592,489
Haywood	19,344,753	10,755,963	30,100,716
Henderson	18,870,003	11,689,605	30,559,608
Hertford	10,034,364	4,364,640	14,399,004
Hoke	3,617,892	2,178,695	5,796,587
Hyde	864,317	814,507	1,678,824
Iredell	30,500,481	17,171,973	47,672,454
Jackson	5,776,332	3,915,972	9,692,304
Johnson	23,765,719	14,574,225	38,339,944
Jones	1,966,992	1,256,441	3,223,433
Lee	19,624,796	14,580,563	34,205,359

(Continued on next page)

327

Table 79 (continued)

Counties	Retail sales taxable	Retail sales nontaxable	Total retail sales reported
Lenoir	34,738,909	18,379,990	53,118,899
Lincoln	11,239,722	6,068,138	17,307,860
Macon	5,836,122	2,846,821	8,682,943
Madison	4,078,636	2,560,977	6,639,613
Martin	11,238,786	4,641,188	15,879,974
McDowell	11,136,376	7,532,556	18,668,932
Mecklenburg	269,811,114	128,096,789	397,907,903
Mitchell	7,811,499	3,011,795	10,823,294
Montgomery	8,159,747	4,396,616	12,556,363
Moore	18,446,358	10,721,288	29,167,646
Nash	33,974,175	12,602,804	46,576,979
New Hanover	63,345,428	25,881,293	89,226,721
Northampton	4,252,241	3,459,809	7,712,050
Onslow	28,060,417	12,759,783	40,820,200
Orange	17,295,565	8,776,988	26,072,553
Pamlico	1,236,062	1,239,666	2,475,728
Pasquotank	18,591,149	7,045,959	25,637,108
Pender	3,317,529	2,026,231	5,343,760
Perquimans	3,544,151	1,070,930	4,615,081
Person	10,815,509	5,209,473	16,024,982
Pitt	34,079,542	15,114,424	49,193,966
Polk	3,411,987	2,528,013	5,940,000
Randolph	28,825,042	13,171,654	41,996,696
Richmond	20,212,509	8,616,542	28,829,051
Robeson	32,703,386	14,916,858	47,620,244
Rockingham	33,586,947	17,164,277	50,751,224
Rowan	45,535,099	26,804,206	72,339,365
Rutherford	20,472,563	9,650,303	30,122,866
Sampson	14,589,925	7,600,335	22,190,260
Scotland	10,212,951	6,286,896	16,499,847
Stanly	20,348,578	11,974,672	32,323,250
Stokes	4,721,363	2,487,687	7,209,050
Surry	29,617,775	11,752,620	41,370,395
Swain	3,312,613	1,801,424	5,114,037
Transylvania	6,138,901	2,970,958	9,109,859
Tyrrell	1,036,494	438,141	1,474,635
Union	19,311,614	12,051,922	31,363,536
Vance	15,980,711	9,532,319	25,513,030
Wake	137,968,908	83,441,311	221,410,219
Warren	5,027,478	4,331,207	9,358,685
Washington	5,438,216	2,115,387	7,553,603
Watauga	7,437,508	3,038,515	10,476,023
Wayne	39,356,001	16,968,068	56,324,069
Wilkes	23,354,085	10,391,729	33,745,814
Wilson	31,920,189	13,596,862	45,517,051
Yadkin	7,655,456	2,713,635	10,369,091
Yancey	2,962,978	1,999,242	4,962,220
Foreign	128,962,969	66,411,369	195,374,338
Totals	$2,603,454,504	$1,315,898,240	$3,919,352,744

Source: *Statistics of Taxation*, 1956, p. 268, Table 62.

Table 80. Assessed Value of All Property Subject to Taxation in North Carolina For Selected Fiscal Years, 1938-39 to 1955-56

(assessments are as of January 1 preceding beginning of fiscal year)

Fiscal year	Real property other than that included in public utility excess (000)	Personal Property				Corporate excess of railroads and public utilities[b] (000)	Total all property (000)
		Tangible other than that included in public utility excess (000)	Bank and building loan shares (000)	Other intangible property[a] (000)	Total other than some tangible property of public utilities (000)		
1938-39	$1,693,971	$430,483	$10,915	$456,207	$2,591,575	$176,599	$2,768,175
1941-42	1,789,431	517,979	12,017	699,794	3,019,221	178,498	3,197,719
1944-45	1,876,668	739,809	12,648	1,067,735	3,696,860	181,999	3,878,859
1947-48	2,082,661	1,056,525	16,398	1,875,831	5,031,416	186,450	5,217,866
1950-51	2,544,455	1,484,145	17,005	2,293,448	6,339,053	206,707	6,545,760
1953-54	3,386,893	2,083,778	17,843	2,649,978	8,138,492	231,962	8,370,454
1955-56	3,731,717	2.154,187	17.887	3,619,563	9,523,334	253,425	9,776,759

Source: *Statistics of Taxation, 1956*, p. 312, Table 111.

[a]Property subject only to state administered intangible property tax.

[b]See text discussion of corporate excess under public utility assessments.

Table 81. Assessed Valuation of Property Locally Taxable by Location of the Property for Designated Fiscal Years

Fiscal year	Assessed valuation		Total
	Rurally located property[a]	Municipally located property	
1945-46	$1,540,991,260	$1,343,320,945	$2,884,312,205
1946-47	1,582,792,133	1,400,043,412	2,982,835,545
1947-48	1,759,708,957	1,582,325,464	3,342,034,421
1948-49	1,932,405,141	1,773,349,480	3,705,754,621
1949-50	2,056,470,309	2,047,745,495	4,104,215,804
1950-51	2,200,277,099	2,052,034,174	4,252,311,273
1951-52	2,429,921,549	2,274,373,599	4,704,295,148
1952-53	2,650,636,751	2,566,080,255	5,216,717,006
1953-54	2,888,468,249	2,832,007,784	5,720,476,003
1955-56	3,148,123,926	3,009,092,377	6,157,216,303

Source: *Statistics of Taxation, 1956*, p. 313, Table 112.

[a]Includes suburban outside corporate limits.

Table 82. Total Property Taxes Levied by All Jurisdictions for Schools and for Other Purposes, by Counties, for the 1955–56 Fiscal Year

County	Total assessed valuation 1955-56	Total levy for schools	City and town levy	Total other than schools: county, municipal, district	Total for all purposes, including schools	Per cent total levy is of assessed valuation
Alamance	$133,882,222	$1,398,227	$1,267,803	$1,924,458	$3,322,685	2.48
Alexander	18,563,061	47,985	40,100	159,182	207,167	1.12
Alleghany	5,509,435	38,566	5,932	61,026	99,592	1.81
Anson	22,570,485	138,100	76,691	340,767	478,867	2.12
Ashe	9,674,559	53,210	27,295	264,321	317,531	3.28
Avery	6,561,919	40,028	9,298	87,385	127,413	1.94
Beaufort	37,536,602	229,266	246,320	542,859	772,125	2.06
Bertie	16,616,189	111,328	56,378	219,217	330,545	1.32
Bladen	26,308,165	205,204	88,803	304,530	509,734	1.94
Brunswick	15,357,311	74,351	35,061	243,920	318,271	2.07
Buncombe	151,682,583	1,636,607	1,314.699	3,196,315	4,832,922	3.19
Burke	75,137.893	432,178	383,426	657,679	1,089,857	1.45
Cabarrus	99,045,456	391,619	348,915	883,362	1,274,981	1.29
Caldwell	71,019,714	280,800	322,583	752,252	1,033,052	1.45
Camden	5,230,623	44,460		47,076	91,536	1.75
Carteret	24,113,262	62,694	202,009	573,353	636,047	2.64
Caswell	12,416,361	142,788	651	62,733	205,521	1.66
Catawba	106,812,170	1,018,254	867,139	1,048,720	2,066,974	1.93
Chatham	32,036,412	190,617	105,845	286,851	477,468	1.49
Cherokee	12,342,800	87,634	77,636	242,289	329,923	2.67
Chowan	12,104,215	76,257	70,358	185,820	262,077	2.16
Clay	3,779,091	15,116	6,892	67,358	82,474	2.18
Cleveland	82,927,833	631,634	399,229	847,950	1,479,584	1.78
Columbus	37,761,714	409,715	198,064	505,822	915,537	2.42
Craven	36,228,148	474,589	264,378	514,353	988,942	2.73
Cumberland	96,577,838	572,738	558,762	1,283,096	1,855,834	1.92
Currituck	11,152,785	96,991		70,301	167,292	1.50
Dare	17,394,366	66,098	21,877	159,271	225,369	1.30
Davidson	106,609,113	582,280	661,771	1,111,981	1,694,261	1.59
Davie	28,754,694	102,798	54,341	201,709	304,507	1.06
Duplin[a]	38,568,387	279,621	149,635	467,824	747,445	1.94
Durham	298,282,868	1,558,215	2,189,732	3,787,633	5,345,848	1.79
Edgecombe	55,637,989	449,336	184,113	545,760	995,096	1.78
Forsyth[b]	577,997,002	3,714,169	3,489,868	5,097,300	8,811,469	1.52
Franklin	23,345,161	115,314	78,173	290,748	406,062	1.74
Gaston	199,769,334	891,406	1,339,933	2,944,558	3,835,964	1.92
Gates	8,759,223	51,550	4,395	71,841	123,391	1.41
Graham	8,757,011	28,898	8,395	88,959	117,857	1.35
Granville	38,559,072	270,837	175,875	392,199	663,036	1.72
Greene	16,396,493	101,101	24,858	128,713	229,814	1.40
Guilford	576,319,612	3,320,023	4,834,456	6,824,938	10,144,961	1.76
Halifax	64,223,317	522,371	502,419	834,374	1,356,745	2.11
Harnett	53,200,838	426,676	225,828	551,474	978,150	1.84
Haywood	39,218,677	403,678	289,069	623,526	1,027,204	2.62
Henderson	43,722,461	177,170	243,168	691,609	868,779	1.99
Hertford	19,660,382	135,657	135,379	271,035	406,692	2.07
Hoke	14,080,292	84,482	62,495	146,977	231,459	1.64
Hyde	8,627,544	34,079		74,197	108,276	1.25
Iredell	77,535,635	560,691	448,191	983,187	1,543,878	1.99
Jackson	17,530,298	82,392	49,075	234,896	317,288	1.81

(Continued on next page)

330

Table 82 (continued)

	Total assessed valuation 1955-56	Total levy for schools	City and town levy	Total other than schools: county, municipal, district	Total for all purposes, including schools	Per cent total levy is of assessed valuation
Johnston	58,242,392	557,852	221,544	623,416	1,181,268	2.03
Jones	6,814,010	47,017	6,710	95,973	142,990	2.10
Lee	32,826,342	273,493	275,655	479,999	753,492	2.30
Lenoir	76,028,726	486,947	410,776	798,523	1,285,470	1.69
Lincoln	32,471,114	192,740	106,366	349,799	542,539	1.67
Macon	15,470,925	58,789	51,995	209,799	268,588	1.74
Madison	11,589,184	92,813	47,344	186,414	279,227	2.41
Martin	27,431,477	263,453	156,426	338,230	601,683	2.19
McDowell	33,887,523	274,489	120,317	269,979	544,468	1.61
Mecklenburg[c]	540,824,610	4,571,361	5,011,688	7,937,576	12,508,937	2.31
Mitchell	10,007,369	46,034	54,326	174,414	220,448	2.20
Montgomery	28,637,572	148,915	121,429	301,846	450,761	1.57
Moore	42,946,283	485,003	276,945	459,143	944,146	2.20
Nash	68,773,819	740,634	590,427	851,767	1,592,401	2.31
New Hanover	109,795,121	782,510	1,465,893	2,000,924	2,783,434	2.58
Northampton	25,754,974	154,082	83,161	268,854	422,936	1.64
Onslow	36,042,263	262,748	267,685	455,609	718,357	1.99
Orange	74,291,878	325,047	224,180	416,127	741,174	1.00
Pamlico	10,664,918	45,859	11,226	104,011	149,870	1.41
Pasquotank	26,803,274	243,278	237,645	393,640	636,918	2.38
Pender	15,097,428	118,062	29,438	168,032	286,094	1.89
Perquimans	8,213,144	52,564	23,194	106,147	158,711	1.93
Person	31,585,658	140,240	118,406	357,193	497,433	1.57
Pitt	69,012,267	505,884	492,197	903,510	1,409,394	2.04
Polk	9,223,997	97,369	46,375	138,056	235,425	2.55
Randolph	81,613,015	662,689	422,127	730,911	1,393,600	1.71
Richmond	50,153,729	272,750	221,983	623,213	895,963	1.79
Robeson	68,985,258	715,503	319,848	878,629	1,594,132	2.31
Rockingham	137,203,200	787,518	797,040	1,194,106	1,981,624	1.44
Rowan	132,066,304	749,461	766,933	1,326,894	2,076,355	1.57
Rutherford	41,757,844	254,722	293,099	769,139	1,023,861	2.45
Sampson	39,432,961	320,459	154,550	517,333	837,792	2.12
Scotland	24,536,616	249,113	133,617	317,028	566,141	2.31
Stanly	48,277,565	333,478	230,940	487,266	820,744	1.70
Stokes	16,493,784	82,469	18,643	183,581	266,050	1.61
Surry	56,365,356	223,029	352,967	777,310	1,000,339	1.77
Swain	7,268,194	26,165	30,685	128,079	154,244	2.12
Transylvania	21,773,402	210,157	76,903	204,234	414,391	1.90
Tyrrell	4,522,794	18,453	15,181	75,786	94,239	2.08
Union	31,175,611	306,294	174,972	442,459	748,753	2.40
Vance	34,473,307	227,524	244,686	415,667	643,191	1.87
Wake	213,522,695	1,793,768	1,960,319	2,878,467	4,672,235	2.19
Warren	15,769,712	126,158	40,700	163,235	289,393	1.83
Washington	12,609,689	56,744	106,426	264,047	320,791	2.54
Watauga	22,301,005	55,752	111,134	256,091	311,843	1.40
Wayne	85,299,489	472,791	575,684	1,099,423	1,572,214	1.84
Wilkes	30,777,696	56,967	161,448	546,169	603,136	1.96
Wilson	54,505,528	546,329	423,951	664,865	1,211,194	2.22
Yadkin	18,831,099	82,857	31,663	174,779	257,636	1.37
Yancey	9,165,567	20,164	36,697	181,513	201,677	2.20
All local units	$6,157,216,303	$42,478,295	$40,300,858	$75,586,909	$118,065,204	1.92

Source: *Statistics of Taxation, 1956*, pp. 354-57, Table 126.

[a]Durham County—The school district levies include $644,910 for Durham (city) and $273,985 for county school system outside of the city.

[b]Forsyth County—The school district levies include $851,792 for Winston-Salem and $513,342 for county school system outside of the city.

[c]Mecklenburg County—The school district levies include $1,999,620 for Charlotte schools and $301,900 for the county school system outside Charlotte.

Table 83. Economic and Social Data for North Carolina

Population

Estimated total population, 1955 4,344,000

Total population born in N. C., living other states 1950 (20.3 per cent) 900,435

Total born in other states, living in N. C., 1950 (11.9 per cent) 475,240
    (Net loss to other states: 423,195)

Growth of North Carolina population	Year
393,751	1790
478,103	1800
638,829	1820
753,419	1840
992,622	1860
1,071,361	1870
1,399,750	1880
1,617,949	1890
1,893,810	1900
2,206,287	1910
2,559,123	1920
3,170,276	1930
3,571,623	1940
4,061,929	1950
4,344,000	1955

Increase in population	
Years	Per cent
1890-1900	17.1
1900-10	16.5
1910-20	16.0
1920-30	23.9
1930-40	12.7
1940-50	13.7

Distribution of North Carolina population, 1950

Urban 1,368,101
Rural nonfarm 1,317,268
Farm 1,376,560
Male population 2,017,105
Female population 2,044,824
White population 2,983,121
Negro 1,047,352
Other 31,455
Foreign-born white 16,134

Ranks in miscellaneous population areas

16th in number children ever born per 1,000 women 15–44 years old 1,594
4th in children ever born per 1,000 women 45–49 years old 3,130
2nd in population per household, 1950 . . . . 3.95
    (Only S. C. above N. C.)
2nd in population per family, 1950 . . . . 4.07
    (S. C. 4.19; U. S. 3.60)
15th in births per 1,000 population, 1955 . . . . 27.0
9th in total number births, 1954 118,338
2nd in deaths per 1,000 population, 1955 (2nd lowest) 7.6
36th in infant deaths per 1,000 live births, 1954 . . . . 30.2
48th in marriages per 1,000 population, 1955 . . . . 6.1
    (S. C. rate 20.4)
11th in total number hospitals, 1954 183
14th in hospital beds, 1954 31,903
10th in patients admitted to hospitals, 1954 486,935
16th in patients in hospitals per mental disease, 1953 9,928
40th in average current exp. per pupil in av. daily attendance, 1952 . . . . $176.00
45th in median school years completed by persons 25 yrs. old or over 7.9
40th in value public school property per pupil in average daily attendance, 1952 . . . . $430.00
9th in number of high school graduates, 1952 32,000
13th in college enrollment 1955 (only Texas in South ahead) 50,652
    (Men 31,293; women 19,359)
9th in value of plants of higher education, 1952 . . . . $228,967,000
    (Wake Forest a major addition since then)

(Continued on next page)

Table 83 (continued)

9th in number institutions of higher education, 1952
    (Full-time staff: men, 3,709; women, 1,498)
28th in total number lawyers with degrees, 1954. 1,726
24th in total number all lawyers, 1954 3,009

Labor

12th in total labor force (persons 14 years of age and over, 1955) 1,555,000
Employed in non-agricultural establishments, 1955 1,036,900
Mining 4,000
Contract const 51,000
Manufacture 456,900
Transportation, public utilities 60,200
Wholesale, retail 207,000
Finance, insurance, real estate 31,100
Service and miscellaneous 92,100
Government 134,600

Major occupation groups and class of worker of employed persons, 1950
Total employed 1,463,352
Professional, technical, etc. 84,427
Farmers and farm managers 226,531
Managers, officials, proprietors, except farm 93,930
Clerical and kindred workers. 97,660
Sales workers 85,030
Craftsmen, foremen, etc. 152,536
Operators and kindred workers 351,083
Private household 55,943
Other service workers 37,653
Farm laborers, unpaid family workers 7,451
Farm laborers except unpaid and foremen 55,978
Laborers, except farm and mine 84,614
Occupations not reported 21,770

Class of workers, 1950
Private wage and salary 941,386
Government 112,626
Self-employed 330,113
Unpaid family workers . . . . 79,227[a]

Hours and gross earnings of workers in manufacture, 1955

	N. C.	U. S.
Average weekly earnings (only Mississippi below N. C.)	$51.46	$76.52
Average weekly hours	40.2	40.7
Average hourly earnings (only Mississippi below N. C.)	$1.28	$1.88

Public Utilities

Electric generating plants in N. C., total, 1954. 3,409
Electric utilities and industrial, fuel 2,352
Electric utilities and industrial, hydro 1,057
    (Privately owned 2461; publicly owned 415, industrial 531)
Production of electricity, total kwh 14,722,000,000
    (Fuel 11,313,000,000 kwh; hydro 3,410,000,000 kwh)
Production of electricity by utilities only kwh 13,411,000,000
    (Fuel 10,233,000,000 kwh; hydro 2,178,000,000 kwh)
Installed capacity hydro stations, 1954, kw 1,057,000
    (Utilities 755,000 kw; industrial 302,000 kw)
Gas utility customers, 1954 75,300
    (N. C. ranks 37th in number of customers)
Gas utility revenue, 1954 . . . . $9,040,000
Estimated undeveloped water power, kw (maximum potential) 1,156,000

(Continued on next page)

Table 83 (continued)

Transportation

Total miles roads, rural and municipal, 1954	76,420
Municipal miles	8,702
Rural miles	67,718
State, rural miles	66,441
Federal, rural miles	1,277
Total highway funds available, 1954	$210,817,000
From motor fuel, vehicle fees, carrier taxes	107,757,000
From Federal funds	12,824,000
Other sources, bonds	90,236,000
Highway disbursements, 1954, total	$130,995,000
Capital outlay, roads and bridges	64,405,000
Maintenance	28,742,000
Other	25,794,000
For local roads and streets	5,719,000
Total motor vehicles registered, 1955 (N. C. 13th)	1,410,000
Automobiles and taxicabs	1,027,881
Trucks and buses (N. C. 10th)	249,856
Publicly owned vehicles (N. C. 7th)	26,515
Trailers	89,695
Motorcycles	7,979
Receipts from motor-vehicle adm.	$25,079,000
Railways, miles of roads, 1955 (N. C. 21st)	4,326
(Some 800 miles have been discontinued since 1930)	
Civil airways mileages, 1955	1,038
Number civil airports and airfields	109

Farms

Number of farms, 1954	268,000
Acres farm land, 1954	18,260,000
Acres crop land harvested, 1954	5,504,000
Average acres per farm, 1954 (N. C. 48th)	68.2
Value farm lands and buildings, 1954	$1,714,975,000
Average value per farm, 1954 (N. C. 41st)	$8,105
Average value per acre, 1954 (N. C. 15th)	$128.13
Per cent of farms operated by tenants, 1954	36.9
White farm operators, 1954	200,998
Nonwhite farm operators, 1954	66,908
(Only Mississippi has more Negro farmers)	
Cash receipts from farm marketing, 1955	$936,800,000
Crops	717,000,000
Livestock and products	219,800,000
Government payments	7,300,000
Farms with electricity, 1954, per cent	93.6
Farms with telephone, 1954, per cent (N. C. 47th)	16.8
Farms with motor trucks, 1954	86,000
Farms with automobiles, 1954	182,000
Farms with tractors, 1954	105,000
Number farms with irrigated land, 1954	2,704
Acres irrigated	25,423

Land

28th in total land area square miles	49,097
(Total land acreage, acres	31,422,208)
Owned by Federal government, acres	1,205,000
Military except air fields, acres	249,000
Federal parks, historic sites, acres	319,000
Federal flood navigation, acres	61,000
Air fields, acres	38,000

(Continued on next page)

Table 83 (continued)

Land (continued)

Indian lands, acres	56,500
Other federal, acres	8,000
State parks (17), acres	35,523
4th in total inland water area, square miles	3,615
(Ahead are Florida, Minnesota, Texas)	
27th in total gross area, square miles	52,712
Number drainage enterprises, 1950	413
Acres in drainage enterprises	1,128,509
Soil conservation districts, 1955	37
Cooperators in soil conservation districts.	77,021
Total area in soil conservation, acres	7,911,000

Forests

Total forest area, acres 19,513,000
    (N. C. ranks 10th in total forest area, 7th in commercial forest area,
    and 2nd in farm forest area)
Live sawtimber volume, 1953 (million board feet) 44,152
    (N. C. ranks 6th in sawtimber volume, evenly distributed between hardwoods and softwoods.
    N. C. ranks 3rd in net annual growth of sawtimber, 2,951,000,000 board feet, 5th in net
    annual cut, 1952, 2,381,000,000 board feet with two-thirds softwoods, and 6th in net volume
    of growing stock, 13,642,000,000 cubic feet).
7th in net area federal forest land purchased through 1955, acres 1,035,000

Federal grants to state and local governments, 1955

Total amount	$70,781,000
Total per capita, (U. S. $18.84)	16.75
Social Security and related purposes	44,476,000
Public assistance	31,224,000
Employment security administration	3,375,000
Health services	3,933,000
Other welfare.	5,944,000
Education	2,549,000
Other.	23,756,000

Public assistance and unemployment insurance

Total amount of public assistance, 1955 . . . . $41,915,000
    Amount of federal grants, 1955 31,128,000

Average monthly payments	N. C.	U. S.
Old-age assistance	$31.78	$53.93
Aid to dependent children per family	62.16	88.61
Aid to blind	40.92	58.09
Permanently and totally blind	37.80	56.18
General assistance (18-65).	20.77	55.01

North Carolina unemployment insurance, funds available for benefits
    on December 31, 1955 . . . . $173,306,000

State wealth and income

Estimated state wealth, 1952 . . . . $21,000,000,000
    (N. C. income is 1.77 per cent of the U. S. total. If its wealth bears same ratio, it amounts
    to $21,000,000,000, since U. S. total wealth in 1952 was $1,210,000,000,000.)
Personal income N. C., 1955. . . . . $5,371,000,000 b
    Per capita income 1,236
    Rank among states 44th
U. S. Savings bonds—Series E and H cumulative sales 1941-55 . . . . $959,057,000
    (N. C. ranks 23rd in total purchases)

Insurance

Life insurance in N. C. 1954, number policies	6,048,000
Amount of insurance in force.	$5,996,000,000
Amount per family (U. S. $6,300; N. C. 34th).	4,900

(Continued on next page)

Table 83 (continued)

Insurance (continued)
Ordinary policies, number 1,610,000
Group policies, number certificates 863,000
Industrial policies, number 3,575,000
Medical care insurance
Number persons covered by hospital insurance 2,196,000
Number persons covered by surgical insurance 2,077,000
Number persons covered by medical insurance 372,000
Per cent of population covered by hospital insurance 52.8

State revenue and indebtedness
Revenue of state and local governments, 1953 . . . . $664,000,000
From federal government 60,000,000
From state sources. 315,000,000
From local sources. 142,000,000
Utility and liquor store revenue 108,000,000
Insurance trust revenue 39,000,000
State payments to local government. 63,000,000
Per capita general revenue of state and local governments, 1953 . . . . 123.72
    (U. S. per capita, 175.30; N. C. rank, 42nd)
Debt of state government outstanding, 1954 . . . . $298,601,000
Per capita debt of state government (U. S., $60.96) $71.22

Public employees
All public employees in North Carolina, 1955 140,700
Federal 28,100
State 82,900
Local 29,600
Rate per 10,000 population, Federal (U. S., 132.3) 65.7
Rate per 10,000 population, state and local (U. S., 307.6) 262.7
State and local government employment, 1955 (full-time equivalent) 102,278
Education 54,025
Highways 10,922
Health and hospitals 9,946
Police and fire 5,725
Public welfare. 1,305
Sanitation 2,465
Natural resources 3,345
Utilities and state liquor stores. 3,108
All other 11,437

Banks and Savings and Loan Associations
All active banks in N. C., 1954 224
Total assets or liabilities $2,550,000,000
Loans and discounts 874,300,000
U. S. Government and other securities 1,017,000,000
Deposits 2,325,500,000
National banks 75
Total assets $631,300,000
State banks. 149
Total assets $1,918,700,000
Number savings and loan associations 178
Total assets. 629,689,000

Retail and wholesale establishments
14th in total number retail stores, 1954 38,054
15th in total retail sales, 1954 . . . . $3,215,000,000
15th in total paid employees, Nov., 1954. 144,229

	Estab.	Sales
Food stores	10,583	$692,000,000
Eating, drinking.	4,132	136,000,000

(Continued on next page)

Table 83 (continued)

Retail and wholesale establishments (continued)

	Estab.	Sales
General merchandise	2,906	$395,000,000
Apparel, accessories	2,331	197,000,000
Furniture, home appliances	2,123	177,000,000
Automotive	2,195	609,000,000
Gasoline service stations	5,176	245,000,000
Lumber, bldgs., mat., hdw.	1,660	255,000,000
Drug stores	1,020	95,000,000
Other retail stores	4,488	331,000,000
Nonstore retailers	1,440	81,000,000

15th in number wholesale estab., 1954	4,750
18th in wholesale employee payroll entire year, 1954	$162,659,000
19th in merchant wholesale sales, 1954	$1,514,000,000
13th in other types wholesale sales, 1954	$2,652,000,000

Industry and manufacturing

12th in number all employees in manuf., 1953	446,265
13th in total salaries and wages paid, 1953	$1,201,031,000
14th in value added by manufacture, 1953	$2,274,019,000
2nd in number cotton spindles in place, 1955	5,994,000
2nd in number spindle hours, 1955	29,892,000,000
1st in bales cotton consumed, 1955	2,511,000
12th in wood-pulp production, 1953 (tons)	585,113
34th in value mineral production, 1952	$38,446,000
(Chief minerals: stone, tungsten, sand and gravel, feldspar, mica)	
Total catch of fish, 1953 (pounds)	326,545,000
Total value of fish caught, 1953	$20,152,000

Miscellaneous

Number all business firms in N. C., 1954	83,000
Total employees	832,627
Total number telephones, 1954	566,000
Business, 166,000; residence, 400,000	
Commercial broadcast stations	165
(AM 121; FM 32; TV 12)	
Number post offices, 1955	920
Gross postal receipts, 1955	$31,159,000
23rd in number hotels, 1948	405
21st in number hotel guest rooms, 1948	18,805
22nd in room rental and sale of meals, 1948	$20,919,000
Total dwelling units, 1955 (N. C. 12th).	820,888
(Increase in units 1940-50, 28.9 per cent)	

Compiled. *Statistical Abstract, 1956.*

[a]This figure is by far the largest of any state, 7.1 per cent of the United States total.
[b]*Survey of Current Business*, XXXVI (August, 1956), p. 10, Table 1.

Table 84.   Life Insurance Statistics and Income, North Carolina,
Selected Years, 1900–55

1. Life Insurance

Year	Life insurance in force in North Carolina	Average life insurance in force per family in North Carolina[a]	Average life insurance in force per capita in North Carolina[a]
1900	$ 53,000,000		$ 30
1905	121,000,000		
1910	178,000,000		80
1915	252,000,000		
1920	576,000,000		230
1925	937,000,000		
1930	1,323,000,000		420
1935	1,253,000,000		
1940	1,662,000,000	$2,100	500
1945	2,412,000,000	2,900	650
1946	2,793,000,000	3,300	760
1947	3,188,000,000	3,700	850
1948	3,448,000,000	3,800	900
1949	3,627,000,000	3,900	900
1950	4,112,000,000	4,000	1,000
1951	4,541,000,000	4,300	1,100
1954	5,996,000,000	5,700	1,425
1955	6,760,000,000	6,240	1,560

2. Income

Year	Per family	Average income payment per capita in North Carolina
1930		$ 255
1935		270
1940	$1,400	316
1945	3,200	757
1946	3,600	808
1947	3,800	860
1948	3,800	898
1949	3,600	852
1950	3,800	956
1951	4,200	1,052
1954	4,760	1,190

Source: *Survey of Current Business* (August issue of each year); Division of Statistics and Research, Institute of Life Insurance, New York, N. Y.

[a]Estimates.

Table 85. Amount of Ordinary Life Policies in Force by North Carolina Home Companies, 1918–49

Year	Home companies	Insurance number	Written amount	In force December 31		Premiums received
				Number	Amount	
1918	10		$ 22,816,698		$ 84,576,478	$ 2,153,445
1920	16		54,360,165		136,345,685	6,209,201
1925	10	14,136	35,519,587	80,606	168,397,430	5,655,521
1930	10	25,350	42,487,925	114,884	242,741,882	7,264,625
1935	11	37,570	39,910,094	134,873	219,447,452	6,207,753
1940	12	45,513	46,795,185	184,775	293,088,463	8,099,049
1945	13	62,452	60,068,426	253,721	397,525,275	11,488,374
1949	13	289,860	155,298,183	490,015	722,600,818	19,537,318

Source: Annual Reports of the Commissioner of Insurance of North Carolina (Raleigh).

Table 86. Amount of Industrial Policies in Force by North Carolina Home Companies, 1925–49

Year	Home companies	Insurance number	Written amount	In force December 31		Premiums received
				Number	Amount	
1925	10	372,954	$ 39,113,954	1,015,665	$ 47,679,299	$ 3,461,805
1930	11	522,441	76,046,785	587,019	77,382,530	4,317,217
1935	8	497,755	81,993,812	687,313	112,236,545	4,046,130
1940	8	527,156	109,446,130	1,071,467	203,416,523	7,474,674
1945	9	448,961	116,652,295	1,643,154	358,157,050	13,218,816
1949	10	452,271	154,252,196	2,006,543	491,260,757	19,797,107

Source: See Table 85.

Table 87.   Life Insurance in Force by States, 1954

	No. of policies (000)	Amount (000,000)	Amount per family	Rank of state
United States[a]	236,536	$333,719	$6,300	
North Carolina	6,048	5,996	4,900	30
Alabama	6,471	4,267	4,800	34
Arizona	635	1,239	3,900	44
Arkansas	1,289	1,627	2,900	47
California	13,323	25,956	5,600	20
Colorado	1,649	2,848	5,700	18
Connecticut	4,091	6,443	8,900	2
Delaware	890	1,151	9,700	1
Florida	6,123	5,759	4,600	37
Georgia	7,564	6,266	5,800	17
Idaho	369	767	4,000	41
Illinois	15,493	24,051	7,600	6
Indiana	6,884	9,408	6,800	9
Iowa	2,680	4,670	5,300	24
Kansas	2,352	3,799	5,600	20
Kentucky	3,920	3,898	4,400	40
Louisiana	4,897	4,291	4,900	30
Maine	1,065	1,458	4,900	30
Maryland	4,963	5,649	6,600	12
Massachusetts	8,036	11,126	6,800	9
Michigan	9,623	15,451	6,800	9
Minnesota	3,138	5,756	5,700	18
Mississippi	1,571	1,718	2,700	48
Missouri	6,345	8,485	5,900	16
Montana	457	962	4,500	38
Nebraska	1,377	2,442	5,400	23
Nevada	136	303	3,700	46
New Hampshire	806	1,107	6,300	13
New Jersey	9,473	15,026	8,700	3
New Mexico	497	910	4,000	41
New York	24,542	43,698	8,100	4
North Dakota	405	768	4,000	41
Ohio	14,274	21,349	7,600	6
Oklahoma	2,140	3,460	4,700	35
Oregon	1,250	2,609	4,500	38
Pennsylvania	21,562	26,809	7,800	5
Rhode Island	1,557	1,902	7,000	8
South Carolina	4,660	3,256	5,300	24
South Dakota	383	807	3,900	44
Tennessee	5,442	5,098	5,100	27
Texas	10,548	15,061	5,500	22
Utah	848	1,409	6,300	13
Vermont	427	641	5,100	27
Virginia	5,682	5,983	5,200	26
Washington	2,041	4,491	4,900	30
West Virginia	2,227	2,856	5,100	27
Wisconsin	4,163	7,055	6,200	15
Wyoming	208	503	4,700	35

Source: *North Carolina Facts*, III (December 10, 1955), 2.

[a]United States totals listed at the top of column include the District of Columbia, which is not shown separately.

Table 88. Bank Failures in North Carolina, 1921–33

Year	Number of Banks	Deposits Involved
1921	14	$ 1,836,000
1922	8	2,874,000
1923	18	3,319,000
1924	11	1,867,000
1925	16	3,198,000
1926	12	2,512,000
1927	14	5,478,000
1928	8	1,852,000
1929	18	6,934,000
1930	93	56,178,000
1931	63	29,791,000
1932	31	14,129,000
1933 (March 15)	10	3,822,000
Total	316	$133,790,000

Source: *Trends in North Carolina Banking, 1927-1937* (Raleigh: Research Committee of the North Carolina Bankers Association, 1938), p. 17.

Table 89. Bank Resources in North Carolina, 1914–56

Year	Bank resources			Aggregate bank resources per inhabitant
	National	State	Total	
1914	$ 71,331,000	$ 81,783,436	$ 153,114,436	$ 64.90
1915	68,567,000	92,384,895	160,915,895	67.17
1916	73,104,000	120,046,244	193,150,244	79.42
1917	93,495,000	156,480,401	249,975,401	101.27
1918	116,944,000	189,632,416	306,576.416	143.96
1919	151,525,000	298,540,408	450,065,408	177.12
1920	183,810,000	271,775,749	455,585,749	176.77
1921	163,937,000	243,046,259	406,983,259	155.71
1922	179,685,000	264,623,024	444,308,024	167.66
1923	175,122,000	298,995,609	474,117,609	176.49
1924	178,798,000	280,618,841	459,416,841	170.40
1925	192,419,000	287,746,807	488,514,207	181.75
1928	202,940,000	331,107,000	534,047,000	184.00
1947	522,795,000	1,484,179,000	2,006,974,000	492.43[a]
1953	627,671,000	1,803,129,554	2,430,800,554[b]	598.45
1956[c]	686,256,000	1,945,414,093	2,631,670,093	600.00

Source: S. H. Hobbs, Jr. *North Carolina: Economic & Social* (Chapel Hill, University of North Carolina Press, 1930), p. 152.

[a]*University of North Carolina News Letter*, XXXV (March 16, 1949).

[b]*Annual Report of the Commissioner of Banks of the State of North Carolina for the Year ending December 31, 1953*, (Raleigh, 1954), p. 41.

[c]Data for 1956 are from a press release dated September 26, 1956, by Commissioner W. W. Jones.

Table 90. Assets of Industrial Loan Agencies, 1945–53

Year	Number	Assets
December 31, 1945	60	$ 1,872,141.90
December 31, 1946	80	4,289,192.48
December 31, 1947	95	6,637,131.36
December 31, 1948	104	9,935,725.14
December 31, 1949	114	5,964,649.86
December 30, 1950	131	7,239,910.26
December 31, 1951	155	11,064,252.40
December 31, 1952	190	12,341,155.09
December 31, 1953	216	13,492,017.21

Source: Annual Reports of the North Carolina Commissioner of Banks (Raleigh).

Table 91. Comparison of Selected States with North Carolina, Total Assets and Number of all Operating Banks, December 31, 1954[a]

State	Assets	Number of banks
North Carolina	$ 2,550,000,000	224
Alabama	1,692,400,000	234
Florida	3,173,900,000	226
Georgia	2,405,800,000	386
Louisiana	2,573,800,000	172
Mississippi	1,042,600,000	197
South Carolina	910,600,000	151
Texas	10,355,500,000	921
Virginia	2,797,700,000	316
New York	59,091,800,000	689
California	19,625,500,000	171
United States	232,684,800,000	14,388

Source: *Statistical Abstract, 1956*, p. 435.

[a]North Carolina ranks twenty-third from the top in total assets of all operating banks. It ranks tenth in population. Its per capita bank assets are about $600, while the average for the nation is about $1,500 in 1956.

Table 92. Average Ratios of State-Chartered Banks, December 31, 1953

	Average Ratios
Percentage total capital to total assets	6.8
Percentage total capital to total deposits	7.5
Percentage total capital to assets less cash and U. S. government obligations	14.1
Percentage of total loans to total assets	34.4
Percentage of total loans to total deposits	37.8

Compiled. *Report, 1953*, North Carolina Commissioner of Banking.

Table 93. Number of Parent Banks, State and National, Classified by Amount of Deposits, North Carolina, 1948-50 (branch banks included)

Year	Deposits of $1,000 M or less	Deposits of $1,000 M to $2,000 M	Deposits of $2,000 M to $5,000 M	Deposits of $5,000 M to $10,000 M	Deposits of $10,000 M to $20,000 M	Deposits of $20,000 M or more	Totals
1948	22	50	66	38	17	15	198
1949	21	49	60	41	15	14	200
1950	37	50	65	44	15	14	225
(North Carolina State Banks Only)							
1953	23	49	61	26	10	11	180

Source: *Trends in North Carolina Banking, 1950*, p. 16; *Report, 1953*, North Carolina Commissioner of Banking.

Table 94. Total and Per Capita Bank Deposits, by County, June 30, 1954

Rank	County	Deposits Total (000)	Deposits Per capita	Rank	County	Deposits Total (000)	Deposits Per capita
1	Mecklenburg	$333,551	$1,542.23	51	Scotland	$ 7,366	$266.36
2	Wake	191,025	1,291.73	52	Richmond	10,835	265.67
3	Wilson	60,093	1,066.82	53	Moore	9,006	264.51
4	Forsyth	138,002	893.27	54	Currituck	1,572	262.70
5	Edgecombe	36,138	685.93	55	Polk	3,025	262.56
6	Guilford	138,085	667.58	56	Harnett	12,703	259.04
7	Durham	72,665	656.23	57	Cumberland	28,722	257.36
8	Pasquotank	16,224	625.10	58	Robeson	23,779	257.33
9	Johnston	39,547	591.99	59	Granville	8,434	256.86
10	New Hanover	38,285	548.55	60	Martin	7,343	255.71
11	Buncombe	65,263	497.98	61	Alleghany	2,041	252.78
12	Vance	16,163	489.63	62	Columbus	13,087	248.19
13	Cabarrus	31,283	476.51	63	Haywood	9,622	247.77
14	Catawba	29,197	441.68	64	Lincoln	7,050	244.37
15	Rowan	33,032	423.34	65	Northampton	6,920	242.91
16	Davidson	27,541	417.19	66	Davie	3,787	242.18
17	Gates	3,800	406.59	67	Stanly	9,361	240.29
18	Wilkes	18,643	403.57	68	Onslow	11,945	228.42
19	Pitt	26,096	402.28	69	Tyrrell	1,095	226.66
20	Iredell	23,631	401.87	70	Washington	3,058	225.76
21	Hertford	8,837	395.46	71	Alexander	3,350	223.02
22	Lenoir	18,941	394.87	72	Cherokee	3,933	217.61
23	Surry	18,619	394.37	73	Ashe	4,540	210.75
24	Rockingham	25,567	377.33	74	Jackson	4,044	210.37
25	Gaston	44,766	370.76	75	Avery	2,754	207.64
26	Alamance	28,366	368.00	76	Sampson	10,204	200.96
27	Anson	9,374	359.47	77	Duplin	8,101	194.55
28	Lee	9,023	353.10	78	McDowell	5,087	189.27
29	Henderson	11,630	352.52	79	Yancey	2,954	185.50
30	Randolph	17,503	327.40	80	Transylvania	3,029	184.15
31	Beaufort	12,075	322.59	81	Watauga	3,200	173.53
32	Wayne	21,276	318.54	82	Graham	1,183	166.94
33	Cleveland	20,872	311.36	83	Warren	3,908	164.85
34	Carteret	7,789	310.49	84	Macon	2,664	163.46
35	Caldwell	13,752	295.32	85	Hyde	953	161.71
36	Craven	16,496	293.14	86	Hoke	2,569	159.52
37	Chatham	7,520	292.86	87	Yadkin	3,501	153.80
38	Orange	11,467	292.05	88	Franklin	4,678	147.34
39	Union	12,627	291.72	89	Swain	1,313	146.54
40	Chowan	3,754	289.83	90	Bladen	4,460	144.86
41	Halifax	16,825	284.36	91	Pender	2,604	139.06
42	Burke	13,756	283.92	92	Jones	1,414	128.10
43	Montgomery	4,948	279.92	93	Nash	7,603	123.12
44	Madison	5,441	276.58	94	Clay	649	111.20
45	Bertie	7,269	273.87	95	Greene	1,927	108.21
46	Perquimans	2,577	270.52	96	Pamlico	1,025	101.32
47	Rutherford	12,599	269.86	97	Stokes	1,847	87.80
48	Dare	1,380	268.84	98	Brunswick	1,690	83.93
49	Mitchell	3,964	268.09	99	Caswell	1,594	75.09
50	Person	6,419	266.61	100	Camden		
					State	$2,011,225	$470.97

Source: *North Carolina Facts*, III (August 6, 1955), 2-3.

Table 95. Growth of North Carolina Building and Loan Associations, 1906–54

Year	Number of associations	Number of shareholders	Total assets
1906	75	17,128	$ 4,353,888
1911	117	25,174	8,375,378
1916	168	37,719	15,904,770
1921	197	64,283	37,666,451
1926	239	96,590	85,715,009
1931	229	95,204	85,348,383
1936	174	87,243	60,313,504
1941	156	131,882	92,356,275
1946	150	142,462	117,646,155
1951	146	202,251	239,332,494
1954	146		387,050,993

Source: Biennial Reports of the North Carolina Insurance Department (Raleigh, N. C.).

Table 96. Growth of Federal Savings and Loan Associations in North Carolina, 1934–54

Year	Number of Associations	Total Assets
1934	4	$ 445,596
1938	16	10,764,644
1942	23	30,095,325
1946	26	65,090,629
1950	29	118,312,320
1952	32	170,513,517
1954	32	242,659,946

Source: See Table 95.

Table 97. State Budget, General Fund Appropriations and Anticipated Revenues, 1957-59

1. General Fund Appropriations

	1957	1959
General Fund		
General Government		
Judicial	$ 1,116,581	$ 1,116,581
Executive and Administrative	5,390,788	5,138,202
Contingency and Emergency Fund	1,750,000	1,750,000
Total, General Government	8,257,369	8,838,048
Public Safety and Regulation	2,470,010	2,422,413
Correction	1,149,243	1,133,232
Public Welfare	8,748,021	8,784,279
Education	159,427,234	162,534,630
Non-Highway Transportation	174,046	176,427
Health and Hospitals	23,874,526	24,331,122
Natural Resources and Recreation	2,720,342	2,714,125
Agriculture	4,438,643	4,668,397
Retirement and Pensions	13,322,426	13,679,706
Debt Service	5,948,458	7,291,283
Capital Improvements	29,861,865	
Salary Increases:		
Public School Employees	18,271,103	18,611,219
Other Employees	6,514,820	6,514,819
Total Salary Increases	24,758,923	25,126,038
Total Appropriations from General Fund	285,178,106	261,699,700
Highway Fund		
Operations	124,401,107	125,903,296
Salary Increases	4,575,354	4,421,468
Total Appropriations from Highway Fund	128,776,461	130,324,764
Agriculture Fund		
Total Appropriations from Agriculture Fund	1,350,658	1,141,060
Total Appropriation from General Fund	285,178,106	261,699,700
Total Appropriations from Highway Fund	128,776,461	130,324,764
Grand Total of all Appropriations	$415,305,225	$393,165,524

2. General Fund Estimated Revenues, 1957-59

		Per cent of total
Tax Revenues	**Tax Revenues**	
Income	$187,742,000	38.83
Sales	158,094,000	32.70
Franchise	48,066,200	9.94
Insurance	24,100,000	4.98
Beverage	23,529,000	4.88
Licenses	13,038,000	2.69
Inheritance	2,100,000	1.68
Savings & loan associations	2,112,000	4.4
Bank taxes	2,076,000	4.3
Gifts	640,000	1.3
Freight cars	132,000	0.3
Miscellaneous	30,000	0.1
	Non-Tax Revenues	
Gas and oil inspection	$ 10,150,000	2.10
Investment interest	4,000,000	8.3
Miscellaneous	1,602,728	3.3
Total general fund revenues	483,471,928	100.0
Excludes Federal fund receipts in amount of	123,969,155	
Total Highway fund revenues*	235,010,000	100.0
*Excludes Federal aid funds in amount of	136,149,992	
Total agriculture fund revenues*	4,131,932	100.0
*Excludes Federal funds in amount of	118,000	

Source: Legislative Survey, Institute of Government Bulletin 87, June 6, 1957 (Chapel Hill); *Digest of the State Budget Recommendations for the 1957-1959 Biennium* (Raleigh, N. C., 1957), p. 6.

Note: Federal highway funds are expected to amount to $136,149,992 for the biennium. Other federal appropriations add many millions to government expenditures in the state.

Table 98. Total State and Local Taxes in North Carolina As Compared to Population and Income for Specified Fiscal Years

Fiscal years	Population	Estimated private income (000)	State and local taxes		Per Capita income and taxes			Per cent taxes constitute of income	
			Total state (000)	Total state and local (000)	Income	State taxes	State and local taxes	Total state	Total state and local
1928–29	3,066,000	$1,194,000	$31,192	$97,103	$389	$10.17	$31.67	2.6	8.1
1937–38	3,456,000	1,077,000	975,947	118,802	312	21.98	34.38	7.1	11.0
1940–41	3,574,000	1,131,000	96,140	141,064	316	26.90	39.47	8.5	12.5
1943–44	3,623,000	2,270,000	127,795	176,176	627	35.27	48.63	5.6	7.8
1946–47	3,730,000	3,012,000	187,768	243,444	808	50.34	65.27	6.2	8.1
1949–50	3,944,000	3,361,000	219,664	306,594	852	55.70	77.74	6.6	9.1
1952–53	4,163,000	4,404,000	294,208	404,090	1,058	70.67	97.07	6.7	9.2
1955–56	4,344,000	5,371,000	358,109	488,489	1,236	82.42	112.42	6.7	9.1

Source: *Statistics of Taxation, 1956*, p. 9, Table 6.

Table 99. Per Capita Revenue State Government, North Carolina and United States, 1955

	N. C.	U. S.
Total general revenue	$96.77	$101.00
Total taxes	72.76	72.33
General sales or gross receipts	13.81	16.44
Motor-fuel sales	19.02	14.68
Motor-vehicle licenses	5.69	6.93
Industrial income tax	9.48	6.82
Corporation net income	8.27	4.60
Intergovernmental revenue[a]	16.35	18.64
From federal government	15.57	17.23
Insurance-trust revenue	10.99	15.66
Unemployment compensation	6.69	8.26

Extracted from *State Government Finances, 1955*, U. S. Dept. of Commerce (Washington, U. S. Government Printing Office, 1955), p. 5, Table 3.

[a]From federal government for public welfare, education, highways, health and hospitals, natural resources, employment security administration, and miscellaneous. Total revenue from federal sources: $65,769,000.

Table 100. Expenditures, North Carolina State Government, 1955

Total for North Carolina, $462,037,000		Per Capita	
		N. C.	U. S.
Total General Fund exp.	427,158,000	$101.10	$107.13
Public safety	10,644,000	2.52	2.97
Public welfare	39,136,000	9.26	16.51
Education	188,675,000	44.66	31.60
Highways	107,151,000	25.36	30.00
Health and hospitals	34,112,000	8.07	9.13
Natural resources	5,266,000	3.33	3.81
Employment security adm.	3,934,000	0.93	1.29
General control	7,445,000	1.76	2.84
Miscellaneous	27,581,000	5.11	8.61
Insurance-trust expenditure	34,879,000	8.26	15.04
Employee retirement	4,366,000	1.03	2.33
Unemployment compensation	30,476,000	7.21	11.10
Workman's compensation	37,000	0.01	1.22

Extracted from *State Government Finances, 1955*, U. S. Dept. of Commerce (Washington: U. S. Government Printing Office, 1955), pp. 22-23, Table 13.

Table 101. Total Local and State Tax Bill in North Carolina for Specified Fiscal Years

Fiscal Year	Local Levies				State Tax Collections					Total all local and state (000)
	County (000)	Municipal (000)	District and township (000)	Total (000)	General fund (000)	Highway fund (000)	Agriculture fund (000)	Payroll (000)	Total (000)	
1928-29	$38,433	$15,568	$11,910	$65,912	$13,706	$17,115	$371		$31,192	$97,103
1937-38	25,031	14,492	3,333	42,855	37,056	30,246	389	$8,255	75,947	118,802
1940-41	26,244	15,377	3,303	44,923	45,521	38,602	478	11,540	96,140	141,064
1943-44	28,203	16,855	3,320	48,378	74,819	32,270	683	20,022	127,795	176,173
1946-47	31,170	20,606	3,901	55,677	117,009	53,360	743	16,656	187,768	243,444
1949-50	46,219	33,304	7,408	86,930	127,808	73,159	710	17,988	219,664	306,594
1952-53	59,605	41,308	8,970	109,882	173,152	99,694	910	20,453	294,208	404,090
1954-55	66,455	43,774	9,749	119,977	182,316	108,548	942	24,371	316,176	436,152
1955-56	73,310	46,514	10,556	130,380	217,279	117,508	919	22,404	358,109	488,489

Source: *Statistics of Taxation, 1956*, p. 4, Table 2.

	(in thousands)
A. Sales and Gross Receipts.	199,970
1. General sales or gross receipts	71,465
Refunds	−58
Use	3,603
General sales.	(67,920)
Apparel	4,785
Automotive	12,745
Food.	9,644
Furniture.	6,374
General merchandise	19,093
Lumber and building material	8,266
Other retail.	6,008
Wholesale	1,005
2. Selective sales and gross receipts	128,505
a. Motor fuels	87,522
Refunds	−1,882
Gasoline	87,536
Special fuels	1,868
b. Alcoholic beverages	13,642
Liquor	6,367
Beer.	6,364
Wine	911
d. Insurance	9,232
General	8,997
Self insurers	115
Fire insurance.	120
e. Public utilities	17,842
Bus and franchise companies	4,272
Telephone and telegraph	4,074
Pullman and freight lines	63
Electric, gas, etc.	9,433
h. Other—laundries	267
B. License	48,517
1. Motor vehicles	25,697
Trucks	10,963
For-hire	1,635
Auto and motorcycle	11,708
Transfer	370
Titles	504
Penalties.	517
2. Motor vehicle operators	1,021
Operators	875
Chauffeurs	129
Duplicates.	17
3. Corporations in general	6,776
Domestic.	3,199
Foreign	3,330
Incorporation.	225
Penalties and interest	22
4. Public utilities—express companies	38
5. Alcoholic beverages	80
Beer	61
Wine.	19
6. Chain stores	263

(Continued on next page)

Table 102   (continued)

	(in thousands)
7. Amusements	590
Theatres	266
Entertainments	108
Billiards and pool	74
Carnivals and circuses	25
Picture film dealers	12
Music machine	92
Other	13
8. Cooperations and businesses, not elsewhere classified	12,579
Feed, seed and fertilizer	750
Agricultural inspection and regulation	549
Insurance	670
Gasoline inspection	3,258
Oil inspection	1,229
Building and loan	919
Installment dealers	823
Automobile dealers	704
Dispensers and weighing machines	394
Loan agencies	345
Professionals and real estate	314
Tobacco and cigarettes	297
Soft drinks	269
Contractors	235
Restaurants	226
Motor fuels distributors	205
Bottlers and distributors	145
Bank examinations	120
Pressers and cleaners	120
Other businesses	115
Cosmetic art	65
Musical merchandise	52
Hotels	63
Nurses	50
Other	662
9. Hunting and fishing	1,473
C. Individual Income	47,810
D. Corporation New Income	44,134
Domestic	18,686
Foreign	24,828
Penalties and interest	620
E. Property	8,071
Intangibles	6,943
Railroad franchise	1,128
F. Death and Gift	3,963
Inheritance and estate	3,548
Gift	415
K. Other—civil process	66
Total (thousands)	352,531

Source: U. S. Bureau of the Census, *Detail of State Tax Collections* (November 19, 1956), p. 21, Table 2.

Table 103. Public School Statistics of the States[a]

STATE	Income per capita	Rank	% Income to public schools	Rank	Income per child	Rank	% School Rev. from state	Rank	C.E. per pupil in A.D.A.	Rank	Av. salary instructional staff	Rank	% Pupils of population	Rank	% A.D.A. of enrollment	Rank	Ratio inst. staff to A.D.A.	Rank
Alabama	$1,091	45	2.85	26	$ 3,904	46	75	3	$150.06	45	$2,537	40	21.9	11	86.5	28	25.4	42
Arizona	1,582	28	3.62	10	6,035	29	27	33	262.71	16	4,021	3	21.4	13	80.9	46	23.9	30
Arkansas	979	47	3.02	24	3,537	47	53	13	123.44	47	1,884	47	22.0	8	84.2	39	26.0	44
California	2,162	6	3.11	23	10,613	6	47	16	260.72	18	4,163	2	16.6	36	96.8	1	26.8	47
Colorado	1,686	22	3.32	18	7,660	20	17	42	253.16	24	3,244	24	18.3	28	83.5	41	20.8	11
Connecticut	2,361	3	1.90	48	11,110	3	27	33	291.25	8	3,937	4	15.0	41	87.7	22	21.9	23
Delaware	2,372	2	2.15	44	11,301	2	86	1	317.83	2	3,919	6	15.2	39	87.9	19	19.9	9
Florida	1,610	26	3.36	17	6,608	27	51	15	206.12	36	3,248	23	18.4	26	85.2	33	23.0	27
Georgia	1,237	39	3.16	22	4,594	43	75	3	165.81	42	2,586	38	21.6	12	84.8	36	24.1	31
Idaho	1,433	34	3.65	9	5,490	36	25	37	211.64	34	2,849	34	22.0	8	88.8	13	24.1	31
Illinois	2,155	7	2.27	42	10,473	7	20	40	291.48	7	3,903	8	13.9	45	88.6	15	21.2	16
Indiana	1,834	13	2.78	27	8,417	15	33	25	253.22	23	3,865	10	18.4	26	85.2	33	24.6	39
Iowa	1,667	23	3.70	8	6,913	26	13	45	260.57	19	2,895	33	18.9	21	87.2	24	18.7	7
Kansas	1,689	21	3.50	14	7,301	21	21	39	245.95	26	2,963	32	19.0	20	86.2	30	18.0	6
Kentucky	1,216	41	2.33	40	4,644	42	42	19	150.65	44	2,393	44	19.6	16	84.8	36	25.4	42
Louisiana	1,302	38	3.60	11	4,941	39	66	6	237.40	29	3,124	27	18.7	22	87.8	21	24.7	40
Maine	1,492	30	2.71	30	6,014	30	26	36	181.31	39	2,269	46	19.1	19	84.7	38	21.4	19
Maryland	1,940	11	2.45	35	8,707	14	31	29	242.62	28	3,903	8	15.7	38	86.6	27	24.4	38
Massachusetts	1,922	12	2.11	46	9,318	9	25	38	266.96	13	3,553	16	13.9	45	87.2	24	20.8	11
Michigan	2,017	8	2.64	32	9,088	11	54	12	267.47	12	3,862	11	17.4	31	89.3	9	24.3	34
Minnesota	1,644	24	3.51	13	6,927	25	40	22	276.92	11	3,327	21	17.0	34	89.5	8	21.4	19
Mississippi	873	48	2.77	28	3,030	48	52	14	95.73	48	1,617	48	24.5	1	88.0	18	28.9	48
Missouri	1,747	18	2.34	39	8,067	17	32	26	211.63	35	2,763	35	16.8	35	84.1	40	22.9	26
Montana	1,729	19	3.92	4	7,252	22	27	33	302.64	6	3,094	28	18.5	25	88.9	12	17.2	4
Nebraska	1,635	25	2.67	31	7,145	23	6	48	245.54	27	2,550	41	17.3	32	88.8	13	16.9	3
Nevada	2,414	1	2.36	37	10,927	4	39	23	262.96	15	3,484	19	22.4	5	75.5	48	21.0	13
New Hampshire	1,605	27	2.42	36	7,694	19	9	47	254.63	22	3,031	29	14.2	44	88.6	15	21.3	17
New Jersey	2,219	4	2.36	37	10,858	5	17	42	312.07	4	3,922	7	14.5	43	86.7	26	20.5	10
New Mexico	1,387	36	3.99	3	5,005	38	84	2	261.18	17	3,621	13	22.4	5	81.6	44	21.6	22
New York	2,163	5	2.28	41	11,517	1	41	21	351.78	1	4,591	1	13.8	47	86.1	31	21.1	15
North Carolina	**1,190**	**43**	**3.77**	**7**	**4,202**	**44**	**74**	**5**	**175.62**	**40**	**3,282**	**22**	**22.0**	**8**	**89.3**	**9**	**26.6**	**45**
North Dakota	1,186	44	3.43	16	5,221	37	30	30	256.21	21	2,535	41	19.4	17	89.6	6	15.5	2

(Continued on next page)

Table 103 (continued)

STATE	Income per capita	Rank	% Income to public schools	Rank	Income per child	Rank	% School Rev. from state	Rank	C.E. per pupil in A.D.A.	Rank	Av. salary instruction- al staff	Rank	% Pupils of popu- lation	Rank	% A.D.A. of enroll- ment	Rank	Ratio inst. staff to A.D.A.	Rank
	1		2		3		4		5		6		7		8		9	
Ohio	1,983	9	2.22	43	9,585	8	32	26	232.44	30	3,537	17	16.2	37	89.7	5	24.3	34
Oklahoma	1,466	33	3.58	12	5,561	35	32	26	226.36	31	3,031	29	22.5	4	79.3	47	21.9	23
Oregon	1,757	17	3.97	3	8,076	16	30	30	316.10	3	3,679	12	18.2	29	85.9	32	19.8	8
Pennsylvania	1,785	15	2.58	34	8,732	13	43	17	264.17	14	3,536	18	15.1	40	89.6	6	23.5	29
Rhode Island	1,823	14	1.94	47	9,219	10	17	42	258.51	20	3,603	14	12.8	48	85.1	35	21.0	13
South Carolina	1,063	46	3.83	5	3,907	45	65	7	153.95	43	2,400	43	23.7	3	83.4	42	24.1	31
South Dakota	1,332	37	3.80	6	5,850	33	12	46	250.72	25	2,351	45	18.7	22	88.2	17	14.5	1
Tennessee	1,212	42	2.61	33	4,786	41	65	7	148.07	46	2,462	42	20.5	15	87.9	19	25.3	41
Texas	1,574	29	2.91	25	6,313	28	57	11	223.29	32	3,213	25	18.2	29	86.3	29	22.7	25
Utah	1,483	31	4.18	1	5,801	34	42	19	196.36	37	3,420	20	23.8	2	90.3	2	26.6	45
Vermont	1,408	35	3.23	21	6,000	31	28	32	219.83	33	2,598	37	17.2	33	89.3	9	21.5	21
Virginia	1,480	32	2.12	45	5,911	32	43	17	168.64	41	2,627	36	18.6	24	87.3	23	24.3	34
Washington	1,949	10	3.32	18	8,882	12	63	10	283.77	10	2,919	6	19.3	18	82.5	43	23.3	28
West Virginia	1,232	40	3.47	15	4,793	40	64	9	183.30	38	2,967	31	22.2	7	89.8	3	24.3	34
Wisconsin	1,706	20	2.77	28	7,802	18	19	41	284.58	9	3,590	15	14.9	42	89.8	3	21.3	17
Wyoming	1,779	16	3.25	20	7,113	24	37	24	311.63	5	3,157	26	20.8	14	81.3	45	17.5	5
United States[a]	$1,770		2.72		$ 7,814		41		$244.24		$3,981		17.3		87.6		23.0	

Source: *State School Facts*, North Carolina Department of Public Instruction, XXVIII (August, 1956).

[a]Years: Col. 1 for 1954; Cols. 2, 4 for 1953–54; Col. 3 for 1953; Cols. 5, 6, 7, 8, 9 for 1952. Includes District of Columbia in United States totals, but the District of Columbia is not ranked with states.

Table 104. Selected Items in Fifty Years of Public Education in North Carolina, 1899-1900 and 1949-50

	1899-1900	1949-50
1. Total school population	657,949	1,095,734
a. White	439,431	760,062
b. Negro	218,518	335,672
2. Total school enrollment	400,452	893,745
a. White	270,447	625,167
b. Negro	130,005	268,578
3. Total average daily attendance	206,918	797,691
a. White	142,413	564,612
b. Negro	64,505	233,079
4. Per cent of population enrolled	60.9	81.6
a. White	61.5	82.3
b. Negro	59.1	80.0
5. Per cent of enrollment in A. D. A.	51.7	89.3
a. White	52.7	90.3
b. Negro	49.6	86.8
6. Number of public high schools	30[a]	958
7. Enrollment in public high schools	2,000[a]	188,753
8. Public high school graduates	200[a]	30,973
9. Number of schools taught	7,391	3,810
a. White	5,047	2,188
b. Negro	2,344	1,622
10. Number of log houses	1,190	0
11. Number of schoolhouses	6,918	3,559
a. White	4,798	1,919
b. Negro	2,120	1,640
12. Value of school property	$1,097,564	$231,008,069
a. White	839,269	196,797,199
b. Negro	258,295	34,211,069
13. Average per schoolhouse	$158.65	$64,908.13
14. Number of teachers and principals	8,320	29,134
a. White	5,735	21,182
b. Negro	2,567	7,952
15. Average annual salary teachers	$83.05	$2,832[a]
a. White	90.90	2,814[a]
b. Negro	66.97	2,914[a]
16. Average term in days	70.8	180
a. White	73.3	180
b. Negro	65.3	180
17. Number of children transported		396,783
18. Number of vehicles used		5,846
19. Total school expenditures	$1,062,303.71	$141,273,663.83
a. Current expense	1,004,903.09	113,272,495.83
b. Capital outlay	57,400.62	28,001,168.00
20. Total state appropriation	$ 100,000.00	$107,661,011.00

Source: *State School Facts*, N. C. Dept. of Public Instruction, XXIV (June, 1952).
[a]Estimated.

Table 105. Receipts and Expenditures for Schools in North Carolina, 1899-1900 and 1949-50

	1899-1900	1949-50
Current Expense Receipts:		
Balance from preceding year	$	$ 3,608,824.42
Poll and dog taxes, fines, forfeitures, etc.	394,724.52	3,820,399.74
A. B. C. boards (liquor license)	75,518.58	167,783.57
Interest, donations		717,640.23
From pupils: fees, tuition		1,066,749.13
Ad valorem taxes—county	454,452.99	6,111,252.86
Ad valorem taxes—district, city	3,067.79	5,272,224.30
Total county and district	$ 927,763.88	$ 17,156,049.83
State school fund (operation)	$ 90,379.73	$ 82,030,262.79
Vocational education—state		1,773,214.13
federal		814,664.04
School-lunch program, federal		2,752,017.52
Veterans, etc. (federal)		8,487,126.69
Textbooks—state		899,999.34
Tax on intangibles, beer, wine		295,726.16
Philanthropic agencies		5,300.00
Total state, federal, philanthropic	$ 90,379.73	$ 97,058,310.67
Grand total receipts, current expense	$1,018,143.61	$117,823,184.92
Capital Outlay Receipts:		
Balance from preceding year	$	$ 10,767,652.80
State aid		5,688,403.86
Sale of bonds		19,532,031.26
Sale of school property		546,535.02
Federal grants		3,101.11
Interest, donations		307,601.42
A. B. C. boards		320,975.31
Tax on intangibles, beer, wine		205,570.37
Ad valorem taxes, county		7,901,974.98
Total	($40,711.54)[a]	$ 45,273,846.13
Availability Debt Service	$	$ 7,678,260.47
Total Availability	$1,018,143.61	$170,775,291.52
Expenditures		
Current Expense—		
General control	$ 50,152.96	$ 2,508,751.68
Instructional service	813,001.70	80,468,793.42
Operation of plant	46,451.26	5,163,646.89
Maintenance of plant		4,837,979.02
Fixed charges		1,284,384.80
Auxiliary agencies		19,008,940.02
Total	$ 909,605.92	$113,272,495.83
Capital Outlay	$ 40,711.54	$ 28,001,168.00
Debt Service		5,990,230.03
Grand Total	$ 950,317.46	$147,263,893.86

Source: *State School Facts*, N. C. Dept. of Public Instruction, XXIV (June, 1952).

[a]Included in current expense receipts.

Table 106. Appropriations for Public Schools

	1954-55	1955-56	1956-57
Support of nine-months' term	$116,524,364	$122,718,752	$126,986,056
State Board of Education	208,000	236,697	239,302
Vocational education[a]	3,572,032	3,542,137	3,605,373
Purchase of free textbooks[a]	2,194,228	1,882,021	1,476,862
Vocational textile-training school	43,806	62,910	63,532
Purchase of school buses	1,977,500	1,324,075	1,810,000
Administration of state school-plant construction, improvement, and repair fund	59,272	63,517	64,817
Subtotal	$124,579,202	$129,830,109	$134,245,942
Department of Public Instruction	396,090	403,911	409,646
Driver education[b]	25,000	25,000	25,000
Total	$125,000,292	$130,259,020	$134,680,588

Source: *State School Facts*, N. C. Dept. of Public Instruction, XXVII (June, 1955).
[a]Includes state administration.
[b]This is a transfer from the Highway Fund.

Table 107. Schoolhouses and Value of School Property, 1900 to 1955

Year	Number of schoolhouses			Appraised value of school property			Average value per schoolhouse			Average value per child enrolled		
	White	Negro	Total	White	Negro	Total	White	Negro	Total	White	Negro	Total
1899-1900	4,938	2,228	7,166	$ 1,335,250	$ 360,000	$ 1,695,250	$ 270	$ 162	$ 237	$ 4.79	$ 2.75	$ 4.14
1904-05	5,115	2,261	7,376	2,712,112	470,806	3,182,918	530	208	432	8.34	3.16	6.71
1909-10	5,325	2,284	7,609	5,185,521	677,448	5,862,969	973	296	708	14.20	4.23	11.27
1914-15	5,640	2,409	8,049	9,270,584	1,163,533	10,834,117	1,643	483	1,163	22.13	6.21	17.21
1919-20	5,552	2,442	7,994	21,670,514	2,387,324	24,057,838	3,903	978	1,978	45.32	11.20	34.80
1924-25	4,655	2,431	7,086	63,434,665	7,271,170	70,705,835	13,627	2,991	8,119	113.40	29.03	87.31
1929-30	3,460	2,365	5,825	98,946,273	11,475,042	110,421,315	28,597	4,852	18,956	162.92	44.20	127.37
1934-35	2,511	2,267	4,778	94,290,164	12,309,808	106,599,972	37,551	5,430	22,311	152.99	44.55	119.42
1939-40	2,123	2,084	4,207	103,724,982	15,154,892	118,879,874	48,858	7,272	28,258	167.36	55.93	133.46
1944-45	1,978	1,918	3,896	114,660,497	18,285,060	132,945,557	57,968	9,533	34,124	204.14	73.08	163.56
1945-46	1,977	1,882	3,859	120,457,515	19,339,763	139,797,278	60,929	10,276	36,226	211.01	76.66	169.84
1946-47	1,951	1,831	3,782	128,308,209	20,609,610	148,917,819	65,765	11,256	39,375	218.01	80.15	176.09
1947-48	1,937	1,782	3,719	142,868,760	23,198,447	166,067,207	73,758	13,018	44,654	239.79	89.21	194.04
1948-49	1,937	1,682	3,619	168,059,603	27,789,180	195,848,783	86,763	16,521	54,117	278.88	106.25	226.64
1949-50	1,919	1,640	3,559	196,797,199	34,211,069	231,008,268	102,552	20,860	64,908	314.79	127.38	258.47
1950-51	1,937	1,519	3,456	235,852,975	46,705,140	282,558,115	121,761	30,747	81,759	370.54	170.91	310.58
1951-52	1,934	1,370	3,304	287,262,871	63,381,987	350,644,798	148,533	46,264	106,127	448.09	232.01	383.52
1952-53	2,012	1,272	3,284	316,483,762	77,408,825	393,892,587	157,030	60,856	119,943	484.94	280.06	423.99
1953-54	1,977	1,220	3,197	349,395,927	89,509,758	438,905,685	176,730	73,369	137,287	511.35	314.31	453.38
1954-55	1,989	1,201	3,190	381,088,651	98,963,164	480,051,815	191,598	82,401	150,486	539.70	336.65	480.02

Source: *State School Facts*, N. C. Dept. of Public Instruction, XXVIII (September, 1956).

Table 108. Number of Teachers in Public Schools in North Carolina, 1944-54[a]

Year	Total	White	Negro	White	Negro	White	Negro
		Total		Elementary		High School	
1944-45	24,534	17,392	7,142	13,252	6,105	4,140	1,037
1946-47	24,999	18,874	7,125	13,207	5,961	4,667	1,164
1948-49	26,266	18,992	7,274	13,923	5,955	5,069	1,319
1950-51	28,395	20,560	7,835	14,937	6,244	5,624	1,591
1951-52	28,916	20,885	8,031	15,134	6,319	5,751	1,712
1952-53	30,100	21,800	8,300	15,847	6,482	5,952	1,819
1953-54[b]	31,056	22,596	8,460	16,449	6,564	6 147	1,896

Compiled from *State School Facts*, N. C. Dept. of Public Instruction.

[a]In this table and Table 109, supervisors are included in the number of principals beginning with the year 1949-50.

[b]Estimated.

Table 109. Number of Principals in Public Schools in North Carolina, 1944-54

Year	Total	White	Negro	White	Negro	White	Negro
		Total		Elementary		High School	
1944-45	1,381	1,086	295	368	102	718	193
1946-47	1,402	1,094	308	388	109	706	199
1948-49	1,414	1,098	316	410	105	688	211
1950-51	1,715	1,296	419	605	204	691	215
1951-52	1,760	1,317	443	635	235	682	208
1952-53	1,820	1,352	468	693	250	659	218
1953-54[a]	1,850	1,367	483	702	264	665	219

Compiled from *State School Facts*, N. C. Dept. of Public Instruction. See footnote "a", Table 108.

[a]Estimated.

Table 110. Average Annual Salaries of Teachers, Principals, and Vocational Teachers, All Funds, in North Carolina Public Schools, 1944-54

Year	Total	Total		Elementary		High School	
		White	Negro	White	Negro	White	Negro
A. Teachers (excluding vocational)							
1944-45	$1,297.33	$1,294.34	$1,304.46	$1,286.03	$1,309.83	$1,327.28	$1,265.45
1946-47	1,700.81	1,689.21	1,729.35	1,678.04	1,731.93	1,727.95	1,713.20
1948-49	2,316.81	2,292.74	2,378.60	2,275.43	2,385.64	2,350.17	2,340.52
1950-51[a]	2,836.33	2,807.74	2,910.26	2,810.72	2,930.16	2,798.17	2,817.11
1952-53	3,177.78	3,150.19	3,249.52	3,153.18	3,273.98	3,140.64	3,145.16
1953-54[c]	3,199.14	3,170.00	3,275.00	3,170.00	3,299.00	3,171.00	3,177.00
B. Principals and Supervisors[b]							
1944-45	2,225.74	2,233.57	2,196.93	2,067.17	2,152.62	2,318.85	2,220.34
1946-47	2,931.38	2,948.23	2,871.52	2,759.29	2,789.57	3,052.06	2,916.41
1948-49	3,868.08	3,877.99	3,833.66	3,654.49	3,810.03	4,011.18	3,845.42
1950-51	4,272.51	4,292.10	4,211.91	4,110.51	4,005.41	4,451.10	4,407.84
1952-53	4,983.30	4,988.08	4,969.49	4,655.63	4,652.88	5,337.68	5,332.59
1953-54[c]	5,023.08	5,027.55	5,011.43	4,649.67	4,691.36	5,419.19	5,394.35

C. Vocational Teachers (including travel)

Year	Total	White	Negro
1944-45	$2,114.29	$2,153.33	$1,960.80
1946-47	2,671.01	2,711.81	2,508.55
1948-49	3,375.89	3,412.14	3,231.55
1950-51	3,850.01	3,896.29	3,676.37
1952-53	4,244.07	4,287.34	4,100.14
1953-54[c]	4,255.00	4,300.00	4,115.00

Compiled from *State School Facts*, N. C. Dept. of Public Instruction.

[a]Contingency salaries applicable to 1949-50 paid to teachers holding Graduate, Class A, and Class B certificates.

[b]Supervisors beginning in 1949-50.

[c]Estimated.

Table 111. Number Employed and Average Salaries of Teachers, Principals, and Supervisors, State Funds, in Public Schools in North Carolina, 1944-54

Year	White		Negro	
	Number	Average	Number	Average
A. Teachers				
Elementary				
1944-45	12,984	$1,249.21	6,075	$1,272.52
1946-47	12,875	1,626.95	5,913	1,686.77
1948-49	13,482	2,206.32	5,912	2,308.82
1950-51[a]	14,380	2,742.52	6,164	2,848.91
1951-52[b]	14,594	3,071.49	6,241	3,170.85
1953-54	15,812	3,084.98	6,467	3,207.70
High School				
1944-45	3,122	1,257.83	814	1,247.49
1946-47	3,523	1,643.75	929	1,648.05
1948-49	3,782	2,223.87	1,066	2,223.62
1950-51	4,243	2,702.85	1,295	2,692.07
1951-52[b]	4,337	2,998.54	1,393	2,971.60
1953-54	4,753	3,058.25	1,544	3,050.82
Total				
1944-45	16,106	1,250.88	6,889	1,269.56
1946-47	16,398	1,630.56	6,842	1,681.51
1948-49	17,264	2,209.99	6,978	2,295.81
1950-51[a]	18,623	2,733.48	7,459	2,821.68
1951-52[b]	18,931	3,054.77	7,634	3,134.49
1953-54	20,565	3,078.80	8,011	3,177.47
B. Principals				
Elementary				
1944-45	333	1,977.42	93	2,082.53
1946-47	347	2,636.48	94	2,746.68
1948-49	375	3,456.37	98	3,604.90
1950-51[a]	418	3,970.80	119	4,049.24
1951-52[b]	448	4,341.64	149	4,408.49
1953-54	508	4,633.05	181	4,687.99
High School				
1944-45	711	2,284.04	191	2,191.36
1946-47	704	2,959.78	199	2,876.09
1948-49	684	3,917.48	208	3,785.87
1950-51[a]	684	4,374.18	212	4,365.28
1951-52[b]	677	4,746.78	210	4,786.63
1953-54	660	5,238.77	216	5,302.99
Total				
1944-45	1,044	2,186.24	284	2,155.72
1946-47	1,051	2,853.04	293	2,834.57
1948-49	1,059	3,754.20	306	3,727.91
1950-51[a]	1,102	4,221.17	331	4,251.66
1951-52[b]	1,115	4,626.57	359	4,629.69
1953-54	1,168	4,975.32	397	5,022.60
C. Supervisors				
1949-50	152	3,052.55	73	3,043.60
1950-51[a]	170	3,435.88	83	3,424.75
1951-52[b]	171	3,920.95	83	3,928.55
1953-54	176	3,996.40	84	4,019.54

Compiled from *State School Facts*, N. C. Dept. of Public Instruction.

[a]Includes "contingency salaries" applicable to 1949-50.

[b]Includes "contingency salaries" applicable to 1950-51.

Table 112. Average Daily Attendance in Public Schools in North Carolina, 1944-54

Year	Total	White	Negro
Total All Schools			
1944-45[a]	713,146	502,550	210,596
1946-47[b]	734,327	521,684	212,643
1948-49	769,405	545,323	224,082
1950-51	816,036	576,117	239,919
1951-52	816,106	578,557	237,549
1952-53	829,720	589,603	240,117
1953-54	874,165	622,951	251,214
Elementary Schools			
1944-45[a]	599,139	412,942	186,197
1946-47[b]	596,023	413,220	182,803
1948-49	617,960	428,711	189,249
1950-51	648,231	449,671	198,560
1951-52	644,847	450,001	194,846
1952-53	652,558	456,821	195,737
1953-54	689,872	485,193	204,679
High Schools			
1944-45[a]	114,007	89,608	24,399
1946-47[b]	138,304	108,464	29,840
1948-49	141,445	116,612	34,833
1950-51	167,805	126,446	41,359
1951-52	171,259	128,556	42,703
1952-53	177,162	132,782	44,380
1953-54	184,293	137,758	46,535

Compiled from *State School Facts*, N. C. Dept. of Public Instruction.

[a]Beginning in 1943-44 elementary schools included grades 1-8.

[b]First year the 12-year system was in full operation.

Table 113.   Percentage Remaining at Each Grade Level of the 1943-44 First-Grade Enrollment, by Race

Year	Grade	White	Negro	Total
1943-44	1	100.00	100.00	100.00
1944-45	2	87.08	58.80	75.11
1945-46	3	86.48	56.15	73.60
1946-47	4	84.58	53.21	71.27
1947-48	5	81.90	48.71	67.82
1948-49	6	77.79	44.62	63.71
1949-50	7	75.11	40.82	60.57
1950-51	8	69.94	37.28	56.09
1951-52	9	64.79	32.45	51.07
1952-53	10	55.28	26.47	43.06
1953-54	11	46.49	21.62	35.93
1954-55	12	41.27	17.90	31.33
Graduates		38.94	16.24	29.28
Post H. S.		17.13	6.62	12.61

Source: *North Carolina Public School Bulletin*, XXI (October, 1956).

Table 114.   Numbers Attending Institutions of Higher Learning, Public and Private, 1900-56

Year	Public	Private	Total
1900	1,766	2,932	4,698
1910	2,581	4,005	6,586
1920	4,751	3,210	7,961
1930	9,324	9,605	18,929
1940	15,233	16,713	31,946
1950	24,061	21,676	45,737
1956	25,968	23,234	49,202

Source: *Higher Education in the Forty-Eight States* (Chicago: The Council of State Governments, 1952), pp. 172–74. The figures for 1956 have been added by the author to those found in this source.

Table 115. Enrollment in North Carolina Colleges, October of Each Year, 1946-56

Year	Men	Women	Total
White			
1946-47	24,403	11,654	36,057
1947-48	26,823	11,677	38,500
1948-49	26,754	11,323	38,077
1949-50	25,832	11,854	37,686
1950-51	23,542	12,353	35,895
1951-52	19,881	12,271	32,152
1952-53	20,342	12,345	32,687
1953-54	21,169	13,092	34,261
1954-55	23,636	13,335	36,971
1955-56	26,199	14,462	40,661
Negro			
1946-47	3,481	4,443	7,924
1947-48	4,300	4,140	8,440
1948-49	4,367	4,010	8,377
1949-50	4,430	4,100	8,530
1950-51	4,345	4,471	8,816
1951-52	3,623	4,841	8,464
1952-53	3,485	5,076	8,561
1953-54	3,318	5,201	8,519
1954-55	3,446	4,780	8,226
1955-56	3,817	4,572	8,389
Indian			
1946-47	69	53	122
1947-48	79	52	131
1948-49	69	47	116
1949-50	68	85	153
1950-51	61	65	126
1951-52	55	68	123
1952-53	47	75	122
1953-54	50	81	131
1954-55	59	102	161
1955-56	61	91	152
Total			
1946-47	27,953	16,150	44,103
1947-48	31,202	15,869	47,071
1948-49	31,190	15,380	46,570
1949-50	30,330	16,039	46,369
1950-51	27,948	16,889	44,837
1951-52	23,559	17,180	40,739
1952-53	23,874	17,496	41,370
1953-54	24,537	18,374	42,911
1954-55	27,141	18,217	45,358
1955-56	30,077	19,125	49,202

Source: *State School Facts*, N. C. Dept. of Public Instruction, XXVIII (February, 1956).

Table 116. Enrollment in North Carolina Colleges, October of Each Year, 1954-56

Institution	Men 1954-55	Men 1955-56	Women 1954-55	Women 1955-56	Total 1954-55	Total 1955-56
Senior Colleges						
1 Public—White						
University, Chapel Hill	4,993	5,411	1,068	1,164	6,061	6,575
State College	4,228	4,738	52	75	4,280	4,813
Woman's College	5	19	2,335	2,338	2,340	2,357
Appalachian Teachers	647	841	805	839	1,452	1,680
East Carolina	1,178	1,405	1,185	1,420	2,363	2,825
Western Carolina	567	671	330	377	897	1,048
Total	11,618	13,085	5,775	6,213	17,393	19,298
Negro						
Agricultural & Technical	1,481	1,644	641	660	2,122	2,304
North Carolina	529	550	877	811	1,406	1,361
Elizabeth City	109	102	330	272	439	374
Fayetteville	159	167	467	350	626	517
Winston-Salem	210	241	586	588	796	829
Total	2,488	2,704	2,901	2,681	5,389	5,385
Indian						
Pembroke	59	61	102	91	161	152
Total Public Senior	14,165	15,850	8,778	8,985	22,943	24,835
2. Private—White						
Atlantic Christian	286	364	210	242	496	606
Belmont Abbey	269	350	1	0	270	350
Black Mountain	10	17	6	10	16	27
Catawba	377	444	162	194	539	638
Davidson	844	845	0	0	844	845
Duke[a]	3,842	3,656	1,184	1,524	5,026	5,180
Elon	669	667	215	200	884	867
Flora Macdonald	9	14	272	306	281	320
Greensboro	12	20	342	371	354	391
Guilford	392	439	182	192	574	631
High Point	554	588	301	296	855	884
Lenoir Rhyne	523	536	359	348	882	884
Meredith	6	1	613	627	619	628
Montreat	2	0	179	189	181	189
Queens	38	25	396	372	434	397
Salem	14	19	322	330	336	349
Wake Forest	1,382	1,427	322	328	1,704	1,755
Total	9,229	9,412	5,066	5,529	14,295	14,941
Negro						
Barber Scotia	1	10	184	193	185	203
Bennett	0	0	450	428	450	428
Johnson C. Smith	304	307	330	347	634	654
Livingstone	137	154	251	266	388	420
Shaw	207	231	314	320	521	551
St. Augustine's	157	195	292	260	449	455
Total	806	897	1,821	1,814	2,627	2,711
Total Private Senior	10,035	10,309	6,887	7,343	16,922	17,652
3. Grand Total Senior	24,200	26,159	15,665	16,328	39,865	42,487

(Continued on next page)

Table 116 (continued)

Institution	Men		Women		Total	
	1954-55	1955-56	1954-55	1955-56	1954-55	1955-56
Junior Colleges						
1. Public—White						
Asheville-Biltmore	210	203	98	114	308	317
Charlotte	177	249	13	25	190	274
Wilmington	137	217	113	61	250	278
Total	524	669	224	200	748	869
Negro						
Carver	123	172	28	46	151	218
Wilmington (Off-campus)[b]	14	28	11	18	25	46
Total	137	200	39	64	176	264
Total Public Junior	661	869	263	264	924	1,133
2. Private—White						
Brevard	89	154	130	126	219	280
Campbell	310	411	142	169	452	580
Chowan	188	187	113	105	301	292
Edwards Military Institute	108	123	0	0	108	123
Gardner-Webb	217	298	139	137	356	435
Lees-McRae	164	177	152	149	316	326
Louisburg	121	220	81	100	202	320
Mars Hill	417	523	445	473	862	996
Mitchell	43	67	74	130	117	197
Oak Ridge	54	68	0	0	54	68
Peace	0	0	212	243	212	243
Pfeiffer	208	321	142	211	350	532
Pineland	0	0	38	40	38	40
Presbyterian	91	108	2	5	93	113
Sacred Heart	2	0	172	222	174	222
St. Genevieve	0	c	82	c	82	c
St. Mary's	0	1	203	221	203	222
Warren Wilson	70	85	73	79	143	164
Wingate	183	290	70	110	253	400
Total	2,265	3,033	2,270	2,520	4,535	5,553
Negro						
Immanuel Lutheran	15	16	19	13	34	29
Total Private Junior	2,280	3,049	2,289	2,533	4,569	5,582
3. Grand Total Junior	2,941	3,918	2,552	2,797	5,493	6,715
Total Senior and Junior						
Public	14,826	16,719	9,041	9,249	23,867	25,968
White	12,142	13,754	5,999	6,413	18,141	20,167
Negro	2,625	2,904	2,940	2,745	5,565	5,649
Indian	59	61	102	91	161	152
Private	12,315	13,358	9,176	9,876	21,491	23,234
White	11,494	12,445	7,336	8,049	18,830	20,494
Negro	821	913	1,840	1,827	2,661	2,740
Grand Total	27,141	30,077	18,217	19,125	45,358	49,202
White	23,636	26,199	13,335	14,462	36,971	40,661
Negro	3,446	3,817	4,780	4,572	8,226	8,389
Indian	59	61	102	91	161	152

Source: *State School Facts*, N. C. Dept. of Public Instruction, XXVIII (February, 1956).

[a]Division according to sex estimated incorrectly in 1954–55.

[b]Sponsored by Fayetteville State Teachers College in 1954–56.

[c]Not operated as a college in 1955–56.

Table 117. Proportion of Population Attending College in the Southeastern States and Nation, 1938-39 and 1949-50

State	1938-39 Number of students	Population per student	State	1949-50 Number of students	Population per student
Louisiana	21,983	108	Florida	39,517	70.1
South Carolina	16,550	115	Louisiana	35,410	75.8
Kentucky	23,441	121	Virginia	40,591	81.8
North Carolina	**27,421**	**130**	Arkansas	23,014	83.0
Virginia	19,493	137	Georgia	41,440	83.1
Florida	13,490	141	Tennessee	39,085	84.2
Tennessee	20,424	143	Alabama	35,508	86.2
Mississippi	15,190	144	Kentucky	33,576	87.7
Alabama	17,571	161	Mississippi	24,102	90.4
Georgia	19,321	162	**North Carolina**	**42,723**	**95.1**
Arkansas	10,773	181	South Carolina	21,624	97.9
Nation	1,220,616	108	Nation	2,486,219	60.6

Source: Gordon Gray, *The President's Report, 1948-1953*, Report of a Five-Year Period from President Gordon Gray to His Excellency William B. Umstead and the Board of Trustees of the University of North Carolina, p. 17.

Table 118.   North Carolina Public-Library Service
(Facts and figures based on 1953-54 statistics)

Total number public libraries				266
County		73		
Regional (19 counties)		7		
Branch		165		
Independent town and city		21		
		266		
Population with access to public-library service			3,878,381	
Population without access to public-library service			183.548	
Total Population			4,061,929	
Total bookmobiles serving 91 counties			94[a]	
Total book stock			2,659,185	
(.65 volumes per capita)				
Total circulation			9,658,629	
From libraries		5,636,372		
From bookmobiles		4,022,257		
(Additional circulation of books left at school and deposit station: 2,212,993)				

Sources of library income:	Total	Per cent		Per Capita
City or town	$681,077	33		.16
County	773,922	37		.19
State aid	390,000	19		.10
Other	241,394	11		.06
	$2,068,393	100		.51
Expenditures:				
Salaries	$1,106,401	57		
Books and periodicals	484,544	24		
Other	364,132	19		
Total	$1,955,077	100		

Counties sharing state aid			92
Libraries with tax vote			19
County		10	
(Anson, Caldwell, Cherokee, Cumberland, Davidson, Pitt, Mecklenburg, Rockingham, Sampson, Union)			
City		9	
(Black Mountain, Granite Falls, Henderson, Hickory, High Point, Mt. Airy, Statesville, Washington, Weldon)			
Counties without county-wide service			8
(Alexander, Ashe, Brunswick, Jones, Madison, Montgomery, Polk, Robeson)			

Compiled. *Report of the North Carolina Library Commission, 1954* (Raleigh, 1955).
[a]Now have 98 (as of June 18, 1955).

Table 119.   Record of North Carolina Hospital Construction and Cost

Table A shows, as of March 1, 1957, the total costs of 247 construction projects approved by the Commission which involve a cost estimated at $95,931,033, supplied by the United States $37,414,723, or 39.0%; by the State $16,862,451, or 17.6%; and by local authorities $41,653,859 or 43.4%.

Table A

Stage of Completion	Total Cost	Federal Share	State Share	Local Share
Completed—203 Projects	$74,751,078	$28,145,452	$15,387,513	$31,218,113
Under Construction—27 Projects	11,781,386	5,722,007	893,214	5,166,165
Planning Stage—17 Projects	9,398,569	3,547,264	581,724	5,269,581
Total Cost of 247 Projects	95,931,033	37,414,723	16,862,451	41,653,859

Types of Construction and Number of New Beds for Patients

Table B shows, as of March 1, 1957, the type and number of hospital facilities that have been or are being constructed in North Carolina with Medical Care Commission aid since Federal and State funds first became available in 1947.

Table B

Stage of Completion	Local General Hospitals Number Projects	Local General Hospitals New Beds	State-Owned Hospitals Number Projects	State-Owned Hospitals New Beds	Health Centers	Nurses' Residences	Diagnostic and Treatment Centers	Rehabilitation Facilities Number Projects	Rehabilitation Facilities New Beds	Chronic Disease Hospitals Number Projects	Chronic Disease Hospitals New Beds	Total Number of Projects	Total New Beds
Completed on March 1, 1957	43[a] 46[b]	2856[a] 1729[b]	2[a] 7[b]	140[a] 587[b]	66	39	0	0	0	0	0	203	2996[a] 2316[b]
	89	4585	9	727									5312
Under Construction March 1, 1957	1[a] 14[b]	100[a] 460[b]	0[a] 1[b]	0[a] 0[b]	6	1	2	0[a] 1[b]	0[a] 30[b]	1[a] 0[b]	80[a] 0[b]	27	180[a] 490[b]
	15	560	1	0				1	30	1	80		670
Planning Stage March 1, 1957	3[a] 8[b]	380[a] 205[b]	0	0	4	1	1	0	0	0	0	17	380[a] 205[b]
	11	585											585
TOTAL: July 1, 1947 – March 1, 1957	47[a] 68[b]	3336[a] 2394[b]	2[a] 8[b]	140[a] 587[b]	76	41	3	0[a] 1[b]	0[a] 30[b]	1[a] 0[b]	80[a] 0[b]	247	3556[a] 3011[b]
	115	5730	10	727				1	30[c]	1	80		6567

Source: Medical Care Commission. *Summary of Activities*, press release March 1, 1957. Raleigh, N. C.

[a] New hospitals and/or new beds.

[b] Additions to existing hospitals and/or new beds added.

[c] The existing 35 spastic and 30 new rehabilitation beds will make a total of 65 beds and the cost will be approximately $636,897.

Table 120. The Growth of Local Health Services in North Carolina, Selected Years, 1911-53

Fiscal year	Number of counties	Expenditures Total	Expenditures Per capita	Fiscal year	Number of counties	Expenditures Total	Expenditures Per capita
1911	1	$ No data	$ —	1936	50	$ 737,000	$0.40
1913	10	"	—	1938[a]	76	1,472,000	0.57
1917	13	"	—	1940	81	1,708,000	0.55
1919	20	132,600	—	1942	87	1,886,000	0.60
1925	29	324,100	—	1944	91	2,253,000	0.68
1929	38	532,800	—	1946	93	2,686,000	0.77
1932	35	387,000	0.25	1948	97	3,393,000	0.97
1934	45	467,500	0.28	1949	100	4,373,000	1.22
				1953	100	5,218,000	1.28

Compiled by W. P. Richardson, M. D., Professor of Preventive Medicine, University of North Carolina School of Medicine, Chapel Hill, N. C.

[a]Data relative to city health departments were not available, hence are not included for the years prior to 1938 but are included for 1938 and subsequent years.

Table 121. Progress in Reduction of Preventable Illness and Death in North Carolina, Selected Years, 1921-53

Selected Diseases	Number of cases 1921	1931	1941	1947	1953
Typhoid fever	2,099	991	197	47	11
Diphtheria	5,136	3,156	1,629	751	130
Whooping cough	9,518	6,992	10,933	2,983	252
Smallpox	2,513	63	4	2	
	Death Rates				
All causes (per 1,000 population)	11.0	10.2	8.7	8.0	7.5
Tuberculosis (per 100,000 population)	104.8	71.5	41.9	28.5	1.0
Diarrhea and enteritis under 2 years (per 100,000 population)	65.2	26.0	19.3	4.5	
Pregnancy and childbirth (per 1,000 live births)	7.3	8.0	4.0	1.8	1.0
Diseases of infancy (per 1,000 live births)	75.0	73.0	59.5	35.2	32.7

Source: Biennial Reports, State Board of Health (Raleigh, N. C.).

Table 122. Payments to Recipients Under the Three Major Public Assistance Programs According to Source,[a] Fiscal Year 1956

Program	Total	Source of funds Federal	State	County
Old-age assistance	$19,369,131	$14,298,556	$2,921,225	$2,149,350
Aid to dependent children	$14,245,549	$11,072,735	$1,747,261	$1,425,553
Aid to the permanently and totally disabled	$ 5,417,749	$ 3,802,454	$ 807,442	$ 807,853

Source: *Biennial Report of the North Carolina State Board of Public Welfare, July 1, 1954, to June 30, 1956* (Raleigh, N. C.).

[a]Does not include vendor payments for medical care.

Table 123.   The Three Major Public Assistance Programs in North Carolina and the United States, Fiscal Year 1956

	Total payments during the year[a]	Source of funds (%)			Number of recipients June, 1956	Average payment June, 1956[a]
		Federal	State	Local		
Old-age assistance:						
North Carolina	$ 19,726,000	73.4	15.3	11.3	51,750	$32.71
United States	$1,633,533,000	54.3	39.3	6.4	2,523,716	$54.29
Aid to dependent children:						
North Carolina	$ 14,412,000	77.6	12.8	9.6	19,954 families	$62.95 per family
					58,993 children	$16.32 per person
United States	$ 639,476,000	56.7	32.1	11.1	613,720 families	$89.27 per family
					1,707,629 children	$24.35 per person
Aid to the permanently and totally disabled:						
North Carolina	$ 5,532,000	69.8	15.1	15.1	13,094	$38.53
United States	$ 165,183,000	49.4	36.6	13.9	258,279	$56.72

Source: U. S. Department of Health, Education, and Welfare.

[a]Includes vendor payments for medical care.

Table 124. Non-Financial Services Rendered During the Month, January, 1957

Type of service	Total services	Services to cases receiving special services only	Services to cases receiving both special services and assistance
Total services	47,479	31,651	15,828
Adult parole supervision	1,691	1,679	12
Investigation of prisoners	60	48	12
Family adjustment service	2,509	971	1,538
Educational and training service	192	99	93
Vocational rehabilitation	983	604	379
Adult mental-problem service	764	533	231
County-home service	407	307	100
Medical and health-care service	9,392	4,305	5,087
Service to individual children	21,881	15,882	5,999
OASI service	606	350	256
Nonsupport of children	785	533	252
Service to adoptive home	1,138	1,136	2
Service to foster home	1,053	1,008	45
Service to boarding home for adults	1,080	763	317
Placement of state hospital patients	75	70	5
Out-of-town inquiry	872	824	48
Referral to other agencies	501	409	92
Other services	3,490	2,130	1,360

Child labor certificates	
Child labor certificates issued	736
Age certificates issued	17
School attendance cases	
Number of cases referred	330
Number of cases on which investigations were made	296
Cases certified as medically indigent	
Under Medical Care Commission plan	1,486
For N. C. Memorial Hospital, Chapel Hill	46
Persons making support payments through department	1,052
Services through community organizations	
Persons aided through Children's Clothing Closet	850
Families aided through Help-a-Home project	61
Cases accepted for legal aid by attorneys	19

Source: *North Carolina Public Welfare Statistics*, XXI (January, 1957), 17.

INDEX

(Bold figures refer to pages on which tables appear.)

Carolina State College, 240–41; University of North Carolina, 240

Fall line, defined, 59
Family, size of, **325**
Farms. *See* Agriculture
Fayetteville, 73, 134, 135
Fayetteville State Teachers College, 234
Federal aid, to highways, 188; to hospitals, 210, 262; to libraries, 256; to public welfare, 184, 209, 272, 273, **335**
Federal Aid Act, 136
Federal building and loan associations, 176–77, **345**
Federal Deposit Insurance Corp., 171–72
Federal Emergency Relief Administration, 237, 272
Federal Housing Administration, 176
Federal Reserve System, 172
Federal Savings and Loan Insurance Corp., 176
Federation of Women's Clubs, 254
Fishing, commercial: growth of, 38; history of, 37–38; inadequacy as income producer, 38–39; rank in U.S., 38, **290;** possibilities for expansion, 39–41; research laboratories and institutes, 39–41; statistics on, **290;**——recreational: 48
Flood control, 24
Flora MacDonald College, 234
Fontana Village, 51
Food processing industry, 59, 95–96, **308**
Forests, annual volume of timber cut, 11, **282–83;** commercial forest area, **282;** federal, 66–67, **283;** growing stock, **283;** kinds of timber, 10–15 *passim;* live saw timber, **283, 335;** in mountain region, 13–14, 68; net volume, **281;** in northern coastal plain, 10–11; ownership of, 11–14 *passim,* **281, 283;** percentage of total land area, 10–13 *passim;* in Piedmont, 12–13, 63; in southern coastal plain, 11–12; in Tidewater, 59
French Broad River, 30
Fulton, Hamilton, 133
Furbearing animals, 44–45, 47–48
Furniture industry, expansion of bank credit to, 169; growth of, 119–20; in Piedmont, 64; production of, 120; promotional activities of, 121; related industries, 121; statistics on, **321;** raw materials for, 120–21; value of, **325.** *See also* Employment, Wages

Game birds, 45–47
Gardner-Webb College, 235
Gastonia Technical Institute, 240
General Fund, 188
Geography, description, 17, 52, 54–68; east–west division, 52–54; forests, 10–13 *passim;* land use, **279–80;** marine subdivisions, 55; seacoast, 37. *See also* Coastal plain, Mountain region, Piedmont, Tidewater

Geological history, 1–3
Gold, Charles F., 164
Gordon, William, 212
Governor, 179, 180–81, 186–87
Governor's Council on Unemployment and Relief, 272
Great Smoky Mountains National Park, 50, 66, 67, 68
Green, John Ruffin, 109
Greensboro College, 234
Grenville, Richard, 71
Growing season, 18–19, 63
Guilford College, 234

Habilston, W. M., 125
Halifax Paper Co., 125
Hamilton, C. Horace, 76–77
Handicapped children, 217, 260, 266, 271
Hanes, P. H., 102
Harbor facilities, 25
Hawkins, Sir John, 107
Health, Board of (county), 198
Health education, 243–44. *See also* Public health service
Hemminger, G. L., 117n
Herring, Harriet L., 185
Higher education, colleges and universities listed, 234–36; Committee on, 232–33; deficiencies in system, 232; enrollment at public and private institutions, 231n, **361, 363;** enrollment by race, **362–63;** expenditures, 231; graduate and professional enrollment, 230n; junior colleges, 231; libraries in, 252–53; percentage of population attending, 365; rank in U. S., 231–32, **332–33;** State Board of, 232–33; teacher-training schools, 231; value of plants, **332**
High Point, 120
High Point College, 234
High Point Furniture Co., 119
Highway Fund, 188
Highway system. *See* North Carolina State Highway System
Hill-Burton Act, 184, 210, 262
History of North Carolina, ethnic, 70–75, **292;** political, 178–79; settled, 70–72
Hiwassee River, 29
Hodges, Luther H., 157
Hodges, William P., 164
Hoke, John, 101
Holmes, J. A., 136
Holt, E. M., 101
Home Security Life Insurance Co., 165
Hosiery. *See* Textiles
Hospitals, Board of, 185; construction statistics, **367;** county, 210; federal aid to, 210, 262; Hill-Burton Act, 184, 210, 262; number of, **332**
Hotels, statistics on, **337**
House of Representatives, federal, 82; state, 179, 182
Humphries, Henry, 101
Hunting, recreational, 42–43

Date Due

NOV 22 '69			
JAN 29 '70			
MAR 26 '73			
NO 5 '80			
AP F 1 '83			
MY 4 '83			
NOV 23 '83			
NO 15 '85			
	PRINTED	IN U. S. A.	